*The Roman
Empire and Its
Germanic
Peoples*

*This book is published in association with
the Center for Medieval and Renaissance Studies
at the University of California, Los Angeles.*

HERWIG WOLFRAM

The Roman Empire and Its Germanic Peoples

Translated by Thomas Dunlap

UNIVERSITY OF CALIFORNIA PRESS
Berkeley   Los Angeles   London

Originally published as *Das Reich und die Germanen*.
© 1990 Wolf Jobst Siedler Verlag GmbH, Berlin

University of California Press
Berkeley and Los Angeles, California

University of California Press, Ltd.
London, England

Library of Congress Cataloging-in-Publication Data

Wolfram, Herwig.
   [Reich und die Germanen.   English]
   The Roman Empire and its Germanic peoples / Herwig Wolfram; translated by
Thomas Dunlap.
     p.   cm.
   Includes bibliographic references and index.
   ISBN 0-520-08511-6 (alk. paper)
    1. Rome—History—Germanic Invasions, 3rd–6th centuries.   2. Rome—History—
Germanic Invasions, 3rd–6th centuries—Historiography.   3. Germanic peoples—Rome.
I. Title.
  DG312.W6613   1997
  937'.09—dc21
                                              96–39741
                                              CIP

Printed in the United States of America
9 8 7 6 5 4 3 2 1

The paper used in this publication is both acid-free and totally chlorine-free (TCF). It
meets the minimum requirements of American Standard for Information Sciences—
Permanence of Paper for Printed Library Materials, ANSI Z39.48–1984.

To my three fathers:
Heinrich von Fichtenau, Gerhart B. Ladner (d. 1993),
and Friedrich B. Wolfram (d. 1993)

CONTENTS

GENEALOGICAL CHARTS

CHRONOLOGIES

1. The Empire and the Vandals

Roman Empire	Vandals
55 and 53 B.C. Caesar crosses the Rhine	
161–180 Marcus Aurelius	
166–180 Marcomannic wars	
211–217 Caracalla	
249–252 Decius	
253–260 Valerian	
253/260–268 Gallienus	
268–270 Claudius II Gothicus	
270–275 Aurelian	270 Vandal incursions into Pannonia, victory of Aurelian
276–282 Probus	
284–305 Diocletian	
285–305 Maximian	
293–311 Galerius	
294 Diocletian's administrative reforms	
306/324–337 Constantine I	
325 Council of Nicaea	
361–363 Julian the Apostate (as sole ruler)	

Continued on next page

1. The Empire and the Vandals—*Continued*

Western Empire	Eastern Empire	Vandals
364–375 Valentinian I	364–378 Valens	
367/375–383 Gratian	August 9, 378, death of Valens at the battle of Adrianople	
	379–395 Theodosius I sole ruler	
395–423 Honorius		
395–408 height of Stilicho's power	395–408 Arcadius	
402 Stilicho's victories over Alaric I at Pollentia and Verona		
		406 Vandals, Alans, and Suebi cross the Rhine
	408–450 Theodosius II	409 Vandals, Alans, and Suebi push into Spain
August 24, 410, Alaric takes Rome		
425–455 Valentinian III		
		428–477 Gaiseric
		429 crossing into Africa
		430 death of Augustine during siege of Hippo Regius
435/436 Aetius destroys the Burgundian kingdom of Worms		435 *foedus* between Gaiseric and the western empire
	438 Codex Theodosianus	
		439 capture of Carthage
		442 treaty with Ravenna
451 Aetius' victory at the Catalaunian fields	451 Council of Chalcedon	
454 death of Aetius		
June 2, 455, Vandals capture Rome		June 2, 455, capture of Rome
455–456 Avitus		
457–461 Majorian	457–474 Leo I	
457–472 Ricimer top-ranking *magister militum*		

Continued on next page

1.   The Empire and the Vandals—*Continued*

Western Empire	Eastern Empire	Vandals
	474–491 Zeno	474 "Eternal Alliance" with eastern empire
476 Romulus Augustulus is deposed by Odovacar, who is elevated to the kingship by federate soldiers		
		477–484 Huneric
480 death of Nepos		
		484–496 Gunthamund
	491–518 Anastasius	
March 493 death of Odovacar		
		496–523 Thrasamund
		500 Thrasamund marries Amalafrida, sister of Theodoric the Great
	518–527 Justinus I	
		523–530 Hilderic
	527–565 Justinian I	
		530–534 Gelimer
	533–534 Vandal War	533–534 conquest of Vandal kingdom by Belisarius
	535–552/555 Gothic War	
590–604 Pope Gregory the Great		
	610–641 Heraclius I	
	626 unsuccessful Avar-Persian siege of Constantinople	

2.   The Burgundians, Franks, and Longobards

Burgundians	Franks	Longobards
	257/258 Frankish incursion via Gaul and Spain to North Africa	
278 Burgundians in Raetia		
	after 286 following victories along the Rhine frontier, Maximian concludes a treaty with the Franks	
413–436 Burgundian kingdom of Worms		
443–534 kingdom along the Rhône		
	466/467–511 Clovis	
Ca. 480–516 Gundobad		
	481/482 death of Childeric, Clovis assumes power	
	486/487 victory over the Roman King Syagrius	
		after 488 Longobards in the former Rugiland
	496 victory over the Alamanni	
	498 baptism of Clovis	
Ca. 500 Lex Gundobada		
501/516–523 Sigismund (Catholic)		
		Ca. 505 Longobards cross the middle Danube
	507 victory over the Visigoths at Vouillé	
	508 Clovis honorary consul	508 victory over the Heruli
		Ca. 510–540 Wacho
517/518 Lex Burgundionum		
		526 Longobards move to Pannonia
	533–547 Theudebert I	

Continued on next page

2. The Burgundians, Franks, and Longobards—*Continued*

Burgundians	Franks	Longobards
534 victory of the Franks, end of the Burgundian kingdom	534 victory over the Burgundians	
	536/537 treaty between Ostrogoths and Franks	
	539 Franks invade northern Italy	
		540/547–560/561 Audoin
		547/548 Longobards are given parts of Pannonia and Noricum in a treaty with Constantinople
		560/561–572 Alboin
		567 great victory over the Gepids
		568/569 trek to Italy
		574–584 rule of the *duces*
	584 incursion into the Po Valley	584 Franks invade the Po Valley
		584–590 Authari
		589 Authari marries Theudelinde
	591 peace treaty between Longobards, Franks, and Bavarians	591 peace treaty between Longobards, Franks, and Bavarians
		591–615/616 Agilulf
		636–652 Rothari
		643 Edictus Rothari
		712–744 Liutprand
	774 Charlemagne becomes king of the Longobards	774 Charlemagne becomes king of the Longobards
	788–796 Franks destroy the Avar kingdom	

3.   The Goths, the Huns, and the Avars

Goths	*Huns*
Since 238: repeated incursions of Gothic groups along the lower Danube	
251 Cniva's victory over Roman army at Abrittus, death of Emperor Decius	
269 victory of Claudius II Gothicus over the Goths at Naissus-Nish	
290/291 Goths split into two peoples	

Visigoths	*Ostrogoths*	*Huns*
332 treaty with Constantine I		
341 Ulfilas consecrated bishop		
369 peace treaty between Valens and Athanaric		
375 Hun invasion	375/376 parts of the Ostrogoths subjugated by Huns	375 Huns cross the Danube and subjugate parts of the Goths
376 crossing of the Danube under the leadership of Alaviv and Fritigern		
August 9, 378, victory in the battle of Adrianople		
	380 treaty with Gratian, settlement in Pannonia	
382 treaty with Theodosius, settlement in northern Thrace		
391 Alaric I elevated to kingship		
394 heavy losses among Gothic *foederati* in Theodosius's army in the battle at the Frigidus		
400 disastrous setback in Constantinople, death of Gainas		
	405/406 Radagaisus invades Italy	

Continued on next page

3. The Goths, the Huns, and the Avars—*Continued*

Visigoths	Ostrogoths	Huns
August 24, 410, Alaric captures Rome, death of Alaric in the same year		
410–415 Athaulf		
Jan. 414 Athaulf marries Galla Placidia		
418–507 kingdom of Toulouse		
		433 Pannonia under Hunnic rule
		435/444–453 Attila
451 death of Theoderid in the battle of the Catalaunian fields	451 defeat of Amal Goths on Attila's side in the battle of the Catalaunian fields	451 Defeat of Attila in the battle of the Catalaunian fields
	451–526 Theodoric the Great	
453–466 Theodoric		
		454/455 Defeat of Huns in the battle at the Nedao, end of the Hunnic Empire
	459–ca. 469 Theodoric as hostage in Constantinople	
466–484 Euric		
468/469–475 war in Gaul and Spain		
Ca. 475 Codex Euricianus	474 Theodoric elevated to kingship in Macedonia	
484–507 Alaric II	484 Theodoric consul	
	488 Theodoric sets out for Italy	
	March 493 Ravenna captured, death of Odovacar	
	497 Theodoric wins imperial recognition as king of Italy	

Continued on next page

3.   The Goths, the Huns, and the Avars—*Continued*

Visigoths	Ostrogoths	Huns
506 Breviarium Alarici-anum, Synod of Agde	506–508 failure of Theodoric's policy of alliances	
507 death of Alaric II in the battle of Vouillé		
511–526 Theodoric the Great, king of the Visigoths	511–526 Theodoric the Great, king of the Visigoths	

Visigoths	Ostrogoths	Avars
	524 death of Boethius	
	525 death of Symmachus	
526–531 Amalaric	526–534 Athalaric (Amalasuintha)	
	534–536 Theodahad	
	535 murder of Amala-suintha, war against Justinian I begins	
	536–540 Vitigis	
	536/537 treaty with the Franks	
	539 Franks invade north-ern Italy	
	541–552 Totila	
	546 and 550 Totila takes Rome	
	end of June/beg. of July 552 battle of Busta Gallorum, death of Totila	
551/555–567 Athanagild		
	552 Teja	552 Turks destroy the Juan-Juan Empire
	October 552 battle at Mons Lactarius, death of Teja	
	555 the last Goths in Italy capitulate	
		558/559 first Avar delega-tion in Constantinople

Continued on next page

3.   The Goths, the Huns, and the Avars—*Continued*

Visigoths	Ostrogoths	Avars
		562 Avars at the lower Danube
		562 and 566 attacks on the Frankish kingdom
568–711/725 Kingdom of Toledo		
568/569–586 Leovigild		
573/586–601 Reccared I		
579–584 revolt of Hermangild		
		582 capture of Sirmium
589 Visigothic kingdom under Reccared converts to Catholicism		
		626 joint Avar-Persian siege of Constantinople fails
653–672 Recceswinth		
672–680 Wamba		
Between 672 and 680 Arab fleet ravages coastal cities in Spain		
694 17th Council of Toledo: height of anti-Jewish legislation		
711/725 Arab invasions put an end to Visigothic kingdom		711/712 Avars cross the Enns, Lorch is destroyed
		Ca. 740: defeat against armies of Bavarians and Alpine Slavs
		788–796 Avar kingdom destroyed in war against the Franks

4.   Britain and Other Tribes

Britain	*Other Tribes*
55 B.C. arrival of first Roman army in Britain	
	258 Alamanni penetrate as far as Milan
	286 earliest unambiguous mention of Saxon pirates
	357 Julian the Apostate defeats the Alamanni at Strasbourg
	368–374 battles against the Alamanni on the Rhine
410 Roman withdrawal from Britain	
429 first incursion of Picts and Saxons	
442 serious Saxon incursions	
	487/488 Odovacar destroys Rugian kingdom
	Ca. 550 first Slavic groups have verifiable contact with Gepids and Longobards
560–616 Aethelbert of Kent, first king to be baptized	
596 Gregory the Great launches the conversion of the Anglo-Saxons with the help of Augustine	

Introduction

"Flourishing cities, an orderly administration, an economy with highly divided labor, lively traffic in the entire region between the North Sea and the Red Sea: never before had the ancient world seen anything of the kind. Cities stood in the countryside unfortified; barely 1 percent of the empire's population was under arms. The army was stationed along the Rhine, the Danube, and the Euphrates and protected the *Pax Romana*."[1] Such was the Roman Empire at its height in the second century. And yet it foundered into the profound crisis of the third century, a crisis it was able to weather only by relinquishing what had been considered indispensable political, institutional, and religious traditions.

In the wake of this crisis, nearly all spheres of life in the empire restored by Diocletian and Constantine I were bureaucratized and militarized to an . unprecedented degree. Added to this was the external threat, first from the Germanic peoples and the Persians, then from the Huns, Avars, and Slavs, and finally from the Arabs. Large areas of the once universal empire were lost or split off from the *res publica*, whose military might (imperium) could no longer protect them or hold them in its orbit. Even where Roman statehood was most strongly preserved, in the East, there arose what was in reality a new empire: *we* call it Byzantium, though its tradition-conscious inhabitants referred to themselves as Romaioi and their country as Romania.

Since that time, countless explanations of the causes behind these truly world-historical events have been advanced and dismissed. Among those causes the important role of the Germanic peoples should be neither exaggerated nor underestimated. Moreover, anyone who has witnessed the fall of world empires and superpowers, as our generation has, will also bear in mind that the Roman Empire simply became too expensive for its

I

inhabitants, who were no longer willing to pay in money and blood for its military power. For centuries the worst defects of the Roman state had been the unresolved agrarian problems and the exploitation of the provinces and client states. Eventually a point was reached when the strains became unbearable. It is no surprise that it was a provincial, Saint Augustine, a native of Africa, who began to have doubts about the greatness of the empire and its pretensions to universality.

To be sure, Saint Augustine, like most Christians, had welcomed the Imperium Romanum as the order of the world and had supported armed struggle to defend it. But Augustine was fully aware of the earthly limitations of the empire, threatened on all sides by a "fraying at the edges," indeed by its utter demise. Moreover, unending warfare was the price for establishing and maintaining a great imperium, and this led Saint Augustine to ask: "Why must an empire be deprived of peace in order that it may be great? In regard to men's bodies it is surely better to be of moderate size, and to be healthy, than to reach the immense stature of a giant at the cost of unending disorders." After all, what were kingdoms but gangs of criminals, and large gangs were worse than small ones.[2]

Saint Augustine lived to see Rome captured by the Goths, and he died (in 430) as Gaiseric's Vandals were laying siege to his episcopal city of Hippo Regius. But a storm was already brewing on the horizon when we began our story with the empire at its height in the second century.

2. THE EMPIRE AND THE GERMANIC PEOPLES

Marcus Aurelius (161–180) had been the last of the "adoptive emperors," men who had risen to power through adoption by their predecessors. This system of succession characterized the second century, which is considered the climax and golden age of the Roman Empire and of classical civilization, perhaps even of world history. Succession by adoption, established by Nerva and Trajan, seemed to have realized once and for all the ancient demand of philosophers that the best man should rule.[3] And so, despite the troubled reality, it had become the theory, indeed the creed, of the Roman world to realize the empire's civilizing mission—*parcere subiectis et debellare superbos* (in the words of Virgil), "to spare the subjected and conquer in war the proud"—and to fulfill the claim to eternal rule.[4] There was simply no conceivable alternative.

Even in the crisis at the end of the fourth century, Ammianus Marcellinus, a Latin-writing Greek of Syrian descent, firmly believed that "Rome will last as long as mankind shall endure"; a conviction that Justinian, the conqueror of the Vandals and future victor over the Goths, was, not surprisingly, very much inclined to share as late as 537.[5]

Throughout its history, Rome had dealt with kings and peoples, *reges et gentes,* subjecting them one by one to direct or indirect rule. In this way the borders of the empire had continually expanded, until they reached, in continental Europe, the Rhine and the Danube. Beyond this watery frontier the Germans had been living since the time of Rome's Gallic wars. Caesar's ethnographic excursuses and the *Germania* of Tacitus described these tribes, shaping the popular image of the Germans right down to the present day. Modern scholarship has, of course, lost the confident certainty of the nineteenth century when it comes to classifying and differentiating ethnic groups. The Germanic problem [the question of the identity of the Germanic tribes] is giving us a good deal more trouble today than it did just a few decades ago.[6]

There was a time when it was possible to say: "The name Germanic peoples refers to those ethnic tribes who spoke a Germanic language."[7] It was also confidently believed that "strictly delineated, sharply distinct, and coherent archaeological cultural regions unquestionably coincided with territories of specific peoples and tribes."[8] Modern archaeology has long since refuted such claims. Rudolf Much, author of a commentary on the *Germania,* already realized that even Tacitus "did not always accord language decisive importance in determining ethnic identity."[9] Even more so than Tacitus, ethnographers who described nomads had to drop language altogether as a criteria of ethnic classification, since they could do little more than note that these peoples were confusingly polyglot. And so scholars limited themselves to questions concerning "customs, the wild way of life, and weapons" (in the words of Ammianus); these, and only these, things could be discovered and had to suffice as yardsticks of ethnographic classification.[10]

Tacitus composed his *Germania* toward the end of the first century A.D. He opened his work with a description of the land of Germania, whose boundaries the ancient ethnographers drew at the Rhine and the Vistula, at the seas in the north, and at the Danube in the south. Tradition dictated that this first chapter be followed by the story of the ethnographic subject's origins. Tacitus divided this story into three parts: first he speaks of the autochthonous character of the Germans. They were pure indigenous inhabitants, their primeval god Tuisto had been born of the earth. This notion of being indigenous to the land, of never having immigrated, of getting along without any outsiders and foreign things, says much about the sense of self-esteem of the Germans who were the author's source of information. To a Latin speaker this information made perfectly good sense; after all, in his language *germanus* meant also something like "having the same parents, brotherly, genuine, real." For despite, or perhaps because of, the reality of a tribal genesis, a process that always embraced a great diversity of ethnic groups, purity of blood and native roots were highly prestigious qualities in the literary world and the real world. The latter is attested, for example, by the complementary names of the Sciri and the Bastarni.

Whereas the Bastarni were a mixed Celtic-Germanic people and were regarded as bastards (Bastarni) by their neighbors, the latter described themselves as the Sciri, "the pure ones."[11] Tacitus's own explanation for the autochthonous character of the Germans is typical for a representative of a high culture and not very flattering to Germania: the Germani were indigenous by necessity since nobody would voluntarily move to their dismal land.

The second part of Tacitus's second chapter contains the actual legend of the origins of the Germani: in their traditional songs they celebrated the earthborn god Tuisto, the "hermaphrodite," whose son Mannus was considered the "origin and founder of the [Germanic] people." Mannus (which means human being or man) had three sons, from whom were descended the tribes of the Ingaevones, Herminones, and Istaevones. However, outside of this ritualized genealogy there existed other "genuine and ancient tribal names" that also boasted divine origin, among them that of the Suebi and the Vandili (Vandals).[12]

Tacitus closes the second chapter with the interesting comment that the Germanic name was a relatively recent additional name that had developed from the specific name for a single tribe. He relates that the Tungri were the first to cross the Rhine on their push westward and were subsequently called Germani by the Gauls. The victories of the Tungri imparted such prestige to this name that it was also adopted by other tribes as a generic name.[13]

Debates concerning the Germanic identity of the Germanic tribes who lived east of the Rhine fill entire libraries, and a good deal of nonscholarly interests have kept the controversy alive.[14] In actual fact, however, the few sentences in Tacitus offer a quite credible and convincing account of what happened. Successful conquerors, whether they already spoke Germanic or not, crossed the Rhine and were called Germani by the Gauls. The name was used first by outsiders, and it remained so even after the Romans had taken it over from the Gauls. However, and here I correct Tacitus, it did not establish itself as the name of all Germanic tribes, just as French Allemands did not become the self-chosen name of the Germans. It was only on Roman territory that a German would call himself or his kind *Germanus,* as the Romans did, that is, only a German on Roman soil who was imitating Roman usage could use the word *Germanus* to refer to himself or his people.

The often-invoked sense of Germanic unity was correspondingly weak. Even the native informants from whom Tacitus learned directly or indirectly about Mannus and his three sons had differing opinions about the universal validity of the threefold ethnogeny, that is, about the meaning of the genealogy that began with the "origin and founder of the people." The descent groups as determined by the number of Mannus's sons simply did not suffice to comprise all of the "genuine and old tribal names," since there were at least five. To be sure, among these units, which the Romans, significantly enough, called "races" or "lineages" (*genera*), there did exist ties that went beyond individual peoples and tribes and could, in fact, even unite several of the recorded descent groups. But it is hardly the case that the traditions of all Germanic peoples—including the heroic saga—were encompassed by the same phenomena, with the possible exception of the fact that in all Germanic languages the southern peoples were called Welsh-Walchs and the eastern neighbors were the Wends-Winds. These outsider names, most likely derived from the Germanic names for the Celtic Volcae and the Veneti (who were probably related to the Illyrians), presuppose a general us-consciousness toward the neighbors and had already undergone the Germanic vowel shift. Regardless of the period to which linguists date the vowel shift, an important linguistic development that differentiated Germans from Celts, by Caesar's time it was already history.[15]

In the eyes of the Romans, a German either lived in Germania or hailed from there. The classical territorial name Germania comprised the tribes that lived within its four watery borders. While the Romans were naturally most interested in their immediate neighbors along the Rhine and the Danube, knowledge about the entire Germanic realm and even beyond grew. For example, there was a rise in ethnographic information about a legendary island called Sca(n)dia-Scandinavia that supposedly lay several days by boat off the continent. In addition, the Gothic migrations expanded the territory ruled or settled by the Germanic peoples beyond the Vistula as far as Sarmatia-Scythia and its eastern boundary along the Don.

As a result, already in late antiquity the Germanic name was limited first to the Alamanni and then to the Franks as the dominant tribal groups in traditional Germania. While the Gutones, the Pomeranian precursors of the Goths, and the Vandili, the Silesian ancestors of the Vandals, were still considered part of Tacitean Germania, the later Goths, Vandals, and other East Germanic tribes were differentiated from the Germans and were referred to as Scythians, Goths, or some other special names. The sole exception are the Burgundians, who were considered German because they came to Gaul via Germania. In keeping with this classification, post-Tacitean Scandinavians were also no longer counted among the Germans, even though they were regarded as close relatives.[16]

It was thus the Romans who borrowed the Germanic name from the conquered Gauls and generalized it to the point of making the peoples east of the Rhine and north of the Danube into the Germans. Prior to that, Greek ethnography, the teacher of the Roman writers, had differentiated among the northern barbarians only the Scythians from the Celts, or at most had mentioned the Celto-Scyths in between the two. Only the Roman Caesar saw from personal experience that a third group of peoples existed as a separate ethnic identity between the Celts and the Sarmatian-Scythian steppe peoples. Though Caesar did not discover the Germans, he added so-lidity to the vague notions the Romans had had about them, thus helping a Germanic ethnography to come into its own. For example, one thing Caesar knew about his great enemy, the Suebian military king Ariovistus, was that Celtic was not his native language.[17]

In 53 B.C., two years after Roman legions had first crossed the Rhine, Caesar advanced into Germania for the second time. To the account of his victorious campaign he added an ethnographic excursus on the Gauls and the Germans. He placed particular emphasis on what he believed were significant "differences between these two nations." Above all, Caesar was convinced that the Germans were far more barbaric and hostile to civiliza-tion than the Gauls. Caesar combined a special political interest with these observations.[18] But he was also simply trying his hand at ethnography, de-scribing primitive peoples from the perspective of a member of an advanced civilization. Such an account contains standard phrases, preconceived no-tions, and traditional classifications, but its purpose was, not least, to hold up a critical mirror to the author's own civilization.[19]

Barbarians, as the conventional view had it, were slaves by nature; and since they lacked the second—the human—nature, they were closer to ani-mals than human beings. They did not have a history but were simply part of the flow of natural history. This attitude has had a long and tenacious life: in the nineteenth century the newly established Department of Prehis-tory in Vienna was affiliated not with the Museum of Art History, but with the Museum of Natural History, as it still is today.

Barbarians were seen as irrational, "two-legged animals." If a storm ap-proached during a battle, they were terror struck by the fear the heavens might collapse upon them; and relinquishing any advantage on the bat-tlefield, they would flee in a panic. At the same time, though, they were driven by a terrible death wish and seemed to delight in death. Even their women took up arms and fought alongside their men. Needless to say, bar-barians were possessed by evil spirits that drove them to commit the most horrible acts.

Barbarians were considered incapable of living according to written laws. Their customs were alien, unpredictable, and dangerous in the worst of them, little more than splendid vices in the best. They had an immense appetite for gold and an unquenchable thirst. They embraced one an-other for the kiss of brotherhood [a customary greeting] but knew no loy-alty to the outsider: for just as the civilized world denied that the barbarians were fully human, they in turn regarded only their own community as the "world of human beings," as the oldest tribal names, in particular, attest. For that reason anybody who left the tribe was beyond the pale.

To Roman or Greek ears, the barbarian language did not sound like the speech of humans, but more like stammering and noise. Barbarian songs were atrocious, and under their assault the classical meter of the learned poet went to pieces. Indeed, Sidonius Apollinaris lamented, how could a poet artfully construct a six-foot verse (hexameter) while a seven-foot-tall Burgundian was yelling and stomping as he danced right outside his house?

But classical observers did generally consider barbarians, Germanic and otherwise, to be good-looking. They were blond and tall, though terribly dirty with abysmal habits of personal hygiene. They greased their hair with butter, preferably rancid butter. Their furs, which they did not take off even in the sunny south, were equally aromatic. Only the Huns were ugly; that was no surprise, as they were considered the sons of evil spirits and Gothic witches expelled from their tribe. The procreative energy of the barbarians was inexhaustible, with the cold climate of their northern homeland and its long winter nights favoring their impetuous urge to reproduce in huge numbers. Just as the next winter was certain to come, the barbarians, too, would return with the regularity of a season. If one of these swarms of locusts was repulsed or even destroyed, the next one presently arose from the swamps and forests of Germania.

So much for the conventional notions. In real life, these tribes were surprisingly small: fifteen to twenty thousand warriors—which means a total of about one hundred thousand people in a tribe—was the maximum number a large people could raise. In defiance of the facts, we hear to this day of barbarian hordes. These people are likewise presented as conquerors of the Roman Empire, even though they constituted a vanishing minority within it. Moreover, since ancient times the various migrations have often been explained on the assumption that a given territory could no longer feed its inhabitants, either because of natural catastrophes or overpopulation, whereupon the entire population or a part of it was forced to leave the land.

To be sure, the notion of a "sacred spring," the *ver sacrum*,[20] when a tribe sent out its young men in search of land, is not mere fiction. Since the barbarian economy was poor and inefficient and was in no way capable of making adequate use of the existing settlement territory, new land had to be continually acquired. A good harvest was reason to hope that one could get through the winter without hunger and disease. Surplus, however, was either nonexistent or useless, since reserves could not be laid in. Barbarian lands had nothing that compared with the giant granaries (*horrea*) of the Roman city territories and imperial domains. And so all barbarians ate the same monotonous diet. If a man outranked others in nobility, if he had a larger share of the products of the primitive tribal economy, in the form of booty or tribute from his underlings, he could purchase gold and hang it around his own neck or that of his wife or horse. Barbarian gold was already proverbial among the Greeks, who did not need treasures to buy bread from the baker. In the old Mycenaean citadels, however, there had been plenty of gold, which still delighted the Macedonian semibarbarians at a time when they became a threat to Greece.[21]

Hunger and want were constant threats to the existence of an individual and of entire tribes. But privation was not the result of an unchecked increase in population or the devastation of the land by natural catastrophes, an assumption that was, to be sure, rejected early on.[22] Rather, it sprang from the fact that barbarian society was in a constant state of war. Peace was the exception; it had to be fixed by treaty. The enemy was not only the tribe living on the other side of a broad border zone. The enemy could be much closer, as close as the neighboring village, the next clan, or the other kin group of the same tribe. It is puzzling that tribal traditions regarded these chaotic conditions as perfectly normal. The explanation must be that the driving force of tribal life was the pathos of heroism. Barbarian traditions are the tales of the "deeds of brave men"—only the warrior matters; tribe and army are one.

Even though the etymology of words like *gens, genealogia, genus,* and *natio* can imply a common biological heritage, the formation of a barbarian tribe was a political and constitutional process that involved the most diverse ethnic elements. When such a "people in arms" migrated, an extraordinary social mobility prevailed in its ranks. Any capable person who had success in the army could profit from this mobility, regardless of his ethnic and social background. Political constitution thus meant primarily the assembling of highly diverse groups under the leadership of "known" families who traced their descent from a god and legitimated their rule by their success in keeping the tribe intact.

Ancient ethnography taught that the earlier a barbarian people introduced kingship, the higher it ranked on the scale of civilization. In reality, however, by the time Caesar came to the Rhine the old form of kingship survived only at the fringes of the Celtic-Germanic world.[23] By comparison, the Germanic kingship that the Romans encountered during the later centuries of the empire, and whose establishment they actually tended to promote in the beginning, represented a new type of rule. Along with these new kings there also arose new political entities that are difficult to grasp conceptually in our language. An "entire people" never comprised all possible members of a tribe. For example, the two main Gothic peoples, the Visigoths of southern France and Spain and the Ostrogoths of Italy, were each made up of ten or more different tribal groups, some of them of non-Germanic origin. Our modern terminology is simply incapable of describing such a reality.

The alternative is to follow the sources and use the word "gens" instead of "people" or "tribe." But even this Latin word should be used more like a cypher for an unknown quantity than as part of a definition, even though such definitions—such as the differentiation between *natio* and gens—were attempted very early on.[24] The bewilderingly diverse ways in which such ethnic units could manifest themselves force us to make observations like the following: "a gens is composed of many gentes and is led by a royal gens," or "the success of a royal gens promotes the creation on Roman soil of an early medieval gens and its kingdom." The reader is forewarned that such confusing statements, which defy any reasonable definition, are in fact the subject of this book.[25]

The philological interest in the Germans in the nineteenth century was greater even than the historical and archeological interest. For example, the division into West Germanic, East Germanic, and North Germanic peoples came from philologists. A historian who all too readily adopts their terminology with its linguistic assumptions falls into a self-created trap. By contrast, a purely geographical division of the Germanic peoples appears quite possible and sensible. For instance, one can speak of the Scandinavians and of Germanic peoples along the Elbe, Rhine, and Danube. In cases where doing so would lead to greater clarity, the artificial term "East Germanic peoples" should be replaced by the phrase "Gothic peoples," which is true to the sources.

At one time, classical ethnography had applied the name "Suevi" to many Germanic tribes. In the first century A.D. it appeared that this native name had all but replaced the foreign name "Germans." However, in the postclassical period, that is to say, after the Marcomannic Wars that were fought and lost mostly by the Suevi, the Gothic name steadily gained in importance. By the end of the fifth century a point had been reached where it was possible to use the name "Goths" to describe the most diverse peoples: the Goths in Gaul, Italy, and Spain, the Vandals in Africa, the Gepids along the Tisza and the Danube, the Rugians, Sciri, and Burgundians, even the non-Germanic Alans.

The most important criteria for an ethnic classification as "Goths" were the shared Arian faith and a language which, thanks to Ulfilas's Gothic translation of the Bible, had developed into a common tongue of the court and the religious cult. It is no surprise that the Catholic peoples of the Frankish kingdom and the Anglo-Saxons stood out as different from the Goths, as did the Scandinavians, who were won over to Catholic Christianity much later.[26] While the Goths, even though they were religious dissidents, sought a direct link to the Roman state, the Catholic Germans achieved the same goal indirectly via Roman Christianity. A remarkable recent book on this period had every reason to open with the statement: "The Germanic world was perhaps the greatest and most enduring creation of Roman political and military genius."[27] From this perspective it mattered little that most migration kingdoms were only short-lived political creations, for their experiences did not disappear with them. By laying the groundwork for the transition from antiquity to the Middle Ages, they created the phenomenon that is called—for better or worse—the continuity of Europe. Hence there was good reason why the rulers and peoples of these kingdoms captured the imagination of posterity, which is to this day fascinated by their meteoric rise and fall.

3. THE GERMANIC PEOPLES AND THE GERMANS OF TODAY

"The triumphs of the Goths, Vandals, and Franks are our triumphs." With these words Beatus Rhenanus (1485–1547) staked out the German claim to the Germanic history of the age of migrations. This jubilant outburst of the humanist Rhenanus is actually one of the more levelheaded statements during eight hundred years of German identification with the Germanic peoples. The highly intelligent and learned Beatus Rhenanus was known for his amiability and objectivity. And yet his words are part of an attitude that, it is hoped, strikes us today as bizarre and incomprehensible. In Nazi Germany, however, it played itself out in all its terrible consequences. As Gollwitzer has noted: "There is a multifarious continuity stretching from the Spanish mythos of the Goths to the Germanicism of the German humanists and the baroque Germanic consciousness in western and central Europe, to Montesquieu and the international cultural Germanicism of the eighteenth century." The latter formed the basis of the political Germanicism of the nineteenth century and of its vulgarized imitations—ranging from the irrational to the criminal—in the twentieth.

In 1776, Thomas Jefferson (1743–1826), later the third president of the United States, suggested the following seal for his country: "The children of Israel in the wilderness, led by a cloud by day and a pillar of fire by night, and on the other side Hengist and Horsa, the Saxon chiefs, from whom we claim the honor of being descended, and whose political principles and form of government we have assumed."[28] By this time this linking of election by God with the Germanic world was already a tradition of long standing; we encounter it in the Gothic history that Jordanes wrote in the sixth century.[29] It was a literary tradition that could excite intellectuals but never had broad resonance or impact. Jefferson's seal was never engraved; Johannes Jensen's dream in 1907 of a "Gothic rebirth of North America" remained just that.

The Nazis, however, were another matter. They renamed the Polish seaport of Gdynia-Gdingen in the Reichs province of Danzig–West Prussia, calling it Gotenhafen. They thought about re-Germanifying what had once been the Gothic Crimea by settling it with southern Tyroleans. Simferopol was to become Gotenburg, and Sevastopol Theoderichshafen. Here the Germanicism of the literary tradition became the impetus for administrative and bureaucratic action. Up to that time such a thing had been unimaginable to the European mind, and it has remained incomprehensible to this day.[30]

But Germanicism did not have to "lead to a final, Fascist phase." In the Anglo-American world the "identification of Germanness with democracy" prevailed, all manner of political dreams notwithstanding. "As a racial and ethnic concept, Germanicism had long since become obsolete when National Socialism revived it one more time" and made it the foundation of its utter disdain for humanity. The collapse of National Socialism has also meant the disappearance of Germanicism as a political or metapolitical factor, as long as "right" Green movements do not revive its memory.[31]

And yet it had all begun so "logically" and in keeping with classical tradition. The tenth century saw the creation of the German people, largely east of the Rhine, between the northern seas and the Danube in the south, that is, in an area that had been traditionally called Germania. The great church reformer Boniface distinguished Germania from Bavaria, which was located south of the Danube and had arisen on the soil of the former Roman province of Raetia. At the same time, this classically educated Anglo-Saxon was following the tradition of antiquity when he included in Germania those Slavic peoples who had settled west of the Vistula.

By contrast, it was clear to the Alamanni and the Bavarians—for example, the "southern Tyrolean" Arbeo of Freising—that their lands were also part of Germania.[32] Charlemagne's grandson "Louis the German" owes his epithet to the fact that since the high Middle Ages, *Germanicus* has been commonly understood to mean "German." But when Louis began to be called *Germanicus* not long after his death, the word still referred to the old Germania and not to Germany. It was meant to indicate that he, among the sons of Louis the Pious, had ruled the part of the Carolingian Empire that was located predominantly on the right side of the Rhine. As a result his "kingdom in eastern Francia," the east Frankish kingdom, was composed not only of Alamanni, Bavarians, Main Franks, Saxons, and Thuringians but also the most diverse Slavic tribes from the Baltics to the Adriatic, and even some descendants of the Pannonian Avars.[33]

The clear and unequivocal equating of the Germanic peoples with the Germans is a little-known result of the Investiture Controversy. It was a defensive move, used by the imperial party in the battle between the papacy and the empire as a way of compensating for its own insecurity and responding to outside attacks with counterattacks.[34] This difficult legacy remained with Germanicism to the very end. For example, as early as the middle of the twelfth century, an Alsatian historiographer invoked the Germanic tradition to fend off French claims and to emphasize the special status of the Germans: as the name of Caesar taught the Middle Ages, he was the first emperor ("Kaiser" in German), and all emperors of the Holy Roman Empire regarded themselves as his successor. According to this view, Caesar also laid the foundation of German history and in particular the origin of the lower nobility of knights and *ministeriales.*

In the *Bellum Gallicum* everyone could read that Caesar had defeated the Gauls-French with the help of the Germani-Germans. And from here imagination carried the story further: after the victorious general had returned to Rome, he supposedly summoned the first German diet. At this assembly Caesar "handed the lower knights over to the princes, on the condition that the princes should not use them like unfree men and servants, but would take them into their service like lords and protectors. This is why the German knights—in contrast to other peoples—are called servants of the empire and *ministeriales* of the princes."[35]

Anyone who in our day and age begins a history of the Germans with the Germanic tribes may find some familiar elements in their constitutional forms and way of life, much as Friedrich Wilhelm Schelling (1775–1854) could still call Germany a "people of peoples." However, a historian today can derive from the Germanic peoples and their history neither special status nor national superiority. He cannot identify with the Germanic peoples either politically, as did the representatives of a committed Germanicism, or in literary terms. The fact that English and modern Greek still use the Germanic name for the Germans and Germany, and that the Russians also use it alongside the common Slavic name, is historically rooted in the medieval mentality and reaches back to the prescholarly study of classical tradition. Only the humanistic rediscovery of the Tacitean *Germania* restored the comprehensive meaning of the Germanic name as it was used by ancient ethnography.

If we pick up the thread of ancient ethnography today, we may include the Germanic peoples and the period of migration to which they gave their imprint in the history of the Germans, but only because the Germanic peoples and their period are as much a part of that history as they are of the history of all European and many non-European peoples. The Germanic peoples have left traces in large areas of Europe and around the Mediterranean, even where their languages have long since ceased to be spoken.

To put it in another way, the present-day Germans have as much a Germanic history as do the Scandinavians, British, Irish, French, Italians, Spaniards, Portuguese, Hungarians, Romanians, Slavic nations, Greeks, Turks, and even the Tunisians and Maltese. To this day Germans draw inspiration from the history of the Germanic peoples, or they are linked with that history by non-Germans. However, historical reality is never merely a matter of dates and facts, but always includes the motivation of the observers. For these reasons, too, the history of the Germanic peoples stands at the beginning of a history of the Germans. But by naively equating Germanic peoples with the Germans, no matter whether it is done positively as a form of self-identification or negatively as a form of disparagement, one loses not only the subject of the "Germanic peoples" and their history but also history *as such,* and eventually oneself. The goal of the present book is to prevent this from happening. It seeks to trace the beginnings of a history of the Germans, even though at the time our story begins there were no Germans—in the sense of *Deutsche*—and wouldn't be for a long time to come.

ONE

Kings, Heroes, and Tribal Origins

1. DEFINING THE PROBLEM

This chapter will ask the reader for a great deal of attention and discrimination. Rarely heard or unknown names of gods and divine tribal ancestors, stories about divine beginnings in distant lands of origin, memories of encounters between gods and humans: all these "existential norms and cultic myths," in the words of Karl Hauck, call for an inordinate amount of patience, indeed almost the suspension of rational thinking, before we can accept them as traditions deserving to be taken seriously.

The problem arises on several levels. From the outset, opinions diverge when it comes to a critical examination of the sources. Some scholars question whether it is permissible to search the accounts of Christian, classically educated writers, most of whom wrote long after the fact, for ideas and conceptions that once constituted a binding reality among the Germanic peoples. If it is permissible to do so, when were "times past" and "the old days"? What did these origin myths mean to those who talked about "the old days," considering that these legends were embedded in a belief in an "eternal return"? We can ascertain the "events of the far distant past" in what is at best a relative chronology by using the names of gods and peoples. Occasionally archaeology might prove helpful. However, when it comes to drawing upon the ethnographers and geographers of the imperial period, we must be very cautious. And what are we to make of all this business about "divine origins" and the "heroic age"?

To begin with, in this day and age no one should think that this bygone era is the world of the author or the wellspring of his motivation as he undertakes the attempt—admittedly unsatisfactory—to make the language of a distant past come alive. This chapter is not about facts and real events, but about equally real motives behind human actions. Today we can recon-

struct these actions only by working our way back from their visible historical results. However, their historical roots and the forces that gave rise to
them elude our grasp. Yet to the extent that these motives are not the
product of random invention but arise from roots that can be attested
across wide regions and are not merely literary, they form the cultic myths of
a tribal group and in this sense reveal something about the group's origins. Such beginnings were history, though not events that could be dated
and located historically; they did, however, become the expression of a collective consciousness. In other words, whether Theodoric the Great was
linked to Scandinavia "by blood," that is, whether or not he originated
from there through some ancestor we can name or ascertain, is not a question for us but for natural history. What is historically significant is that he
wanted to give himself a Scandinavian descent, and that he expressed it and
established it with motifs that were believable to his age. It is not surprising
that even today some find this sort of history a nuisance while others identify with it.

The critical attitude toward this past has always done far less harm than
the identification with the Germanic peoples; in fact, compared to the latter, it has so far been completely harmless. Moreover, it is certainly correct
and necessary to evaluate every written source first in its entirety and as a testament to the period in which it was created. Nevertheless, literature based
on oral tradition can also present a story that contains more than only contemporary elements, a story that is not "invented" but shaped and controlled by the expectations of the intended audience.[1] It would thus be a
serious methodological error to regard all sources exclusively as literary
works belonging to the time of their composition, and to deny the possibility that the "songs of the ancestors" (carmina maiorum) ever constituted a
genuinely binding reality (religio). The battle cry "down with critical exege-
sis," which is being raised anew today and is meeting with resounding enthusiasm, is after all nothing new, but rather an echo from the dark ages of
nineteenth-century positivism.

2. THE KING

The Germanic peoples "choose [that is, elect] their kings [reges] for their
noble birth [ex nobilitate], their commanders [duces] for their valor [ex vir-
tute]. The kings have no absolute and arbitrary power, the commanders
rely on example rather than the authority of their rank."

This is how Tacitus begins the seventh chapter of his Germania and with it
his discussion of the constitution of the Germanic peoples. Though he appears to describe the simultaneous existence of royal and military (ducal)
authority, he was in fact recording two forms of Germanic kingship that
supplemented, indeed succeeded, one another. Such an interpretation of

this famous, and brief, passage may seem at first glance more than bold. Both Caesar and Tacitus describe a phenomenon that modern scholarship has called the "Gallic–West Germanic revolution."[2] It refers to the fact that around 50 B.C., precisely the most advanced and best organized peoples on both sides of the Rhine no longer had kings, even while they still had royal families. Initially it was one of the maxims of Roman policy to support those oligarchic powers that sought to prevent a restoration of the kingship. Not a few members of the old royal families perished because they were suspected of wanting to become kings "again." Arminius, from the tribe of the Cherusci, the "liberator of Germania," was even done in "by the treachery of his own relatives" on this pretext, and he was not the only one to suffer that fate.[3] Later the Romans supported the formation of kingdoms provided they could choose and install the barbarian princes; in this way one of Arminius's nephews, and probably a great-nephew as well, became for a few years kings of the Cherusci—contested kings, to be sure. Of course, their rule had little in common with the old-style kingship.

In contrast to the oligarchies at the center of the Celtic-Germanic world, a type of "ancient" kingship survived at its outer edges: on the British Isles, in Scandinavia, among the East Germanic peoples, and in the eastern Alps. Not infrequently we find dual kingship, which was religiously depicted by two helper gods (Dioskouroi), as it had been in ancient Sparta. The kingship of the premigration era strikes me as archaic. Its holders possess a high degree of sacral responsibility and are responsible for a "small region" that is ethnically relatively homogeneous.

This observation draws support from the oldest titles, which are formed the same way in various languages and have the same meaning. For example, the Latin tribal word *tribus* is complemented by the office of the *tribunus;* the Gothic word for "people," *thiuda,* by the office of the *thiudans;* the word for "race, lineage," *kind,* by the office of the *kindins;* and the Frankish word for "army" (people in arms), *druht,* by the office of the *druhtin.* To be sure, the Roman tribune did not remain a tribal chieftain, but came to occupy many offices, including even that of commander of a regiment in the army of the later Roman Empire. The *thiudans* of the Ulfilas Goths did not remain a tribal king. In the fourth century, the Gothic *kindins,* too, contrary to the original meaning of the word, was no longer a clan chief. Among the Danubian Goths he had now become the judge who, elected for the duration of a specific threat and limited in his authority to the territory of the tribal confederation, exercised special monarchical power. History could thus carry a word far away from its original meaning, its etymology. Nevertheless, the fact that the old titles continued to be held testifies to the durability of what was once a life-sustaining connection between a group conceived as a descent group and its representatives.

When Ulfilas set out to translate the Bible into Gothic, his aim was surely not to furnish historians of Germanic constitutional history with the linguistic equivalents they so desperately needed. Still, Biblical Gothic, the language into which bishop Ulfilas and his assistants translated the Bible after 350, is one of the most important sources for investigating the Germanic constitution. The reason for this is that the various layers of language in Biblical Gothic reflect past influences and cultural contacts. There are Celticisms in the important military and political sphere that appear only in Gothic and no other Germanic language.[4] Every single time their Greek text spoke of a *basileus*, the Bible translators and their successors used the word *thiudans*. However, this *thiudans* does not represent the Gothic people and its land, the *Gútthiuda*. Instead, he is the Roman emperor or a Hellenistic king of the Gospels. But above all he is God the Father and Christ as King of the Jews. Absorbed into the sphere of sacral language, the old word for king increasingly lost its connection with worldly politics. Though the legendary hero-king Beowulf is still celebrated as *theoden*, (lord), we are more likely to find the word in the Anglo-Saxon and Old Saxon praises of Christ.

Biblical Gothic used the Celtic word *reiks* (pronounced *rix*, singular and plural) to describe the kings of this earth and the rulers of nations. The other East Germanic peoples adopted this Celtic royal title from the Goths, as the many personal names with the root word *reiks* reveal. The Merovingians too used such names after they became related in marriage to the East Gothic Amals, even though a Frankish king was not a *reiks* but a *kuning*. But we are told that Theodoric the Great—the *thiuda-reiks*, the tribal king par excellence—was a *reiks*, "which is what the barbarians customarily call their leaders." The African Vandals also attest to this practice.[5]

In Ulfilas's time the Burgundians, considered an East Germanic people, still had two types of king side by side. On one side was a group of *hendinos*, princes who were entrusted with responsibility for the tribe. If the fortunes of war were unfavorable or the bounty of the harvest declined, they were deposed, possibly even killed. Opposite them stood an "elder," *sinistus*. At the time our source was written, the only function he still exercised, as *rex sacrorum*, was that of high priest. Originally the Burgundian "elder" had no doubt been the sacral tribal king. Despite, or precisely because of, the restriction of his activities to the sacral sphere he continued to hold the status of monarch. The *hendinos*, by contrast, had to share his power with several competitors.

The same was true for the Gothic *reiks* as well as the *kuning* or *cyning* of the West Germanic peoples, because the peoples along the Rhine and the Elbe had lost the old tribal kingship even before the great migrations began. Ariovistus, Caesar's Suebian adversary, had already been a king of the new type, the king a migrating army made up of different tribes. But even those members of old royal families who supposedly or actually sought to obtain the kingship would not have been trying to renew the original form of rule over a single people but attempting a greater monarchy based on a victorious army composed of many tribes. The sign that Arminius (a Cheruscian) wanted to become a king as *dux* (leader of the army) was not his successful defense against the Romans in the battle against Varus and in the long struggle that followed. What signaled his ambition was his offensive war against and victory over Marbod, king of the Marcomanni in Bohemia.[6] Arminius had led a tribal confederation against Marbod, who in turn had been supported by some Cherusci under the command of Arminius's uncle Ingomer.

While the "king by noble birth" (*rex ex nobilitate*) was the descendant of divine royal ancestors and thus the representative of a largely ethnically homogenous society that was territorially small, the "commander by valor" (*dux ex virtute*) had to fight for his rise to the kingship as leader of a victorious polyethnic army. The holder of this younger type of kingship could be of royal as well as nonroyal descent. He was "chosen" by the army, that is to say, by peoples in migration, because of a decisive victory that brought the tribe new land. A heroic achievement, a primordial deed from which a given group derived its identity, gave proof that the commander was fit to be king. While the old tribal king was the successor of kings who had ruled a tribe "since time immemorial," the king of a victorious army was a founding king from whom both a new royal family as well as a new people took their origin.

With the replacement of tribal kings by kings of migrating armies, the representatives of the new kingship had to take on rights and responsibilities of the older form of rule. The tasks and sacral responsibilities of the "elder" devolved upon the Burgundian *hendinos*-kings. "In accord with ancient custom" they were held accountable if they failed. The Gothic military kings were concerned early on to continue the traditions of the *thiudans*-kingship. Under the leadership of military kings, the Goths moved from the Baltic Sea to the Black Sea and from there attacked the empire. In the battle with Rome the oldest Gothic military kingship and the unity of the tribe were destroyed forever.

Among the western Goths power was taken over by an oligarchy. There was a group of *reiks* who, in an emergency, subordinated themselves to the monarchy of a judge, *kindins,* whose authority was limited in duration and territorial extent. Among the eastern Goths, the Amals succeeded in capturing the kingship and held on to it until the assault of the Huns. The best known and last of these kings was Ermanaric. In all likelihood, however, he was also no longer called *thiudans:* he did not represent a people, a *thiuda,* but as a royal *reiks* ruled over many peoples of different ethnic backgrounds. Likewise, the word *Gútthiuda* did not describe a single Gothic people but the western land of the Goths, which was inhabited by many peoples.

The assault of the Huns accelerated the migrations of the Germans and led to the founding of their kingdoms on Roman soil. The sequence of tribal kingship to military kingship became irreversible. This gave rise to a greater kingship that did not revive either the Gothic *thiudans* or the Burgundian *sinistus* or any of the other names of the old tribal kings. The Visigoth Alaric, the Vandal Geiseric, and the Ostrogoth Theodoric firmly established the monarchy of the *reiks*. In much the same way Kuning Clovis became the sole Frankish king, while a number of Anglo-Saxon kings tried to achieve something similar.[7] Beowulf's designation as *theodcyning* (tribal king) has the same meaning as Theodoric's name. The "eastern" word *reiks* was nowhere able to displace the West Germanic *kuning*.

Among the northern Germans, however, there was a faint memory that the royal title borrowed from the Celts was older than the "king." Generations later a learned poet systematized what was known by declaring that the true father of the first king had been the god with the revealing name, or rather title, *Rígr* (*reiks*).

Defining and contrasting the two types of kingship is fraught with all the dangers of generalization. To be sure, the clarity with which the sources attest the military kingship leaves nothing to be desired. The archaic tribal kingship, however, becomes only dimly visible in old names and tales of abandoned cults. Moreover, the military kingship was not a constitutional form exclusive to the age of migration. It not created during the migrations, nor did it come to an end with them.

The assertion that military kings like Theodoric, Geiseric, and Clovis were not "of good family" is false; precisely the opposite was the case. But being an Amal, a "long-haired" Hasding, or a Merovingian—that is to say, someone who was unquestionably *ex nobilitate*—would not have been sufficient in itself to found a large kingdom on Roman soil. The military success that was the precondition for this was the product of valor (*ex virtute*). It goes without saying that the two types of kingship did not prepare a uniquely Germanic development. Both appear in at least the entire Euro-Asian sphere,[8] and may in fact represent a form of political organization common to all mankind.

In his search for the system underlying the Indo-European pantheon, Georges Dumézil found a pair of complementary gods that corresponded to the two types of kings. One was a charitable, "normal" god. He maintained a geographically small, stable system of laws and traditions by ensuring fertility and peace. His counterpart was a wild, dangerous, even chaotic god. Warlike communities, migrating tribal armies, and individuals consecrated themselves to him, their lord and leader.[9] Among the Germanic peoples of the north and west, Wodan-Odin embodied this duality, which the disintegrated *thiudans*-society had already dissolved before the "new peoples" appeared at the borders of the Roman Empire. The Goths—or more accurately, the Amali—who had left the north before the "arrival of Odin" were led by his predecessor Gaut, who was also a god of military kings and their warrior bands.

However, in all these social and political systems there also existed the outsider, who embodied the chaotic contradictions of the war god to such an extent that he was regarded as someone consecrated to that god, indeed utterly surrendered to him. This figure, both tragic and necessary, was the hero.

3. THE HERO

Kings of wandering armies dissolved the structures of life belonging to territorial, small tribal kingships, and in the process the deed of the individual displaced the "eternal return" of traditional order. At the same time, through the figure of the hero and the tests he had to endure, the individual had his earliest and most profound experience of himself as a being active in the flow of history and in command of himself.

While every king had to look after the community entrusted to his care and was responsible for its survival, the hero stood opposed to the community and demonstrated that he was "unattached, unreasonable, that he violated the rules." The hero is lonely, often someone banished from the community; he is, to use the German word, a *Recke*. The term lives on in the English *wretch* and in the French *garçon*. Someone who can hardly be distinguished from the *Recke* was the *Kämpe*, the hired champion who made his living by fighting judicial duels for other people. And he was the sort of person one would think perfectly capable of using evil practices, invoking magical chants, and otherwise being up to no good.[10]

A king had divine and royal ancestors—Theodoric's daughter Amalasuintha was said to have "as many kings as ancestors" in her genealogy[11]—or he was himself venerated as the founder of a royal clan, *stirps regia*. By contrast, if the hero failed to become a hero-king—the *theodcyning* Beowulf was one hundred years old when he met his death in the battle against the dragon, the final deed for his people[12]—he died a king-hero, young and without offspring.

The Scandinavian hero Starkad reached old age only because his god Odin raised him in person and endowed him with three human life spans. This gift, however, did not go unchallenged by Thor, the god of "normality." He did the logical thing and placed on Starkad the curse of childlessness and the condition that he would perform a "nithing's deed," a dishonorable and base deed, in each lifetime. If the war god gives him the best weapons and clothes, Thor denies him the lordship over land and people, prerequisites for the founding of a kingdom. If Odin bestows on him victory in every battle and the ability to surpass the best fighters, Thor inflicts serious wounds on him in every fight and strikes him with the fate of being hated by "normal" people.[13] Thus Starkad is kept from becoming a hero-king; he serves kings and their peoples to their advantage, but he also brings them death and destruction, just as the curse said he would. Starkad is an ardent defender of the good old days and knows that one must neither "consider wealth as noble birth and treasures as ancestors, nor measure good fortune by one's possessions instead of by one's descent."[14] He outlines the perimeters of "what a human being can do in extreme circumstances."[15]

Only the interplay of kings and the power of fate allows creation of the heroic saga. The saga derives its theme from the heroic pathos of a threatened or dying kingdom. The historical King Ermanaric, overcome by despair over his defeat by the Huns, sacrificed himself to the god whose name he bore and who had nevertheless abandoned him, which meant that he could no longer be a king to his people. Ermanaric's reward was a place in his people's heroic saga.

The collapse of the Gothic kingdom in southern Russia seemed to be repeated in the downfall of Theodoric the Great's Ostrogoths in Italy after Theodoric's death. The heroic saga made the two kings contemporaries and antagonists, even though Theodoric, the historical model for the Dietrich von Bern [Theodoric of Verona] of the saga, the refugee and exile, lived and died more than a century and a half after Ermanaric. Their fate sees the reversal of the life of a hero-king: both men become king-heroes left to their own devices as the tragic end of their kingdom and their people approaches.

The Goths of Ukraine, the Ostrogoths, were also called Greutungi. This tribal name reached Scandinavia as part of the heroic lore and there entered into a strange union. In the Nordic *Hervarasaga,* which includes the "Song of the Battle of the Goths and Huns," we find a demonic armorer of the Gothic king. When the Huns try to seize the sacred object of the Goths, "the radiant stone on the banks of the Dnieper," he confronts them and with his spear consecrates them to the war god Odin. This armorer of the Gothic king bears three names, which are of special significance: he is called Gizzur the Old, Greutungian warrior, and Gaut. The names reveal his true identity: he is Odin himself.[16]

The confusing quid pro quo of identities and identifications is in keeping with the history and nature of Odin-Wodan, who absorbs older gods and takes over the themes they represent. Thus the military kings are his men and descendants, as is attested in most genealogies of the Anglo-Saxon kings; while those genealogies begin with Wodan, some can even reach back beyond him to Gaut-Géat. At the same time, however, the heroes and military kings are the creatures of Odin-Wodan, who determined their success and caused their tragic downfalls. For no apparent reason he turns on them and bestows life and victory on the enemy. Faced with death, the defeated can do little more than utter an angry complaint: "If I could meet him, the faithless fiend, that battle would bring him ignominy and disgrace! If my fist could grab the false conniver, I would tear the war god to bits like the cat a mouse."[17]

The demeanor of the hero who is consecrated to death is comparable to that of Prometheus in rebellion, who does not deny the power of the gods but seeks to conquer it. "The heroic saga is thus an eminently secular form of poetry in a much deeper sense than merely in its subject matter."[18] It tells the story of the outsider with superhuman powers who once lived, and who must live time and again, in order for this world—*Midjun-Gards,* the "house in the middle"[19]—to become and remain habitable for humankind. Prometheus brought fire to humankind; Hercules with his club cleansed the world of monsters. The Scandinavian Thor, in this case himself a lonely hero, fought the *Midgard*-dragon and the giants who were a threat to the world. Thor must have been swinging his hammer as the god Donar ("the Thunderer") of the West Germanic peoples already during the imperial period, since Tacitus equated him with Hercules.

What gods and demigods embodied, the heroes had to live out. As individuals they proved themselves outside the rules so that the community might live by the rules. Just as Thor seeks to stem the advance of age and tries in vain to halt the inevitable end of the world,[20] the hero fights the battle that cannot be won but must always be joined anew lest the world with all its gods, kings, and peoples come to ruin. He is the lonely guard at the shore and riverbank, in the wooded mountains and the moor, at the boundaries of the land where humans dwell. And he is condemned to fail and by his failure bestow life: "Think of it: the hero endures. Even his ruin was but an excuse to be: his final birth" (Rainer Maria Rilke, "First Duino Elegy"). The origin of a people and its existence over time, however, was the work of gods and kings; the longer their line, the longer the life of the people.[21]

4. THE ORIGINS OF A PEOPLE

When a Latin author speaks about a barbarian people he usually calls it gens or *natio*. Both words are related to birth and begetting. Etymologically they describe a community of descent, though at times they refer to different organizational forms of a tribe: for some authors, *natio,* "the people of a single blood," stands for the subgroup of a gens; gens embraces also

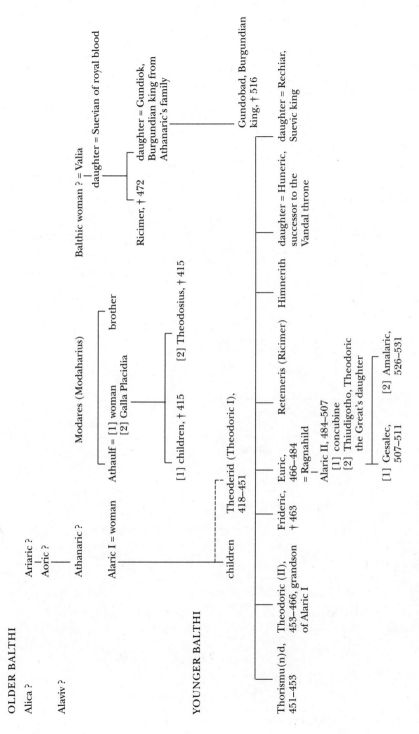

Figure 1. Genealogy of the Older and Younger Balthi

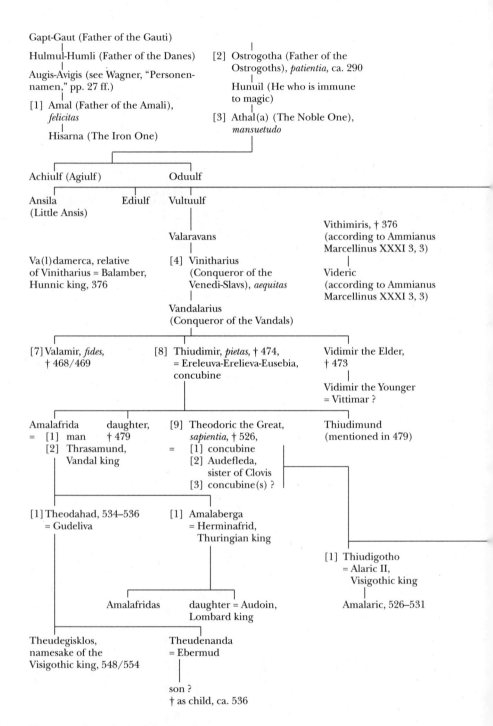

Gapt-Gaut (Father of the Gauti)
|
Hulmul-Humli (Father of the Danes)
|
Augis-Avigis (see Wagner, "Personen-
namen," pp. 27 ff.)
|
[1] Amal (Father of the Amali),
    felicitas
|
    Hisarna (The Iron One)

[2] Ostrogotha (Father of the
    Ostrogoths), *patientia*, ca. 290
|
Hunuil (He who is immune
to magic)
|
[3] Athal(a) (The Noble One),
    mansuetudo

Achiulf (Agiulf)   Oduulf

Ansila   Ediulf   Vultuulf
(Little Ansis)
                            Valaravans
                            |
                            [4] Vinitharius
                                (Conqueror of the
                                Venedi-Slavs), *aequitas*
                            |
Va(l)damerca, relative
of Vinitharius = Balamber,
Hunnic king, 376
                            Vandalarius
                            (Conqueror of the Vandals)

Vithimiris, † 376
(according to Ammianus
Marcellinus XXXI 3, 3)
|
Videric
(according to Ammianus
Marcellinus XXXI 3, 3)

[7] Valamir, *fides*,   [8] Thiudimir, *pietas*, † 474,   Vidimir the Elder,
    † 468/469   = Ereleuva-Erelieva-Eusebia,   † 473
                                    concubine |
                                                                        Vidimir the Younger
                                                                        = Vittimar ?

Amalafrida   daughter,   [9] Theodoric the Great,   Thiudimund
= [1] man   † 479   *sapientia*, † 526,   (mentioned in 479)
  [2] Thrasamund,   =   [1] concubine
      Vandal king   [2] Audefleda,
                                       sister of Clovis
                                   [3] concubine(s) ?

[1] Theodahad, 534–536   [1] Amalaberga
    = Gudeliva   = Herminafrid,
                                     Thuringian king

                                                                    [1] Thiudigotho
                                                                        = Alaric II,
                                                                          Visigothic king
                                                                    |
              Amalafridas   daughter = Audoin,   Amalaric, 526–531
                                   Lombard king

Theudegisklos,   Theudenanda
namesake of the   = Ebermud
Visigothic king, 548/554 |

                               son ?
                               † as child, ca. 536

Figure 2. Genealogy of the Amali

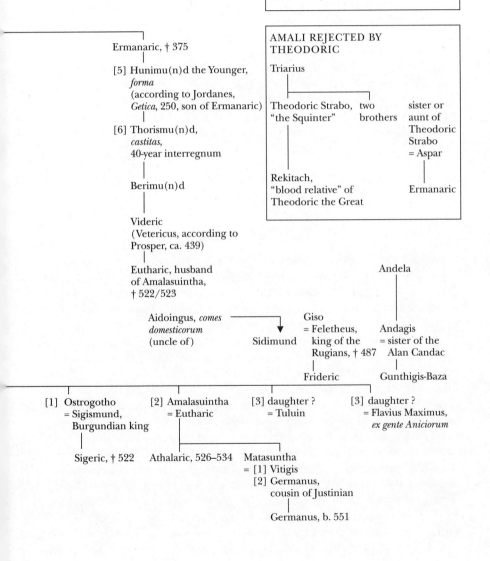

AMALI ACCEPTED BY
THEODORIC

Hunimund the Elder

Gesimund (one or two persons;
if two, second is Amal, son-in-arms)

Hunimund, king of the Danubian
Suevi Amal, son-in-arms

Ermanaric, † 375

[5] Hunimu(n)d the Younger,
forma
(according to Jordanes,
Getica, 250, son of Ermanaric)

[6] Thorismu(n)d,
castitas,
40-year interregnum

Berimu(n)d

Videric
(Vetericus, according to
Prosper, ca. 439)

Eutharic, husband
of Amalasuintha,
† 522/523

AMALI REJECTED BY
THEODORIC

Triarius

Theodoric Strabo, two   sister or
"the Squinter"   brothers   aunt of
                              Theodoric
                              Strabo
                              = Aspar

Rekitach,
"blood relative" of   Ermanaric
Theodoric the Great

Aidoingus, *comes*   Giso
domesticorum   = Feletheus,   Andagis
(uncle of)   Sidimund   king of the   = sister of the
                                  Rugians, † 487 Alan Candac
                                  Frideric   Gunthigis-Baza

Andela

[1] Ostrogotho   [2] Amalasuintha   [3] daughter ?   [3] daughter ?
= Sigismund,   = Eutharic   = Tuluin   = Flavius Maximus,
Burgundian king   *ex gente Aniciorum*

Sigeric, † 522   Athalaric, 526–534   Matasuntha
                                      = [1] Vitigis
                                        [2] Germanus,
                                            cousin of Justinian

                                      Germanus, b. 551

the "outsiders, guests, and immigrants" and thus becomes a political entity that presents itself militarily as a "people in arms."[22]

The origin of a people—*origo gentis, initia gentis*—is divine; indeed it is a god. This is how we must translate two specific passages in Tacitus, even taking into account the author's "condensed" style. The divine beginnings have no ultimate goal, they are celebrated in religious observances and are thus confirmed and renewed as an "eternal return."[23] The same holds true for the leading family (or families) of a people. Tradition does not differentiate between these two manifestations of tribal political life. The sources call the people, as well as its royal family or the old noble clans, gens or gentes; in either case we are dealing with the same constitutional reality. The Hasding Vandals gave rise to the royal family of the Hasdingi, who were able to maintain themselves as kings despite grave defeats and to preserve the Vandals as a people. The Hunnish mercenaries of Aetius destroyed the Burgundian King Gunther "along with his people and the royal clan." This catastrophe formed the core of the *Song of the Nibelungs*, though historically it was redeemed by the birth of a new Burgundian people. The royal family of the Merovingi, the "long-haired kings," stood for the Franks; the Balthi represented the western Goths (see Figure 1); and the Amali were the "family of the eastern Goths" (see Figure 2).

The Descent of the Amali

When the Amal Goths—so we read in Cassiodorus-Jordanes—recognized the divine charisma of their leaders, they acclaimed and venerated them as Ansis, as "Aesir." Both Ansis and Amal probably mean the stake or piece of wood used to carve the figures of gods: the two oldest Dioskouridean pairs of kings of the Vandals bear similar "woodnames" that are of divine origin.[24] Thus the Amal Ansis embody a descent of the clan and the people that is "by no means purely human." However, the genealogy of the Amali in Cassiodorus-Jordanes does not begin with an Amal, as one would expect, but with Gaut, the Scandinavian war god and ancestral god of many peoples. The Gauts, a Scandinavian people after whom Götaland (a region of southern Sweden) is still named, derived their name from him. However, Gaut had not merely stayed behind in the homeland, he had also gone out with the migrating peoples. The great Longobard kings Audoin and Alboin called themselves Gausi (Gauti). Hathugaut-Hathagat, the founding father of the Saxon tribe on the continent, had a name in which Gaut formed the root. Gaut-Géat headed the genealogies of Anglo-Saxon kings whenever the goal was to extend the genealogies back beyond Wodan-Odin. Gaut is older than Odin, and in the Scandinavian sources the latter thus boasts of his earlier name, Gautr. Odin had only become the "Gautic god" and had taken over the leadership of the gods at the head of the Aesir after the Ansis Amals had left Scandinavia. The Gaut of the Amals had not yet been a Wodan-Odin, though he did represent and legitimate the strong Gothic kingship organized around warrior bands. Odin had very specific ideas about what his followers had to do. They had to enter Valhalla fully armed. By contrast, we can identify the Gothic graves of the pagan period by the absence of weapons. Apparently they were of no use to a dead Goth in the hereafter; he did not need them to serve his god Gaut.

After Gaut, the Amal genealogy lists his son Humli; his name could be identical with the primeval ancestor of the Danes and Angles. Celtic connections are also evident. Only the fourth link in the genealogical chain is occupied by Amal, "from whom the race of the Amals is descended." The name belongs to a period when the Amals had not yet joined up with the Goths of southern Russia, for Amal's son is Hisarna, "the Iron One"; he embodies a Celtic phase of the race and in all likelihood reflects a time when the Goths were subordinated to the Celts. The influence of the latter on the politico-cultic sphere of the Goths can be easily substantiated; it begins around the time of Christ's birth, when the Gutones in Pomerania, the precursors of the Goths of southern Russia, were part of a Celt-dominated cultural community in the heart of Silesia. This influence continued and was renewed when the Goths in the third century encountered Celts and Bastarni along the lower Danube.[25]

The long Celtic era of Hisarna was followed by Ostrogotha, the founding father of the Ostrogoths, as the Goths of southern Russia called themselves. The Amal genealogy thus made Hisarna the father of Ostrogotha. Tradition knows the latter as the eponymous hero, the name-giving founder of the eastern Goths, the Ostrogoths. In connection with Ostrogotha there are reports of historical events that we can date to around 290 and which show that a new royal clan had come to power among the eastern part of the Goths, who had been divided into two peoples.

Ostrogotha is the father of Hunuil, "he who is invulnerable to magic," whose name manifests something of the special charisma of the Amali. Hunuil's son is Athala, "the noble one"; his oldest grandson is called Ansila, "little Ansis," a name that reflects the Ansic tradition of the royal family. Ansila is the older brother of Ermanaric and thus belongs to a generation with which the Amal-Gothic history enters the full light of history. In the middle of the fourth century, the Ostrogothic King Ermanaric ruled for many decades over a realm that stretched from the Black Sea to the Urals and the Baltic. With Ermanaric's death, in 376 at the latest, ended the older line of the Amali, the last Gothic kingdom outside the empire, and for many decades the independence of the Goths. Those Goths who were unable to seek refuge in the empire became subservient to the Huns.[26]

The genealogy of the older Amali up to Ostrogotha embodies a succession of tribal formations that are fleshed out as divine ethnic origins. Older than Ostrogotha, the king of the Black Sea Goths, and thus older than the Ostrogoths, are Amal and the Amali. But older than Amal and the Amali are Gaut and the Gauts. The Amals become Goths no earlier than appeared the youngest tribal ancestor Ostrogotha, which is why Gothic tradition knows of pre-Amalian origins of the Goths. The descendants of Gaut, Amal, and Ostrogotha were not called Gautungs or Amalungs—only West Germanic epic poetry could give the Goths such names—or Ostrogothungs, but Gauts, Amali, and Ostrogoths.

Such "strong" tribal names are both grammatically and semantically nothing other than the plural of the name of an original ancestor, whereas the "-ingen (-ungen)" derivation would express only an association as subordinate followers or at times even as slaves. Gauts, Amali, and Ostrogoths were thus not servants of a god or a deified tribal founder, but his sons, his reincarnations. With the Amali the Gautic-Ansic tradition reached the eastern Goths.

The Origins of the Goths

The oldest story of tribal origins (*origo gentis*) to not merely present a Germanic people as the object of ethnographic interest but to glorify it was Cassiodorus's *History of the Goths*. Cassiodorus, a high official in the service of Theodoric the Great and the Italian Gothic kings who followed, wrote an *origo Gothica* at Theodoric's request. He presented his work as the family tradition of the Amal royal clan, and it served the Byzantine Goth Jordanes as the source for a work he himself called an excerpt from Cassiodorus's book. Jordanes compiled his work in Constantinople in the winter (probably) of 551, and unlike its model, which is known to us only by title, has survived. Moreover, we know that Cassiodorus was trying—in a manner exemplary for the future—to make his Gothic history, his *origo Gothica*, into Roman history, *historia Romana:* that is, he tried to detach the history of Gothic origins from the "eternal return" and give it a goal in the Christian-teleological sense. To that end he combined two traditions, the ancient literary tradition and the oral memories of the Goths. The result strikes us as a magnificent grotesque.

Gothic history, we are told, lasted 2,030 years, precisely from 1490 B.C. to A.D. 540. In 1490 B.C., led by a king, the Goths supposedly used three boats—the Saxons too came to Britannia in three boats[27]—to sail from Scandinavia to the estuary of the Vistula. In A.D. 540, King Vitigis surrendered to the imperial General Belisarius.

Soon after the Goths had landed on the continent they clashed with the Rugians and Vandals, who eventually had to withdraw from the area close to the coast. Here is where "Gothic Scandinavia," *Gothiscandza*, arose, and it provided a home for the Goths until "their fifth king, approximately," led his people to southern Russia. In their new home, "in the fruitful meadows" (*Oium*), they had to face severe trials and tribulations. Most of all, however, their history now became part of classical ethnography with its preconceived explanatory models and stock phrases. For Cassiodorus presented his Gothic history as a *Getica*, the history of the Getae, and Jordanes did not change this in any way. What this means is that he claimed for the Goths the entire history of the Getae, a people related to the Scythians and settled at one time in what is modern-day Romania, whom he understood to be Goths because of their similar-sounding name.

To be sure, Cassiodorus did not invent this "ethno-etymological" equivalence; however, he was the first to use the *Getica* of the Greek writer Dion Chrysostomos (now also lost) and other texts to create an unbroken Gothic history spanning more than two thousand years, which he embedded between a longish pre-Amal and a shorter Amal epoch.

The Amal Gothic history, we are told, reaches from the days of Emperor Domitian (81–96) to 540, when the *origo Gothica* finds its culmination and fulfillment; through the "fortunate defeat" at the hands of Belisarius, it now becomes truly part of Roman history. This interpretation may have been already added by Cassiodorus himself or a little later by Jordanes. By contrast, the Amal *Origo Gothica* begins with a glorious victory over the Romans. Cassiodorus can make his claim because he turns the defeat that one of Emperor Domitian's generals suffered against the Getae in Dacia into the primordial deed, the beneficent founding act of the Amal kings. Even though Cassiodorus must thereby base all of Amal Gothic history on what was in reality a non-Gothic event, he fills this gap of about seventeen generations with the names of a line of kings and gods that is derived solely from the Amal family tradition.

In the older, pre-Amal section of his work, Cassiodorus goes back an elegant distance beyond Domitian and fixes the year of the Gothic landing, that is to say the primordial deed of pre-Amal Gothic history, in the year 1490 B.C. This brought one nearly to the era when Moses "led the Jewish people in the desert"; at the same time it showed that the first deeds of the Goths were older than the Trojan War (calculated at about 1180 B.C.), from which the Romans traced their descent. Finally, equating the Goths with the Getae made it possible for Cassiodorus to Gothicize also all of classical knowledge about the Getae. And so the Goths were given a Thracian-Greek as well as an Asiatic-Egyptian past; no wonder that in this scheme even the Amazons were Gothic warrior women.

When the Ostrogoths made the Amali their kings, they probably also adopted their religion, even though a change of cult is not explicitly mentioned. Such a conversion is documented, however, for the Longobards.

The Origins of the Longobards

The Germans knew two families of gods: the older, settled Vanir, who bestowed fertility, practiced marriage among siblings and a pronounced matriarchal way of life, and counted helpful twin gods among their own; and the younger, warlike Aesir, headed by Odin-Wodan. Against this backdrop unfolds the saga of Longobard origins: lots were drawn to select a group of Vinnili who had to leave their homeland. The archaic sacral king apparently remained behind, for the emigrants followed the two commanders (*duces*), Ibor and Agio, a Dioskouridean pair of brothers who were accompanied and counseled by a wise woman—their mother—who was knowledgeable about the gods. The first crisis on the way to the formation of a new tribe was a clash with the Vandili-Vandals. Incidentally, the same motif dominates also the heroic founding event of pre-Amal Gothic history.

Before the decisive battle, the chief Aesir god, Wodan, prophecies that the Vandal commanders, the enemy Dioskouroi Ambri and Assi, would be victorious. The Vinnili priestess, however, wins the support of her goddess, Frea-Freja, who contrives to make Wodan—in an untypical move the Vanir goddess is made into Wodan's wife—fulfill his prophecy *against* the Vandals. One of Wodan's many names was "longbeard." The Vinnili women and their Vanir goddess trick the god of war into involuntarily naming the threatened tribal group after himself—longbeards-Longobards (Lombards). The story goes as follows: "Frea had advised the women of the Vinnili to let down their hair and arrange it in front of their faces like beards. Then they were to appear early in the morning along with their men and stand where Wodan would have to see them when he followed his usual habit of looking out the window toward sunrise. This was done. When Wodan beheld the women at sunrise, he exclaimed: 'Who are these longbeards?' Whereupon Frea added that he must give victory to those to whom he had given the name." This name-giving had trapped Wodan, he was forced to give victory to the "new" people of his name. Originally he had done the usual thing among gods and had decided in favor of the stronger battalions of the Vandals.[28]

The story is part of the saga of the origins of the Longobards. Sagas like this should not be questioned too closely for their historical content, their chronological horizon, or their geographical location. Their subject matter is strongly altered: chronologically disparate events are synchronized, sons are given fathers who lived hundreds of years earlier.[29] However, the story of the Vinnili shows clearly what a change of name and cult implied, what its preconditions and consequences were: an ethnic group leaves its homeland and takes along traditional ideas about the gods and tribal institutions. The Dioskouridean princes and the importance of female goddesses represent ancient Vanir ways of life and belief, which were quite comparable to those of the Vandals; for example, the tribal saga of the Longobards recounts that their enemies put up resistance under the leadership of the two generals Ambri and Assi.

Already Tacitus speaks in the same breath of the central Vandili cult site ("a sacred grove of ancient worship"), which was presided over by a priest dressed like a woman, and of the Alci-Alces, two deities he equates with the Dioskouroi Castor and Pollux.[30] The clash between Vinnili and Vandili, who were both committed to the same way of life, was settled in favor of the homeless invaders. Both peoples were ready to take on the militarily more successful organizational form of the wandering tribe (the Vandals Ambri and Assi approached the god of war first), which means, in the language of mythology, to turn toward Wodan, the god of warrior bands. At that moment the Vinnili women, the goddess Frea, and her priestess not only prepare this change of cult and name but also actively pursue it, thus gaining victory for their men. As representatives of the Vanir tradition they sacrifice their own past and cultic existence for the welfare of the tribe and thus legitimate the new ethnogenesis. No wonder the saga of Longobard origins made its first monarchical king the son of the second Vinnili dioskouroi and general, Agio.

The Literary Genre of the Origo Gentis

Despite the classical literary constructions that dominate his *origo Gothica,* all of Cassiodorus's work attests to the vitality of a Gothic tradition that reached far into non-Mediterranean regions and pre-Roman times. Yet we must be wary of too readily synchronizing the tribal *memoria* with the accounts of the classical ethnographers of the first centuries A.D. Precisely those passages of Cassiodorus's Gothic history that scholars like to use in this way contain the comment "still today." Every event tagged in this way is thus dated to the sixth century and is not suited for comparisons with classical ethnography before and after the birth of Christ. What, then, is the historical value of an *origo gentis,* the story of a tribe's origins, if we cannot compare it with the statements of writers contemporary with the alleged origins? Are these constructions not an abomination for any historian concerned with the "true" provenance of a people? Would it not be better to do without all tribal histories—from Cassiodorus's Longobard *origo* and the *origo* of Paulus Diaconus, all the way to Widukind's Saxon history and Saxo Grammaticus's history of the Danes (which mentions Hamlet and an early version of Wilhelm Tell)?

It is easy to expect too much from the literary genre of the *origo gentis.* To ask about the "true" origin of a people is already the wrong question, since it is as little amenable to a historical answer as the biological question about which came first, the chicken or the egg. The oral tradition of the tribal *memoria* always recounts origins and beginnings in a way that presupposes other origins and beginnings. The emergence of the Wodan-Longobards presupposed the existence of the Frea-Vinnili. And before the Amali entered Gothic history there were other Goths who venerated non-Amal founding kings; however, the first of those kings did not come out of nowhere but is said to have led the Goths from Scandinavia across the sea. The Franks raised up their "long-haired kings" after they had crossed the Rhine; and before the Hasding royal family of the Vandals came into existence an entire tribe bore that name.

Long before it was put into writing and altered from the classical-biblical perspective, the tribal *memoria* had already selected and distinctly changed its material; it conceived of tradition telescopically, that is to say, it condensed it and presented it in the accelerated style of a time lapse technique. The tradition can in fact reach back many generations and contain genuine names; it can report tribal formations and theogonies of which we would otherwise be ignorant. Like the later heroic saga in which Ermanaric and Theodoric are made into contemporaries, the older tribal *memoria* too can assign the first Longobard king a father who may be five hundred years "older" than his son. That is to say, the chronological horizons of two historical tribal princes are related to each other, and we can spare ourselves the question whether or not we are dealing with the names of two historical individuals.

Cassiodorus had to tackle this sort of material by using the tools of classical ethnography, with the specific goal of legitimating the Amal kings as the rightful rulers of Italy in the eyes of both the Roman and the Goths. Nothing illustrates his approach better than the way in which he structured the generations of the Amal genealogy: just as there were seventeen Roman kings from Aeneas to Romulus, Theodoric's grandson Athalaric ruled in the seventeenth generation after the divine primordial ancestor Gaut. The example of the Goths was followed by the Longobard King Rothari, who justified his law code of 643 with three references to the tribal *memoria:* first, the saga of Longobard origins itself; second, his own Harudian descent in the tenth generation (which alluded to Scandinavian origins); third, the knowledge that he was the seventeenth Longobard king.

Traditions of this kind provided motives for concrete action, so there is no need to ask to what extent they are based on historical dates and facts. This said, it is a fact that stories of origins involving "old names" are found only among those Germanic peoples of the north and east who appear already in the Roman imperial sources up to about A.D. 150, and who presented themselves at that time as "small" peoples and bore names that can be linked to the root word *theudo* (people). Such names are, for example, Gútthiuda, for the homeland of the Danubian Goths, and the old English Saexthéod, for England. Finally, all these peoples had kings whose family traditions were absorbed into the Germanic heroic sagas, usually with tragic content. The death of the Gaut King Beowulf means also the end of his kingdom, just as the kingdoms of Ermanaric and the Burgundian Nibelungs perish along with their rulers. By contrast, the kingless Alamanni and Bavari did not produce their own heroic sagas; their songs told of foreign hero kings, like the Longobard Alboin. The same holds true even for the Franks. Though the Merovingians possessed comparable traditions, Clovis occupied only fourth place in the succession line of royal lineages; compared to Longobard, Anglo-Saxon, Gothic, let alone Scandinavian genealogies, this was very modest indeed.[31]

Stories of origins speak of "genuine and old names":[32] Goths and Gauts, Vinnili and Vandili-Vandals, Longobards and Hasdingi are names of this kind. They depict their bearers as reincarnations of divine founders of the tribe.[33] By contrast, the names of the Alamanni, Franks, and Bavarians reflect later forms of tribal formations. Their meaning is transparent; they are not derived from divine origins but represent events that can be historically grasped and reconstructed—Alamanni: the union of all men; Franks: the union of the free; Bavarians: origins in Bohemia. While reports about these peoples come mostly from outside observers, the "genuine and old names" sum up their origins in three motifs: First, once upon a time there was a small people—the Goths, the Saxons, the Longobards. As their homeland could no longer feed them, they set out under divine guidance. The first test demanded the performance of the primordial deed, be it the crossing of a sea like the Baltic or the North Sea or a river like the Rhine, Elbe, or Danube, be it a victorious battle against mighty enemies—or both, as it was in most cases. In a situation that seems all but hopeless, divine aid is given to a select group of the homeless tribe. Thus the eastern Goths realized that their Amal leaders were Aesir, "with whose good fortune they were wont to win."[34] The Vinnili turned toward the longbeard Wodan and became Longobards. The Franks experienced the charisma of the Merovingians on Roman soil. In this way the primordial deed establishes a new tribal identity, which derives its legitimacy and attraction from the nucleus of tradition, that is to say, from the group of leaders with better gods and organizational structures than exist in the world around them. Both qualities establish the superior status (*nobilitas*) of a people over its neighbors. In this case "smallness ennobles," something the—only seemingly—paradoxical statement *paucitas Langobardos nobilitat* teaches us.[35] The success of the "noble" Longobards led to the creation of a new tribe that grew rapidly in numbers.

Second, as is reported of the Longobards and of Clovis's Franks, and as we can infer for the Goths both from the story of their landing and from the Amal victory, a change of religion and cult takes place during the primordial deed; tradition presents this process also as a singular event.

Among the Longobards, Wodan, the divine leader of warrior bands, replaced Dioskouridean twin gods and a Vanir religion that tended to be matriarchal. After the decisive victory over the Alamanni, Clovis and his core followers underwent baptism.

Third, if the primordial deed was a victory against mighty enemies, those remained the "model enemy" par excellence, either in keeping with later history or quite contrary to historically verifiable events. For Goths and Vinnili the Vandals filled this role, for the Longobards both the Heruli and the Gepids, for the Saxons not the Franks—as one would expect—but the Thuringians. What lived on in these sorts of stories was the memory that one's own gens had once been a subordinate subgroup within a larger tribal confederation from which it had broken away by force, thus triggering or accelerating the confederation's disintegration and downfall.[36]

TWO

The Empire and the "New" Peoples

From the Marcomannic Wars to the End of the Third Century

1. THE LEGACY

When Marcus Aurelius died on March 17, 180—probably near Sirmium, the capital of Pannonia—the Marcomannic wars, which had raged for nearly fourteen years, had also come to an end.[1] Rome had fought four successive campaigns to maintain the frontier along the middle Danube. Sheer endless suffering had befallen the inhabitants between present-day Franconia and Transylvania. The Danubian provinces of Raetia, Pannonia, Moesia, and Dacia, as well as northern Italy, lay ravaged. At the very end a devastating epidemic, the "plague," had driven the horrors beyond the threshold of what was bearable. The Roman Empire appeared shaken to its very foundation.

Yet the philosopher-emperor Marcus Aurelius was able to control the external enemy and master the internal crisis. The measures he took to restore and secure the imperial borders included the construction of new legionary camps in Castra Regina–Regensburg and Lauriacum-Lorch at the mouth of the Enns River. The transfer of border troops to the stretches of the Danube in Raetia and Noricum was a highly significant move, because previously not a single legionary had been stationed between Vienna and Strasbourg. The emperor's decision would have lasting consequences (of course unforeseen at the time). Many centuries later the tribe of the Bavarians coalesced around the camp at Regensburg and made it its political center, while the Carolingian march grew up around Lauriacum-Enns.

Marcus Aurelius had inflicted such a crushing defeat on the Germanic-Sarmatian peoples that Rome even announced the establishment of two new provinces: Sarmatia and Marcomannia. These were intended to link up with Trajan's province of Dacia north of the Danube, thereby eliminating the dangerous "funnel of peoples" formed by the interfluve between the Danube and Theiß rivers. Moreover, the annexation of what are today the

Czech and Slovak republics and of the northern part of Lower Austria would have substantially expanded—following the model of Gaul—the hitherto exceedingly narrow approaches to Italy.

After the emperor's death these ambitious plans were not carried out. Marcus Aurelius's son Commodus essentially returned to the Augustean defensive policy along the Rhine and Danube, motivated probably less by an inability to conceive long-term plans than by an accurate assessment of the real strength of the empire, even if it was victorious at the moment. And so when the young emperor celebrated the triumph over the vanquished enemies in the fall of 180,[2] one could have said, in the words of Tacitus, that once again, as so many times before, Rome was celebrating total victory over Germania.[3]

2. A FAULTY THEORY

Though the Germans were known to the Romans before his time, it was Caesar who discovered them for a broader public[4] and at the same time placed them into the chaos of "the other world." There was a long literary tradition as well as an immediate political reason for situating the Germans in this way: Caesar wanted to explain to his listeners and readers why he had not conquered Germania as he had Gaul. The forested wilds of Germania were home to unreal and fabulous wild beasts (like unicorns and jointless moose); barbarians lived there who were not fully human in Roman eyes, which is why any effort to civilize them was pointless. The conquest of a wholly other world like this could never have lasted; it was thus meaningless, not worth the price of a single Roman legionary. Merchants too had no business with such savages, since they lived in such a primitive primeval state that buying and selling were foreign concepts. Such were the mental framework and stereotypes of classical ethnography; even a man like Tacitus could not fully escape them.

The literary tradition thus blocked the Romans from grasping reality and gave rise to almost ludicrous contradictions. Remarkably good knowledge of the geographic and ethnographic details of Germania came precisely from Roman traders and merchants, whose travels in the country took them far into the Scandinavian north and who were certainly engaging in lucrative exchanges. Their information was used by the same ethnographers who, owing to the prevailing dogma, had to deny that their informants had in fact penetrated so deeply into Germania, because everyone was sure that there was nothing in that country worth trading for.[5]

And so contemporaries were taken in by their own prejudices; a false theory often provided the sole basis for making political and military decisions. To civilized Romans the Germanic peoples offered the spectacle of a "world turned upside down." One could be pleasantly horrified by this world or make fun of it, but is was not necessary to know, let alone understand, it. The result of this attitude was numerous misjudgments. Already at the beginning of the Marcomannic wars, several thousand Longobards had crossed the Danube and invaded Upper Pannonia. From about the time of Christ's birth it had been known that this people lived along the lower Elbe River.[6] To be sure, Romans also noted that the Longobards had played a leading role among the Germans who had attacked in 167. However, it didn't occur to anyone to draw inferences from this, for example by raising or investigating the question of whether intra-Germanic movements might have caused the outbreak of terrible battles and whether one should not prepare for even worse to come.[7] Two generations later, when there were growing indications that the "barbarians sitting on top of Dacia"[8] had become restless, it also did not occur to the responsible authorities in Rome to take suitable measures to counter the impending threat.

Taking countermeasures would have presupposed an understanding of the barbarian world that the Romans did not possess.[9] They thought they knew that new barbarians did not and could not exist: they had always been the same, and as Scythians and Germans they confronted the Romans "like the irrational and the uncontrolled confronts reason."[10] And so it was a popular and often-used policy to destroy barbarians with barbarians, Germans with Germans. Beyond that, how could a government in Rome take the correct preventive measures if its "foreign policy" experts were literati who described the Goths, the Vandals, and the Huns as Scythians, thus equating them with the long-extinct people of the steppes of southern Russia? And for the situation along the Rhine the Romans also had traditional categories at hand: Alamanni and Franks continued to be seen as Germans in the meaning that the word had in the early imperial period; alternatively, in keeping with the pre-Caesarean practice of the Greeks they were even regarded as Celts or Celto-Scyths.

And so all the Old World could do was react to the challenge of the new world; there was nothing to be learned and nothing was learned, even when the Imperium Romanum was thrown into the "world crisis of the third century,"[11] lost the battle of Adrianople on August 9, 378, and suffered the sack of Rome on August 24, 410. The catastrophe that befell Emperor Valens at Adrianople did not register with contemporary Romans. A billionaire senator who had just seen—and one would think, understood—the reality at the Germanic frontier along the Rhine apologized in a letter to a friend for making a big to-do about the events of 378, after devoting half a sentence to them. Our letter writer, in any case, reports in far greater detail about his poor health and need to rest.[12] And long after Rome had been conquered by the Visigothic King Alaric, a story made the rounds which—whether true or invented—is an excellent reflection of the indolence of the Roman leadership: Honorius, the emperor of the western empire, was an avid chicken breeder; his favorite chicken was called Roma. When the fall of the Eternal City was reported to him as the death of Roma, he supposedly broke into violent lamentations and calmed down only after he had been told the message "merely" meant that the Goths had taken Rome.[13]

3. AN OBSOLETE DEFENSIVE DOCTRINE

For centuries the legacy of Augustus determined Roman frontier and military policy. As far as the Germans were concerned, this policy entailed the defense of the Rhine and Danube and the creation of the *limes* in the provinces of Upper Germany and Raetia, a project begun at the end of the first century and fully completed under the early adoptive emperors. The *limes*—a system of light barriers, watchtowers, and small forts—shortened the approaches that had to be defended between the Danube and the Rhine and formed a policing line that stretched from Brühl on the Rhine to a little below Krelheim on the Danube.[14]

The basis of the Augustinian doctrine was the decision to station the Roman army—with its legions, auxiliary units, and irregular troops, about three hundred thousand men or between .5 and 1 percent of the population of the empire—almost exclusively along the borders of the empire. This rigid line took the place of an in-depth defense. The presence of the army in the border regions led to their Romanization. The Rhine and Danube provinces, in particular, were Romanized in this way from the periphery to the center, as a result of which pre-Roman traditions maintained themselves more strongly in the hinterland than along the banks of the two rivers.

If the imperial government was planning offensive wars or had to take defensive measures, the army on the border had to contribute certain detachments, *vexillationes,* to the operational forces that were raised ad hoc. Once the campaign was concluded, the intervention troops were dissolved again and the detachments usually returned to their parent units. This strategic concept got by with remarkably few troops. It functioned during the glory days of the empire as long as Rome had the initiative, whether it was the aggressor itself or had to repel barbarian invasions. However, strains of the magnitude of the Marcomannic wars turned into catastrophes, not to mention the fact that Rome was never in a position to conduct lengthy wars on several fronts at once.

And so the inevitable happened when "new" peoples attacked along the Rhine and Danube, and at the Black Sea, when the old and new Persian enemies invaded Syria after the fall of the Parthian Empire in 224, and foreign barbarians were also ravaging Britain and Africa: the Roman Empire lost its credibility as the protective power of the civilized world. It seemed to dissolve into individual realms separately fighting for their own survival. What manifested itself in the third century as the age of the soldier-emperors was in reality the prelude to a profound transformation of the Roman world.[15]

4. ALAMANNI, FRANKS, AND GOTHS: THE "NEW" PEOPLES OF THE FIRST LINE

The newly attacking tribal groups followed each other in quick succession: the Goths appeared in 238, the Franks in 257/258, and, along with the Franks around the middle of the third century, the Alamanni.[16] These gentes must have appeared to the Romans like three large tribes very much alike, the sole difference being that they penetrated the imperial borders at different points. Their names were new to realistic observers among the Romans; of the three, the Franks could most readily be linked to known peoples.[17] The Alamanni were considered "an ethnically mixed tribe"; this explanation presupposed a knowledge of the Germanic language or Germanic contacts.[18] As for the Goths, for another generation they were given exclusively the name Scythians, until Emperor Claudius II in 269 assumed the triumphal title *Gothicus* and thus announced to the Roman world for the first time the name of the tribe he had in fact defeated.[19]

None of the classical ethnographers made a connection between the Danubian–Black Sea Goths and the Gutones of Pomerania. The Gutones had stepped onto the stage of history at the time when the Romans were penetrating into free Germania. In those days their settlements were strung along the southern coast of the Baltic Sea from Pomerania to the Passarge River in eastern Prussia. Archaeologists assign to this people the products of a culture named after the eastern Prussian town of Willenberg-Wielbark.

This highly distinct, apparently indigenous culture was already characterized by a peculiar practice that would also identify the later Goths during all their migrations: dead Gutones, like dead Goths, were buried without their weapons. This presupposes a belief in the afterlife that was vastly different from that held by neighboring peoples and cultures. All the pagan neighbors of the Gutones, as well as the later Goths, were laid to rest heavily armed; the Gutones had no need of such equipment. Other than that, however, the Gutones were no different from the world in which they lived, either in terms of armaments or institutions; even their kingship they had in common with their East Germanic neighbors. Their kings, however, were special and enjoyed an unusual degree of authority by Germanic standards. To join the Gutonic kings one had only to be a good warrior and maintain a certain measure of discipline. In this way a body of royal retainers must have developed, with the help of which the Gutones surpassed the military capabilities of the surrounding peoples. This also explains the apparent contradictions that had already come to characterize the early history of the Gutones. The Gutones, so the story goes, were initially a dependent and, supposedly for a long time, also a small tribe, yet they occupied an expansive settlement area. Around A.D. 150, no later than five generations after they are first mentioned, they settled on the eastern, Sarmatian bank of the central reaches of the Vistula. Here the Gutones became the core of the barbarian avalanche that led to momentous changes in the Sarmatia–Black Sea region in the last third of the second century and eventually to the collapse of the Roman border along the Danube.

Taking the Roman point of view, we still speak of the Marcomannic wars, a term that does not do justice to the full dimensions of the events. The Gutones who penetrated into the region between the lower Danube and the Don at the end of the second century were, in any case, no longer a small people. They asserted themselves successfully against the native inhabitants and soon stood—always under royal leadership—at the head of very warlike tribal federations. Together with other Germanic and non-Germanic gentes they threatened the Roman Empire. In their newly acquired settlement areas the Gutonic emigrants had become Goths at the moment the Old World considered them Scythians. Their archaeological legacy is called the Cherniakhov culture and has links with the Wielbark culture in what is today northern Poland. Nevertheless, if it weren't for Cassiodorus's *origo Gothica,* in the Jordanes version from the mid-sixth century, probably no historian would venture to expand the history of the Goths to take in that of the Gutones.[20]

The Alamanni bear a name that—all scholarly objections notwithstanding—can be easily interpreted to mean "all men" or "all of mankind." They were a composite of "many peoples." A sixth-century source, drawing on a source three hundred years older, makes a connection between the name of the Alamanni and their polyethnic character. As late as the beginning of the seventh century one still spoke quite as a matter of course of the *nationes Suevorum,* the "peoples of the Suevi." To be sure, the equating of Suevi and Alamanni is not attested prior to the year 500. Still, one could imagine a connection between the appearance of the Alamanni name and that of the Suevi, much older and also composed of many peoples; after all, this connection has remained intact to this day in Swabia. The first mention and meaning of the name thus suggests that the Alamanni were a confederation of warrior bands, not least of Suevic origin, that was newly formed around the middle of the third century, at the latest. However, they either did not call themselves Alamanni but were given that name by their Germanic neighbors, or their self-chosen name as "all of mankind" was reinterpreted by those neighbors pejoratively to mean "half-breeds." To be a bunch of "half-breeds" and "newcomers" from God-knows-where was, after all, incompatible with a people's pride and anything but honorable. The following story is evidence of that: When we meet the Juthungi for the first time in 270, they vigorously deny—in view of the Alamanni name whose meaning was transparent to them—that they are "half-breeds" and not "pure and genuine." At that time the Juthungi were not yet Alamanni; only in the fourth century were they too counted among the Alamannic tribal confederation.[21]

For a long time tribes with the names Hermunduri and Naristi had been neighbors of the Romans along the *limes* in Upper Germania and Raetia. Their Alamannic-Juthungian successors were certainly not "old barbarians" under new names. Instead, they were for the most part immigrants from the Elbe region of Germania who displaced the Hermunduri name without having driven out or slaughtered every last Hermundurus. Genocide is a phenomenon of the modern world; the constant shortage of people in the tribes was reason enough why genocide did not accompany the formation of barbarian tribes. Thus many a Hermundurus and Naristus must have become an Alamannus or Juthungus, while their old names lived on in changed form and outside their original areas of settlement.[22]

Until now, "attempts to explain the emergence of the new tribes of the third century have focused too one-sidedly on Germanic roots." "In war and peace the Franks dealt mostly with the command staffs of Lower Germany in Cologne." The Alamanni looked toward Mainz, and the Juthungi, as successors to the Hermunduri, developed a close relationship with Augsburg and thus with the provincial administration of Raetia. "Frequent meetings between certain Germanic chieftains in Cologne, Mainz, or Augsburg may have led to joint action and eventually to a confederation. Since the Alamanni were increasingly pushed toward the south, they gradually occupied Raetian territory too. This gave rise to an Alamannic-Juthungian community of shared interests, which eventually led to the absorption of the Juthungi into the Alamannic tribal confederation."[23] This scenario accords with the fact that the Romans, after giving up the *limes,* called the Germans of the upper Rhine Alamanni and those of the lower Rhine Franks.[24]

Among the three "new" peoples the one most important for the future was the Franks. Frank and free: is the Frank a free man or the free man a Frank?—this has been the topic of endless scholarly controversies. Already in the fourth century the name was interpreted to mean "the wild" or "the brave," but also "the protected," which agrees with the meaning "the free." The older view is thus the most plausible: when those Germanic tribes along the right bank of the lower Rhine who had remained free, who had not been subjected—the Chamavi, Bructi, Ambivarii, Chattuari, and probably also the Chatti and other small tribes—formed a confederation (around A.D. 200) against the teetering Imperium Romanum, they had called themselves the Free. The Salians, however, who later held the pre-eminent place among them, did not become Franks until the fourth century; the creation of their kingship, one distinguished in many ways, required as the primordial deed the crossing of the Rhine.[25]

5. SAXONS, VANDALS, AND BURGUNDIANS: THE "NEW" PEOPLES OF THE SECOND LINE

The Saxons, Vandals, and Burgundians were just as "new" or "old" as the Goths when they became the object of Rome's politico-military interest in the course of the third century. Ptolemy had probably been the first to mention the Saxons, around the middle of the second century. The first unequivocal mention of Saxon pirates, however, comes only in the year 286, when they had plundered what was then the Roman coast of the English Channel. Their name is almost certainly derived from the "sax," the short, cutting sword that classical authors had first noticed among the peoples in northeastern Germany.[26]

The Vandals, who had originally formed one large ethnic group (like the Suevi), bore "a genuine and old tribal name."[27] The Longobards arose in the struggle against the Vandals. The Gothic tribal saga too reflects centuries of conflict between Goths and Vandals. True to its bias the saga celebrates the very first clash as a Gothic victory. In reality, what took place was probably not a singular incident but a longer process that freed the Gutones from dependence on the Vandals. Pliny the Elder still knew the Gutones as a subgroup of the Vandals-Vandili. The Gutones are also mentioned in connection with the Lugians, and even Tacitus speaks of Lugians and Vandals in one breath.

In all likelihood the Lugians and the Vandals were one cultic community that lived in the same region of the Oder in Silesia, where it was first under Celtic and then under Germanic domination. What was for the most part considered "Celtic" around the time of Christ's birth was considered "Germanic" a century later. The Lugian name was preserved, and so Tacitus could simultaneously recognize the importance of the Vandals, locate the Gutones—from the perspective of the Danubian frontier—"beyond the Lugians," and include many Lugian subtribes among the Vandals.

At the end of the first and the beginning of the second century, the Gutones separated from the Lugian-Vandal community and moved from Pomerania to the Vistula. The Vandals (assigned by archaeologists to the Przeworsk culture) meanwhile expanded southward from what is today central Poland. The Sudeten Mountains became the "Vandal Mountains"[28] and demarcated the land of one of the Vandal subtribes, the Silesian Silings. To their east we can make out the other Vandals, the Hasdingi, the "long-haired," whose ancient customs and institutions probably reach back into the Lugian period. For example, the first three generations of their royal line are pairs of military kings: Ambri and Assi ("alder" and "ash") resist the Longobards, Raus and Rapt ("beam" and "reed") request permission in 171 to enter Trajan's Dacia, and even two hundred years later Hasdingi warriors invade the Roman Empire under the leadership of two kings whose names are unknown to us.[29] The Hasdingi in the narrower sense can be compared to the Gothic Amals, who were also considered to be Aesir: for one thing, both names represent the ethnic group from which "the kings are chosen"; for another, the name of the Amal Aesir probably means the same as the names of the Vandal dual kings Raus and Rapt, namely, a log or tree from which stake idols were carved.[30]

While the majority of the Silings remained beyond the Sudeten Mountains, Hasding groups had already crossed the Carpathian Mountains southward by the time of the Marcomannic wars. We are told that they joined the great Gothic military King Cniva around 250; in 270 they penetrated from the upper reaches of the Tisza River all the way into Pannonia.[31] Just as the Saxons backed the Franks, the Vandals backed the Goths in the conflict with Rome. The Burgundians—coming from the region of the middle reaches of the Oder River—deployed behind the Alamanni. Generally the name of a new people becomes known after its first penetration into the Roman Empire. In 278, Burgundian hordes, who had been joined by Siling Vandals, appeared in Raetia and were defeated by Emperor Probus.[32] But more than a century later the Burgundians—against the conventional doctrine—were "a new name of a new enemy."[33]

To be sure, the Burgundians were above all bitter enemies of the Alamanni. This made them interesting to Roman imperial policy; the Burgundians seemed good candidates for an alliance, provided they didn't operate along the Rhine in too great numbers. The special relationship between Rome and the Burgundians was in keeping with the belief of the latter that they were relatives and descendants of Romans, who for their part derived the name of this tribe from the fact that the Burgundians had provided the garrisons of the *burgi,* the typical late-antique border fortifications. This feeling of closeness also kept a Roman observer from dismissing the peculiar Burgundian kingship as barbaric; instead, he compared it to the sacral responsibility of Egyptian pharaohs.[34]

6. THE BARBARIAN SETTLEMENT IN THE BORDER PROVINCES OF THE EMPIRE

From the very beginning, the imperial government had to deal with barbarian chieftains and their bands, indeed with larger groups, who petitioned for admission and settlement on Roman soil or sought to achieve this by force (usually without success). The motives of the petitioners were varied: losers in tribal feuds sought protection against their victorious opponents; dispersed units saw no other way of ensuring their physical survival; many others were enticed by a better life within the borders of the empire, just as today people from the Third World are drawn to the First World. However, none of these groups pushing into the empire saw themselves as conquerors, and the same holds true of barbarians who sought glory and booty at the expense of Rome and launched plundering raids into the border provinces.

The Goths

More than a generation had to suffer the disastrous Gothic assaults that ravaged the entire Balkan Peninsula and Asia Minor beginning in 238. In 250, the Goths launched a campaign lasting several years against the provinces of Dacia, Moesia, and Thrace. The operation was led by a mighty king named Cniva, who was able to muster, in addition to the Goths, a number of other tribes of Germanic as well as Sarmatian origin; even Roman deserters seem to have joined him.

Cniva proved himself a general who had more than just a primitive knowledge of tactics and strategy. His kingship was so strong that he could accept losses and defeats without having his followers desert him. Eventually the Roman army of the Danube, along with the emperor and his son, would be defeated by Cniva's huge barbarian force.

After some initial successes, the Romans—probably in June of 251—met the main Gothic army around Abrittus-Hisarlak near Razgard in modern Bulgaria. Cniva lured the enemy into treacherous marshland he knew well. Here he could divide the Gothic force into several tactical units with which he sought to encircle the imperial troops. The maneuver was successful and the emperor and his son were killed in the ensuing battle. The Goths moved on, laden with a rich booty of prisoners and goods, and Rome even had to agree to annual payments.

About the same time a plaguelike epidemic broke out and ravaged the land for years. The empire's strength was nearly exhausted. But neither Cniva nor any of the other attackers had indicated that they wanted to settle on Roman soil; in fact, even Trajan's Dacia was not conquered, though it was all but defenseless. The booty taken was an incitement to further raids, which revealed that the behavior of the attackers was both murderous and suicidal.

Barbarian ruthlessness, an old motif of the classical authors, was taken to new heights when Gothic attacks from the sea injected an entirely new element of warfare into the conflict. In 257, Gothic pirates ravaged the southwestern coast of the Black Sea for the first time. A barbarian invasion of unprecedented size was launched in the spring of 268, and the combined Gothic-Herulian fleet was able to break through into the Aegean. But only a few months later, in 269, Emperor Claudius II, after some initial successes in Thrace, won a great victory at Naissus-Nish. Only a fraction of the Gothic warriors who had originally set out returned to their homeland. Claudius II was the first Roman emperor to assume the triumphal title *Gothicus*.

The next victor over the Goths was Claudius's successor Aurelian, who crossed the Danube in 271 and defeated the Goths in several engagements on their own territory. Now the Gothic danger seemed averted for good. Aurelian certainly deserved his triumphal title *Gothicus Maximus*, for he had not only gained victory over the enemy but had also won peace: "Defeated by Aurelian, the stern avenger of their misdeeds, the Goths kept quiet for many centuries."[35]

In fact it was only for a century that the Gothic question seemed to have been essentially solved. However, this does not in any way detract from Aurelian's achievement. From a position of strength the emperor could decide to give up Trajan's Dacia administratively, a province he still had in firm control. How correct Aurelian's decision had been became clear during the following decades. The Goths had their hands full taking possession of Dacia, dividing the land with their allies, and defending it against their enemies. But there certainly was no violent conquest of the most recent and only Roman province north of the Danube.[36]

The Alamanni

The loss of the *agri decumates*—essentially the area of modern-day Baden-Württemberg, southern Hessia, and northwestern Bavaria—was also not the result of a planned conquest by the Alamanni; rather it was the consequence of intra-Roman conflicts in the course of which the imperial government abandoned the parts of Germania Superior and Raetia that were located on the right bank of the Rhine. Though the name of the Alamanni is not securely attested before 289, the Germans who broke through the *limes* at several locations around the middle of the third century were most likely already Alamanni.[37] In the west they succeeded in pushing across the Rhine all the way to Trier, in the south they crossed the Danube and reached as far as the northern foothills of the Alps. The imperial border had little protection as Rome's best troops had been sent to fight yet another war with the Persians. As soon as the Roman army—reinforced by units from the East—had returned to the West, they were quickly able to drive the Alamanni back across the *limes*. Thereafter the Alamanni launched a plundering raid every five years, until the Roman imperial defense was withdrawn to the line running from the Rhine to lake Constance, to the Iller and the Danube.

Emperor Gallienus had proved himself a capable general in the fight against Alamanni and Franks, and his favoritism toward the West had been so blatant that it led after 258 to an estrangement between him and his father, Emperor Valerian. Then, in June of 260, Valerian fell into Persian captivity, from which he would never return. "Raetia lost under the princeps Gallienus"—this was the high point of Rome's misery.

Gallienus reacted with appropriate measures. Among the accomplishments to his credit was the abandonment of the obsolete defensive doctrine that said that the empire was to be defended exclusively at the borders. At the end of 258, or possibly as early as 257, Gallienus had used his newly established striking force in a victory over Germans along the upper Rhine, who probably already considered themselves Alamanni. The emperor chose Milan as his central base and stationed there heavy cavalry led by a special commander. Moreover, it is likely that Gallienus no longer sent legionary *vexillationes* (detachments) back to their units but kept them in his vicinity as a permanent reserve. The redeployment of mobile units into the interior of the empire and the abandonment of another doctrine, according to which the legionary soldier fighting on foot formed the backbone of the *exercitus Romanus,* constituted revolutionary measures that went hand in hand with the concurrent ousting of senators from the ranks of officers in the army.

The Germanic invaders in 259/260 were also dispersed and soon after annihilated in Gaul and northern Italy. Still, Gallienus was not able to reestablish the old imperial border: before the ill-fated year 260 was over, the Roman governor of Upper Pannonia, Postumus, usurped power and established a separatist Gallic state, drawing his strength primarily from Germanic warriors. Shortly before, Gallienus had already begun constructing a new border defense in Upper Germany behind the Rhine and in Raetia behind the Danube. For example, the dilapidated legionary camp of Vindonissa-Windisch in the Swiss canton of Aargau was rebuilt.[38]

Alamanni and Goths were the first Germans who succeeded in winning Roman territory. However, it would be more accurate to say that their success "happened" rather than that they were explicitly aiming for this. There is a noticeable difference, though, between East and West: while the Goths in the subsequent period remained largely quiet (with the exception of a few raids by individual bands), the Alamanni did not stop their large-scale raids into the Imperium Romanum even after they had pushed their way into the *agri decumates.*

This difference probably had to do not least with the different political structures of the two large tribes. Until their serious defeat at the hands of Claudius II and Aurelian, the Goths had had a strong kingship that ruled the area between the Romanian lands of the Danube and the Crimea. Five thousand warriors perished along with the last pre-Amal Gothic king, whereupon the kingship that was common to the whole tribe came to an end. The western Goths established themselves as the oligarchic Tervingi-Vesi, while the Amal must have succeeded around this time in setting themselves up as the kings of the eastern Greutungi-Ostrogoths. Around 290/291 the division of the Goths into these two tribes was an accomplished fact. Approximately the same time the Gepids made their appearance in the Carpathian region; the Goths regarded them as close and hostile relatives.[39]

The Goths fought for their survival as a divided people deprived of their common kingship. Though a military kingship, it had taken over so much from the duties and meaning of the archaic *thiudans*-kingship that it possessed considerable sacral prestige. By contrast, the Alamanni had no comparable institution, no old nuclei of tradition that could create large-scale tribal organizational forms just as easily as they could drag them along in their own downfall. Even after 260, bands of Alamannic predators—apparently organized on the basis of retainership—continued their plundering expeditions into the Roman Empire, while the Alamannic gentes settled the abandoned Roman territory only slowly and hesitantly. With the exception of the Juthungi who later became Alemanni, no tribal group brought with it an ancient name. Though many kings and chiefs are known by name, none came from old families.

The advance of the Alamanni resembles in a certain respect the much later Slavic settlement between the Baltic and the Mediterranean. In both instances the new arrivals moved in numerous groups without a monarchical leadership, they clung tenaciously to their common name and took their special names from the occupied lands, the *patriae*.[40] However, as one would expect, the first special Alamannic names are not attested until a century after the first settlement on Roman soil.[41] Thus it is not before the middle of the fourth century that we find the Lentienses, the inhabitants of the Linzgau on the northern shore of Lake Constance,[42] the Bucinobantes on the right bank of the Rhine across from Mainz,[43] the Brisigavi in the Breisgau, and finally the Raetovarii, the "people from Raetia," that is to say, from the Ries around Nördlingen.[44]

These territorial names—most of them known to us characteristically enough as the names of Roman elite units—can frequently be assigned to one or more kings who formed the leadership stratum of the tribes. However, there are three times as many *reges* with clearly defined territories under their rule as there are territorial names. These kings concluded treaties with one another as well as with the Romans; at no time, however, were they all united in fighting the Romans, and yet they all appear to have been related and to have attended more or less regular gatherings. "An overarching organization under a common military king recognized by all is not attested for the period of settlement around 260 to the conflict with the Franks. Evidence for the unifying idea of an Alamannic sense of community is lacking."[45]

It is difficult to say how much of this tribal structure from the middle of the fourth century reaches back into the third century. A constitution without a unified leadership but a multitude of power centers was as much an Alamannic legacy as the general name. From the moment these Germans ceased to be mere brigands and became instead both enemies and servants of Rome, the traditional structures had to be adapted to Roman conceptions. The various Alamannic tribal groups assigned themselves to specific territories with Romano-Celtic names.

The Franks

In recklessness and boldness, the first Frankish advances into the empire surpassed everything the Romans had previously come to expect from the Germans on the other side of the Rhine. At their first appearance in 257/258, bands of Frankish marauders roamed across all of Gaul. South of the Pyrenees they destroyed the city of Tarragona on Spain's Mediterranean coast; here they probably got hold of some boats, using them to advance as far as the coast of North Africa. Only a few years later, Franks took part in the Alamannic invasions of the year 250 and fought with varying success against the Gallic Emperor Postumus.

Postumus, a Roman general, had usurped the imperial power over the large province of Gaul, and his method was typical of this period: in 258, Emperor Gallienus had to leave the Rhine border to fight foreign and domestic enemies in Illyria. He left his young son behind in Cologne in the care of a tribune and transferred the command in Gaul to his capable and trusted general, Postumus. Following the victory in 260 over the invading Alamanni and Franks, the question was what to do with the booty that had been recovered from the defeated Germans. Against the tribune's objections, Postumus advocated that the plundered goods not be returned to their original Roman owners but instead be distributed among the soldiers. That did it: the Rhenish army rebelled, Postumus seized the purple, and the emperor's son and his protector were killed.

The question to whom the booty recovered from the barbarians belonged was addressed around 270 in the "canonical letter" of a bishop from Asia Minor. The frequent Gothic-Sarmatian invasions of Asia Minor had been used not only by the impoverished and oppressed to change the existing distribution of property in their favor. Members of the upper class too had sought to enrich themselves by organizing militias and fighting back the attackers, something the regular army, whose resources had long since been overtaxed, could not do. Not least at stake was the booty recovered from the Goths. And we hear not only of money and goods, but also of captives who passed from the hands of the Goths into the hands of their Roman "liberators" without regaining their freedom. The bishop condemned such outrageous behavior in the strongest possible terms, declaring that the community of Christians could not tolerate it under any circumstances. Still, in the fifth century Roman legislation tried in vain to impress upon the leaders of successful militias that they had to return all booty recovered from the barbarians to the rightful owners. The conduct of Postumus, a Roman officer of regular units, reveals to what extent even the Roman army had ceased to be under control of the state.

By the time Aurelian was able to return Gaul to the fold of the empire in 274, the territory east of the lower Rhine had been ravaged and Tongeren destroyed; a little while later Trier shared the fate of Tongeren. Emperor Probus, Aurelian's immediate successor, restored the imperial border in serious fighting that inflicted heavy casualties on the enemies. During the conflict, Frankish prisoners of war were dragged off clear across Europe to the Black Sea, where they were supposed to be settled as dependent peasants. But the captive Franks seized some ships, and after an adventurous "Viking expedition" through the Mediterranean and the Strait of Gibraltar, they returned to their homeland on the lower Rhine.

This period also witnessed the first Frankish-Saxon pirate raids against the coasts of the Roman channel. Expeditions of this sort are reminiscent of the Gothic-Herulian raids in the Black Sea and the Aegean. These plundering raids at sea stand in striking contrast to the later unseaworthiness of the Goths and Franks.

The fighting continued with frightening regularity. After Emperor Diocletian had charged the capable Maximian with the conduct of the war in the western provinces, first as Caesar and after 286 as Augustus, the old enemies of Roman Gaul—including Franks, Alamanni, Burgundians, and even Heruli—suffered heavy losses; in fact, so devastating were the losses that "the Rhine might well run dry, flow along in a barely perceptible trickle, and yet there was no cause for fear, since everything I behold on the other side of the Rhine is Roman."[46]

Beginning in 286, Maximian had gone on the offensive and twice crossed the lower Rhine with his troops. Eventually a Frankish king, reportedly Gennobaudes by name, submitted to him, promised peace, and returned a large number of prisoners. In return Maximian allowed the Franks to conclude a regular *foedus*, a treaty concluded in accord with the Roman *ius gentium*. It is no coincidence that the first mention of a Frankish king and the oldest known *foedus* of the Franks coincide chronologically: through the treaty Gennobaudes "recovered his kingship" from the emperor "and received it from him personally."[47]

7. AN INTERIM ASSESSMENT

The history of the third century unfolded with dreadful monotony: usurpations at home, Germanic attacks in the West, Gothic advances in the East, and all this punctuated by the never-ending Persian wars. The barbarians invaded the land, sowed devastation, and made off laden with booty. Often the Romans succeeded in luring them into a trap, encircling them and inflicting heavy or even devastating losses; but it didn't take long before the invaders were back. The land was destroyed, those whom the enemy had not killed or driven off fell victim to famine and plague.

The Christians, however, a growing minority, suffered simultaneously at the hands of the empire and the barbarians. The general trend toward regionalization and the fracturing of the res publica coincided with the critical attitude of the Christians toward the Imperium Romanum. For instance, a bishop from Asia Minor called on his parishioners to show solidarity not as Romans and citizens of the empire but as Christians and Pontici, inhabitants of the Black Sea region.

The transformation of the empire led to the restoration during the era of Diocletian and Constantine. And the "new" peoples were not immune to this transformation. The barbarians suffered from a chronic lack of manpower, which they tried to remedy with captives. Even if they were successful in doing so, the tribal economy still remained an economy of plunder and scarcity. Hunger and deprivation ruled. Revealingly enough, the members of the leading stratum, as for example the Burgundian *hendinos*-kings, were probably answerable with their lives for success in war and the blessings of a good harvest.

War and harvest were the forms of economic life that ensured the survival of the gens, even if the plundering expeditions cost the lives of many members. However, there was a limit beyond which an economy of plunder turned into life-threatening overexploitation. When this happened the chance opened up for the military kings, either as monarchs or as the leading stratum of the consolidating gentes, to find a modus vivendi with Rome, that is, to conclude a treaty. Thus Aurelian signed on the defeated Vandals in 270, Maximian the Frankish King Gennobaudes, and in the 290s, at the latest, the Goths came aboard.[48] To be sure, this did not solve the Germanic problem in politico-military terms. In fact, clashes between the empire and the external foes actually became more fierce, as annihilating battles outside Strasbourg in 357 and Adrianople in 378 would show. Still, the possibility of turning the "new" peoples into federates in the conventional sense allowed for an accommodation between the world of antiquity and the other world of the barbarians. For now this instrument of Roman foreign policy was used only for the Germans beyond the empire's borders; nevertheless, for a century it was enough to get the "savages raging" against Rome to adopt a peculiarly ambivalent attitude, one that made them in equal measure dangerous enemies and servants of the empire.

THREE

The Germanic Peoples as Enemies and Servants of the Empire in the Fourth Century

1. AN OUTLINE OF THE ORGANIZATION AND SOCIAL STRUCTURE OF THE EMPIRE

The Organization of the Empire

Though their religious policy toward the Christians could not have been more different, the emperors Diocletian (284–305) and Constantine the Great (306–337) had one thing in common: with an iron hand they put an end to the principate ("rule of the emperor as the first citizen"), which had degenerated into the emperorship of generals, and reorganized the empire as a far more strictly regimented dominate ("rule of the lord"). While Augustus, in keeping with the original theory, had seen himself as the first man in the state and the citizenry, and his successors too had committed themselves to this principle, the emperor now became the unquestioned lord and master. As such he assumed toward the community the same position which previously only the master over slaves had held: *Dominus est, cui est servus*—"He who has a slave is a lord."[1]

The emperor's word was law. Legislative power lay in his hands: the dominus stood above the law, *princeps legibus solutus est,*[2] and established the law. *Leges* originated as written answers (*rescripta*) from the emperor to questions from offices and magistrates. Only the highest officials had the power to issue decrees with legal force for their region (*edicta*); the Italian kings of the sixth and seventh century made use of this right, since they saw their regnum as part of the empire and thus recognized the emperor as the sole legislator.

The Diocletian-Constantinian reform effort dealt primarily with imperial administration and military organization. The entire executive was organized on military lines; in fact, it *was* the army, though here, contrary to Roman tradition, a functional division was established between civilian

authority and actual military power. During the following centuries the civilian bureaucracy was seen as the *militia Romana* that was open only to citizens of the empire, preferably those with legal training. By contrast, armed
might, *militia armata,* was opened up far more extensively than before to the
barbarians inside and outside the empire. Many of them had successful careers in the army, indeed they found their home here.

Emperor Diocletian had already augmented the troop strength; we are
told he increased the size of the army fourfold; in reality, though, he probably doubled its strength. Those units who continued to serve at the border,
the *limes,* each stood under the command of a sector commander, a *dux
limitis,* and in 363 they were for the first time called *limitanei.*[3] Then there
was the mobile army, which was organized as imperial retainers, *comitatus,*
and whose units, also called marching army or field army, were structured
by military worthiness and rank: Next to the guard troops, the soldiers
closest to the emperor were the "palace people," *palatini,* who were composed of certain legions and the barbarian auxiliaries. The second group of
the mobile army was made up by the actual retainers, *comitatenses,* which
comprised the remaining legions and detachments, *vexillationes.* The lowest
rank in the mobile army was held by the *pseudocomitatenses,* who were formed
from the border troops as the need arose and were thus withdrawn from the
borders, a move that diminished the valor of the *limitanei.*

On the basis of organizational forms that had been developed already in
the third century, Constantine created the guard of *protectores (et) domestici,*
who were organized into "schools" (*scholae*), each consisting of two cavalry
squadrons and an infantry regiment of five hundred men. Around 400,
under Emperor Honorius, the household troops were commanded by one
comes domesticorum equitum for the cavalry and one *comes domesticorum peditum*
for the infantry.[4] These commanders were *comites illustrissimi* of the highest rank, second only to the army chiefs. While the troop strength of the
guard units did not increase, their number did: after 400 there were seven
scholae palatinae in the East and five in the West.

Since service in the guard brought with it certain privileges, higher pay,
and more splendid trappings, the rank of a guard was also bestowed as an
honorific and thus lost much of its military character in the course of the
fifth century. This necessitated the formation of new guard troops, while the
old ones marched out only for parades or were simply sent into retirement
(Theodoric the Great retired his old guard troops). The increasing demili-
tarization of the palace units was undoubtedly also furthered by a typical
late Roman dual command: in peacetime the guard was led by a civilian official, the *magister officiorum;* though he was also responsible for the armament factories, in wartime he had to yield the command to the two *comites
domesticorum.*[5]

Already under Diocletian, the number of provinces was nearly doubled through numerous subdivisions; we hear on one occasion of 94 provinces, on another of 114. Several of these new provinces together formed a diocese; at first there were twelve, later fourteen of these larger administrative bodies, whose name lives on to this day in the organization of the Catholic Church. While the Diocletian tetrarchy, the rule of four emperors over four portions of the empire, was a passing phenomenon, the formation of large-scale administrative units became unavoidable. However, it was only Constantine who created the territorial prefectures, which were to fill this administrative need. The prefecture of Gaul comprised the entire West from Mauretania to Britannia, inclusive of Spain and Gaul. The center was formed by the prefecture of Italy, Illyria, and Africa, which initially stretched from Milan to Sirmium–Sremska Mitrovica and from Carthage to Thessalonica. The prefecture of the East was made up of Thrace, the Asian provinces, and Egypt, along with Lybia and Cyrenaica.

When the Imperium Romanum was divided at the end of the fourth century into a western empire with the capital at Milan, later Ravenna, and an eastern empire with the capital at Constantinople, the unity of Greater Illyria, which stretched from Salzburg to Sofia, came to an end. The two provinces of Noricum and the four provinces of Pannonia, along with Dalmatia, went to the West as the diocese of Illyria-Pannonia; the two dioceses of Dacia and Macedonia formed the prefecture of Illyria which belonged to the eastern empire.

The Diocletian-Constantinian organization basically envisaged that the military offices not only ranked behind their civilian counterparts but were also dependent on them. Thus the entire system of provisions and supplies for the army, the armaments factories and horse farms, indeed for a while even the guard troops, were under civilian supervision. The provinces were governed by civilian officials with the title of a higher-ranking *corrector* or a lower-ranking *praeses*. At the tops of the dioceses were the vicars. One or more border provinces formed a single military district, the commander of which was a "military commander" in the true sense and carried the title *dux*.

Whereas the modern separation of powers envisages a judiciary alongside the legislative and the executive, in the late-antique state judicial power fell within the executive's sphere of authority. Every officeholder was therefore simultaneously judge over those subordinated to or within his jurisdiction. Military officers sat in judgment over their soldiers, and the heads of the central, regional, and local authorities sat in judgment over the lower bureaucracy and the citizens of the empire. High magistrates, however, drew upon the services of career judges when it came to the administration of justice.

The traditional *cursus honorum* of the Roman high bureaucracy had been characterized by a well-balanced service that put its members to use as military and civilian administrators both at the center and the periphery of the empire. A man's career began in Rome, and following an appropriate period of service in the provinces, he returned to the capital to advance to higher positions. Via the highest provincial posts, the career track eventually led back to the center and to the top echelons of the Roman bureaucracy. However, such a career generally presupposed descent from a senatorial family; the career of the *equites,* the second order, culminated below the very top level.

In the third century the privileges of social rank had at times turned into a distinct disadvantage, and at the beginning of the dominate they were legally abolished. What mattered most now was proximity to the ruler; membership in the *comitatus* determined how the various imperial "followers" would be used. Such a *comes* in the true sense of the word began his career not infrequently at the center and then had to prove himself as a representative far from the court. Thus *comites provinciarum* were used to supervise the various diocesan administrations, a mandate which, in the case of the *comes Orientis,* even developed from a temporary appointment into a permanent institution.

In the mobile army, *comites rei militaris* held the higher posts of command and could rise to be *comes et magister militum.* In the beginning, each emperor had a single, higher-ranking infantry commander, *magister peditum,* and a subordinate cavalry commander, *magister equitum.* In the course of the fourth and at the beginning of the fifth centuries, the number of commanders rose; their positions were regionalized along the lines of the prefectures and, as needed, also along the lines of the dioceses. When the emperorship became "domesticated," that is to say, when those who held it for some time after the death of Theodosius I in January of 395 did not play a role as active generals, there arose in the East and the West the office of the imperial commander in chief; as *comes et magister utriusque militiae praesentalis* he combined in his person a previously unimagined amount of power. Not only did he unite both branches of the army under his command and carry the highest honorary title of a patrician, in violation of the Diocletian-Constantinian arrangement he also exercised an increasing measure of civilian authority.

Beginning around 400, to enforce their claims to power the generals drew support from their own guard troops, the *buccellarii.* From the start this unit was open to both Romans and Goths; the name comes from the *buccella,* a better variety of bread that was given to these troops. In the East, the highest-ranking generals were not able to take the step from holding a magistracy to being rulers; in the West, by contrast, this development became institutionalized in the function of the *patricius occidentis.*[6] It is no surprise that the kings of the Roman-barbarian realms took the vice-emperorship of the western generalissimi as their starting point, indeed frequently using attainment of this position as a precondition for the institutionalization of their power or taking this supermagistracy as their model.

Every revolution, whether an overthrow from below or a restoration from above, has to live with the contradiction that it can be "radical" only when it comes to the elimination of individuals and groups, while being unable to bring about a change in the traditional structures. Roman society was founded on wealth, rank, and class; at its head stood senators and *equites*. The more individual emperors had to fear senatorial opposition, and the less "family" they had themselves, the more they were interested in packing the senate with their own supporters or in cutting back its influence. The *equites* pushed into the resulting political and social vacuum.

At the beginning of the fourth century, the senate seemed to be more a time-honored tradition than a necessary institution, let alone one with a future. A fundamental change occurred with Constantine the Great, for there was now a senate in Rome and one in Constantinople, and—to put it in simple terms—the entire upper stratum of the empire formed the new senatorial nobility. The criteria of selection were a balanced combination of birth and proven ability in government service.

However, since admission into the imperial *comitatus* took place essentially without regard to social class, and since the comitatus served as the pool of appointees to the most important offices of the state, including even senatorial offices, it was always possible that capable careerists would be added to the senators, in fact would greatly increase their numbers. Once someone had attained senatorial dignity by way of the successful tenure of some appropriate magistracy, one of the most important mechanisms of the dominate kicked in: all social rankings and professions were to a large extent heritable. Now all male descendants were also senators, though they had to confirm and preserve their inherited dignity as servants to the state. One result of this was that the rank of *equites* lost its inherited status and was awarded by the emperor to those in question after their service as *militantes* and *officiales,* midlevel military and civilian civil servants. At the same time the regional and local upper classes, the heritable *curiales* of the cities, sought to rise into the senatorial rank and thus enjoy the privileges that came with it.[7]

The notion that the dominate was a centralized despotic state not only ignores the fact that it lacked the necessary systems of communication, it is also refuted by the historical evidence. While it is true that the dominate sought to regiment and supervise society, tie people through inheritance to occupation and soil, and set and freeze prices and wages, it had to rely on a largely decentralized administration to accomplish these goals. As a res publica the Roman Empire was always composed of a multitude of autonomous communities, the *civitates,* cities and their surrounding territories. At the head of the *civitates* stood the members of the municipal "councils" (curiae), who were called *decuriones* and *curiales* or "possessors" (*possessores*). Among other things they were responsible for collecting the taxes assessed on their districts. Since they had to make up shortfall from their own wealth, and since imperial legislation was naturally most interested in seeing to the proper collection of taxes—by far the most extensive part of the *Codex Theodosianus* deals with the curiales (200 laws out of a total of 438)—one can easily get the impression that this duty became an unbearable burden that destroyed the cities and their upper classes.[8] In actuality, however, the curiales not only collected the taxes, they also distributed them locally, a task that concentrated a considerable degree of economic power in their hands.

One-third of the tax revenue was spent on the municipal administration, while one-third each was reserved for the central bureaucracy and the army. However, the monies did not travel in long wagon trains or on ship to the respective imperial capitals; instead, they were at the disposal of the praetorian prefect or the military officers on a local or regional level. The instructions of one prefect to the curiales in Istria shows that they were to purchase grain with the third reserved for the central administration and have it transported to Ravenna by boat.[9] To even out fluctuating values as much as possible, taxes were calculated in gold according to the Constantinian solidus, though they could be paid in cash, in kind, or in the form of public service. In principle the curiales were tied to their rank by a hereditary bond, which, given their multifarious responsibilities, opened up many possibilities of social advancement as well as decline. In regions where the senatorial nobility disappeared, the curiales formed the sole Roman upper class to which the sources could be referring when they speak of senators.[10]

In 212, Emperor Caracalla, by means of the Constitutio Antoniana, had granted Roman citizenship to all inhabitants of the empire. Excluded from this measure were "foreigners and subjected peoples," those who belonged to the barbarians within and outside of the borders and who had either been settled on Roman soil after a formal surrender (known as the *dediticii*), or their descendants, who were called *laeti.* These non-Romans were separated from citizens by a number of legal distinctions; most of all, however, they were prohibited from marrying them and were excluded from careers in the civil administration. Subjected peoples and *laeti,* who were under the authority of the military administration, were to till the soil like the peasant underclass of the "civilian" coloni and were to provide the necessary recruits for the army. The establishment of the procedure of "surrender," *deditio,* had at times led to a considerable barbarization of Roman areas even before the actual tribal migrations got under way.[11]

Beyond the imperial borders, but certainly within the extended sphere of Roman power, were those kings and peoples who had concluded a treaty, a *foedus* (noun, plural *foedera*) with Rome. The *foederati* who were tied to Rome in this way had agreed to respect the borders of the empire, to send a prescribed number of warriors, and, under certain circumstances, to pay tribute in kind. In return, Rome made certain payments, allowed commerce, and offered protection that was phrased in rather general terms. The barbarians, for their part, saw the treaties mostly in personal terms. Hence when the emperor who was party to the treaty died, they regarded the agreement as having come to an end; they would then behave accordingly and the Romans consequently regarded them as disloyal. For the most part the imperial government interfered only very cautiously in the internal affairs of the federates, who retained their tribal constitution and remained outside the provincial administration.[12] It was theoretically unthinkable that federates could settle inside the empire, for if a gens ever attained federate status on Roman soil, that would mean it had established a state within the state, which would invariably lead to the transformation if not the destruction of the Roman system. While this consequence was not intended by the parties involved, this is precisely what happened for the first time at the end of the fourth century.[13]

The Social Structure

The senators formed "the nobler part of humankind."[14] But even in the upper stratum of Roman society there existed a multitude of graded—at times highly confusing—distinctions of rank, wealth, and influence. This diversity had always been true of Roman society, which was never based on anything other than fundamental inequality and was dominated not least by the dichotomy of "free" vs. "unfree." This legacy was passed on to the Middle Ages and the modern era, and it lives on to this day in the European nobility. Yet "despite its complicated ranking system, late-antique society was certainly not a caste system";[15] the frequent reiteration of imperial laws that sought to force sons into the rank and profession of their fathers shows how futile this effort was. Instead, there was a relatively strong middle class, whose ranks, owing to a high degree of social mobility, were constantly joined and increased in size by foreigners as well as liberated slaves.

The differences in rank had their counterpart in an enormous disparity in the distribution of wealth; in our own day comparable examples would be hard to find even in the Arab oil states and in the United States. Around 400 lived Saint Melanie, the daughter and heir of the Valerii. Having made the decision to renounce the world and lead a radically Christian life, she intended to dispose of all her worldly possessions. Her hagiographer lists in detail what they were: Melanie drew a yearly income of 1,600 pounds of gold from properties, namely, ones that lay not only in Rome itself or in central and southern Italy, but were scattered also in Britannia, Spain, Mauretania, Numidia, and proconsular Africa. Melanie's real estate holdings in the home town of Saint Augustine exceeded the town's own property. The total number of her slaves is estimated to have been between fifty thousand and one hundred thousand, eight thousand of whom she is said to have freed. However, not all the liberated slaves were happy with this and they remained with Melanie's brother, from whom they expected work and protection. Melanie's townhouse on the Mons Caelius in Rome was too expensive even for Serena, niece of the emperor and wife of Stilicho. Part of the magnificent complex has been excavated; in the process archaeologists uncovered a hoard of silver which was probably buried in 410 to hide it from Alaric's Goths. Bronze tablets that were also recovered provide information on the large number of the Valerii's clients.

As immense and impressive as the possessions of the Valerii may have been, there were senatorial families whose income was more than three times as large.[16] This enormous wealth was combined with pride in one's ancestors and a pronounced conservatism of values, which caused the senators in Rome to be pagans for a long time. In contrast to these powerful social positions was the fact that participation in the imperial government was dependent on the emperor's goodwill. Senators could rule their latifundia, maintain outward trappings of unimaginable splendor and magnificence, and spend on traditional games as much as an entire yearlong imperial military campaign would cost[17]—yet as long as the ruler did not appoint them to high posts in state government or at court, they could hold only pseudo-offices.

For all its dislike of barbarians, the senate of Rome could thus be won over by barbarian generals and kings as soon as they seemed to grant this venerable body real power. Added to this was the fact that senators and Germanic princes shared the same high value they placed on descent and family, an attitude that rarely held any appeal for the emperors: "Just as the person descended from you is called a senatorial noble, the person who is brought forth of the royal clan has proved himself the worthiest candidate for [royal] rule." With these words Athalaric informed the senate of his "rise" and combined it with the declaration that nothing outshone the splendor of Amal blood.[18]

Senators were prohibited from engaging directly in trade and commerce; but as patrons they could exercise territorial lordship as well as participate in mostly urban activities through dependent individuals, corporations, and guilds. Thus the generalissimo and three-time consul Aetius was also the patron of the highly important guild of pig dealers in the city of Rome, and he made a decision that was important for them in a number of ways.[19] Senators could be patrons of entire cities, with their interests spread throughout the entire empire. They formed the imperial aristocracy, which differed fundamentally from the urban upper classes in terms of rank, wealth, and sphere of duties. If we can generalize from an African source from the time of Emperor Julian, for each senator there were ten members of the curial municipal aristocracy.[20]

The *curiales* were also, though on a much more modest level, owners of expansive estates that enabled them to look after the town's commonweal entrusted to them and to supervise in a responsible manner the collection and distribution of taxes on a local and regional level. Without their work the acceptance and integration of Germanic newcomers would have been impossible. Together with the urban hierarchy they formed the *episcopi et possessores* who, in the wake of the withdrawal or disappearance of senators from a given part of the empire, became and remained the sole representatives of the Romans. Thus they took the place of the vanished upper classes and were not infrequently called senators themselves.[21]

All aspects of trade, commerce, and transportation in the cities, as well as education, medicine, and the arts, were in the hands of what was for the most part private enterprise organized into numerous guilds and corporations. Money was to be made here, and there were many opportunities that ambitious people often took advantage of. For example, the prefect of Rome in 389 was the son of a simple peasant, and as Sidonius Apollinaris said, "[T]he man of education is as much above the boor as the boor in his turn above the beast."[22] Education had given him the opportunity for his social advancement. Around the same time a famous physician and medical writer was governor of the rich province of Africa and held the rank of imperial *comes,* which he apparently shared with several of his colleagues. But even among the unfree, physicians ranked at the very top; only well-educated eunuchs cost more, by about 16 percent.[23]

Thoughts of the Roman Empire conjure up visions of a vast and differentiated network of cities. In reality, probably nine out of ten people lived on the land, and among them the peasant class of dependent coloni formed by far the overwhelming majority. Their right to own property was restricted, and they had all but lost their freedom of movement. At the same time, however, the coloni's ties to the soil provided a certain safeguard for their existence. Those who had fulfilled their obligations for thirty years were released from them, as was the person who succeeded in avoiding them for the same length of time. Up until the fifth century coloni could enlist as soldiers or become clerics. But once this escape route had been legally closed off, the coloni fell into the *servilis conditio* and differed but little from slaves.[24]

At the bottom of the social ladder stood the mass of the slaves, still enormously large in late antiquity. The existence of slaves was the reason simple human labor was, by today's standards, unimaginably cheap.

A freeman was considered poor if he could not afford either a house or a marriage and had to get by with no more than three slaves.[25] Slaves were regarded as objects. They had no standing before the law and were subject to degrading and cruel punishment or modes of interrogation (such as torture). However, in keeping with the humanitarian tendencies of the time, late-antique legislation also addressed itself to the slaves. Though Christianity did not reject slavery in principle, it did demand that the treatment of individual slaves adhere to the commandment to love one's neighbor. While some church fathers advocated that slavery be retained, others were hoping for its gradual disappearance. To be sure, Gregory of Nyssa (331 to after 394) was the only one among the fathers who came out unequivocally for the abolition of slavery.

As a rule neither slaves nor freedmen were ordained as priests, but as early as the third century a former slave occupied the papal chair. Documents and law codes attest that slavery lived on in the barbarian states that succeeded the Roman Empire, though it had lost much of its importance and was transformed into a limited kind of unfreedom. In much the same way the word *servus* disappeared from the Germanic-Romanic languages and was replaced by the ethnic term "slav(e)." However, contrary to a widely held belief, this process did not begin in early medieval Byzantium but took place only in the region of Germanic-Slavic contact in the tenth and eleventh centuries.[26]

"A person is either free or unfree; there is no third option in between." This was still how Charlemagne justified his response to a request for legal advice. Free or unfree was a condition that came with birth; the legal theory was crystal clear. Legal reality, however, provided for a rich differentiation between the conditions. The modern notion of the ancient state of slaveholders was long based on the terrible experiences of modern slavery, especially in non-European regions, and it applied to the distant past the criteria of the bourgeois or Marxist concept of liberty. In our eyes unfreedom violates the most basic human rights. Any differentiation within this state of "being a nonperson" thus becomes unthinkable, a view that seems to find confirmation both in the statements of classical philosophers as well as in ancient and medieval laws.

In actuality, the notion of a homogenous mass of the unfree is as inaccurate for antiquity and the Middle Ages as the claim that society was rigidly divided into lords and servants. Both the Middle Ages as well as antiquity knew a rich differentiation of the social structure, one that comprised freedom and unfreedom and in which—even by modern standards—a high degree of mobility upward and downward was possible. The landed lordships of late antiquity and the early Middle Ages alone required many skilled services in order to function. Those who provided them always had the chance to acquire possessions, and not only material goods but also cash, which eventually gave them economic and social mobility.

It is true, however, that the period of the migrations returned the social structure to a more archaic state and sought to reduce it to the duality of lords and slaves. But there was a strong countermovement, namely, qualified military service, which allowed social advancement and prevented social decline. Of course it is difficult to gauge the percentage of unfree in early medieval armies. And it differed from one tribe to the next: for example, probably more slaves served in the army of the Spanish Visigoths than was the case among the Franks or Lombards. But even if the precise percentages were known, this would not change the basic argument.

In any case, the unfree element increased in the armies of medieval fiefholders. Thus the military change of the Carolingian period (the creation of an army of heavy-armed horsemen) required that the individual warrior acquire expensive armament—a mail shirt alone cost the equivalent of a medium-size estate—as well as superb training in order to fulfill his task. However, since the free vassals were in no way numerous enough to serve as heavy-armed horsemen, the king as well as secular and ecclesiastical magnates had to equip a corresponding number of their unfree men and free them up for the necessary lifelong training.

As a result of the peculiar constitutional development of the high medieval empire, the German emperors' military leaders were dependent most of all on the contingents of the Ottonian-Salian imperial church. The early forms of the so-called *ministeriales* thus originated from the imperial church as an extended royal patrimony and from the imperial domain in the narrower sense. Thus unfree men rose not only into the social middle stratum but even into the nobility, without for the time being shedding their unfree status.

The vast majority of contemporary German nobility is descended from these *ministeriales,* who were once able to transcend the barriers which the antique-medieval dichotomy of "free-unfree" had erected. The institution of the *ministeriales* was recognized early on as a typical manifestation of the constitution of the German Empire. It establishes a visible bond between the "Roman Empire and the Germanic peoples" and the "Medieval Empire and the Germans."[27]

2. GERMANIC POLITIES AT THE PERIPHERY OF THE RES PUBLICA

Two states existed in the world, the Imperium Romanum and the kingdom of the Persians. A world ruler therefore had to subjugate both, an ambition that was attributed to Attila at the height of his power.

When Rome in 363 ceded territory to the Persian king, those provinces were in fact abandoned; their inhabitants had to leave their homes and property and "a disgraceful treaty" was concluded, one "without parallel in the annals since the founding of the city." So much for Rome's relationship to the Persian kingdom, which was recognized as an equal state. By contrast, the empire could lose (*amittere*) provinces and lands to barbarian polities, but could not abandon them (*intermittere*) to these "nonstates." That is why the retreat to Hadrian's wall in Britain, the withdrawal from Dacia and the *agri decumates,* the military surrender of the upper valley of the Nile over a length of nearly one thousand kilometers, and the loss of Frisia and the estuary of the Rhine were "hardly worth mentioning"; there are no Roman sources that discussed these events at length, let alone complained about them the way they did about the peace terms of 363. Even if the barbarians conquered Roman territory and held it as *possessio* by virtue of occupying it, they would never be able to exercise full dominion (*dominium*) over it in terms of constitutional and civil law.[28]

The sources of the fourth century are full of incessant fighting along the Danube and the Rhine, of terrible battles and ghastly bloodshed. As enemies of the empire they name in the first place Goths, Alamanni, and Franks, only secondarily the North Sea Saxons, the Burgundians in central Germany, or the Marcomanni, Quadi, Sarmatians, and Vandals along the middle reaches of the Rhine, and last the smaller tribes like the Naristi, Sciri, or Heruli.

The whirlwind of events, indeed their apparent meaninglessness, did unfold with a certain order that was, despite all contradictions, the tried and tested system of Roman-barbarian relations. Those relations rested on treaties that were regularly broken but then just as regularly renewed. This book thus deals primarily with *foederati,* to whose kings and princes the imperial government extended visible recognition by sending them—following the imperial model—special insignia of lordship, such as fibulas and diadems.

The intra-Roman struggle over the emperorship forced the various contenders to use the army against their rivals: the court armies followed their commanders and the defenders of the imperial borders were withdrawn from their posts. Franks, Alamanni, and Goths crossed the Rhine and the Danube and ravaged the provinces, either driven by their own desire to take advantage of a good opportunity or called in by one of the would-be emperors.

The most capable imperator eventually prevailed, turned his hapless rivals into usurpers who had to die, and ended the civil war by punishing the barbarians who had invaded. The first step was to ruthlessly purge the imperial territory of these barbarians, no matter if they—like the Alamanni after 350—were already settled 50 kilometers west of the Rhine and in control of a strip of Gallic land another 150 kilometers long. If the armies met in battle, as they did near Strasbourg in 357, the Germans lost with terrible casualties. In the third stage of the operation the Romans crossed the border rivers and ravaged the enemy's tribal lands until new treaties were concluded.

The greater the bloodletting the longer the defeated gentes kept quiet; sometimes an entire generation passed before they returned. For example, the *foedus* that Constantine concluded with the Danubian Goths in 332 remained in force far beyond one generation. At the Rhine too the Alamanni and the Franks, mindful of the Roman successes of the great emperor here during his lifetime, held back their attacks for nearly a quarter of a century.[29] To intensify the effect of their offensives and make them last, the emperors from Constantine the Great on up to the brothers Valentinian I and Valens strove to establish strongholds in the barbarian land, preferably on abandoned imperial territory.

In the summer of 328, Constantine opened a stone bridge across the Danube between modern-day Gigen (Oescus) and Sucidava (Celeiu) in Romania. The construction of the bridge was considered a first-rate military event; the emperor was celebrated as the renewer of Trajan's Dacia. At the same time the fortress of Daphne was erected downstream; it was supplied with the help of a large ferry from Transmarisca-Tutrakan on the right bank of the Rhine. Good roads leading from the hinterland to the fortified sites were repaired or newly built. While the bridge at Oescus linked the empire with Little (i.e., Roman) Walachia, which was intended as a buffer zone and was for the most part successfully defended as such, Daphne and its environs protruded like a thorn into the territory of the free Danube Goths.[30] After the battle of Strasbourg in 357, Emperor Julian drove across the Rhine into the *agri decumates*, where he had one of Trajan's old fortresses restored. As a condition for peace and a treaty with the Empire, the neighboring Alamanni not only had to tolerate this *munimentum Traiani*, but also had to provision the Roman garrison stationed there.[31]

On June 26, 363, Emperor Julian, "the Apostate," succumbed to the injuries he had suffered during a campaign against Persia. Neither the enemy, who was ready to talk, nor the Roman army had wanted this war. Following impressive victories over Franks and Alamanni along the Rhine, the Roman officers wanted an offensive at the lower Danube. The western Goths on the other side of the river, in particular, would have deserved an emphatic reminder of the punishment they had received at the hands of Constantine. But these Goths, too, had honored their obligations under the treaty of 332 and had furnished a contingent of tribal warriors to fight the Persians. Still, the wish of the Roman generals would be fulfilled very soon. Along the Rhine, and especially along the middle Danube, the Roman armies launched new attacks against the Germanic-Sarmatian neighbors.

The policy of force, which contemporaries criticized (though only after it had failed), reached its final culmination under the rule of the brothers Valentinian I (364 to 375) and Valens (364 to 378).

Along the Danube

In early summer of 364, Valentinian I and Valens met at Nish. Here they divided the army and the empire: Valentinian, the older of the two, took over Milan and the West, his younger brother took Constantinople and the East.

After the border fortifications along the Danube had been strengthened, a first line of defense was constructed north of the river. The defense of the approaches was aimed especially against the Suebian Quadi and their Sarmatian neighbors, who differed but little in their way of life and appearance. After one of the Quadi kings had met his death while negotiating with the Romans, the old enemies attacked. Just like the mounted nomads from the great Scythian steppe, they sprang from an ambush—riding shaggy horses and carrying long lances, they were protected by scale armor of horn plates—and cut down the Roman soldiers. In response, Valentinian I launched his Quadian-Sarmatian war, choosing, like many emperors before him, Carnuntum as his command post. Carnuntum, by this time a "dilapidated, filthy hole,"[32] was now relatively strongly fortified. With a base at Savaria-Steinamanger in the interior of Pannonia I, Valentinian opened his offensive. But then insolent Quadi envoys at the peace negotiations in 375 upset the emperor so much that he suffered a stroke and died. Despite the untimely death of the older Augustus, the middle Danube retained its function as the northern border of the empire.

The younger brother Valens had fought a Gothic war in the years 367/369 and had carried his attacks into the land of the barbarians, into Bessarabia-Moldavia and Romania. A triumphal procession in the capital of Constantinople and the assumption of the victorious title *Gothicus* was the total yield of the war, which was but a pale reflection of the concurrent Alamannic campaigns of Valentinian I. Both conflicts, however, were brought to an end by treaties similar in form and substance. In September of 369, Valens concluded with Athanaric, the leader of the Gothic confederation of the Danube, a peace as between equals. The treaty was negotiated on boats anchored in the middle of the Danube; it replaced the *foedus* of 332 and put an end to the "Gothia Romana" in terms of constitutional law.

The Romans for their part restricted the previously open trade between the Danubian provinces and the Goths to two border posts and stopped the *foederati* payments. The Goths handed over hostages, and Athanaric was given free reign to persecute Christians (which he did until 372), that is to say, to fight his domestic enemies who were regarded as pro-Roman. Athanaric's attempt to detach from Roman rule the tribes entrusted to him—even at the price of economic sacrifices—was aimed at the consolidation of his monarchy, which previously had been of limited duration. The experiment came to grief in the onslaught of the Huns, shortly after the Gothic judge had been able to prevail against strong opposition from within the tribe which was seeking to revise the treaty of 369.[33]

Along the Rhine

Valentinian I had been forced to wage war against the Alamanni very soon after assuming power. In 368 even Mainz had been taken and plundered. In a splendid counterattack the emperor crossed the Rhine into enemy territory and inflicted a serious defeat on the Alamanni. At that time the old professor of rhetoric and princely tutor, Ausonius (who was about fifty-eight years old), came into possession of his "war spoils": Bissula, an Alamannic girl who delighted his heart. He set her free and gladly submitted to her: "She has no words of blame for her fate or homeland. Set free on the spot from a servitude never known to her before, she has now traded it in for the amenities of Latium [Rome]. In her appearance she remains a German, though, with dark blue eyes and blond hair. Now her language, then her outward appearance make the girl an enigma; the latter extols her origin from the Rhine, the former her origin from Latium."

Valentinian's victory and the fifth anniversary of his rule, the quinquennial, were festively celebrated at Trier in February of 369. The oration was delivered by the eminent Roman senator Symmachus. He had followed the emperor to the Rhine and had thus witnessed the intensive building of fortifications on the left bank of the river as well as the establishment of bridgeheads in the land of the Alamanni. That same year the emperor tried to envelop the enemy by mobilizing their neighbors and enemies, the Burgundians, against them and advancing a Roman army from the Danube. Even though the army operating from Raetia was successful, there were serious setbacks, both with the building of fortifications east of the Rhine and with the Burgundian allies.

Around this time the Bucinobantes King Macrianus, who had already given Julian all kinds of trouble a decade earlier, reemerged and refused to continue recognizing Rome's dominion as set down in the treaty. The confrontation with the unruly and dangerous prince in the vicinity of the Rhine dragged on until just before Valentinian's departure from Gaul. Eventually negotiations did take place in the fall of 374 in Mainz, which the emperor conducted by boat with the Alamannic prince and his retainers, who were encamped on the right bank of the Rhine. The outcome was a treaty, the details of which are unknown to us, but which is illuminated by Macrianus's subsequent activities in the service of Rome: the Alamannic king was from now on, so we are told, a faithful ally, until 380 when he met his death in an attack on the Franks, which was, if not incited, then at least tolerated by the imperial government. Ironically Macrianus was killed by a Frankish king who had made a career for himself both as a high Roman military officer as well as a tribal prince.[34]

The destroyer of Macrianus was Mallobaudes; in 378 he held the high military office of a *comes domesticorum* and as such ranked immediately below the general in charge of Gaul. At the same time, however, Mallobaudes was also a Frankish king and thus remained rooted in a tribal society. In his double function Mallobaudes embodied, like no one else of his time, the noble German as servant and enemy of the empire. His ambivalent attitude probably went back to an experience he had had as a young tribune in the Gallic army under Silvanus. Silvanus, all but forced to usurp power in 355, was fully assimilated; he was a Christian, and as the son of a Frankish officer of Constantine the Great he had been born in Gaul. Before he reached for the purple, he tried to escape the intrigue that was being plotted against him by arranging his flight to the Franks on the right bank of the Rhine. However, one of his officers, also a Frank, convinced him that in the homeland of his ancestors he would be either killed or handed over to the emperor. Mallobaudes and other Franks, who were "at the time both large in numbers and influence at the imperial court," had tried in vain to intervene on behalf of their fellow Frank; but even after the catastrophe of Silvanus, no one besides Mallobaudes returned to the homeland.[35]

Of course the era of the all-powerful generals of Frankish background— Merobaudes, Bauto, Richomeres, Arbogast—did not start winding down until the seventies. Their enormous influence began under Valentinian I and ended in 394 with the battle at the Frigidus. At this tributary of the Isonzo, the Catholic eastern Emperor Theodosius the Great defeated the army of the West and thereby put an end to the usurpation of Arbogast's creature, Eugenius, and to the pagan reaction spearheaded by Eugenius and his general.

The "Frankish" generals fought very harshly against Alamanni and Goths, and not least against their own tribal brothers. But this was not the reason why the path Mallobaudes had taken was closed to them; rather, as consuls and members of the pagan—and Christian—upper class they had cut themselves off completely from their roots. Their paganism had nothing to do with the traditional Wodan religion, but was the intellectually sophisticated and very modern Neoplatonism of the educated circles in Rome and Gaul. The somewhat younger Danubian Goth Fravitta can be considered their counterpart in the East.[36]

No Alamannus ever attained the prominent position of the Franks, even though it seemed around the middle of the century as though three Alamannic officers "held the state in their hands." In 354 all three were suspected of conspiring with their tribal brothers; yet at least one of them went on to a respectable career in the East, and another died of natural causes in the same year. The accusations were more likely part of the usual court intrigues, whereby a certain hostility to foreigners may have played a role. Moreover, people switched sides as much for their own advantage as from outside pressure. For example, Fraomarius, the defeated enemy of Macrianus and an Alamannic king by Rome's graces, left his tribe and fled across the Rhine into the empire, where he was made tribune and sent to Britain along with his Alamannic retainers.[37]

The Goth Fravitta had a predecessor in the Thracian General Modaharius. The latter came from the "royal lineage of the Scythians"; he was thus related to Athanaric, though this did not keep him from taking tough action against his former countrymen and from being a good Christian. In spite of, or perhaps precisely because of, the fact that the Goths won the battle at Adrianople, Modaharius joined the army of Theodosius and advanced very quickly.[38] One who failed, however, was the Gothic Christian Gainas. In the fierce summer of 400 in Constantinople, he lost his imperial generalship and tried to escape his defeat against Fravitta by returning across the Danube to his old homeland. There he met his death in the battle against the Huns.[39]

Barbarian kings, unable to hold on to their power, switched to the Roman side and became commanders of auxiliary units. They could even rise to become generals for a time, provided they were at the same time kings. Returnees of the highest rank, however, were unable to hang on to their lives, let alone become kings. Some were Christian, some Roman pagans (probably of the Neoplatonic variety). One Alamannic king had become a follower of Serapis; another, along with his wife, had converted to Judaism.[40] The Germanic tribal religions along the Rhine and the Danube were in a process of complete dissolution, as were the social structures of the peoples on the periphery of the Roman world.

3. GERMANIC TRIBAL STRUCTURES
AT THE RHINE AND DANUBE

"All the warlike peoples were led by Cnodomarius and Serapio (his nephew), who were more powerful than the other kings (of the Alamanni)." "They were followed by the next most powerful kings, five in number, by ten petty princes, and by a considerable number of noblemen." Next came many thousands of armed men "who had been recruited from various tribes, partly for pay, partly on the basis of treaties of mutual aid." "And suddenly there was heard the clamor of the Alamannic foot soldiers, who cried out with a unanimous and angry voice for the kings and princes to get down from their horses and join them, so that they might share the fate of all in whatever happened. Cnodomarius immediately leapt from his horse, and the others followed his example."[41]

Such was the organization of the Alamannic army that was destroyed in 357 in the battle of Strasbourg. Shortly before this battle, Cologne had returned to Roman control following successful negotiations with several kings of the Franks.[42]

A plurality of kings ruled also over the Danubian Goths and the Tisza-Vandals, and as was the case with the Alamanni, ancient observers noted among the Danubian "Scythians" a ruling class broken down into kings and nobles. There were clear differences of rank within the group of kings, some were of greater nobility than others. The family that rose to prominence in the course of a campaign or intertribal conflict furnished the highest king of kings. The leading class wore royal insignia and enjoyed special honor and family descent.[43] Their family members formed the royal family. The various kings ruled over subdivisions or subtribes which could unite for joint undertakings. The Alamannic force at Strasbourg came together not only on the basis of mutual treaties but also had to be "bought together."[44]

Compared to the Alamanni, the contemporaneous oligarchy of the Danubian Goths had much more strongly institutionalized the process of joining the forces necessary for joint expeditions. To counter the external and internal threats, a monarchy of limited duration and which embraced the entire tribal confederation was created in the fourth century. The person holding this power was a judge, *kindins,* who was not permitted to leave the tribal territory. He received his mandate from a tribal council composed of royal princes and magnates; the kindins was supposed to execute the decisions of this council. This Gothic judge was responsible for three areas: religious life, the administration of justice, and the waging of defensive war. Though there is no direct connection, the Gothic judgeship resembles the centuries older function of the Gallic *hegemon,* the *vergobretos* of the Haedui.

But as was the case with the Gallic political constitution during Caesar's time, there also developed among the Goths the office of a military leader whose function was limited to the military sphere. And while the monarchy of the various judges was a dead end from the point of view of constitutional history, the function of the tribal military leader, who had every right to leave the tribal territory and had to do so, was the preliminary stage to the later military king. However, the military mandate is, characteristically enough, attested south of the Danube only at a time when the judgeship had already ceased to exist.[45]

"Cnodomarius immediately leapt from his horse, and the others followed his example": the mounted Alamannic kings and nobles had to respond instantly to the demand from the great majority of their troops, who were foot soldiers. Even in the face of the enemy, the mightiest of the kings, who led the army, had no absolute authority. The upper stratum was dependent on its people. When the Alamannic tribes rose against Rome, two royal brothers wanted to remain faithful to the *foedus* of 354. The more powerful and probably also older king was murdered by the "hawks." Thereafter his people joined the attackers, since the younger brother was also not able or willing to keep his tribe from breaking the just recently concluded treaty and resuming hostilities.[46] And as late as the sixth century there were peoples, like the Heruli, over whom a king exercised a dominion that was as venerable as it was chaotic and ridiculous in the eyes of the Romans.[47]

4. THE CONFEDERATION OF THE DANUBIAN GOTHS

Of all the Germanic polities that emerged and endured at the edge of the Roman world in the fourth century, the confederation of the Danubian Goths is of singular importance, for two reasons: First, there was no Germanic people in which the classical authors, Romans as well as Greeks, took a stronger interest than in the Gothic tribal confederation on the soil of modern-day Romania. Contemporary observers examined its political and religious institutions, its levels of social and economic development and the resulting patterns of behavior, its military possibilities and expansionary tendencies. They were familiar with the two special names of the Danubian Goths, who called themselves "the Good," *Vesi,* and whom their neighbors—the "splendid" Ostrogoths or Greutungian "steppe and grass dwellers"—called *Tervingi,* "forest people."[48]

Second, we have the Gothic translation of the Bible. It was written by Ulfilas and his helpers around the middle of the fourth century in a language which, despite its strong dependence on the original Greek source, embodied the idiom of the Danubian Goths. Needless to say, the New Testament is historically situated in Roman Palestine around the time of Christ's birth. At that time Jewish tribal traditions were in conflict with the tradition of the great Hellenistic-Roman state: the Roman emperor and his governor shared the historical stage with Hellenistic kings, ethnarchs, tetrarchs, and the oligarchic organs of Jewish self-government. To all this we must add the personal power wielded by the rich and noble, and structures that determined a person's descent and membership in a particular clan.

This multifarious New Testament "politics" unfolded against a backdrop of a Mediterranean culture that was based on public literacy, had an advanced money economy with a system of banking and taxation, and was familiar with the latent tensions between city and countryside. The way in which the language of the Danubian Goths translated the biblical text and thus interpreted this foreign world, the question of whether Gothic terms were available or whether foreign or borrowed words as well as loan translations were necessary, and the matter of which of the classical languages they came from—all this conveys information about the social and material levels of development of the Danubian Goths' tribal culture. The vocabulary that was required can be compared with the information that their contemporary or near contemporary classical authors—both Greek and Latin—supply about the Tervingi. The picture which thus emerges is eminently suited for a comparison with the accounts available about the similarly structured tribal confederation of the Alamanni.[49]

Located as it was in immediate proximity to the great Roman state, the tribal society of the Tervingi was exposed to tremendous tensions and was in a process of transformation at the time Ulfilas and his helpers translated the Bible. Both written as well as archaeological sources reveal a growing social differentiation into rich and poor. As had happened in pre-Caesarean Gaul and was happening among the contemporary Alamanni and Franks, the aristocratic tribal structure of the Danubian Goths seems to have developed at the expense of the political, social, and economic importance of the free lower classes. The vertical element of lordship was further strengthened by the fact that the tribal confederations at the time were made up not only of subdivisions of the same people but of many peoples of Germanic and non-Germanic origin. This fundamental polyethnic tribal system diminished the importance of the community of descent and favored the expansion of the system of retainership.

The spheres in which the life of the people took place reveal how numerous and varied the social frames of reference were. We can identify the following units and structures: first came the *Gútthiuda,* the land and the people of the Tervingi as a political entity. Though etymologically the word meant merely "Gothic people," it had long since ceased to mean a community of shared descent. Instead, it referred to the territory ruled by the Danubian tribal confederation (the *Gothi*) or the Tervingian "homelands" (*genitales terrae*) of the Latin and Greek accounts.

Next there was the *kuni.* It was not only the regional subdivision of the *Gútthiuda* but had remained in part a community of descent. A Goth belonged to the *kuni* as an *inkunja,* that is, as a member of the tribe in the original sense. The number of the Tervingian *kunja* is unclear. Only a few of them can be located. Each *kuni* had its own shrines and priests and no doubt also its own cult. With the fall of the old Gothic monarchic kingship the Tervingi seem to have lost their common tribal religion. This would explain why the concept of what constituted a community of descent shifted from the level of the *Gútthiuda* to that of the *kuni.* Although this opened the Tervingian tribal confederation to non-Gothic elements, it was at the same time politically and cultically fractured. The task of the judge was to prevent the dissolution of the gens in times of crisis; accordingly, we know from Athanaric's period both politico-military and religious measures aimed at stopping the disintegration of the tribe or even reversing it.

House and fortified residence, *gards* and *baúrgs,* represent the authority of the Gothic lord over the members of his family, his free retainers, dependent clients, and semifree and unfree peasants of Gothic and non-Gothic origin. *Gards* and *baúrgs* were the seats of local clan organizations and the centers of aristocratic lordship. They formed a vertically structured community, which conceived of itself as a kin group inclusive of the servants and armed retainers. The *baúrgs* was most likely the larger, "fortified" house, the place where—as among the Alamanni—a tribal chieftain lived, while the common nobleman lived perhaps in a former Roman manor that was unfortified or surrounded at most by a stockade.

The members of the house and the *baúrgs* were bound to the lord by oath, which created a mutual obligation of loyalty, a bond. The economic basis of the house was the land passed down in the family, the *haimothli* (the "Hoamatl" as the farm is still called in the Austro-Bavarian dialect). This word reveals at least the beginnings of the formation of landed lordship, an institution that became possible especially after the occupation of the Dacian province.

Compared to the firmly established organizational forms of house and *baúrgs,* the *sibja,* the clan, the community of descent par excellence, strongly recedes into the background. However, it is clearly visible as a legal community. Adoption (so important for tribal societies), states of lawlessness and outlawry, but also reconciliation with one's brother, were described with phrases that mention the clan or with terms that contain the word's root.

The village, *haims*—preserved in the French *hameau* and borrowed back into German in addition to being present in the word *Heimat*—or *weihs,* formed the social world of the Gothic freeman. The land of the Goths, the subtribe, the *baúrgs,* and the house were dominated by the Gothic magnates. The instrument of their rule was the bands of retainers, in which the differences between free and unfree disappeared because each retainer had to obey a lord. In competition with these forms of lordship was the communally organized village. Here the free Goth must have felt "at home," *anahaims.* Outside of the village he or she was in exile, in a strange land—*afhaims.*

Even the free villagers did not participate in the decisions of the magnates in the tribal council or in the process of formulating the political objectives of the *kuni.* If the village assembly of free Goths did not agree with the decisions of the tribal council, it had only the timeless methods of peasant resistance: deceiving the authorities and sabotaging their decrees. But if a delegate of the tribal council came into the village with his armed retainers, he had the power to put down communal self-government with an authoritative command. There would then be no more room for village self-government and its institutions.

Saba's Village

We know something about the life in a Germanic village of the fourth century because the Goth Saba suffered martyrdom in the river Musaeus-Buzau on April 12, 372, at the age of thirty-eight, and the story of his *passio* was written down at about the same time. Although Saba was poor and, in the eyes of one Gothic magnate, a political nobody, he was nevertheless a freeman who took part in the decisions of his fellow villagers and could resist them successfully even as a single person. It is clear from the story that the village assembly was dominated by a group that made suggestions, guided the decision-making process, and acted as the executive organ.

The people in this group were also in charge of consecrating the sacrificial meat, that is, they were responsible for the cult and ritual affairs. These men were probably individuals whose prominence was a function of their prestige and economic power, but who could not make decisions without the other villagers, even if, like Saba, they owned nothing more than the shirts on their backs. The village notables were still all pagans, which is shown both by the name used for them as well as the fact that they prepared and carried out the sacrifices. A Christian was thus not fit to exercise any function on the village level. However, the villagers demanded of their pagan dignitaries that they protect the Christians whom they considered their relatives.

Saba's village, led by the village spokesman, decided one day to serve the Christians unconsecrated meat during the sacrificial meal prescribed by the magnates. When Saba resisted this "pious ruse" he was banished. After some time Saba returned to his village; his exile had been only temporary. The village elders then tried by all means to protect Saba against princes who ruled the village from outside. There had thus been a change of sentiment in favor of the steadfast Christian. The notables reacted with great sensitivity to public opinion in the village. Now they were even willing to perjure themselves by swearing that there were no Christians in their *haims*. Saba, however, sabotaged this subterfuge, as well, whereupon the elders swore to a representative of the *kuni* that they had only one Christian in the village. With this move they protected their Christian relatives but at the same time exposed the saint. Saba's second banishment was pronounced by the same prince who had mocked him for his poverty. But Saba survived this exile also, returned once more to the village, and fell victim finally to the third wave of persecution under another monarchic lord.

The author of the Saba legend sided not only with the persecuted Christians but also with the pagan lower classes. Despite the villagers' weakness he feels sympathetic toward them and grants human feelings to the retainers who were very reluctant to kill Saba and did so only after he had reminded them of their lord's orders. In a scene of daily life the author paints a portrait of the woman who set Saba free when his captors had fallen asleep and who in return enlisted him to help cook breakfast and wash the dishes, delaying him so long that the retainers of the bloodthirsty *reiks* caught him again. It is quite possible that the author, or at least his informant, called a Gothic village his home.

Cult and Religion of the Goths

The ritualistic and religious life of the Danubian tribal confederation was centered in the individual village communities and was determined and overseen by the *kuni* and its representatives. The village was the special sphere of peace established and maintained by the ritual sacrificial meal of the villagers. Whoever excluded himself from that meal violated the religion and thus broke his ties with the community, which responded by banishing the sacrilegious person, who was guilty of denying the divine origin of the tribe. Such apostasy could be more readily accepted and dealt with by the communally organized village, where everyone was in fact related, than by the vertically structured *kuni*. The denial of the tribal tradition was a threat especially to the upper stratum of princes and kings, who saw themselves as the bearers of the ethnic traditions which they managed to all but monopolize.

It is within this context that we must place the Amal deification of their Ansic ancestors; however, the Danubian Goths too opened battle by intoning songs in praise of their ancestors. The wooden idol that Athanaric had ordered taken around the land for worship might have represented the—or, better, an—original ancestor of the Tervingi. Each Gothic subtribe had its own special sacred objects, which were looked after by priests and priestesses. Tervingian paganism was an exclusive tribal religion. One did not talk to outsiders about it, and outsiders had no part in it. A Christian priest who was persecuted along with Saba escaped with his life because he was not a Goth and could therefore not violate the tribal law, just as he could never have become the object of a pagan mission.

None of the pagan priests participated in the persecutions of the Christians in the fourth century. Decisions concerning religious policy and their execution lay in the hands of the tribal princes, the Gothic judge, and the *reiks*. This had been the custom since time immemorial. Already Filimer, king during the migration period, had to expel from the tribe Gothic witches (*haliurun(n)ae*), that is "women who engaged in magic with the world of the dead," whereupon they entered into union with the evil spirits of the steppe and gave birth to the Huns. The historical significance of the witch expulsion is quite comparable to that of the persecution of the

Christians. Banishment was the punishment a pagan society meted out to those who had violated its norms through sorcery, by which we must understand ritual and practices not recognized by the tribe. However, black magic was not all there was. There existed also the beneficial force of the person who was graced with the power of doing good and who filled a tribal society with life. Pagan charisma was no doubt meant when one person wished another *hailag*, as is attested by the runic inscription on the necklace from Pietroasa-Bucharest.

The reversal of a blessing into a curse (sacral polarity) was inherent in the nature of the oath. The person who swore an oath appealed to fate and cursed himself should he violate the oath. There are numerous reports of utterly false oaths. We are told, for example, that the Goths who crossed the Danube in 376 came with the express intent of breaking, at the first chance they got, the oath they had sworn to the emperors as a guarantee. The Goths in Saba's village were perfectly willing to commit perjury to protect their Christian relatives. A tribal society, however, did not owe any loyalty to the outsider, and an outsider was anyone living beyond the village lands. This is the only way to interpret the story that Galatian slave-traders during the age of Julian conducted veritable slave hunts among the Danubian Goths, something that was possible only in the wake of interethnic tribal feuds.

The gods of the Goths, both of the western Tervingi and the eastern Greutungi, can be known only by inference: it is likely, for example, that both Gothic peoples knew an Ansis-Aesir ancestral cult. At the head of the Aesir stood Gaut, whom the Amal royal clan, in particular, venerated as its ancestral god. The first high God of the Danubian Goths was probably the war god Teiws (pronounced *Teeoos*), who manifested himself in the form of a sword, something that had been a tradition of faith already among the pre-Gothic peoples of this area.

The Danubian Goths apparently named this sword god after their tribal name, Terving, though they even equated him with the Scythian-Thracian Ares-Mars. The Tervingi seem to have carried out a similar acculturation with the thunder god, whom they may have called in Gothic *Faírguneis*, "oak god," and probably also Jupiter in Latin. We cannot rule out the worship of an *Ing* god and an *Irmin* god. In all likelihood a Gothic Wodan-Odin did not exist. The Danube may have been venerated as a god in the traditional manner; the river god received human sacrifices and oaths were sworn to his name.

The Tribal Army

Tribal armies were small—three thousand men was apparently considered the standard size—and were composed of specialized elite warriors. Armies were raised both by the individual *kunja* and the entire *Gútthiuda*. Our sources speak explicitly of warfare within the Gothic tribe. We can also make out expeditions of various chiefs with their retainers. If the *Gútthiuda* was in a state of war, the Gothic judge had supreme command of the army insofar as defense of tribal territory was concerned. Operations outside of the territory, however, were conducted by his officers.

In the Gothic and Vandal armies we find subdivisions of "one thousand" and "one hundred," though these did not correspond to actual numerical divisions (such as multiples of one hundred, for example). It is likely that the numerical units go back to non-Roman influences, probably to structures found among mounted steppe nomads. While the Tervingian tribal armies were composed mainly of unmounted warriors, the armored lancer, who covered enormous distances and fought hand-to-hand on horseback, had already become the norm for the Ostrogothic warrior. His world included hawking, shamanism, and religious practices and experiences that in Christian times were still reflected in the eagle fibulas; the political manifestation of his world can be recognized in the Amali's adoption of the Sassanian royal insignia.

The way of life of the Iranian-Turkish steppe peoples was, after all, part of the enormous realm ruled by the great Ostrogothic-Greutungian military king, Ermanaric. His conquests and the extent of his domain suggested to ancient observers a comparison with Alexander. In the territory under his rule, which was centered in Ukraine but which extended to the Urals and across the Wolga to the Baltic, there lived, alongside his Goths, also Fins, Slavs, Antes, Heruli, Alans, Huns, Sarmatians, and Aesti.[50]

The Conversion of the Goths and Bishop Ulfilas's Translation of the Bible

The Goths at the Danube and on the Crimea were the first of the Germanic tribes who made contact with Christianity as an entire people. The cause of this encounter was the Gothic attacks that swept over the Balkan Peninsula and Asia Minor in the third century, ravaging what were at that time the most strongly Christianized regions of the empire.

Tribal societies always suffer from a lack of manpower, most especially a shortage of workers and trained personnel. That is why the booty of the Goths included prisoners, whom they carried off to their Danubian and southern Russian homelands. This is how, probably in 257, the non-Gothic ancestors of Ulfilas came from Cappadocia into the Gothic land north of the lower Danube; and like those before and after them they were among the many enslaved people "who turned their masters into brothers [in Christ]."

It is an exaggeration to speak of an early and intensive Christianization of the Danubian Goths, as some historians have, since the vast majority were pagan in 376; still, the captives of the third century and their descendants planted the seeds for the Christianization and Romanization of the Goths.

Ulfilas is a prime example. The future Gothic bishop was born around 310, which means he belonged to the second or third generation born north of the Danube. There is no doubt that he was a Goth. Some have read his name, "little wolf," as a sign that he was of lowly origins, but the early stages of his biography already reveal that this was not so. Those who maintain that Ulfilas's Cappadocian ancestors were on his mother's side and that his father was a Goth argue on the basis of inferences from similar cases but not from any direct evidence. In any case, the Cappadocian Christians who were dragged off in 257, as well as their descendants, became western Goths who remained Christians and probably also continued to be multilingual.

It is most likely that Ulfilas was baptized after birth and raised trilingual, since it does not appear that he learned Latin and Greek only later "at school." The Gothic bishop was able to compose theological tracts and exegetical writings in Latin and Greek. This would indicate that he had gone through some kind of training in rhetoric, which in turn would have presupposed a native fluency in these languages. After all, during nearly the entire fourth century there was lively contact and a constant exchange of ideas and people between the Danubian Christians and the churches of Asia Minor, especially those of Cappadocia.

It was probably in the year 341 in Antioch that Ulfilas was consecrated "bishop of the Christians in the land of the Getic land," with Eusebius, the imperial bishop of Constantinople, performing the ordination. The mere fact that Ulfilas was not given an absolute but a relative ordination as bishop, meaning that he became the Christian leader in and for a specific and identified area, presupposes the existence of a Christian community in the Gothic land. Moreover, the translation of the Bible also attests to the efforts of both Latin and Greek missionaries among the Goths prior to Ulfilas. The Cappadocian Eutyches, for example, whom the Catholic tradition made into the "apostle of the Goths," was probably an older contemporary of Ulfilas's, and among the Fathers who gathered at the First Ecumenical Council in Nicaea in the year 325, a certain Theophilos from Gothia is mentioned right after the bishop of the Crimea. In all likelihood this bishop was the predecessor and perhaps even the teacher of Ulfilas. Last but not least, the language of the Gothic Bible reveals that Ulfilas and his helpers could build on existing foundations.

The translation of the Bible, created after 350 on Roman soil, made Gothic by far the earliest Germanic language to reach the written stage. Biblical Gothic drew specialized Christian liturgical terminology from Greek, either directly or through the mediation of Latin. The terms for the cultural achievements of Mediterranean civilization, however, rest almost exclusively on a Latin basis. This linguistic heritage reflects the life of a barbarian society whose peasants, traders, and warriors came into contact with the greater Roman state and its civilization.

The Goths cut their hair (*capilli*) in the Roman style (*kápillon*). Luxury articles and the words to describe them were nearly all imported from the Roman Empire. The physician (*lekeis*), "he who casts spells on disease," used herbs and spices, the former derived from Gothic tradition, the latter supplied by the Roman model. The cloth he used was identified by a Gothic word, the sacks and bandages he cut from it reveal the classical loanword. Purely Gothic are the words for domesticated cattle, while those for poultry, the domesticated dog, all kinds of game, the donkey, and the camel (misunderstood as an elephant) are derived from the classical languages.

The biblical parables paint a vivid picture of the life of a people who made a living from agriculture, cattle breeding, and fishing. Ulfilas needed virtually no loanwords to translate these scenes into Gothic. Nearly all terms in biblical Gothic for fruit, types of grain, weeds, manure, the plow, and all other tools and peasant activities rest on a Gothic basis. From the same Gothic roots comes the rich terminology of cattle-breeding herdsmen. The fact that wealth meant literally "livestock" (*faihu*) is something Gothic has in common with other ancient languages. But horticulture and viticulture too seem strongly Gothicized in spite of basic Latin words, with the exception, however, of vinegar (*aket*). Of the names for Mediterranean fruit-bearing trees, that of the olive was borrowed very early, perhaps from the Illyrian-Venetian languages. The palm tree was called "pointed tree" in Gothic, the fig may have been taken from a Caucasian language, and only the name for the "mulberry," simply "the berry tree," was a Gothic creation. The carob was named after its shape—"horn." It is quite remarkable, though, how few foreign elements Ulfilas needed to translate the great number of biblical crafts and trades into Gothic. Although he could not always get by without borrowed concepts, even taxes and tax collectors, money changers and scribes are wrapped in Gothic garb.

Ulfilas translated from the Greek; his model for the New Testament is likely to have been the so-called koine version of the fourth century. Our knowledge of biblical Gothic derives primarily from the famous Codex Argenteus, a manuscript that was produced only later in Theodoric's Ostrogothic Italy. Ulfilas and his helpers used a Gothic alphabet of their own creation, which incorporated elements from Latin and Runic writing into a base of Greek letters. Ulfilas's translation of the Bible was of epochal significance for all "Gothic" peoples—the Goths proper, the Gepids and Vandals, the Rugians, Sciri, Heruli, and even the originally non-Germanic Alans.

Ulfilas followed the creed of the emperors with whom he had the closest dealings, and they all professed the subordination of Christ to the Father and of the Holy Spirit to the Son. In simplified terms this position was called, then as now, Arianism; it maintained that Christ was not of identical essence (*homoousia*) but only of similar essence (*homoiousia*) to the Father. In 360 Ulfilas opted for a compromise which spoke only of the resemblance of the divine persons but declined to say anything about their essence (*ousia*).

Still, on his deathbed Ulfilas declared his belief "in one God the Father, solely unbegotten and invisible, and in the only begotten Son, our Lord and God, the creator of all creation who has no equal—and thus one is God the Father of all who is also the God of our God, and in the Holy Spirit, the giver of life and holiness, who is, however, neither God nor Lord but the faithful servant of Christ, and not equal to him but subordinate and obedient to the Son in everything, as the Son is also subordinate and obedient to God the Father in everything."

In the long run such a profession of faith could not compete with the theological sophistication of the Nicene Creed. Fifth-century critics were thus not entirely wrong when they conceded that, at most, Ulfilas was well-meaning or when they spoke of his intellectual inability to understand his error. The Goths, in any case, following Ulfilas's teaching and his community, became Arians. Of course this development came to full fruition only when the Goths, Vandals, Burgundians, and finally the Lombards had raised up kings and established kingdoms inside the Roman Empire. The kings became the heads of the Arian tribal church, which thus took the place of the old tribal religion. In the Arian kingdoms, as everywhere among the Germanic peoples, doctrine and church organization worked "from top to bottom." This, however, was a complete reversal of the original conversion of the Goths, which had begun "from the bottom up," a unique occurrence in the entire Germanic world. Christianization and Romanization went hand in hand in the Danubian Gothic land and provoked a corresponding reaction from the pagan upper class. As a result, this region saw in the fourth century the only "state"-sponsored persecution of Christians in all of Germania.

The Gothic persecutions were no different from their Roman counterparts, leaving aside the fact that they were decreed not by the imperial government but by the tribal council of Gothic magnates headed by the Gothic judge. It was probably Athanaric's father who in 348 hounded the Ulfilas Christians until the Gothic bishop and his flock left the land. Emperor Constantius II took in the refugees and gave them a place to settle in the north of modern-day Bulgaria near the city of Nikopolis–Stari Nikub. Here Ulfilas was active as bishop and tribal chief (*pontifex ipseque primas*) until his death in 383. The emperor is said to have called him the Moses of his time; Ulfilas was also compared with Elijah, which reflects similar ideas of a savior of threatened ethnoreligious identities.

A number of martyrs are known to us from the first persecution. The second persecution claimed even more victims, and their names are also better attested. This persecution was launched by Athanaric following his peace treaty with Emperor Valens in the summer of 369, and it lasted at least until 372. During his first Gothic war, Valens had Eudoxius, bishop of the imperial capital, at his side in the field, evidently in order to deploy him also on a mission to the barbarians north of the Danube. The unsuccessful campaigns of the Roman military meant at the same time a setback for the conversion of the Goths: the Gothic leadership launched a fierce persecution against Christians of all creeds for being supporters of Rome and destroyers of the sacred tribal order.

Though the Christians were a minority, they were a force that had to be increasingly reckoned with. It must have given some magnates pause when Athanaric had his mandate of power, originally granted for the defense of the tribal territory against the Romans, extended indefinitely to fight the enemy at home. How easy it was for the temporary judgeship to turn into a permanent kingship. In response a *reiks* by the name of Fritigern took the side of the Arian Christians—in a pro-Valens sense—and took up arms against the Gothic judge. It is likely that Fritigern was personally bound to Valens by a treaty. These inner-Gothic struggles must have come to an end before the assault of the Huns in 375/376, for at that time Athanaric had completely regained his monarchical power, though as previously it was temporally and territorially limited.

Catholic authors of the early fifth century made Ulfilas into a supporter of Fritigern and an enemy of Athanaric. The latter was undoubtedly the case, though we have no evidence for this or for a direct cooperation between Fritigern and Ulfilas before or after 376. But if Fritigern adopted the emperor's position, Ulfilas's Goths were essential if he wanted to actually implement the emperor's offer of accepting the imperial creed. At the time only Ulfilas and his people had the personnel and the means to undertake missionary work. However, this means that Fritigern's decision in favor of imperial Arianism represented the first internal Gothic encouragement for the work of conversion which Ulfilas had begun so long ago.[51]

5. THE INVASION OF THE HUNS AND THE RESUMPTION OF THE GOTHIC MIGRATION

After subjecting the Indo-European Alans, who live to this day in the Ossetians of the northern Caucasus, large Hunnish bands crossed the Don in 375 and attacked the realm of the Greutungian King Ermanaric. Following several defeats, the prince of the eastern Goths, whom heroic legend later turned into the contemporaneous enemy of Dietrich von Bern, took his own life. He probably sacrificed himself to the god whose name he bore, in this way rendering a final service to his tribe. And so after the death of their king the Greutungi did not give up the fight, and they chose a successor from his Amal clan. The resistance of the eastern Goths lasted about a year, when this new king too was killed and the Greutungian defensive struggle collapsed for good. Now most of the members of the tribe were subjects of the Huns. However, a group of Goths and a group of Alans escaped subjection and retreated jointly toward the borders of the Roman Empire. This tribal confederation was led by two nonroyal chiefs, the Goth Alatheus and the Alan Safrax, who had also been joined by Hunnish bands. This confederation of three tribes followed in the political tradition of the last Ostrogothic Amal king, which was reflected in the fact that Alatheus and Safrax took the young son of the dead king with them.

Already at their first appearance west of the Don, which according to ancient geography formed the boundary between Asia and Europe, the Huns displayed a lack of political cohesion and, like the Alans, the ability to join all kinds of different ethnic groups. To be sure, in the battle with the Ostrogoths there appeared a Hunnish military king who held the top command and who was able to legitimate his rule over the Ostrogoths through his marriage to a relative of the Amal king, whom he claimed to have killed with his own hands. But this did not by any means establish a Hunnish monarchy in a lasting way.

In the summer of 376, Athanaric led a strong army from Moldavia through Bessarabia to the western bank of the Dniester. Here, at the old border between the two Gothic peoples, the Gothic judge built a fortified camp to await the Huns. Then he ordered two noble chieftains to lead a vanguard about twenty miles east across the river into the land of the Greutungian neighbors. The Huns, however, bypassed this small force and made a surprise attack on Athanaric. Still, the Gothic judge managed once again to retreat with only negligible losses. Already in the war against Valens he had proved himself a master at such maneuvers. The Gothic line of retreat was also covered by the Bessarabian forest zone into which the Huns were unable or unwilling to follow.

Athanaric gathered a large part of the Danubian Goths between the Siret and the Prut and began to fortify the exposed southern flank of the central Moldavian plateau with a long rampart. While Athanaric was pushing ahead with his "well-planned work," the Huns launched another surprise attack. This time the assembled army would have met its fate had the enemies not been encumbered by the booty they were dragging along. The clash took place at the northern edge of the wedge between the Siret, Prut, and Danube, that is, right where the forest zone turns into open country. The fact that the Huns showed up here loaded with booty must have meant they were on their way home after far-ranging plundering expeditions that took them deep into Greater Walachia.

The Gothic food supply collapsed. But hunger was not the only thing that plagued the Goths; they no longer had hope of surviving in an utterly devastated land that a new type of enemy could destroy at will and without advance warning. No one, not even Athanaric, knew how to defend against such an enemy. At that very moment the leaders of the opposition, who were friends of Rome and Christians, that is, the old enemies of the Gothic judge, offered a credible alternative.

Athanaric's monarchy had now lasted close to ten years, and it had brought strife at home and warfare against the Romans and the Huns. Though the war against the emperor between 367 and 369 had cost few casualties, the land had suffered heavily by that time. Then the persecution of the Christians between 369 and 372 and the subsequent tribal feud split the *Gútthiuda*. Finally, the events in the summer of 376 had demonstrated that Athanaric was not able to protect the tribal territory against the Huns. Fritigern seized the initiative and promised flight into the Roman Empire as the only means of salvation.

A few months later the main group of Danubian Goths was in fact admitted into the empire. When their leaders were named, Alaviv was mentioned first. It was only after Alaviv's death that Fritigern gained the supreme command over all the Goths admitted into the Empire. Fritigern was a tribal *dux* in the true sense of the word, a leader of the army "who ruled in place of a king." He was never a Gothic judge nor did he ever become a monarchic king, even though his position was clearly a preliminary stage of military kingship. Fritigern had the authority to negotiate and conclude treaties with the emperor as well as with other tribal groups.

Athanaric, who had originally intended to follow Alaviv and Fritigern, learned of the difficulties encountered by all Gothic refugees who could not or would not show themselves to be Christians like Fritigern, and he abandoned his plan. The former Gothic judge therefore decided to leave only his immediate homeland. Between 376 and 380, he and his people remained in the "Caucaland," a mountainous region originally inhabited by Sarmatians and located either west or east of the Carpathians. However, in the fall of 380, Athanaric was driven out by his own people at the instigation of Fritigern. Now he fled to the empire, in fact directly to Constantinople, where the emperor gave him a splendid reception on January 11, 381. But only two weeks later Athanaric died.[52]

The reception of foreign peoples into the empire was certainly no longer a novelty in 376. What the Romans expected from the foreigners was submission, *deditio,* which meant that they laid down their arms and at the same time declared their readiness to be settled as tax-liable subjects (coloni, *tributarii*) at the emperor's discretion. This is what had happened a few years earlier to Alamannic prisoners, who had been transplanted into the Po Valley.[53] And already around the middle of the century, Franks had found a homeland on the same conditions in Toxandria on the left bank of the Rhine.[54]

At about the same time, Sarmatians had submitted to Emperor Constantius II by "humbly asking for peace. They arranged themselves in battle formation. Then their leader stepped forward, laid down his arms and threw himself to the ground. After the emperor had indicated to him that he should rise, his people also threw away their shields and weapons and stretched out their hands as a sign of submission." They were then given the status of coloni and were supposed to be settled in distant regions. It goes without saying that it was not necessary to conclude a treaty with the Sarmatians who had submitted. As coloni they could be drafted without limitations for military service. Had they been settled on land of the imperial treasury, they could have also been given the status of *dediticii* in the first, and that of *laeti* in the second generation, a status that differed from that of coloni only in that the former were directly subject to the military administration.

The admission of the Fritigern Goths and the planned settlement of the Sarmatians thus did not differ in any fundamental way but only with regard to the special situation in 376, when the Goths arrived in unusually large numbers and it proved impossible, owing to the incompetence of the Roman magistrates, to disarm them or commit them to the status of coloni.

The admission of an entire people overtaxed the abilities and integrity of the Roman officials. They were unable to handle the food supply for the Goths administratively and did not shrink from exploiting the Goths' difficult position and profiting from it. Since the emperor was on yet another campaign against the Persians, he and this army were far from the Danube in Asia Minor. The Thracian regional army, however, was not only badly officered but also numerically much too weak to carry out the authorized crossing of the Fritigern Goths and prevent the unauthorized crossing of the river by other Gothic groups. And so the inevitable happened. The Romans lost control, and the end result was murder and mayhem, war and destruction.

News from Thrace really could not have been any worse. The regional army had been simply overrun by the rampaging Goths. Roman and barbarian slaves as well as Goths in Roman service joined Fritigern, who in turn had entered into an alliance with the mounted three-tribe confederation of Alatheus and Safrax. And to make matters worse, neither Emperor Valens nor his court was able to assess correctly the extent of the danger.

The Gothic war of 367/369 was less than a decade old, and at that time the Danubian Goths and their allies had barely dared to defend their homeland, let alone move against the Romans offensively. What could have possibly changed with these savages, whom Emperor Julian had already considered an enemy unworthy of the Roman army? He was going to keep them in check using Galatian slave-traders.[55]

Once again the Roman government failed when it came to making a realistic assessment of a barbarian threat. The tribal armies of the Danubian Goths had indeed been small and had been composed of noble elite warriors. Now, however, the assault of the Huns was causing a *levée en masse*, with the result that every last peasant from Saba's village who could hold a spear became a warrior fighting for his survival. The consequences of this were not considered, let alone foreseen.

In the fall of the 369, the rhetorician Themistius had praised the emperor's philanthropic policy toward the Goths and their treatment in a way that was reminiscent of the contemporaneous glorification of the victory of the Alamanni which the emperor's older brother Valentinian I had just celebrated in Trier. Since the third century, Goths and Alamanni had been settling on Roman territory from which the imperial administration had, without abandoning it, withdrawn. Though the two groups were not considered citizens of the empire, they were seen as its subjects, a notion that the Roman army knew how to drive home by making its presence known in those lands for short periods of time.

The Roman senator Symmachus, a member of the high nobility, praised the emperor with these words: "The inhabitants of Alamannia live for you, Valentinian. The people whom you remove from the sword you add to the empire. It is enough that you have changed the nature of the tribes through your gentle actions. What independence is left to them, whose well-being is dependent on your kindness and whose lands are dependent on the Roman forts? They are free by law, but captives in the consciousness of their shame. Will they perhaps move to distant lands, wither follow not only your standards of war but also new cities? . . . Inhospitable land, in what state were you found so very recently? Without knowledge of ancient cities, unattractive with houses of twigs, roofs of grass. What I tell you now is to your benefit: you have been defeated. Like the other provinces of the empire, you too now show yourself fortified with towers. More fortune does it bring the lands to serve my emperor than to resist him."[56]

In the end, however, both Valens and Gratian, who had succeeded his father Valentinian I in the West in 375, were forced to realize that the Goths in Thrace could be neither starved into submission nor ignored, that it was necessary to fight and destroy them if it was not possible to subject them. While the "barbarians acted like savage beasts that have sprung their cages,"[57] Valens led the entire eastern court army from Asia Minor to Thrace. He had between thirty and forty thousand elite troops at his disposal, which represented a concentration of military force such as had not been seen in this area for a long time. At the same time Valens asked his nephew Gratian for help. Gratian ordered his army to march east in the winter of 377/378, but a sudden Alamannic invasion prevented him from going through with his plans. Though Gratian was able to win a splendid victory, he lost valuable time before the western court army was able to set out to unite with the troops of Emperor Valens.

Still, the western army had already reached Castra Martis–Kula, on the Danube in present-day Bulgaria, by the beginning of August 378, when the eastern war council reached the decision that it was imperative to attack and defeat the Goths without outside help. A number of favorable rumors, along with a reconnaissance report that the Goths were only ten thousand strong, made everyone believe that the battle had already been won. The euphoria drowned out cautious counsel from a group of imperial officers whose speaker was an old cavalry general, a Sarmatian by birth who had served as an envoy to Athanaric in 366. Based on his experiences he advised the emperor to wait until the two court armies had joined. Valens, however, who was jealous of his nephew's victory over the Alamanni to begin with, paid more heed to the flatterers who reminded him of his earlier victories over the Goths and of the recent clashes they had won.

Probably on August 5, 378, it seemed for a moment as though Valens would reverse his hasty decision. A messenger from Gratian arrived in Adrianople and conveyed the urgent request of his lord to await his arrival and attack Fritigern with combined forces. The western army had good reason to send this warning: while Gratian's advance troops had been encamped at Castra Martis, it had been suddenly attacked by Alanic horsemen from the Alatheus and Safrax group. The Romans suffered only very minor losses, but this strange "blitz attack"—a phrase that was to become one of the standard ways of describing Gothic battle tactics during the next two centuries—had made a lasting impression on the western legions, who had rarely, if ever before, seen anything like it. None of the Romans had been able to strike back successfully, since the enemy was operating with feigned flight outside of the Romans' range.

Still, Valens insisted on his decision to begin the battle immediately. Even the news from Castra Martis did not impress him. Perhaps he was thinking of the clash in the summer of 369, when the troops under his command had been the first Romans to meet up with Greutungian horsemen. The Roman army had been attacked in the steppe between the lower Dniester and the delta of the Danube, but it easily fended off the foreign cavalry. Once again we get the impression that it was the earlier successes against the Goths of the Danube and Ukraine that made it impossible for

Valens to recognize the full extent of the threat. And so the event was played out like an ancient tragedy: the messenger came to warn the hero of his doom, but the hero, blinded by hubris, would not and could not listen.

After a few more attempts on Fritigern's part to resume talks with "his emperor," the Roman army set out from Adrianople on the morning of August 9, 378, leaving behind the baggage train, the imperial treasure, and the insignia. The Goths awaited the Romans entrenched behind their wagons. The Roman troops had to cover a distance of eleven miles in full armor, with no water or food, in the blazing heat of the southern Thracian August sun. The road was poor and the Goths had set fire to the withered grass and brush to add to the distress of the Romans. In this situation the emperor discovered the poor job his reconnaissance service had done: it was not ten thousand men that awaited him, but a Gothic army several times that size.

Once more a messenger from Fritigern arrived, the extended line of the Roman army slowed down, the emperor hesitated and spoke to the enemy's envoys. Suddenly it appeared as though a peaceful solution would be found at the last moment. Since Valens wanted to talk only with the leaders, the western Goths demanded a high-ranking Roman officer as a hostage for the duration of the negotiations between Valens and their chiefs. After some hesitation the Frank Richomeres, the future *magister militum* but at that time a high officer on loan from Gratian, agreed to go. But it was already too late. Two Roman units had begun hostilities without orders, and they dragged the rest of the army into battle in a disorganized manner.

The battle had hardly begun when the day was carried by the "blitz attack" of the Gothic cavalry. Alatheus and Safrax had no sooner returned from foraging than they threw themselves into the fray. As from an ambush the Gothic and Alan horsemen attacked the right flank of the Romans and rolled it up from the side or perhaps even from the rear. Then one detachment of the Gothic cavalry withdrew, went round the Romans and fell on their left flank, where it repeated its tactics. By now the Gothic foot warriors had left their circle of wagons and were attacking from the front. The Roman cavalry fled immediately, and the tactical infantry reserves did the same. There was no chance of reestablishing the battle lines. The Roman army, surrounded on all sides, was cut down, and with it the emperor and most of his generals and field officers. Only a third of the Roman troops managed to escape, among them the cavalry. This meant that the legions, which at that time still formed the most valuable part of the Roman army, had been largely destroyed.

The battle of Adrianople has been called the great turning point in western warfare. But August 9, 378, had no such impact on the history of warfare, and it is also easy to exaggerate its impact on the history of the late Roman Empire. The Romans of the fifth century, who had lived through the horrors of the previous generation or two, saw Adrianople as the beginning of the end. This perception was shared by Edward Gibbon, whose view has shaped the picture to this day. But the immediate contemporaries of Adrianople thought differently. Emperor Valens died among his soldiers, probably struck by an arrow. Some stories had it that the mortally wounded emperor was carried into a log cabin where he and his companions were burned to death. The fact that the body of the hated Arian emperor was never found was linked with the story of his death by fire, which symbolized the eternal flames of hell. To Catholic Christians it was soon very clear that the devil had taken Valens, nothing more had happened.

However, when a pagan contemporary mentioned the battle of Adrianople in the same breath with the battle of Abrittus in 251, in which Emperor Decius and his son were killed, and when he compared August 9, 378, with Cannae, it was clear what he meant: after Cannae came the battle of Zama, where Hannibal lost the war, and Abrittus was followed by the victories of Claudius II Gothicus and Aurelian, victories that destroyed the first kingdom of the Goths between 269 and 271, ended their unity, and very nearly wiped them out.

And in fact the Goths were not able to exploit their victory at Adrianople in any major way, indeed they were not even able to take the city that housed the imperial treasury. Most other cities in Thrace likewise resisted the Gothic assaults, and it hardly needs mentioning that the barbarians had no hope of taking Constantinople. "I wish to keep peace with walls" was the lesson that Fritigern had to learn very quickly. But behind the walls lay not only the riches of the Romans but also the food which the Goths so urgently needed. Once again the tribe began to go hungry.

But August 9, 378, did set in motion three important changes. First, the battle led to a profound transformation of the tribes of the Danubian Goths. A new ethnogenesis began at this time. As Fritigern's Goths saw it, it was the cavalry that had won the great battle and a few smaller clashes before and after. And though these mounted warriors were Goths or Gothicized nomadic horsemen, they were outsiders. Their obvious success promoted the acculturation—or better, reacculturation—of the Danubian Goths to the eastern, "Scythian" way of life. It is one of history's ironies that the Goths returned to the ways of their eastern neighbors only on Roman soil: it was south of the Danube that the Danubian Goths became the mounted Visigoths who carried the traditions of the eastern steppes to the far western corners of the Roman Empire. All at once there is a change in the archaeological finds in the *castra* and *castella* [camps and fortresses] from the estuary of the Danube to that of the Inn and far beyond. It is often impossible to tell whether an artifact from the fifth century comes from the Crimea, from Untersiebenbrunn near Vienna, or from Normandy.

The western Gothic adoption of eastern customs continued also after the Greutungian-dominated three-tribe confederation separated from Frit-igern's Goths in 380. Both Gothic groups continued to remain in close contact. Thus the sources mention at least three different occasions on which the eastern Goths joined the Visigoths. Among them were even Amals, that is to say members of Theodoric the Great's own royal family.

Second, the battle of Adrianople set in motion the final Christianization and especially Catholicization of the Roman Empire, however paradoxical this may sound. Without the destruction of the Arian Emperor Valens and without the establishment of the Arian Goths on Roman soil, there probably would never have been this solidarity effect under Emperor Theodosius, who, in the battle at the Frigidus in 394, succeeded in helping Catholic Christianity prevail over pagans and Arians.

Third, the battle of Adrianople brought about a change in Roman policy toward the imperial barbarians. The accommodation between the classical and nonclassical worlds that Constantine the Great had begun experienced another fundamental shift. Now one had to get along with the assimilated groups, no matter that one had defeated them. No supernatural power—whether a god or an anonymous law of history—determined the fall of Rome. There was still freedom to make good and bad decisions.

The man who was able to muster enough imagination to respond to the challenges of the time was Theodosius, the "friend of peace and of the Gothic peoples."[58]

6. THE GOTHIC TREATIES OF 380/382 AND THEIR CONSEQUENCES

Shortly after the death of his coemperor, Valens, Gratian took steps to bring the Spaniard Theodosius, who had withdrawn to his native country and into private life following the judicial murder of his father of the same name, closer to the throne again. The emperor's attempt at reconciliation was successful; Theodosius was promoted at least to the position of *magister equitum* of Illyria and he took over the defense of the *limes* in Upper Moesia and Dacia, which he knew from earlier commands. In the final months of that unhappy year 378, he was still able to inflict a crushing defeat on the Tisza Sarmatians, who had taken advantage of the destruction of Valens's army to penetrate into the empire. Theodosius thus legitimated himself as a general, an imperator in the truest sense of the word. And so on January 19, 379, in the Illyrian capital of Sirmium–Sremska Mitrovica, Gratian elevated him to the rank of coemperor and put him in charge of the East, including the newly created prefecture of Illyria. His sphere of authority had thus been expanded as far as the rivers Drina and Neretva.

The most pressing task of the new emperor was to replace the destroyed eastern army. Peasants, miners, Asian and African federates, even Goths were recruited in large numbers to quickly raise a new field army. But in spite of a few victories, Fritigern's Goths and their allies, the horsemen of Alatheus and Safrax, could not be defeated, let alone subjected or even annihilated. Then, in 380, the horsemen of the three-tribe confederation left Fritigern's Goths and once again attacked the region of western Illyria—Pannonia. This put them inside Gratian's imperial territory. Gratian was also quick to realize that a military solution was impossible, and he settled the Ostrogothic-Alan-Hunnish horsemen as federates at the river Save in Pannonia. The legal basis for this was the conclusion of a treaty by which the foreigners on Roman soil were given special status. Gratian had probably consulted Theodosius about this treaty, who for his part reached an agreement with Fritigern's Goths on October 3, 382: "an entire gens of the Goths along with its king [Fritigern] surrendered to Romania."

Even if the treaty of 380 was a precedent for the *foedus* of 382, the latter loses nothing of its epochal significance. And this holds true even if in fact, as some have conjectured, Emperor Julian had already tolerated Salian federates in Netherlandish Toxandria south of the Rhine.[59] In some way or another there were thus undoubtedly precursors to the treaties of 380/382. Still, it was only at this time that a new page was turned in the book of Roman institutional history, since nothing compares to their historical significance. The Goths were recognized as federates in the heartlands of the empire and formed, in relatively close proximity to the capitals Constantinople and Ravenna, separate constitutional entities that would invariably develop into "states within the state."

The Franks' penetration into the territory of the empire is not really comparable. What the Franks did was more like conquest and settlement, even if interrupted by constant setbacks, and prior to 508 we cannot point to a single treaty between Frankish tribes in Gaul and the central government that would have provided a legal safeguard for what they were doing. If the Franks west of the Rhine were federates at all prior to this date, they were federates of rebellious local Roman generals and not of the empire. However, this is not to say that the Frankish way of establishing a kingdom on Gallic soil was not successful. On the contrary, it had a great future ahead of it, as the imperial recognition in 508 shows. But the impulse for the constitutional transformation of the western empire and its replacement by Roman-barbarian kingdoms came not from the Rhine but the Danube.[60]

The terms of the treaty of 382 must have been as follows: First, the Goths became subjects of the empire but remained foreigners and as such had no right of intermarriage (*connubium*) with Romans.

Second, the Goths were allotted tax-free settlement land in the northern part of the dioceses of Dacia and Thracia, that is, between the Danube and the Balkan Mountains, though they did not hold this land as property (*dominium*) as defined in Roman law.

Third, while the land assigned to the Goths remained Roman sovereign territory, the Goths were considered to be autonomous, that is, they were ruled by their own tribal princes.

Fourth, the Goths were obligated to render military assistance to the Romans, but their own tribal leaders would receive only subordinate commands. King Alaric I, for example, stood under the supreme command of regular Roman generals when Theodosius in 394 marched out the eastern army against the usurper Eugenius.[61]

Fifth, the Goths lived "under one roof" with the provincials, who were partners to the treaty; this arrangement was undoubtedly not meant to be permanent and is reminiscent of the Roman practice of *hospitalitas* (billeting of soldiers). The Goths' livelihood was to come from the allotted land, which they had to work themselves. This solution did not have much of a future and was—except in Britain—rarely tried again after the beginning of the fifth century. In addition, the Goths were entitled to annual payments of unspecified amount.

7. STILICHO AND ALARIC

Stilicho was born in 360 or shortly thereafter, Alaric around 370. The younger of the two spent his childhood in the barbarian land; the older one was a Roman citizen all his life. Stilicho came into the world as the son of a Vandal who served as a cavalry officer in the army of Emperor Valens, though probably not until after his son's birth; Stilicho's mother was a Roman. His parents could have married only with dispensation, and the emperor who gave it—indirectly through a high-ranking bureaucrat or directly—must have been Julian or even still Constantius II. Around 383, Stilicho, though "barely past his youth," took part in a delegation to Persia as an officer of the imperial household troops. Upon his return he was married to Serena, Emperor Theodosius's favorite niece, and simultaneously promoted to master of the stable. About two years later, probably as early as 385, Stilicho rose to the rank of general and became chief of the guard; the young man was now only one step away from becoming *magister militum*, commander in chief of the army.

Stilicho's rapid advancement is not all that surprising following his marriage into the Theodosian house. But how did this close relationship with the imperial family come about in the first place? It is true that as a small boy Stilicho had already been entered into the roster of the court guards. While his parents had thus ensured the beginning of a splendid career, they could not have influenced the speed of his advancement and his rise to dizzying heights; those things were determined solely at the emperor's discretion.

Evidently Stilicho must have come to know Theodosius early on and must have struck him as a particularly promising young man. Perhaps there had already been some kind of connection between the fathers of the two men. The elder Theodosius had served in Pannonia, where he fought against the Sarmatians. In the process he must have also had dealings with Vandals. It is interesting that an imperial law forbidding marriage between Romans and barbarians had been addressed to the elder Theodosius. But such a marriage had been contracted at least ten years before by Stilicho's parents.[62] Is it possible that the elder Theodosius had exceeded his authority too generously in granting dispensations, with Stilicho's father as one of the beneficiaries?

The poet Claudius Claudianus (who died around 405) reports that Alaric was born on the Danubian island of Peuke (S. Georghe), which had passed into Roman literature as the home of the Bastarni, long since expelled by the Goths. We would thus be well advised not to presume that the poetic statements refer to the estuary of the Danube; other passages mention only Alaric's descent from the "paternal Ister." There is, in any case, no doubt that he was born north of the Danube, or that he was a member of the clan of "the bold," the Balthi. Together with the "even nobler" Amals, the Balthi were among the oldest Germanic royal families of recorded tradition. They were older than the Vandal Hasdingi, who only in the fifth century developed from a tribal name into the name of a royal family. Most of all they were older than the Merovingians, who rose to become the sole Frankish royal clan at the end of the fifth century.[63]

Alaric was probably related to the Gothic judge Athanaric, but the name of his father is not recorded. If my reading of a passage in Claudianus is correct, Athanaric learned how to wield arms and shoot the bow from a foster father "instead of his father," which may indicate that he lost his biological father at an early age. If we look for an eminent Danubian Gothic reiks whose name is related to that of Alaric and who died in the late seventies, the natural candidate is Alaviv, who together with Fritigern (though mentioned as the higher-ranking of the two) led the Goths into the Roman Empire, and who must have died in 377 at the latest.

When Stilicho and Alaric encountered each other for the first time, they had both taken a decisive step forward. In the late summer or early fall of 391, various tribal groups had crossed the Balkan Mountains and penetrated into the interior of Thrace. The colorful band was composed of Moesian-Gothic federates as well as of invaders from north of the Danube, and it followed its leader, Alaric, who was here mentioned by name for the first time. Theodosius, who had just returned from the West, was prevented from crossing the Maritsa and was very nearly captured in the process. The danger was averted one more time, but the Romans found themselves forced to conduct a costly war against Alaric's group, until Stilicho was able in 392 to corner and encircle Alaric at the Maritsa River. Although Alaric and his people were let go on the emperor's order, they had to renew the *foedus* of 382 with the same conditions. Two years later the Goths marched as federates against the West in Theodoric's army, and Alaric was not given an independent command.[64]

So much for the events which formed the framework for the actors. Stilicho had been promoted to *magister peditum praesentalis* of the East in 391;[65] probably that same year (and not in 395), Alaric I, for his part, established the first Gothic kingdom on Roman soil. This kingdom was undoubtedly based on the polyethnic bands of 391 who had made Alaric their military king. At first this fundamental institutional change[66] was of little consequence. Hitherto barbarian kings had not had great careers in the Roman army. It was quite an achievement when one king rose to be a commander of the guard;[67] as for the others, the post of commander of border troops at the Arabian *limes* (*dux Phoeniciae*) was the end of the career for one king of the Alamanni,[68] while another got no further than regimental commander (tribune) in Britannia.[69]

Alaric broke with this tradition; he was the first Germanic king who became general of a regular Roman army, even though in 391 he had not yet succeeded in revising the restrictive provisions of the treaty of 382.

In the spring of 392, Valentinian II, the son of Emperor Gratian and the person who had elevated Theodosius to the rank of an augustus, died under mysterious circumstances. The Frank Arbogast, chief of the army and almighty generalissimo, who had long since risen to be the true ruler of the West, tried at first to get Theodosius's blessing for his position. But the Christian emperor did not want to accommodate the pagan Arbogast and his followers, even though, or precisely because, their faith had long since ceased to be a primitive tribal religion. When all attempts at mediation failed, Arbogast decided at the end of August 392 to have Flavius Eugenius, a former teacher of rhetoric and kindred pagan spirit who was Christian only outwardly, proclaimed emperor by the army.

What Theodosius thought of all this is revealed by his decree of November 8, 392, which outlawed all pagan cult activities throughout the empire. Still, Eugenius continued to negotiate until the eastern emperor had completed his preparations and, by the middle of 394, marched against the West with a powerful force. His army included an unusually large contingent of Gothic federates. The Gothic tribal warriors, approximately twenty thousand strong, stood under the command of Alaric, though beyond leading his own troops Alaric was not given any Roman military command.

Rather, the Balth was subordinated to three regular Roman troop commanders, who in turn had to follow the orders of the generals Timasius and Stilicho. One of the three commanders was Gainas, a Goth like Alaric but without "family."

Battle was joined on September 5 and 6, 394, at the Frigidus-Wippach-Vipava, a left tributary of the Isonzo. While the eastern army's vanguard, which was composed mostly of Goths, suffered such dreadful losses on the first day of fighting that it was reduced by half, a divine judgment on the second day decided the outcome in favor of the Christians. The Bora, a feared wind, roared down from the very mountains on which the troops of Eugenius had erected statues of Jupiter and struck them in the face with such terrible force that it impeded their fighting, while it spurred the forces of Theodosius and gave them victory.

Alaric must have distinguished himself highly during the fighting, because he was granted the title of *comes*. But the dreadful losses among the Gothic warriors, which even seemed intentional on the part of the imperial military leadership, and the continuing refusal to grant their leader a higher Roman military office, greatly heightened the tensions among the federates. It would take only a spark to cause this powder keg to explode. However, the Goths remained within the formation of the combined Roman armies at least until January 17, 395, that is until the death of Theodosius. But after that nothing could keep them. Stilicho had to discharge them even before he was able to begin the orderly return of the eastern army.

Formally Stilicho had participated in the battle at the Frigidus while still second general, though in all likelihood he lead the decisive attack on the second day of fighting. Since Theodosius had been planing to return to Constantinople as quickly as possible, his highest-ranking general had already gone on ahead when the emperor died unexpectedly in Milan. Stilicho was now the highest-ranking officer commanding both armies, the victorious army of the East and the defeated army of the West. This meant, however, that he was the de facto ruler of the western empire, to whom the emperor had entrusted the child Honorius and supposedly also responsibility for the already eighteen-year-old eastern Emperor Arcadius. This changed the entire situation: it seemed only a question of time before the West, so recently humiliated, would triumph over the militarily defenseless East. Added to this was the revolt by Alaric and his Goths in the East.

The federate warriors returning from the West must have simply picked up their tribal brothers who had remained behind in Moesia and continued right on their way, so fast did they all set out toward Constantinople, where they arrived in the first half of 395 under the leadership of their king, Alaric. The death of the emperor had ended the treaty of 382/392. The purpose of the Gothic expedition was thus the conclusion of a new *foedus*, one that would guarantee the tribe better living conditions and its leader a permanent place in the Roman military hierarchy.

While the federate warriors had been fighting and dying in the struggle against Eugenius, and while the survivors had been stationed in northern Italy for months after, Hunnish horsemen had crossed the frozen Danube and assaulted the Moesian homeland of the federates. If the Goths remained in their allotted settlements and if their warriors continued to be thoughtlessly sacrificed by non-Gothic Roman generals, their very survival as an ethnic entity was seriously imperiled.

Alaric's negotiating partner was the East Roman praetorian prefect Rufinus, first adviser to the emperor Arcadius and keenest rival of Stilicho. Rufinus and Stilicho were probably also personal enemies. With the remnants of the eastern army fighting against the Huns who had invaded Asia Minor in 395, Rufinus had no choice but to come to an arrangement with the Goths. The result was a new treaty that granted Alaric a high military office, perhaps already that of *magister militum* of Illyria. If this is true, and it is highly likely that it is, the treaty would have overturned the most humiliating clause of the *foedus* of 382/392 while at the same time pronouncing a new territorial authority of the Gothic federate army. In any case, the Goths withdrew from Thrace; the immediate threat to Constantinople had been removed.

Of course this masterful diplomatic move came at the expense of eastern Illyria; though it was still firmly under east Roman control in the spring of 395, Stilicho claimed it for Honorius and the western empire in fulfillment of an alleged testamentary disposition of the deceased emperor. In any case, the Goths marched to Greece, to the Diocese of Macedonia, and after surmounting local pockets of resistance they arrived on the plain of Larissa, where they fortified themselves behind their wagons to await Stilicho. The latter had already marched to the East with both mobile armies in the spring of 395, and during the summer months he caught up with the Goths southwest of Mount Olympus. Here the troops of Alaric and Stilicho stood facing each other for several months, a tactical maneuver that was used in most cases of inter-Roman conflicts. After all, the armies of Stilicho as well as the federate warriors of Alaric were Roman armies; their commanders were duly appointed Roman generals. From the standpoint of traditional law, Stilicho had less reason to be in eastern Illyria than Alaric, who had been appointed by Arcadius. Eventually Stilicho accepted the jurisdiction of the eastern emperor, gave up his position in Thessaly at the command of Arcadius, and returned to Italy with only the western troops. The eastern field army marched off to Constantinople under the leadership of the *comes* Gainas.

The troops were ceremoniously welcomed outside the gates of the capital on November 27, 395. Rufinus would not survive this event, and it is not impossible that the long arm of Stilicho struck: a group of soldiers fell upon Rufinus, who was standing next to the emperor, and literally hacked him to pieces. The chief chamberlain Eutropius now took the place of the prefect Rufinus, whose death put the Goths into a treatyless limbo. Gainas became chief of staff while Alaric lost his Illyrian magistracy. This made Alaric and his army into rebels once again, and they behaved accordingly. It is possible, though, that the Gothic king crossed Thermopylae while he was still a loyal federate and Illyrian military chief, since he was the duly appointed superior of the commanding officer put there very recently by Rufinus. In that case the commander of the troops at the Thermopylae pass would not have committed treason, as one so often reads, when he let Alaric and his army through.

Once across the pass, the Goths swarmed over Boeotia: they avoided Thebes but were able to capture Piraeus. Athens, however, was saved: Pallas Athene and Achilles were said to have appeared on the walls of the city. But undoubtedly what impressed the Goths more were the large sums with which the Athenians bought them off. The Goths then moved across the isthmus and ravaged the land. For more than a year Alaric and his hordes remained in the Peloponnesus, creating the impression that he intended to settle there for some time, if not for good.

In the meantime, however, Eutropius and Stilicho had come to an agreement whereby Illyria was divided in 396, with the two dioceses of Dacia and Macedonia remaining part of the eastern empire as the prefecture of Illyria. This relieved Ravenna of the need for and responsibility of concerning itself with the former Gothic federates. But as a result of the relative amity between East and West, Stilicho was ordered to march eastward once again with the western field army to support Arcadius in his struggle against the Huns and Goths.

The western army landed on the coast of the Peloponnesus in the summer of 397 and began to move against the Goths in the tried-and-true way. After clashes in which they suffered heavy losses, Alaric and his men were surrounded northeast of Olympia; it seemed only a matter of time until the rebellious federates would capitulate. But the expected end did not come; Stilicho entered into some unknown agreements with Alaric and withdrew from Illyria. In response his erstwhile ally Eutropius had him declared an enemy of the eastern empire, though he was now forced to deal with Alaric on his own.

The Goths crossed the gulf of Corinth and invaded Epirus. After terrible devastation to the land, Constantinople was ready to conclude a new treaty: the Goths were settled as federates in the Macedonian heartland between the rivers Haliacmon and Axius west of Thessalonica, and Alaric was appointed—probably for the second time—*magister militum* of Illyria. In this way an institutional model was created that would appear time and again in the future: a few relatively small centers of compact barbarian settlements were formed within a larger Roman administrative unit, which as a whole was placed by imperial orders under the authority of the representatives of tribal groups. Since the federates came under military administration, it was necessary for both sides that the barbarian leaders be given high Roman military positions. But in principle such a military office did not also confer legitimate civil authority on the barbarian leader, and it was the civilian authorities who were responsible for feeding, arming, and provisioning any military unit on Roman soil.

The highest-ranking military commanders, the likes of Arbogast and Stilicho, held vice-imperial positions and thus were also in de facto command of the civilian bureaucracy. A regional commander, however, which is what Alaric became probably in 395 and for certain in 397, had no such authority, even if he was a king. Imperial recognition of the kind of barbarian institution the kingship represented was extended only through the bestowal of a post as regional *magister militum,* later as general *magister militum.* When this recognition did take place around 400, it was the first time in the history of Roman-barbarian relations.

Between 397 and 401 all was quiet between Stilicho and Alaric. The Gothic king sought to consolidate his position in Illyria, while the generalissimo of the West had his hands full securing the realm of Honorius and solidifying his authority. The quashing of an African revolt brought so much money into the state's coffers that ten new bodies of troops could be raised and the imperial borders along the Rhine and in Britannia could be fortified. At the same time, however, Stilicho moved the seat of the prefecture of Gaul from Trier to Arles, even though new treaties with Franks and Alamanni in the late summer of 398 had secured the Rhine border in an impressive way.

Stilicho deposed a Frankish king not agreeable to him and simply banished him to Etruria. When his brother then tried to break the treaty he was killed by members of his own tribe. Peace abroad gave Rome time for internal reforms. In 400 Stilicho entered into his first consulship and thus stood at the height of his life and career. Now he was also the father-in-law of Emperor Honorius, to whom he had given his daughter Maria in marriage after putting down the African rebellion.

But the picture already began to darken as the year 401 went by. While Stilicho was busy in Noricum and Raetia dealing with Vandal-Alan invaders from Pannonia, Alaric's Goths left their Macedonian homeland and marched unimpeded to Italy, where they appeared as early as November 18,

401. After that they leisurely crossed the Po Valley and even threatened the imperial residence of Milan. Stilicho, however, acted quickly. At the beginning of March 402, he forced his way across the river Adda, whereupon Alaric had to give up the siege of the capital. The shock caused by the presence of the Goths before the walls of Milan led to the permanent transfer of the imperial residence to the impregnable and easily provisioned city of Ravenna.

Alaric, however, did not withdraw to the East but continued marching westward, whereupon the war had to be conducted with the fronts reversed. Soon troops from the Rhine and Britannia approached, posing to the Goths the danger of catching them in a pincer. Eventually Alaric pitched his camp near Pollentia-Pollenzo, where the imperial troops launched a surprise attack on Easter Sunday, April 6, 402. Stilicho handed over the supreme command of his troops to the pagan Alan chieftain Saul, who immediately opened battle while the Goths had their minds on celebrating the resurrection of Christ. The battle ended in a draw, even though Alaric suffered great tangible and intangible losses; many members of the tribe, including even women and children of his relatives, were taken prisoner by the Romans. Stilicho was able to stand his ground, but he had to let the powerful Gothic cavalry, in particular, depart unimpeded and undefeated.

The Goths abandoned Italy south of the Po and in fact seemed ready to beat their retreat. But Alaric halted near Verona; it appears that he was trying after all to get to Gaul across the valley of the Etsch and the Raetian Alps. Stilicho had had enough: now he wanted the Gothic king dead or alive.

In July or August of 402 the second great battle of the year was fought near Verona. It turned into the worst defeat Alaric would ever suffer. Though he was able to preserve the core of his tribe, he suffered such great losses that he had to withdraw from Italy and settle "in the barbarian land next to Dalmatia and Pannonia." The Goths were now in a situation where they had no treaty with either Ravenna or Constantinople. And so they proceeded to ravage eastern Illyria, until Stilicho provoked another break with Constantinople and had Honorius conclude a *foedus* with the Gothic king. It was probably in 405 that Alaric became *magister militum* of Illyria—probably for the third time, though this time he was appointed by Ravenna. This step was a serious violation of the sovereignty of the eastern empire. Honorius even appointed the prefect of Illyria in violation of the agreement on Illyria between the two imperial brothers.

But for the time being the invasion of Radagaisus and his barbarians prevented both Stilicho and Alaric from carrying out their plans. The Gothic king kept quiet, while many tens of thousands, who were mostly of Gothic background and seeking to escape Hunnish rule, invaded the Roman Empire via Pannonia and penetrated deep into Italy. In the summer of 406, Stilicho confronted the Radagaisus warriors near Florence and inflicted a decisive defeat with the help of Hunnish troops led by Uldin and Gothic supporters of Alaric's opponent Sarus. The Roman troops were made up of thirty *numeri*, which could mean nine thousand men just as easily as three times that number.[70]

Only in 407 could Stilicho once again think of attacking the eastern empire. The Illyrian *magister militum* Alaric had already invaded Epirus and was to be supported by a fleet. At that very moment the imperial defenses along the Rhine collapsed completely. It seemed impossible to stop the hordes of Alans, Vandals, and Suevi who poured into Gaul, which "lit up like one gigantic pyre." At the same time rumors about Alaric's death spread.

Stilicho now showed himself conciliatory, and while the policy of reconciliation between East and West made only slow progress, Alaric and his Goths had become dispensable. This meant the break of the treaty with the Goths, whereupon Aetius and the other hostages, who had been guaranteeing the treaty between the empire and the Goths since 405, probably returned home. In the spring of 408, Alaric's warrior, rebels again, marched once more against the West. At first they occupied the Norican part of present day Slovenia, Carinthia, and southern Styria, as well as the adjoining area of western Hungary. At the same time Alaric demanded an indemnity of four thousand pounds of gold and threatened to invade Italy.

This sum, enormous by public Roman standards, would have allowed more than ninety thousand people to live comfortably for one year. This figure agrees with the presumed size of the tribe, which is generally estimated at one hundred thousand people. Moreover, four thousand pounds of gold amounted to the yearly income of a senator of the wealthy, though not the wealthiest, class in Italy. Was Alaric trying to buy his way into the Roman nobility?

Whatever the answer, Stilicho acknowledged that the demands were legitimate and pushed them through against the most vehement opposition from the senate. The Balth was also once again taken into Roman service: as military commander of Gaul he was to lead regular Roman troops and his Goths against a Gallic usurper.

None of these plans were carried out. Stilicho was toppled on August 14th and executed on August 22, 408; thousands of barbarians who were living in Italy and trying to assimilate were killed in the subsequent manhunt. At this very moment a military king at the head of his warriors stood ready—within striking distance, as it were—to present himself as the savior of the persecuted barbarians: many tens of thousands of non-Romans are said to have joined Alaric, among them the twelve thousand elite troops that

Stilicho had taken over from Radagaisus. Alaric thus became the heir to Stilicho the barbarian, but he could not follow in the footsteps of Stilicho the Roman.

Stilicho's downfall is perhaps less puzzling than it might seem at first. The calamity was probably caused largely by the alienation between the emperor and his top general. The reason for this alienation was presumably the simple fact that Stilicho had not had any success since throwing back the invasion of Radagaisus in 406. The entire greater prefecture of Gaul had since fallen to usurpers and barbarians. Stilicho's downfall was set in motion by the death of the eastern emperor. Arcadius had died on May 1, 408, and both Honorius and Stilicho wanted to personally assume the regency for the emperor's minor son, Theodosius II.

In this situation, Stilicho's opponents tried to discredit the generalissimo by claiming he was trying to win the emperorship of the East for his own son. This rumor was sown among the troops that were gathering in Pavia for their departure to Gaul. The troops rebelled on August 13, 408, and lynched their officers, who were considered supporters of Stilicho. The imminent betrayal of the sacred Theodosian dynasty was too much for the army to bear, which might have just been willing to follow a Gothic king as military commander of Gaul into his sphere of command. On August 14, 408, Honorius signed the arrest warrant; eight days later Stilicho was dead, after the Gothic dissident Sarus had overpowered his Hunnish bodyguard. Killed along with Stilicho were most of his supporters and family; and Alaric marched on Rome.

In the fall of 408 Alaric reached the pinnacle of his career. Standing outside the walls of Rome he extorted payment of an enormous tribute and the joining of thousands of barbarian slaves to his forces. Still, lasting success eluded him. Though Honorius let his subjects pay, he wouldn't dream of concluding a new treaty and ending the treatyless situation. In response Alaric marched on Rome for the second time in 409; in November or December he wanted to reach an agreement with the senate, in doing so showing himself Stilicho's able student. The Gothic king got the senate to declare the urban prefect Attalus emperor; Attalus had been working for a reconciliation between the imperium and the Goths since 408. But already his very first measures must have been a deep disappointment to Alaric.

Though the Balth was once again made commander in chief, he had to share this honor with an open enemy of the Goths. In addition, Attalus appointed the spokesman of the anti-Gothic senatorial party as praetorian prefect of Italy. To these appointments, Attalus added his persistent refusal to conquer Africa with Gothic participation. Although African grain fed Rome and the heartland of the western empire, it seemed that the emperor by the grace of Alaric preferred failure to yielding on this issue, which in fact presented an intractable problem. If the Goths gained a foothold on the other side of the sea, they no longer needed Attalus and his senate. But if the expedition was attempted without the Goths, it would lack the necessary military power to force the African governor into union with Rome. A weak consolation remained to Alaric in that "his" emperor abandoned his paganism and converted to the Gothic faith.

As expected, the African venture collapsed; Attalus's rule could not last much longer, for the Gothic people were going hungry. Eventually the Gothic king's patience ran out and he once again drew closer to the legitimate augustus. In the camp near Rimini, Alaric had the hapless Attalus publicly stripped of his office, and he sent the diadem and purple robe to Ravenna.

All this led to a meeting between the Roman emperor and the Gothic king. But the imminent agreement fell victim at the last moment to a daring coup by Alaric's enemy Sarus, who launched a surprise attack on the Goths and inflicted a defeat on them. Honorius immediately reversed his policy; the reckless Sarus was received with honors, while Alaric marched against Rome for the third time, this time determined to take matters to the bitter end.

On August 24, 410, the Goths forced their way into the Eternal City. The swift capture was blamed on treason. A certain lady of high rank was even suspected of having secretly opened the gates, supposedly because she did not want to see so many people suffer in the siege. During the three-day plundering of the city the Goths seized vast treasures, among them probably part of the Jewish temple treasures that Titus had brought from Jerusalem to Rome. Alaric's brother-in-law Athaulf personally captured Galla Placidia, the emperor's sister, unless the report we have was a later invention because she eventually became his wife.

The capture of the city was a profound shock to Latin contemporaries. Was this the punishment of the Christian God or were the pagan gods avenging the abandonment of the old religion, the foundation of *Roma aeterna*? Augustine, in his *City of God*, created an eschatology in which the fall of Rome was endowed with providential significance.

In fact the Goths did not remain in the Eternal City for long. It was said that a demon had compelled Alaric to take the city. Perhaps he was even driven to do it for the sake of his own destruction. Since Alaric died in 410, these two events—the fall of the city and the death of its conqueror—gave rise to a tradition-forming motif that would influence the course of future actions, as is attested in the case of Attila.

At first Alaric's march south was successful. Cities like Capua and Nola were taken, but time was running short. And then the Strait of Messina confronted the Goths with an insurmountable obstacle. Inept attempts to reach at least Sicily with unsuitable vessels failed. Now the Gothic army began its retreat, marching northward toward Campania. We know for certain that the Goths spent the winter there and were not quick to give up the African plan even when Alaric died in Bruttium before the year was out.

To this day little has changed in the special fondness of German historiography for Alaric I. According to the *origo Gothica* "his people mourned out of love for their leader." Such sentiments were nothing unusual, however: when Attila died, his peoples too mourned, and the death of an Amal ruler supposedly caused such intense grief that the Goths did not elect another king for forty years. The "grave in the Busento" is also part of this conventional motif. The *origo Gothica* reports that Alaric was buried in the Busento near Cosentia-Cosenza after the river's waters had been diverted. The laborers who did the work were supposedly killed afterward. But this source reports the same thing also of Attila's burial. The "nocturnal" burial of the "young Gothic hero" became part of the cultural tradition of Romanticism through Platen's well-known poem. Judging from the type of burial chosen for the migratory king—the "young hero" was of course forty years of age—the Goths wanted to leave Italy. There are numerous Scythian parallels for the "grave in the river." In fact the Busento must have yielded up Alaric's grave already in the following season, when the river turns into a modest streamlet or dries up completely.

What Alaric meant to his tribe emerges far more clearly from the fact that he was able to suffer several serious defeats without being deserted by all his people. Alaric was not a savage any more. He was an Arian Christian. He was ambitious, proud of his noble ancestry, and he prevailed with his Balthic identity against Romans and Goths. If anyone offended him or his people, he became the barbarian who jumped up and ordered the march on Rome. But he was also a good organizer and recognized the value of Roman administration. He was aware of the importance of regular supplies, and he solved the kind of logistical problems that had so quickly led to the downfall of Radagaisus.

Even by Roman standards Alaric proved himself a good—though not a superior—general. He was never completely defeated, but then he was also never able to defeat a Roman army that was halfway intact. However, just as he himself was not able to establish a royal clan, something that was achieved only by the younger Balthi after serious setbacks, Alaric I also did not solve the question of how a lasting reconciliation could be achieved between the Roman emperorship and the barbarian kingship. Alaric's unsuccessful attempt to integrate Gothic statehood into the empire was the reason his policy seemed to waver so abruptly between enmity toward Rome and readiness for accommodation and compromise.

Stilicho and Alaric embodied the attempts by two barbarians to work at the top of the Roman state and possibly even control it. But Stilicho, a consul several times, became a Roman, whereas Alaric never attained Roman citizenship. Stilicho, the son of a Vandal, pursued the road of total integration, and like his Frankish-pagan predecessors he cut himself loose from all tribal ties. He was an ardent Catholic and served the imperial family loyally, as he understood the word. Alaric, by comparison, had combined his Gothic identity with Arian Christianity and a new kingdom on Roman soil. If it proved possible to obtain, on the basis of these three elements, imperial recognition, and a solution to the economic question satisfactory to all, Alaric's plans would be blessed with a long life, as measured in human terms, even if he himself would not live to see it.[71]

FOUR

Emperorship and Kingship
on Roman Soil

1. CONSTITUTIONAL THEORY AND CONSTITUTIONAL REALITY

Ravenna tried to rid itself of the invading barbarians in the same way Constantinople was able to during the fifth century. In politics, however, intention and achieved result cannot be considered apart. This is the reason why, after the death of Emperor Theodosius, the gap separating the barbarian policy of the East from that of the West steadily widened. At first glance it seems strange that this should have been so, since the starting position of the eastern half of the empire appeared weaker for a number of reasons: First, at the end of the era of Theodosius, as at the beginning, Constantinople had only a strongly reduced court army at its disposal. In 379, the new emperor had to depend on the demoralized remnants of the battle of Adrianople, and in 395 the eastern elite units stood in northern Italy under Stilicho's command.

Second, Theodosius, like his predecessor Valens, had been initially only the "younger" augustus. And while Gratian strengthened his coemperor by ceding to him the Illyrian prefecture with the dioceses of Dacia and Macedonia, to which was added Pannonia in 392, in 395 Stilicho, invoking the alleged last will of the emperor, reclaimed the three dioceses for the western empire.

Third, East Roman territory was home to the largest and most dangerous federate settlement of the new type: the regnum of the Thracian Goths, which would not remain without a king for long.

And yet the East must have already gained the upper hand, for a variety of reasons: First, Theodosius broke with tradition and transferred the East to Arcadius, since he was the older emperor. In the process he even seems to have asked Constantinople to give up Illyria; apparently it was felt that without it the younger Augustus Honorius would not have gotten his fair share in being placed in charge of the western empire, and he was to be compensated for it.

Second, it gives one pause for thought that a civilian, without the elite units and without making even the attempt to employ military means, succeeded in prevailing upon the rebellious Alaric Goths to give up their siege of Constantinople. This man was the praetorian prefect Rufinus, who had good connections to the rebels. Rufinus, who appeared in Gothic garb and warlike dress to meet with Alaric, understood their mentality. But this can hardly have been enough to convince the Gothic king, any more than it would be enough today for a civilian to don the uniform of a marshal or a five-star general to persuade an invading army to turn around.

Third, Stilicho reacted much like Alaric had in his dealings with higher authority. Having surrounded the Goths in Thessaly in 396, Stilicho was ordered by Emperor Arcadius to give up his position. Stilicho obeyed, recognized the authority of the eastern emperor, promised to return the eastern army, and even renounced eastern Illyria. When Stilicho returned to the east with an army in the spring of 397, he was already doing so at the behest of Constantinople, and he was declared an enemy of the state by the eastern government after he had taken it upon himself to come to an agreement with Alaric.

It is hardly possible to list all the reasons and motives that determined the "game of the powerful." However, one explanation above all forces itself upon us: the economy, society, and political structure had become far stronger and more resilient in the East. Although himself still the prime example of the fourth-century military emperor, Theodosius nevertheless initiated the development that lead the East to do away with *militaris potentia,* military dictatorship. At the same time the civil bureaucracy retained its importance.

How very different the situation in the West. The attempts of its ruling class to use the Roman-barbarian kings to preserve the res publica failed. And the patrician chiefs of the military, equal in rank to kings and mostly from the same families as they,[1] were also not able to stop the general process of dissolution and breakdown. In fact, often they themselves deliberately promoted that process, as demonstrated by the example of Ricimer (457–472), the top military commander and patricius of the West of Gothic-Suebian background.

In Constantinople, by comparison, the senate and the people had remained the true emperor-makers of the eastern empire. These two forces above all, alone or along with the palace and sometimes also the army, chose and raised up the emperor. It is true that the "domestication" of the emperorship did not produce any great rulers, but it also prevented the militarization of the state. And it is only a seeming contradiction that the Byzantine armies were nearly always tactically and strategically superior to the barbarian armies. There were a number of reasons for this: First, as the events of the summer of 400 showed, the masses of Constantinople were numerically strong and politically active enough to quash the revolt of a seemingly almighty military chief and to reduce the influence of the military. When the latter had regained much of the lost ground two generations later, the capital was once again the birthplace of the countermovement, which in 471 resulted in the toppling of the patrician generalissimo at the time. Constantinople had simply become "the city" in which comparatively huge masses of people lived.

Second, quantification is today a popular activity, and sometimes it does in fact offer astonishing insights. Of course the data in the sources is very meager for the early period. We are forced to estimate, and estimates of late antique and early medieval data, especially of population figures, are always a matter of luck—in fact they are actually impossible if one demands absolute figures. Still, results obtained with the same method can be compared and are of some value. If the estimates for Constantinople around the year 500 are placed at three hundred thousand to five hundred thousand inhabitants, the figure for contemporary Toulouse is assumed to have been only fifteen thousand. This means, in other words, that in the capital of the Westgothic kingdom, and thus of the better part of the former prefecture of Gaul, there lived fewer people than made up the Gothic army, which is estimated at about twenty thousand men. By contrast, more people lived in Constantinople than ever comprised the entire Roman military force.

Third, this quantitative-demographic example finds its counterpart in a qualitative-economic observation. Once Theodoric the Great secured domestic peace in Italy, the still-rich land filled the treasury in Ravenna. After his death, his daughter Amalasuintha inherited—after subtracting the returned Westgothic royal treasure—40,000 pounds of gold. This sum corresponded to two annual budgets of the West Roman Empire of the middle of the fifth century. By comparison, the yearly income of the eastern empire is estimated at 270,000 pounds of gold, of which 45,000 pounds, more than twice the entire yearly budget of the West, was spent on maintaining the army. That is why the sum that Theodoric was able to amass in thirty-three years of unchallenged rule seems modest compared to the eightfold amount, 320,000 pounds, which Anastasius I left behind after a reign of twenty-seven years.

To be sure, numbers of this kind do not explain everything, but they illustrate why the western imperium, during the late fourth and early fifth century, declined to the rank of Constantinople's territorial and institutional junior partner. For example, around 450, about 60 percent of the yearly tax revenue of the western empire, but not even 5 percent of the eastern budget, would have been required to pay for thirty thousand elite soldiers. And needless to say, with an army of this size, Ravenna could have intervened—with prospects of success—either in Gaul or Africa; doing both at the same time would have been impossible.

And if the western imperial government had found the 12,500 pounds required for thirty thousand men, it would have had at its disposal only the same sum that three rich—but not "superrich"—Italian senators could expect each year from their estates. In Byzantium, "private" incomes were evidently not as high. Here 1,200 gold pounds was the yearly income of a senator, which was in keeping with his status even if he were a former Gothic king. In 535, Theodahad declared himself willing to renounce the Gothic-Italian kingship in favor of Justinian; in return he demanded exactly the sum of 1,200 gold pounds and permission to settle in Constantinople.

The disproportion between public poverty and private wealth thus forced the western empire to recognize new forms of statehood. The res publica gave rise to the regna of senators, various *curiales,* and barbarian kings, who in the end retained the upper hand.

At all times *connubium* (marriage) served the upper class as an instrument of politics. The same is true for adoption. In both cases the imperial government had to be concerned to block any claims that might have arisen. The Byzantine marriage and adoption policy was thus only a way of appeasing and stalling the barbarian partner to a treaty. A "kinship table of the late Roman military nobility" begins with the name Diocletian and ends with that of Justinian I. In between we find everybody who was anybody: Constantine the Great and Theodosius the Great as well as the kings of the Goths, Vandals, Burgundians, and Franks, and the military chiefs of the most diverse backgrounds.[2] In real life politics, however, all these kinship ties meant little.

Alaric's successor, Athaulf, tried to legitimate the establishment of his kingdom on Roman soil by linking himself in marriage to the Theodosian dynasty. In 414, "the queen of the south" married "the king of the north," as contemporaries interpreted the marriage of Athaulf to the emperor's daughter Galla Placidia in accordance with the prophecy of Daniel. The following year Galla Placidia gave birth to a son, and the child was given—as expected, one is tempted to say—the imperial name Theodosius. But the child died soon after and thus fulfilled for the experts another part of Daniel's prophecy, namely, that the couple from north and south would have no offspring.

Two generations later, however, there was offspring when the Vandal pretender to the throne married an emperor's daughter whom he had likewise "brought back" from Rome. Out of this marriage between Huneric and Eudocia, the granddaughter of the onetime Gothic queen Galla Placidia, came the next-to-last Vandal ruler and last legitimate Vandal king, Hilderic. His downfall showed once again how little importance attached even to marriage into the Theodosian dynasty. The path Athaulf had tried did not lead to the desired goal even if a half-Roman and grandson of an emperor became king of the tribe.

The following story may explain why this was so, regardless of whether it was true or merely Ravenna court gossip: Honoria, the sister of the western Emperor Valentinian III, had chosen Attila as her fiancé and savior when her colorful love life at the imperial court had gotten her into trouble. In response the king of the Huns asked for her hand and the emperorship. There were people at the court in Ravenna who thought one could establish marriage ties with barbarian kings like Attila or Gaiseric as a way of conducting politics. In the end, however, the traditional view prevailed: from Ravenna came the answer that the emperor's sister had no share of the rulership, since only men were eligible for the Roman emperorship.[3]

Another reason marriage between the imperial and royal families remained essentially unsuccessful politically lay in the fact that the question of descent played a far less significant role in the elevation of emperors than it did in the kingship of the time. The "families of kings and heroes" were as much entitled to the kingship as the senatorial high aristocracy was to its Roman honors and offices. What proved an illusion, however, was the attempt by both groups to use the "splendor of lineage" as a political instrument in the struggle for the emperorship, as the fate of the Gallic "Gothic emperor" Avitus reveals. "Nobility and blood," *nobilitas et sanguis,* was enough for the barbarian kings. Something quite different was expected of the emperor; he also had to possess (philosophical) virtue, *virtus.*[4] That is also why the marriage between Matasuntha and Germanus, Justinian's cousin, did not fulfill the expectations placed in it. Germanus died still in 550 while preparing the invasion of Italy. His work was finished by the eunuch Narses, who for obvious reasons was hardly a candidate for dynastic marriage ties, while Germanus's posthumously born son, Germanus II, never attained any political importance.

Characteristically enough, Matasuntha's cousin, the granddaughter of Theodoric's sister Amalafrida, was far more successful. After the death of her Thuringian royal husband, she first fled with her mother, Amalaberga, to Ravenna, then went to Constantinople and was finally given by the emperor in marriage to the Longobard King Audoin, Alboin's father, as his second wife. Via the Thuringians the "splendor of the Amal blood" had thus still reached and exalted the Longobards.

In practice, imperial policy had to chart a path between the claims of the Roman-Germanic kings and the attempt to maintain the Roman imperial administration to the greatest possible extent. The federate kings sought as well to put their own armies institutionally in place of the Roman military.[5] Where the imperial administration had to allow this to happen, the Roman res publica was temporarily or permanently suspended. The Germanic regna on Roman soil were simply a fact of life; they wouldn't go away and had to be dealt with. Likewise, the barbarians who had been admitted into the empire could not be destroyed or driven back across the Rhine and the Danube, as Synesius of Cyrene might demand in the style of the old pagan Libanius, or even Ammianus Marcellinus on occasion might dream about.[6]

Constantinople solved the dilemma through an extremely flexible, even creative, use of treaties; the treaties always extended the recognition of a barbarian state for a limited period of time only and tied it to inner-tribal legitimacy. Though the political tradition of the kings entered in this way into the respective treaties, the relationship between the imperium and a regnum was by no means settled once and for all. Even the special treaties that Gaiseric had concluded with Emperor Zeno and Theodoric with the emperors Zeno and Anastasius did not have unrestricted validity, in spite of their transpersonal quality. When one of the partners to the treaty changed, the various stipulations of the treaty had to be at least confirmed or even renegotiated.

The existence of a barbarian kingdom was thus always an open question, and it was threatened above all when the tribal leaders had to ask the court in Constantinople if the emperor would be willing to accept a planned succession arrangement.

While the West fought for its survival with treaties of every kind—from settlements of federates to marriages—the East, confident in its strength, always saw the policy of appeasement only as a temporary solution. In the first half of the fifth century, the pressure of the Huns lay heavily on the provinces of the Danube and the Balkans. After the collapse of Attila's empire, Pandora's box was opened anew, and Gothic peoples in the broadest sense of the word had to be settled in the East Roman Empire. But even at this time, Constantinople succeeded in settling the majority of the free-floating gentes as conventional federates. Those who defeated the Huns remained outside of the empire at the left bank of the Danube, even though they did live off the provincials on the right bank.

Under these circumstances, Byzantine policy toward the German kingdoms was able to concentrate increasingly on securing Italy and the central Mediterranean. Though Constantinople had been compelled, like Rome, to recognize the Vandal kingdom, it would never dream of considering itself permanently bound because of it. And the same was true for Italy. At first Constantinople sought to secure the western heartland by sending emperors or imperial candidates to Ravenna. In 476 a *rex* replaced the imperator; in so doing he created an institutional fact that called for different strategies on the part of the Byzantines.

What had preceded the constitutional change in Italy had been the destruction of the *exercitus Romanus,* which was stationed on the peninsula, at the hands of "the armies of Odovacar." Even though the king also appointed Romans to officer ranks and continued to fill Roman military offices, his army was composed of federates, his "hordes" were considered barbarians, *externae gentes*. All these features also characterized the army of Theodoric and his successors, so that some ancient authors let the rule of Gothic kings in Italy begin with Odovacar and not with the Amal King Theodoric.

Latin and Greek sources that had not yet absorbed the experience of the great Gothic War left no doubt about the fact that Theodoric the Great had gone west in his capacity as an imperial representative with the rank of a top military chief *and* candidate for the kingship. To be sure, when the Goths elevated their leader to the kingship in 493, Constantinople was irritated, since the victorious federate army had not waited for "permission" from the new Emperor Anastasius. Yet there was never any talk of a breach of the treaty between Theodoric and Zeno. For now the *foedus* of 488 had a transpersonal quality, that is to say it did not automatically lapse with the death of one of the contracting parties. Thus Theodoric was not regarded as a usurper, especially since he could invoke the fact that the situation of *praeregnare,* which was provided for in the treaty, had occurred and that he had to exercise the regnum for a legitimate emperor.

Only when the balance of power had changed clearly in Constantinople's favor did Belisarius maintain that Theodoric had been a usurper like all the others. Now Byzantium interpreted his assumption of power in Italy as the unintended exchange of "one tyrant for another." Procopius, however, was objective enough to report also the argument of the Gothic negotiators: as patricius and consul, Theodoric had been chosen by the emperor to revenge Augustulus against Odovacar and to rule the land with the Goths legitimately and justly. After the Romans had lost Italy to Odovacar, Theodoric, with permission from Emperor Zeno, had waged war against him, defeated him, and subsequently possessed the entire western empire according to the laws of war.

Such views were held far from the court, even in Constantinople: Theodoric, Procopius tells us, had been a legitimate king, or *rhix*. It was only before his march to Rome at the emperor's request that the ex-consul and *magister militum* had acted as a tyrant in Thrace. Theodoric's successor and grandson, Athalaric, now had the same rights as his grandfather.

However, the fact that the Greek author Procopius used the Latinism *rhix* with the meaning of *rex-reiks* only twice in his monumental work means something. The first passage deals with the king of the Heruli and his feeble power. The second reports that Theodoric had been called *rhix* by his peoples. Thus the kingship of a *rhix* remained in the eyes of Procopius a purely barbarian, basically irregular and unlawful constitutional form that had nothing to do with the Roman state.

Procopius thus dissociated himself from the regnum as an institution that could expect lasting recognition from the imperial government. There was a good reason for this, even though Constantinople sometimes "forgot" about it: the regnum was, after all, the one late-Roman institution whose occupants were not appointed by the Romans. Neither the palace, nor the *senatus populusque Romanus,* nor a Roman army was, by itself or jointly with the other imperial institutions, authorized or capable of constituting a regnum on Roman soil. The authority to do this lay solely in the hands of a tribal assembly, a federate army, even if it may have been composed of "former Roman soldiers." What applied in this case was not the saying "the army makes the emperor" but the maxim "the federate army makes the king."

One might call this regnum the "Flavian kingship," after Theodoric's title of *Flavius-Theodoricus-rex,* first attested in 501. Just as the older Flavians possessed the emperorship, the younger Flavians sought to embody the kingship. Secondary in this was the question of which legal status the chosen had, whether he was to be considered a Roman citizen or a foreigner. However, it would seem that a *civis Romanus* like Theodoric or his son-in-law Eutharic had an easier time obtaining the necessary imperial recognition than did a tribal king without citizenship rights, even if he held high Roman military offices.

As a rule Constantinople granted only temporary recognition and linked it to a ruler's legitimacy within the tribe. Odovacar proved himself an avid student of this policy when he attacked and drove away the Rugian federates at the Danube in 487/488 because they had departed from the grounds of their own legitimacy.

The only Roman institution capable of offering effective resistance to the establishment of a kingdom was the army under the leadership of the legitimate emperor. A king therefore had to split them up, to try and eliminate the *exercitus Romanus,* indeed if possible have it dissolved by the imperial government. At the same time he had to secure recognition from the emperor and settle it by a treaty.

Imperial prerogatives—such as the use of the title of imperator, the wearing of the imperial robes, the decreeing of laws and judicial authority over senators and the high clergy, the full right of minting, and the promulgation of statutes—remained formally untouched until the end of the sixth century. When a Merovingian king like Theudebert I (533–547) usurped some of these rights and had gold coins minted with his image, his pretensions were considered scandalous and isolated actions. South of the Pyrenees, Leovigild (568/569–586) was the first who carried out an *imitatio imperii* that attracted wide attention.

Justinian I was resolute and uncompromising in carrying out his restoration policy against Goths, Vandals, and other barbarians as soon as they themselves departed from the ground of their own legitimacy. When Theodahad had his cousin Amalasuintha killed, Justinian considered the principle of Amal legitimacy broken and launched his Gothic War, which nothing—neither the death of Amalasuintha's killers nor the elevation of her daughter Matasuntha to the kingship—could stop.

But the Goths still possessed the right to chose the ruler over Goths and Romans. And Justinian, though in a state of war, accepted this decision even in the case of Vitigis, such was the continuing force of Zeno's treaty. In order to remove any remaining doubt that Zeno's treaty with Theodoric, which had evidently not lapsed with the death of the two contracting parties, had lost its validity, Constantinople had to try and bring about the circumstance in which a king, legitimately chosen by the Gothic army, handed himself and his realm over to the emperor. Fate would have it that Vitigis and not Theodahad would be the king of Goths and Italians, who had to bend to the emperor's will.

In 534, Justinian I had already used a breach of legitimacy to conquer the Vandal kingdom. Gelimer had violated a succession arrangement, and Constantinople—basing its decision on the old treaty between Gaiseric and Zeno—declared him a barbarian usurper. Finally the end of Balthic-Amal legitimacy must have offered Justinian an additional pretext for attacking the Visigothic kingdom and occupying at least parts of Spain.

The Catholic Franks remained beyond Justinian's military reach. Still, they felt threatened, for they "did not consider their possession of Gaul secure as long as they did not have the emperor's recognition of their claims signed and sealed." Justinian's troops fought the Franks only in Italy, and then more by accident than design. Only his successors would try, if in vain and only with diplomatic means, to regain a foothold in Gaul.

The Imperialization of the Germanic Peoples

Though the Gothic-Germanic kingdoms on Roman soil had their roots in the traditions of "foreign peoples," *externae gentes,* they were late-Roman institutions. They absorbed the highest magistracy of the late-antique military organization and the vice-imperial position associated with it; not infrequently they were ruled by Roman consuls. However, they did not become offices with regional authority but territorial lordships that abolished the Imperium Romanum within their sphere of jurisdiction.

A Gothic gens was therefore not merely an *exercitus Gothorum* but a Roman federate army as well. As successor to the Roman court armies, it had the right—if a territorially limited one—of transferring power. The Italian federates, the Goths, did not raise up an emperor but a king equal in rank to the emperor. From the perspective of the Roman constitution, the barbarian kingship was that anomalous entity that reconciled the practice and theory of the anomalous late-antique statehood. With its help the gens was cast into an institutional—or one might say, imperial—mold.

In this sense Theodoric the Great took the Imperium Romanum as the measure for his regnum. The Gothic regna and the other Roman-barbarian kingdoms of the migration period were as much an embodiment of late-

Roman constitutional developments as the Roman kingdom of Syagrius in Soissons (destroyed by Clovis), the "tyrants" of Britain after Rome gave up the island, the Breton Loire kingdom conquered by the Visigothic King Euric, or the African realm of a "king of the peoples of the Moors and Romans" at the beginning of the sixth century.

Just as in the modern state the opposition is part of political life, the Gothic-Germanic peoples were part of late-Roman statehood. Their regna were not barbarian states shifted onto Roman soil. A Roman-barbarian federate kingdom of the fifth and sixth centuries could, in fact, not survive without the imperium and its provincials. Even though experiences gathered outside of the Roman world were important elements of barbarian political theory, the Roman foundations remained vital and indispensable. Thus the defeated Heruli were not able to establish a kingdom in the Rugian land along the Danube in Lower Austria, a region devastated and largely emptied of its Romans, whereas the Longobards, who came directly from the barbarian lands, found it quite livable there. There is also an economic reason why Gregory of Tours reports that the Franks raised up "long-haired kings" only after they had crossed the Rhine, that is, on Roman soil.

But the establishment of the Roman-barbarian regna also offered the imperial government a certain advantage: the western part of the empire, which had become virtually ungovernable, retained in this way a reduced though predictable political structure with fixed borders. The emperorship, whose sole bearer since 476 was Constantinople, was given breathing space and at the same time the possibility of revising all the existing treaties. Constantinople could recognize a kingdom within Roman borders, accept the Gothic regnum *Italiae* as the successor to the *hesperium* regnum, and, in fact, even lose formerly Roman territory to barbarian states. But given the right circumstances and balance of power, Constantinople regarded these polities as provisional entities and the result of usurpations, and those who founded and ruled them as tyrants. The emperors reserved this option for themselves much earlier than Justinian, although he was the first who was able to make use of it. And when he did even the Franks had to fear for their lands, should Justinian follow in the footsteps of the earlier emperors and seek to conquer Gaul. In the end that did not happen. The kingdoms of the Franks, like Visigothic Spain, survived the Justinian reconquest. And even the Longobard kingdom, which had shifted to Italy, had to be accepted by Constantinople at the price of dividing the peninsula.

Justinian's successor synthesized a new policy from his predecessor's successes and failures. The regna of the "blond peoples" had become a permanent reality, and realities were something Constantinople had always accepted. The kings of these realms now formed the "family of kings" that had to respect the emperor as its paternal lord. Thus a modus vivendi had been established between East and West, which lasted until one of the barbarian kings, Charlemagne, had the audacity to reestablish the western imperium. Of course in Byzantine eyes this king of the Franks and Longobards got even the ceremony wrong: instead of being anointed emperor, he had himself anointed "from head to toe," that is to say, he received the extreme unction. And so Byzantium, with a disdainful smile and backed by a protective fleet, could survive Charlemagne's crowning on Christmas Day in the year 800, in theory as well as in practice. Only the West insists to this day on calling that totally "mis-anointed" king its Emperor Charlemagne.[7]

2. RECOGNITION AND INTEGRATION

The Economic Basis of the Roman-Barbarian Kingdoms

In 1844, Theodor Gaupp, going against the prevailing theory of catastrophe and conquest, advanced the thesis that an orderly policy lay behind the settlement of the Germanic tribes within the empire. From that time until quite recently, the following model of the economic foundations of the barbarian kingdoms on Roman soil held sway as virtually the only acceptable view: In 418, the Goths, as the first of the Germanic peoples, were settled in Aquitaine on the basis of the Roman billeting laws and with the consent of the region's ruling class, and this made them into co-owners of the property of their hosts. The disorder after the death of Emperor Honorius in 423 supposedly shifted the balance of power in favor of the Goths, and for the first time in Roman history barbarian co-owners proceeded to actually divide the land. The Goths received two-thirds of the cultivated land. To this was added half the fallow land, the virgin forests, and the pastures, though the Gothic owners had to pay an appropriate compensation if they developed or improved this land. Moreover, a third of the labor force was also said to have fallen to the Gothic allotment, the *sors Gothica*. Finally, the Romans may have been given the right of first choice in the billeting.

This "*hospitalitas* system" fails to explain the assumption that the Romans would have given up one-third or even two-thirds of their property without resistance. After all, the Visigoths and Burgundians, unlike the Vandals and Longobards, certainly did not enter the land as conquerors; instead, they were settled deep inside the Roman borders at the command of the Roman generals who had subjugated them. In the case of the Visigoths and Burgundians, a prior agreement was made between the military central authority and the Roman magnates affected by the intended settlement. As for the Ostrogoths, they had even been sent to the land of their permanent settlement by a legitimate emperor.

On the whole, however, the sources have so little to report about the modalities of the settlement that we can only infer that the method used was familiar and by no means oppressive and unacceptable. By contrast, encroachments by the Loire Alans, who did in fact expropriate, expel, or even kill Roman landowners led to indignant outcries in the otherwise terse Gallic accounts of the fifth century.

As for the late-antique laws on billeting, they described only how mobile military units were to be housed and not how their livelihood was to be financed. They regulated merely the traditional, temporary *hospitalitas*, which, as the personal obligation of most homeowners, was not a permanent arrangement. What remained of this practice after the permanent settlement of the Germanic peoples, however, was the language of the sources. They depicted the relationship between barbarians and Romans as that of "guests," *hospites*, most likely because they were to be housed in accommodations provided by the provincials.

In actual fact, not a single Roman was legally expropriated. Instead, in the territory of the kingdom of Toulouse and the kingdom of the Burgundians, two-thirds of the Roman tax revenue went to the newcomers as tax-exempt *sortes*, while the "one-third of the Romans" was earmarked for maintaining the administration in the Roman *civitates*. Responsibility for collecting and distributing the taxes lay in the hands of the municipal *curiales*, the land-owning regional upper class that formed the curiae of municipal self-government. Whereas the Italian Ostrogoths were satisfied with one-third of the tax revenue, the Visigoths and Burgundians, while claiming the same amount from the poll tax paid by each coloni, demanded double the amount from the general land tax.

This probably had something to do with the fact that the customary distribution of the revenue—one-third for the army, one-third for the central authority, one-third for curial self-government—could be continued only in the Italy of Odovacar and Theodoric, who took over the entire Roman apparatus including the regional and central provincial administration. By comparison, the Gallic kingdoms were composed only of *civitates*. Roman administration functioned here only down to the level of the *curiales*, while the central organs had to be created by the barbarian kings—though naturally not without Roman help—and appropriately funded. That is the reason two-thirds of the tax revenue went to the kings of the Visigoths and Burgundians.

The type of Gothic settlement devised in southern Gaul constituted a viable compromise between the demands of men like Alaric I and Athaulf and the attempts of the imperial government—doomed to fail—to settle the invading Germans at the borders or in uninhabited regions. The Gothic army was, after all, a Roman federate army, the maintenance of which could in traditional fashion be left to the curiae.

The fundamental novelty, however, was the fact that this army was on the land to stay and formed the basis of a kingdom. The same was true later for the Anglo-Saxons in Britain and for the federate Burgundians after they had been moved from the Rhine to the interior of Gaul, to Savoy and the valley of the Rhône. But even the African Vandals and the Italian Longobards were given shares of the taxes, though they came as conquerors. To be sure, expropriations and confiscations occurred everywhere in the Roman-barbarian kingdoms; but no matter how painful and how numerous they may have been in some places, they remained isolated instances, unsystematic excesses, or punishment for resistance and rebellion. The "new" order itself, however, was based on the "old" principle that the army was entitled to one-third of the land taxes.

In general, the process of assigning troops to the civitates and billeting them was also attended by injustices and acts of violence. *Hospes,* "billeted barbarian," became a dreaded word, as many a deep groan of despair from the Romans reveals. The federates formed a state within the state and also changed their Roman environment: not infrequently they caused old wealth to disappear and new wealth to arise. But most senatorial nobles retained their importance in the Gothic domains and remained as powerful as before. The landholdings of some Italian, Spanish, and Aquitanian senators were unimaginably vast—sources contemporary to the times called them "kingdoms."

How very apt that description was would be demonstrated as late as the sixth century by a Spanish lady of the senatorial class, whose wealth allowed her husband to raise thousands of soldiers, thus laying the groundwork for his elevation as king of the Visigoths. But the senators of the Auvergne, too, had enough wealth to defy Euric's Visigothic kingdom for four years. Thus the royal tax demands were a far greater threat to the wealth and freedom of the *curiales* than to the status of the senators. But no ruler in control of the treasury, be he emperor or barbarian king, could have had any interest in diminishing the ability of the provincials to pay their taxes or to see them "flee into the forest." Legal protective measures were therefore necessary, and they were taken especially by the kings of the Goths and Burgundians.

If the issue was one of punishing an offense, if for example a Goth was trying to obtain the Roman share in violation of the law, the "judges of the various *civitates*" or the managers of the royal estates intervened. Oaths and the testimony of witnesses were permissible as evidence. However, the legal rights of the plaintiff were protected by more than just an inquisitorial trial in the presence of the plaintiff and the judge; in keeping with the Roman structure of the Gothic administration, there were also written records. The existence of such records is clearly assumed by Gothic legislation and by the following story told in the memoirs of an intellectual driven from his homeland.

The author, Paulinus, a native of Bordeaux, lived an impoverished and lonely life in Marseille, a city that was still Roman at the time. Decades had passed since the Goths under Athaulf had entered his hometown for the first time. Suddenly, out of the blue, an unknown Goth sent him the purchase price for a small piece of property. The buyer must have discovered that a certain Paulinus was the rightful owner of the land. Of course the story also shows that a "foreigner," a Roman provincial living beyond "the borders of the Gothic allotments," had no choice but to accept whatever was offered. There was no negotiating about the price, let alone the Roman's willingness to sell; a Goth simply sent the money and that was that. But Paulinus's legal title of possession could have been preserved only because it was entered in an urban land register, *gesta municipalia,* where the Goth discovered it and accepted it as legally valid, since he himself wanted to become the properly registered owner of the property in question.

Whatever the members of the Gothic army did not consume they could invest in landed property. As landowners they became—though not without resistance—subject to taxation. The settlement of the army of the Ostrogoths is the best documented case. It could have a variety of different consequences for the individual Gothic warrior and his followers as well as for the Roman "neighbors and partners." Together with his property a Gothic warrior received a charter drawn up by an official authorized to do so. King Theodoric set as the cutoff date August 28, 489, the day he had crossed the Isonzo with his Gothic army. Thus already in the second decade after his entry into Italy, Theodoric made all illegal or irregular acquisitions prior to this date subject to the thirty-year statute of limitations.

From the outset, members of the royal family, and possibly other Gothic magnates as well, were given possession of land and people, and their property was called *patrimonium,* like the senatorial family estates. It is hard to imagine that these latifundia (*massae*) were subject to regular taxation. The king himself took over the royal *patrimonium* Odovacar had created. It comprised and administered the former imperial landholdings as well as the private property of the ruler, which included entire provinces. The domains of the Gothic kings can be attested in the Po Valley, in Apulia, and in Sicily; in addition, a very rich royal *patrimonium* lay in Tuscany.

However, leaving aside the king, his family, and the leading nobles, the following arrangements were made to satisfy the "victorious Goths":

1. Eligible Goths were assigned to certain *civitates,* where they lived side by side with the Romans and received from the curiales lodging as well as an appropriate tax-exempt share (*sors*) of the third (*tertia*) of the regular land tax (*annona* or *canon*). Nothing is said about the size of the yearly payments beyond the fact that they "fed" the Goths. The sources are also silent about the criteria that entitled a Goth to such an allotment, but personal freedom as well as a certain rank and level of wealth were no doubt prerequisites.

2. The customary pay (also called *annona*) was given to the conscripted units, both to the troops quartered in barracks for an indefinite length of time, as well as to any member of the first group as soon as he served active time in the army. The warriors stationed in the royal patrimonial provinces were paid from the *patrimonium,* which after all collected the taxes of the provincials who lived there. The Goths who made up the units quartered in barracks for extended periods, perhaps even permanently, may have been made up of economically weaker groups, for example younger sons, who were not entitled to a *sors.*

3. Extraordinary donatives were paid to the members of the first group, as well as to special units such as the free sailors of the fleet that was built in 526. Moreover, between 511 and 526, Theodoric gave the entire income from Spain as a "yearly gift" to the Spanish army, which was made up of Ostrogoths and Visigoths.

4. All Goths and barbarians who had acquired property "no matter under what title" were in principle subject to taxation.

5. Free and unfree retainers were to be maintained by their respective lords.[8]

The Organization of the Roman-Barbarian Kingdoms

All Roman-barbarian kingdoms rested on two preconditions: one was the military kingship of the migrating Goths, Vandals, Burgundians, Franks, and Longobards; the other was Roman administration, multilayered and based on literacy and the rule of law. This gave rise to the union of Roman magisterial structures and Germanic lordship structures. However, the personal element in the exercise of power was derived not only from barbarian tradition but also had roots in the regime of the late-antique military emperors.

Except for Odovacar and Theodoric, none of the Germanic kings were faced with either the problem or the option of taking over an undiminished administration that comprised the provincial administration inclusive of the office of the prefect. In fact, both the Vandals and the Franks even destroyed the Roman tax registers so that they might put in place their own order, though this order too was cast in the Roman mold. Thus in all kingdoms outside Italy the only element of the territorial structure that was retained was the urban district, the classical *civitas.* Despite this difference, which appears to be a fundamental one, the Italian kings organized the kingship side of their royal administration in the same way as their neighbors across the sea or the Alps. Goths, Vandals, Franks, or Burgundians: they all employed personal agents (*comites*), which they used—much as the late-antique emperors had—to intervene in and supervise the bureaucratic channels.

The rich sources of Ostrogothic Italy show that this traditional element was here expanded and developed into a veritable *comitiva Gothorum*. Those occupying these positions, who were taken from the leadership stratum of the Gothic army, entered into deliberate competition with the Roman hierarchy of officials. A *comes Gothorum* had the right to use the staff of the regional authorities. He was charged with military tasks and possessed the judicial power that accompanied them, though in disputes between Goths and Romans he could exercise this authority only in consultation with Roman legal experts. Theodoric had thus added an ethnic element to the system of overlapping spheres of authority that Diocletian had set up. We are reminded of attempts that were made in the recent past after revolutions and seizures of power to simultaneously unsettle and control the existing bureaucracy through political officials or a parallel party bureaucracy.

In peacetime a *comes* was primarily responsible for a municipal district in Italy, as was also the case in the kingdoms of the Visigoths and Burgundians, in the Romanized part of the Frankish kingdom created by Clovis, and among the Vandals in Africa. In those *civitates* that had few or no Ostrogothic-barbarian settlers, but which had mobile units stationed in them, the competence of the city-*comes* could be expanded over an entire province. But nowhere was it the case that several Ostrogothic *comites civitatis* were ever subordinated to a *comes Gothorum provinciae*. The one *comes* mentioned with this title was a "*comes civitatis* with an extended command." Thus the *comes* of Salona commanded the united provinces of Dalmatia and Savia, the *comes* of Syracuse all of Sicily, the *comes* of Naples at least the entire coast of Campania, the *comes* of Marseille Ostrogothic Provence or at least its southern half, and the *comes* of Sirmium the attached province of Pannonia II.

Such *comites* were—like the nonruling members of the Amal royal family, the Roman prefects, and the patricians—*viri illustres*, members of the highest rank of the class of *illustri*. In contrast, the city-*comes* without an extended competence was only a *vir spectabilis,* but that still made him equal in rank to the Roman border generals and the Roman provincial governors of the highest rank.

Gothic city-*comites* with and without expanded competence had to enjoy the king's special confidence for them to assume positions of considerable power far from court and thus outside his immediate sphere of authority. A number of high-ranking and top-ranking *comites* existed also at the court itself, and among them the sword bearer (*comes armiger*) occupied a special position. A *comes armiger* could go very far, even though he usually did not come from one of the best families. Up to the middle of the sixth century, nearly all non-Amal Ostrogothic kings belonged to such families of sword bearers. To be sure, the migration period and the establishment of a strong kingship did not make the old nobility fade away, but wealth and office determined a person's rank, which was in turn defined by proximity to the king.

Theodoric the Great was the only one among the kings of the Roman-barbarian successor states who had also taken over the imperial *comitatus*, whose most important task lay in its function as a palace court. Romans and Goths without distinction had to answer to the *comitatus*. Later even the appointment of bishops was decided by the *comitatus*, in which Goths held the majority. The "chief of the royal bedchamber" was also an Ostrogothic court-*comes;* he supervised the court chamberlains and court eunuchs and administrated the royal treasury. The court office of the *comes patrimonii*, however, was open to both Goths and Romans.

The *patrimonium* had been created under Odovacar in order to take the management of the separate royal wealth in land holdings out of the hands of the "regular finance minister." This innovation proved so useful that it became an imperial Roman institution under the East Roman Emperor Anastasius. The western *patrimonium*, however, competed not only with the regular financial administration but also with the normal provincial administration. The head of the provinces was the *praefectus praetorio*. All provinces that Odovacar took over when he assumed power remained under the authority of the prefect, and Theodoric did not change this. But whatever the two kings conquered within the Italian prefecture they regarded as their private property. Thus Sicily (after 476), Dalmatia (after 481), and Pannonia II (after 508) were administrated by the *patrimonium*.

The holders of the *comitiva Gothorum* made sure that the interests of the court and the army were protected far from the court. Among them was a lower-ranking group of envoys whom the king sent from the court into the provinces. As Goths they were members of the military, but in the name of the king they could take on military *and* civilian tasks. They were called *saiones*, retainers in the true sense of the word. All officials of the Gothic military and Roman civil hierarchies were directed and supervised by the *saiones;* even the *praefectus praetorio* could not escape this supervision. And yet the *saiones* certainly did not come from the best families; on the contrary, most of them did not go on to careers as *comites*.

The king as leader of the army was *the* quintessential *dux*. As the Roman-barbarian kingship increasingly became cast in an imperial mold, the kings had authorized *comites* take their places; as independent military commanders these *comites* were then given the same title as their king and were called *duces*. In addition, there was a *dux* who had a specific function within the Roman military hierarchy: he was the commander of a *ducatus*, a military district in charge of one or more border provinces. In the Ostrogothic kingdom, the traditional *ducatus* were retained along the comparatively secure northern border, in Raetia and Noricum, and they were headed by local Romans as *duces*.

The military conquests begun by the Visigoth Theodoric (453–466) and largely completed by his younger brother Euric (466–484) gave rise to new organizational forms; since Roman military districts were absorbed in the course of these conquests, these new forms also incorporated Roman military personnel.

Following these conquests the kingdom of Toulouse was composed not only of many city districts but of entire Roman provinces. Still, no separate Gothic provincial administration combining several city-*comitatus* was set up. Instead, as in Theodoric's Ostrogothic kingdom, some *comites civitatis* were assigned an entire province as an expanded sphere of authority. However, many of the recently conquered provinces had already been organized as *ducatus* to prevent an expansion of the Goths. In all likelihood, therefore, Euric absorbed the existing Roman institution into his realm, in not a few cases even along with the Romans who held this office. And so already at the end of the fifth century, the title *dux provinciae* was given to a *comes* in command of a larger jurisdiction.

With the expansion of the Merovingian Frankish kingdom across Roman-Gothic-Burgundian Gaul, this structure was taken over in the conquered territories and initially maintained. However, the *dux* steadily gained in importance as an agent of the Frankish king who now stood above the *comes*. A similar development must have taken place in Visigothic Spain, since the legal sources of the seventh century provided for the possibility of appealing a decision of the court of the *comes* to the court of the *dux*. The *comes civitatis* disappeared completely in the Italian kingdom of the Longobards; when the tribe invaded, *duces* were installed everywhere—probably in imitation of Byzantine practice at the time.

Nevertheless, in terms of constitutional history the *comes civitatis* is the bridge between late antiquity and the Middle Ages. No matter what name was given to the office and the officeholder, for centuries it was simply one of the necessities of political life that in endangered border regions several administrative districts be placed under a unified military command. Thus the functions of the late-antique *duces* and *comites* gave rise to the medieval dukes and counts. However, how tenacious these roots were can be seen from the fact that the Carolingian restoration made *dux* and *comes* interchangeable once again, and that subsequently down to the beginning of the high Middle Ages every *dux* was in principle also a *comes*. In all of this, the title *dux* emphasized the kinglike element of independent military leadership, while the *comes*, who was joined around 700 as an equal in rank by the previously subordinate Frankish *grafio*, always functioned as a regional deputy of the king.

We have virtually no information about the commanders of the smaller units of the Italian Gothic army, while a "leader of one thousand" (*millenarius*) existed among the Visigoths and the Vandals. It is also known that the Visigothic *exercitus* was structured according to the decimal system, in a way that had no parallel elsewhere. Thus the legal sources speak of the numerical commanders *decanus, centenarius, quingentenarius, millenarius,* and—with the exception of the unit of five hundred—of troop units that corresponded to these commanders. None of these troop commanders were entrusted with an independent command, though they did act as judges and possessed judicial powers as well as police authority.

As at the other royal courts, we also find in Toulouse and later at Toledo the usual court offices, the holders of which were responsible for the ruler's well-being, finances, and security. Among these *comites*—most of them designated with a Latin name—we find the *comes scanciarum,* the chief cupbearer. This position had a good old Gothic name; after all "to drink like Goths" had long since become proverbial.[9]

If we seek to describe the leadership stratum not only of a Gothic but of every other Roman-barbarian kingdom as well, it is not enough to name only the royal officials. Instead, it was the agents of the king *and* the preeminent men of the tribe, *comites et primates gentis,*[10] who represented the army and thus the realm after and with the king. However, they owed their position not only to the exercise of power in the king's service, but also to their own lordship; and the strength of this lordship depended on the size of the lord's following, how many private warriors he could keep and raise. While the emperors did not tire of prohibiting bands of retainers, the Visigothic kings were the first to institutionalize this form of dependent warriorship. Consequently the practice of keeping retainers was not only tolerated but given special attention.

The Visigoths knew two types of dependent retainers: the *buccellarius,* the higher-ranking of the two, who, despite his Latin name, is not directly comparable to his Roman model, and the *saio,* the Gothic retainer in the true sense of the word. The *buccellarii* were permitted to use, for the duration of their service, the weapons and other gifts they had received from their lord. If they left their lord's service and looked for another employer, which nobody could prevent them from doing, they had to return to their lord everything they received along with half of whatever they had acquired. This obligation did not change even in the second or third generation, and it applied equally to male and female descendants of the *buccellarii.* Daughters could retain possession of whatever was given in "loan" if they "remained in the power of the lord" and married a man acceptable to him.

By contrast, the *saio* had full freedom of movement and also full possession of the weapons given to him. But whatever he acquired during his time of service remained without exception his lord's property if he decided to seek another patron. Without doubt the *buccellarius* had the best social and economic position among the retainers; as late as the seventh century, his was probably the normal case of a dependent freeman. Even if the *buccellarius* betrayed his loyalty he could keep half of what he had acquired during his service. The *saio,* by contrast, had no economic and social guarantees. While the Visigothic *saio* could be the retainer of any lord, the Ostrogothic *saio* was exclusively an agent of the king. Even during the time when Theodoric the Great ruled both kingdoms there was no change in this functional difference.

During the last decades of the Visigothic kingdom in Spain we hear of a royal retainer of high rank who was called *gardingus* and who, after *dux* and *comes,* belonged to the people at court.

At the bottom of the royal and noble retainers stood the unfree barbarians. They were used militarily within a Longobard unit (*fara*) and as Gothic *servi in expeditione* (as "slaves on campaign"), and thus had the chance to improve their status economically, socially, and legally.

Even though the terminological, and probably also the legal, differentiations of Visigothic law have no counterpart in the other Roman-barbarian kingdoms, the situation in those regna was certainly comparable, if not identical. Thus being a Goth, enjoying the "freedom of the Goths," and marching in the Gothic army were one and the same thing. However, nobody was immune from losing that freedom. If a Goth felt that his status was threatened, proof that he had served in the army was sufficient to protect his personal freedom. Moreover, anyone serving in the Gothic army was legally of age.

We know the name of honor of the Gothic freemen from their songs: they were called the "curly-haired or long-haired ones," *capillati.* However, in Ravenna there was apparently a tendency to understand by that term all able-bodied barbarians who belonged to the Gothic army. If that was indeed the case, the term would herald the transformation of the Gothic army with its various peoples into a general class of subjects bound to the king by an oath.

The army on the march held out the promise of social mobility and attracted the native underclasses. At the time of migration this attraction seemed very useful, as it helped to relieve the chronic shortage of manpower. But in Italy, Gaul, Spain, and Africa the coloni were needed in the fields and not on the battlefield. Theodoric the Great, for example, staked his future on consolidating and stabilizing his kingdom, which is why he prohibited the Roman peasant underclasses from joining a Gothic army.

However, the old attraction was still alive when the Gothic kingdoms were fighting for their survival. At the battle of Vouillé, a contingent of Roman magnates from the Auvergne with their free and unfree *clientes* fought on the side of the Visigoths. This unit was led by a Catholic senator and son of the former bishop of Clermont. The Ostrogothic King Totila not only accepted Roman slaves and coloni into the Gothic army, he even mobilized them against their senatorial masters with promises of freedom and ownership of the land. In so doing the king gave the Roman underclasses a chance and an excuse to do what they had been ready and willing to do since the third century: "to become Goths" out of despair over their economic and social condition.[11]

FIVE

The Hunnic Alternative

1. THE BEGINNINGS IN EUROPE

In 375, the Huns, a steppe people difficult to classify ethnically, crossed the Don River and with it the border between Asia and Europe. The belief that this event triggered the Germanic migration has long been among the historical truths deeply embedded in our culture's consciousness, truths that have indeed become banal and yet stand up to every scholarly examination, though in the process they do lose their sloganlike quality in favor of a more subtle meaning.

Much the same holds true for the invasion of the Huns and their advance all the way to eastern central Europe. Although they ravaged Greater Walachia as early as the summer of 376 and may have even reached the Olt, it still took more than a human lifetime before a Hunnic polity was able to take shape along the imperial borders from the bend of the Danube in Pannonia to the river's estuary.

The basic organization of the Huns had not changed significantly since their first appearance at the Don. In the eyes of classical observers, already in 375 these "new Scythians" were no longer a tribal unit. Their followers included the Iranian Don-Alans, who had joined the Hunnic "tribal swarm"[1] quite against their will before they jointly attacked the Ostrogothic kingdom of Ermanaric. After its conquest the Huns continued to be dominated by a central Asian element,[2] but for the first time they were now joined by Gothic peoples alongside Sarmatians, Balti, and Fins.

This ushered in an intense and reciprocal assimilation between the eastern Goths and that branch of the Huns whose glory days and end would eventually be linked with Attila, the bearer of a Gothic name. It was thus only logical that it was the Attilanic Huns who, for the Germanic and Germanicized peoples along the Danube and the Rhine, formed the high point and end point of a development that had already begun with Ermanaric's death: in these Huns there arose an alternative to the Imperium Romanum and, to a lesser degree, to the Persian Empire. Or in other words, the tribes had to decide whether they wanted to become Roman or Hunnic Goths, Gepids, Heruli, Sciri, Burgundians, indeed even Franks. Those who sought to avoid making this decision had to count on the combined enmity of Romans and Huns.

The chaos that descended upon the entire region between the Danube and the Don after the Gothic defeats of 375/376 also prevented a consolidation of Hunnic rule. The next generation therefore witnessed repeated breakaways by Gothic groups and their crossing onto Roman territory. In fact, the first confederation of Ostrogothic-Alan groups to do so had been joined even by Huns, who together with these non-Hunnic horsemen decided the outcome of the battle of Adrianople in 378 and two years later were settled as Roman federates in Pannonia.

These first Roman Huns were to have many successors; they all fought with great determination against the creation of a Hunnic monarchy at the periphery of the Roman Empire. Thus Huns joined with Germanic Sciri and Dacian Carpi to escape the emerging greater Hunnic realm and find a home on Roman soil. This attempt was an utter failure. But shortly afterward, in 386, a certain Odotheus was at least partly successful when he crossed the Danube with a large number of well-armed Ostrogoths in order to become Roman. To be sure, the strange-looking Germans were lured into an ambush in which many were killed. But Emperor Theodosius withdrew the survivors from the Danube and settled them in Phrygia. With this move the Gothicization of the Danubian provinces had spread even into Asia Minor.

Until 392, at the latest, there was normal border traffic between the Roman Empire and a Gothic realm located across the Danube and not under Hunnic control. Only the attempt by Gainas, after an initially successful but eventually failed Roman career, to return to the Gothic land north of the Danube and create a kingdom, called the Huns onto the scene. After this time only two kinds of tribal geneses were possible: that of the Roman Goths inside the empire and that of the Hunnic Goths at its doorstep. And the same was true for most other gentes.

In the winter of 394/395, Hunnic units had attacked both the Balkan provinces and—by striking across the Caucus—Asia Minor, causing great devastation. In 398, a *comes* by the name of Tribigild had earned great credit by successfully fighting the Huns while serving at the head of cavalry divisions that had been recruited from among the Phrygian Goths. When his demand for an appropriate reward was turned down by the imperial government in an insulting manner, he rebelled in 399 and began to ravage the provinces of Asia Minor.

His victorious campaign soon came to a momentary halt. A local commando, led by an urban notable, lured the Goths into an ambush and inflicted a devastating defeat on them. Tribigild was able to escape with three hundred men only because an officer of the Roman units that were supposed to support the irregulars accepted a bribe. This incident shows how problematic it was to try and fight rebellious barbarians with seemingly loyal barbarians.

Asia Minor had plenty of unhappy Goths; the Roman army was full of them, and Tribigild had only to make use of their dissatisfaction as soon as they marched against him. After yet another Roman army had been defeated, or rather, had switched sides, Gainas, military chief of Visigothic origins, was given command of the operations against his relative Tribigild. Tribigild was probably out to win a position much like that of Alaric I, which would have entailed the creation of a Gothic people in Asia Minor. Gainas, however, was reaching for the power in Constantinople itself; Tribigild—like other barbarian chiefs—was probably merely a means to this ambitious goal. Be that as it may, in the winter of 399/400, Gainas dropped his disguise, joined forces with the rebels in Asia Minor and crossed the straits into Europe. At the same time Tribigild's name disappears from the sources.

Gainas marched to Constantinople and occupied the city. Of course the capital was a size too big for even the most successful of all barbarians in Roman service. Gainas, a zealous Arian, demanded a Catholic church for the services of his people. The imperial Bishop John Chrysostom, backed by popular opinion, vehemently opposed this plan. Rumors flew that the banks would be plundered. Next the imperial palace was suddenly in flames. The unrest intensified into street fights and eventually into full-fledged panic.

Gainas had quartered only half his troops in the city; when he attempted to unite his troops by withdrawing from Constantinople, the masses attacked the Goths and a general manhunt was on. On July 12, 400, seven hundred Goths fled into a church, not an Arian one, as one might have expected, but a Catholic one near the imperial palace. There they were surrounded and on the personal order of Emperor Arcadius either hacked to pieces or burned to death. Gainas was able to escape. His attempt to cross back over to Asia Minor with his troops failed for lack of appropriate transportation; Fravitta, Gainas's successor as military chief and former fellow tribesman, appeared with a Roman fleet and destroyed the primitive rafts of the Goths.

Despite this catastrophe Gainas refused to give up. With the remnants of his followers, among them also regular Roman troops, he marched through Thrace toward the Danube with the intention of trying to create a kingdom in his old homeland. He discarded everything Roman and staked all on the ethnic card. On crossing the Danube he had the Roman soldiers sacrificed to the river god. Barely across the river, Gainas got caught up in some fierce fighting with the Huns under their chief, Uldin. After a number of clashes, Gainas met his death on December 23, 400. Uldin, the first known ruler of the European Huns, sent the head of Gainas to Constantinople, where it arrived on January 3, 401. The Hunnic-Gothic war came to an immediate end.

The imperial government of the East showered Uldin with gifts and rewarded him with the first treaty between Rome and the Huns. Uldin honored the treaty also in his dealings with the western empire when a huge avalanche of tribes rolled across the imperial borders less than five years later. The hordes under the leadership of a certain Radagaisus were the last large, Gothic-dominated group able to escape Hunnic rule. All Roman observers speak of the suddenness and magnitude of this assault, whose destructive force struck northern and central Italy toward the end of 405. Prior to that the Illyrian region had felt the blow; scores of Roman refugees poured into Italy. The storm of Radagaisus was broken near the Florentine city of Fiesole and ended with its leader's death at the hand of the executioner on August 23, 406. The victor's name: Stilicho. But the enemy could not have been destroyed without help from the Alans, the Uldin Huns, and the Sarus Goths who had broken away from Alaric.

And so the years 405 and 406 saw a repeat of the political constellation of 400. As before, the Roman federates under Alaric I remained neutral, a Roman Goth defeated the Gothic enemy of Rome in the decisive battle, and Uldin destroyed him. Uldin was always ready and willing to repel renegade Goths, but he never sought a direct confrontation with Alaric's Roman Goths. Rome and Uldin, who, among the Hunnic chieftains, was the one more than anyone else able to expand and consolidate his rule, had arrived at a modus vivendi, and the peoples on either side of the imperial border had to live by it.

But even in the subsequent years there was not a single, all-powerful military king who led the Huns in a monarchical manner. At no time were all the Huns ever subject to one king; at no time was there ever *one* Hunnic people. Just as Gaiseric did not rule over all the Vandals and Theodoric the Great never ruled over all Goths, Attila, even at the height of his power, was not able to unite under his rule all the Huns and the peoples subject to them. Even when he was at the height of his power, the Romans were not willing to hand over to him all or most of the "deserters." After all, Huns had been serving in the Roman army for more than a generation, not so much as regular units but as federates in Gaul, Italy, Africa, or Britain.

The Huns inside and outside the Roman Empire were under the leadership of their own chieftains, whose titles are not known. The best Latin and Greek sources record titles one could take to be Gothic and read as *reiks*.

These *reiks* were distinguished by rank and prestige, for it was said of a certain Charaton in 412/413 that he was "the first of the kings."[3]

Charaton must have already pushed his realm as far as the Pannonian Danube. The chiefs of the individual Hunnic groups were still willing to collaborate with the Romans. The imperial General Aetius, for example, who in his youth had been a hostage to the Huns, successfully fought the Ravenna court clique in 425 and 433 with Hunnic help, put down rebellious Noricans, broke apart the Burgundian kingdom of Worms soon after that, and, in Gaul at the end of the thirties, kept in check the Visigothic kingdom of Toulouse and the native rebels known as the Bagaudae.

2. THE HUNNIC REALM ALONG THE MIDDLE DANUBE PRIOR TO ATTILA

The settlement of the Hunnic peoples inside the arch of the Carpathians was completed in the first third of the fifth century. Already before 427 the Hunnic sphere of influence extended to Pannonia, for at that time we hear about the Roman reconquest of Pannonia after nearly fifty years of Hunnic occupation. However, this highly controversial report does not distinguish between the various, even mutually hostile groups.

The Roman success, in any case, was short-lived, and a consolidated Hunnic realm, whose center lay between the Danube and the Tisza, extended also across Illyrian territory, whether or not we assume a formal separation of Pannonia in 433. From this time on, at the latest, there is truth to the description in the Gothic history that the Ostrogoths were the subjects of the Huns in a Scythian land that had shifted from Ukraine westward across the Carpathians and now also comprised Roman territory. This new Scythia was composed of "Dacia and Pannonia, where the Huns lived with various other peoples they had subjected."[4]

In the generation before Attila, his uncles Octar and Ru(g)a ruled the Huns. In 433, Aetius, the imperial general of the West, had to fear not only for his position but also his life. He fled via Dalmatia and Pannonia to the Huns, into the land between the Danube and the Tisza, where Ruga at the time held the highest position. Aetius concluded a treaty and returned to the western empire with strong Hunnic forces. Not only did Aetius receive back his old post as *magister militum,* promoted to the rank of *patricius* he also went on to exercise, unopposed, a vice-imperial function until 454.

Ruga was the first Hunnic ruler to succeed in forcing Constantinople to conclude a treaty promising annual payments. The agreement was for 350 pounds of gold, not a large sum considering the salaries of the top civil servants or the vastly larger yearly incomes of the senatorial upper class. Still, this sum was evidently enough to purchase from the Ruga Huns their "right of making acquisitions by war" until the next incident. That incident was not long in coming. Larger numbers of Hunnic tribes had crossed over to the Romans. This prompted Ruga shortly before his death to send an embassy to Constantinople to demand the extradition of these and all other deserters and refugees. It was explicitly said that nonfulfillment of this demand would amount to a breach of the treaty.

3. ATTILA (435/444–453)

Ruga did not live to hear the answer. But his successors, the brothers Bleda and Attila, concluded a new treaty with a Roman representative near Margus, a site east of modern-day Belgrade. Constantinople had to agree to hand over all Hunnic refugees as well as all former Roman prisoners who had failed to pay ransom to the Huns before returning to the empire. However, the Roman refugees would be exempted from this clause if eight solidi—roughly equal to a low yearly income of a member of the middle class—were paid for each former Roman prisoner. Constantinople furthermore promised not to form any alliance with a barbarian people with whom the Huns were at war. Next, the treaty guaranteed that fairs would be held, and finally the imperial government doubled the annual subsidies from 350 to 700 pounds of gold (25,200 to 50,400 solidi).

The fate of two young men of royal blood reveals what Attila and Bleda intended to do with the Hunnic refugees: after their extradition they were crucified. The treaty of Margus formed one of the cornerstones of Attila's later Hunnic Empire, one to which he came back time and again. The Scythian trade in human beings and the killing of returned refugees are an unpleasant reminder of current events.[5]

Like their predecessors, Bleda and his younger brother Attila ruled jointly for a few years. Fratricide brought Attila sole power in 444/445, and he led the empire of the Huns to the height of its unity. The fact that Attila succeeded in rising to power by murdering Bleda may be attributed to a number of causes. First of all, Attila's act was surely motivated by his lust for power. Let us compare a similar case: the three sons of Theoderid, king of the Visigothic kingdom of Toledo, ruled in succession, and only the first of them did not commit fratricide. Neither victim lost the kingship because he was incompetent. But that may not have been true of Bleda: Constantinople did not fulfill the treaty of Margus as the Huns had expected. To be sure, in the ensuing warfare Illyria and Thrace suffered terrible devastation, the entire defensive system along the Danube and the Save collapsed, and Sirmium was captured.

But then something must have suddenly happened to the Hunnic armies to prevent the horsemen from reaping their spoils. Was it an epidemic like the ones later in 447 and 452? Was it an uprising or rebellion by subjected peoples who may have attacked the Hunnic heartland? Whatever the reason, all victories turned into setbacks, and Bleda was responsible for this evidently divine punishment. Eventually Constantinople felt strong enough, beginning in 444 at the latest, to completely suspend payment of annual subsidies to the Huns. This must have sealed Bleda's fate, and Attila showed what a successful king of the army was capable of doing and obligated to do.

A chronicle of the year 447 contains four alarming entries: (1) in a terrible war more ferocious than the first, Attila crushed nearly all of Europe to dust; (2) the walls of Constantinople came crashing down during an earthquake but were rebuilt within three months; (3) Attila got as far as the pass of Thermopylae; (4) Arnegisclus, a Thracian general of Gothic descent, fell in a battle against Attila in the Danubian province of Dacia ripensis after fighting bravely and killing many enemies.

In the fall of 447 the war was over. It had begun with uncoordinated attacks by Hunnic forces and ended with the greatest victory the Huns ever won against the empire. Although some of the attackers had been struck down by a disease, the Hunnic victory had become Attila's victory. From 447 until his death, Attila was *the* Hunnic ruler, the scourge of God, chief general and chief judge of most Huns and their peoples. But even at that time he was worth only 2,100 gold pounds to the imperial government, only a hundred pounds more than Emperor Leo would promise Theodoric Strabo in 473.

For this reason alone one ought to refrain from seeing in Attila Hegel's "world spirit on horseback." "After the murder of Bleda, Attila was sole ruler of the Huns, lord of the Goths and Gepids, a mighty warrior and for some years more than a nuisance to the Romans, but never a real threat."[6] This verdict is correct, even though the treaty of 448 was costly for Constantinople: 6,000 pounds of outstanding back payments; 2,100 pounds annual subsidies; twelve solidi for each Roman fugitive; extradition of all barbarian refugees and the promise not to admit any in the future.

This time Constantinople largely fulfilled the provisions of the treaty. Terrible scenes are said to have occurred. The imperial government took gold wherever it could get its hands on it, and not a few Romans even of the upper class came away impoverished. Fugitives preferred death at the hands of Romans to being returned to the Huns. Among the unfortunate fugitives there were once again members of the Hunnic royal clan who had evidently resisted Attila's autocratic rule and had taken refuge with the Romans. In some places the Romans had stopped taking any Hunnic prisoners to avoid having to turn them over to Attila's people.[7]

In addition, Constantinople had to relinquish a strip of territory—five days' journey wide—south of the Danube, stretching from Pannonia to the Moesian city of Novae-Svistov. The Hunnic-Roman border was pulled back to around Naissus-Nish, which is also where the market for Hunnic-Roman commercial traffic, hitherto set up at the Danube, was to be held. When Priscus, a member of the embassy from 448/449, came to this city he found it deserted and destroyed, with Christian hostels full of sick people. Unable to spend the night there, the envoys moved downstream along the Morava and halted at the first "clean site": up to that point the banks were littered with the bones of men killed in the fighting.[8]

Roman Envoys at the Court of Attila (448/449)

Priscus has left behind a vivid description of life at Attila's court, where he also met West Roman envoys. Negotiations proved to be exceedingly difficult; on several occasions the embassy seemed to end in failure before the Hunnic king had even received them: Attila was preparing for war "on the pretext that not all fugitives had been given up." But eventually the envoys did manage to cross the Danube, and the hitherto very frosty climate seemed to improve. The account of Priscus was frequently translated and in an excerpted form also made its way into Gustav Freytag's *Scenes from the German Past*. This is not surprising, since the report of the Roman envoy is detailed, vivid, and in need of little in the way of explanation:

> In the late afternoon we were taking our dinner when we heard the clatter of horses coming toward us, and two Scythians arrived and told us to come to Attila. We bade them first join us for dinner, and they dismounted and were well entertained. On the next day they led us on the road, and we arrived at Attila's tents (of which there were many) at about the ninth hour of the day. When we wanted to pitch our tents on a hill, the barbarians who had come to meet us prevented us because Attila's tent was on low ground. We encamped where the Scythians thought best. . . .

But this by no means meant that the embassy achieved a breakthrough. On the contrary. The East Roman envoys were already preparing to return in a very dejected mood, when at the last moment the magnates in Attila's entourage, among them Odovacar's father Edica, were swayed with money and good words to speak to Attila in favor of receiving the delegation. After the most compromised member of the embassy had left, "Attila summoned us. . . . and we came to his tent, which was surrounded by a ring of barbarian guards. When we were granted entrance, we saw Attila seated on a wooden chair. We halted a little before the throne, and Maximinus [the leader of the delegation] advanced, greeted the barbarian, gave him the letters from the Emperor and said that the Emperor prayed that he and his followers were safe and well. He replied that the Romans would have what they wished from him. . . ."

> For a while we traveled with him and then turned off onto a different road at the command of our Scythian guides, since Attila was to go to a certain village

where he wished to marry a daughter of [the shaman?] Eskam.⁹ (Although he
had many wives, he was marrying her according to Scythian custom.) From
there we traveled along a level road over a plain and crossed navigable rivers. . . . These we crossed in boats made of single tree trunks, which those living near the rivers used; the others we negotiated on the rafts that the barbarians carry on their wagons because of the marshy areas. At the villages we
were abundantly supplied with foodstuffs, millet instead of wheat and instead
of wine what is called by the natives *medos* [mead: Priscus was hearing the
Germanic word]. The attendants in our train also carried millet and the
drink made from barley that the barbarians call *kamon*.

Having completed a long journey, in the late afternoon we encamped
near to a pool containing drinkable water that supplied the inhabitants of the
nearby village. Suddenly a wind and a storm arose with thunder and a great
deal of lightning and rain, and it not only collapsed our tent but blew all
our baggage into the pool. Terrified by the tumult that was raging in the air
and by what had already happened, we fled the place and scattered, each of us
in the darkness and the downpour taking the path that we thought would be
the easiest. Arriving at the huts of the village (which we all reached by our different routes), we gathered together and began to shout for the things we
needed. At the uproar the Scythians rushed out, kindling the reeds that they
used for fire and making light, and asked us what we wanted with our shout-
ing. When the barbarians who were with us replied that we were panicked by
the storm, they called to us and took us into their own homes and, burning
a great quantity of reeds, gave us warmth.

The woman who ruled the village (she had been one of Bleda's wives)
sent us food and attractive women for intercourse, which is a mark of honour amongst the Scythians. We plied the women generously from the foods
placed before us, but refused intercourse with them. We remained in the
huts and at about daybreak we went to search for our baggage and found it all,
some in the spot in which we had happened to halt the previous day, some
at the edge of the pool, and some actually in the water. We gathered it up
and spent the day in the village drying it all out, for the storm had ceased and
the sun was shining brightly. When we had taken care of the horses and the
rest of the baggage animals, we visited the queen [Bleda's widow], thanked
her, and repaid her with three silver bowls, red skins, Indian pepper, dates
and other dried fruits that the barbarians value because they are not native
to their own country. Then we called blessings upon her for her hospitality
and departed.

When we had completed a journey of seven days, on the orders of our
Scythian guide we halted at a village, since Attila was to take the same road and
we had to follow behind him. There we met some western Romans who were
also on an embassy to Attila. [Among them were the father and father-in-law
of Orestes, who himself was Attila's secretary and was to become the father of
the last West Roman emperor, Romulus Augustulus.]

Since we were on the same journey, we waited for Attila to go ahead and followed with our whole party. Having crossed some rivers, we came to a very
large village in which Attila's palace was said to be more spectacular than

those elsewhere. It was constructed of timbers and smoothly planed boards and was surrounded by a wooden wall that was built with an eye not to security but to elegance. The buildings of Onegesius were second only to those of the king in magnificence, and they too had a circuit wall made of timbers but not embellished with towers, as was Attila's. Not far from this wall was a bath that Onegesius, whose power amongst the Scythians was second only to that of Attila, had built fetching stones from Pannonia. For there is neither stone nor timber amongst the barbarians who inhabit this area, but the wood that they use is imported. The builder of the bath had been taken prisoner at Sirmium, and he hoped to gain his freedom as a reward for his inventive work. But he was disappointed and fell into greater distress than slavery among the Scythians. For Onegesius made him bath attendant, and he waited upon him and his followers when they bathed.

In this village, as Attila was entering, young girls came to meet him and went before him in rows under narrow cloths of white linen, which were held up by the hands of women on either side. These cloths were stretched out to such a length that under each one seven or more girls walked. There were many such rows of women under the cloths, and they sang Scythian songs. When Attila came near to Onegesius's compound, through which the road to the palace passed, Onegesius's wife came out to meet him with a crowd of servants, some carrying food and others wine (this is a very great honour amongst the Scythians), welcomed him and asked him to partake of what she had brought out of friendship. In order to please the wife of a close friend, he ate while sitting on his horse, the barbarians who were accompanying him having raised aloft the platter that was of silver. When he had also drunk from the cup of wine that was offered to him, he proceeded to the palace, which was higher than the other structures and built on a rise.

We waited at the compound of Onegesius as he had ordered, for he had returned with Attila's son. His wife and the most important members of his clan received us, and there we dined. Onegesius did not have time to dine with us, since immediately upon his return he had gone to speak with Attila to report to him upon the business for which he had been sent and upon the accident suffered by Attila's son, who had fallen and broken his right arm. After the meal we left Onegesius's compound, moved closer to Attila's palace and camped there. . . .

At daybreak Maximinus sent me to Onegesius to give him the gifts, both those that he was giving and those that the Emperor had sent, and to learn where and when he wished to speak with him. I arrived with the servants who were carrying the gifts for him and, since the doors were still shut, I waited until someone should come out and report our arrival.

As I was waiting and walking about before the circuit wall of the palace, someone, whom I took to be a barbarian from his Scythian dress, approached me and greeted me in Greek, saying, *"khaire"* ["hello"]. I was amazed that a Scythian was speaking Greek. Being a mixture of peoples, in addition to their own languages they cultivate Hunnic or Gothic or (in the case of those who have dealings with the Romans) Latin. But none of them can easily speak Greek, except for those whom they have taken prisoner from the sea coasts of Thrace and Illyria; and whoever met them could easily recognize them from their tattered clothes and filthy hair as persons who had fallen into adversity. This one, however, was like a well-cared-for Scythian with good clothing and his hair clipped all around.

I returned his greeting and asked who he was and where he came from to the land of the barbarians and why he took up a Scythian way of life. In reply he asked why I was so eager to know this. I said that his Greek speech was the reason for my curiosity. He laughed and said that he was a Greek and for purposes of trade he had gone to Viminacium, the city in Moesia on the river Danube. He had lived there for a very long time and married a very rich woman. When the city was captured by the barbarians, he was deprived of his prosperity and, because of his great wealth, was assigned to Onegesius himself in the division of the spoils; for after Attila the leading men of the Scythians, because they were in command of very many men, chose their captives from amongst the well-to-do. Having proven his valour in later battles against the Romans and the nation of the Akatiri and having, according to Scythian law, given his booty to his master, he had won his freedom. He had married a barbarian wife and had children, and, as a sharer at the table of Onegesius, he now enjoyed a better life than he had previously.

He continued, saying that after a war men amongst the Scythians live at ease, each enjoying his own possessions and troubling others or being troubled not at all or very little. But amongst the Romans, since on account of their tyrants not all men carry weapons, they place their hope of safety in others and are thus easily destroyed in war.

There follows a lengthy discussion between Priscus and the Roman Hun, a discussion that some scholars have depicted, probably wrongly, as mere fiction and the Roman envoy's hidden criticism of the Roman system. Finally the doors of the palisade open for Priscus; he is led to Onegesius, is able to present his gifts and ask for his intercession. Priscus also pleads his cause with Attila's wife Hereka, who had given birth to three sons for the Hunnic king. In addition there was an exchange of views between Priscus and the West Roman envoys, who discussed above all what Attila's new plans might be.

When we returned to our tent, Tatulus, the father of Orestes, came to us and announced, "Attila invites you both to his banquet. It will begin at about the ninth hour of the day." We waited for the time, and those of us who had been invited and the envoys of the western Romans presented ourselves. We stood at the threshold facing Attila, and, as was the custom of the land, the wine waiters gave us a cup so that we might make a prayer before taking our seats. When we had done this and tasted from the cup, we went to the seats where we were to sit for dinner.

All the seats were arranged around the walls of the building on both sides. In the very middle of the room Attila sat upon a couch. Behind him was another couch, and behind that steps led up to Attila's bed, which was screened by fine linens and multicolored ornamental hangings like those that the Greeks and Romans prepare for weddings. The position of those dining on the right of Attila was considered the most honorable, that on the left, where we were, less so. Ahead of us sat Berichus, a Scythian noble, for Onegesius sat on a chair to the right of Attila. Opposite Onegesius two of Attila's sons sat on a chair; the eldest one sat upon Attila's couch, not close to him but right at the end, gazing at the ground out of respect for his father.

When all were seated in order, a wine waiter came up to Attila and offered him a wooden cup of wine. He took the cup and greeted the first in the order. The one who was honored with the greeting stood up, and it was the custom that he not sit down until he had either tasted the wine or drunk it all and had returned the wooden cup to the waiter. When he had sat down, all present honoured him in the same manner, taking our cups and tasting them after the greeting. Each guest had a wine waiter in attendance, who had to step forward in line after Attila's waiter retired. When the second had been honoured and the rest in order, Attila greeted us with the same ceremony according to the order of the seats. When all had been honoured with this greeting, the wine waiters withdrew and, beginning from Attila, tables were set up for three or four or more persons, from which each could partake of what was placed on the platter without leaving the line of chairs. Attila's servants entered first bearing a plate full of meat, and after him those who were serving us placed bread and cooked foods on the tables. While for the other barbarians and for us there were lavishly prepared dishes served on silver platters, for Attila there was only meat on a wooden plate. He showed himself temperate in other ways also. For golden and silver goblets were handed to the men at the feast, whereas his cup was of wood. His clothing was plain and differed not at all from that of the rest, except that it was clean. Neither the sword that hung at his side nor the fastenings of his barbarian boots nor his horse's bridle was adorned, like those of the other Scythians, with gold or precious stones or anything else of value.

When we had finished the foods on the first platters, we all stood up, and no one resumed his seat until, in the order as before, we had each drained the cup full of wine that was given to us and prayed for Attila's health. When he had been honoured in this way we resumed our seats, and a second platter, containing different dishes, was placed on each table. When all had partaken of this, again we stood up in the same manner, drank a cup of wine and sat down. Since it was now evening, pine torches were lit. Two barbarians came and stood before Attila and chanted songs that they had composed telling of his victories and his deeds of courage in war. The guests fixed their eyes on the singers: some took pleasure in the verses, others recalling the wars became excited, while others, whose bodies were enfeebled by age and whose spirits were compelled to rest, were reduced to tears.

After the songs a Scythian whose mind was deranged came forward and, by uttering outlandish, unintelligible and altogether crazy things, caused all to burst into laughter. After him Zercon the Moor entered. . . . Now, during the banquet he came forward and by his appearance, his clothing, his voice and the words that he spoke all jumbled together (for he mixed Latin, Hunnic and Gothic) he put all in a good humour and caused all to burst into uncontrollable laugher, except Attila [Zercon had been Bleda's favorite]. He remained unmoved with no change of expression and neither said nor did anything that hinted at laughter, except when his youngest son, whose name was Ernach, came up and stood by him. Then he drew him closer by the cheek and gazed at him with gentle eyes. When I expressed amazement that he paid attention to this son while ignoring the others, the barbarian who sat next to me and who knew Latin, warning me to repeat nothing of what he would tell me, said that the prophets had foretold to Attila that his race would fall, but would be restored by this boy [which did not come to pass]. Since they were spending the night over the banquet, we departed, not wishing to continue drinking for a long time.

When day came we went to Onegesius and said that we ought to be dismissed without any pointless delay. He said that Attila was willing to send us away. After a short time he deliberated with the leading men upon Attila's views and had the letters drawn up to be delivered to the Emperor. Present at this transaction were his own secretaries and Rusticus, a man from Upper Moesia who had been captured in war and who, because of his literary skills, was employed by the barbarian in drawing up letters.

When he came out of the meeting, we asked him to free the wife of Syllus and her children, who had been taken prisoner at the capture of Ratiaria [Arcer on the Bulgarian Danube]. He did not object to their freedom, but wished to sell them for a high price. When we begged him to think of their previous happiness and have pity for their current misfortune, he went to Attila and dismissed the wife for five hundred *solidi* and sent the children to the Emperor as a gift.

Meanwhile Hereka, Attila's wife, invited us to dine at the house of Adamis, the manager of her affairs. We went there together with some of the leading men of the nation and were generously received. He welcomed us with gracious words and an array of foods. With Scythian hospitality each of those present stood up, handed us a cup full of wine, and after we had drunk, embraced and kissed us, and took back the cup. After the dinner we returned to our tent and turned to sleep.

On the next day Attila again invited us to a banquet, and in the same manner as before we presented ourselves and took part in the feast. On this occasion it was not the eldest of his sons who was seated next to him on the couch, but Oebarsius, his paternal uncle. Throughout the banquet Attila addressed friendly words to us and he bade us tell the Emperor to give to Constantius, who had been sent to him as secretary from Aetius, the wife whom he had also promised to him. When Constantius had come to the Emperor [Theodosius II] in the company of the envoys sent from Attila, he said that if Theodosius gave him a wealthy wife, he would ensure that the peace between the Romans and the Scythians would be preserved for a long time. The

Emperor agreed to this proposal. . . . After nightfall we left the banquet and three days later we were dismissed, having been honoured with appropriate gifts.[10]

The Battle on the Catalaunian Fields (451)

Attila had made Constantinople pay dearly: many hundreds of thousands of gold solidi went from the mints of the eastern empire to the Danube, where they served as ornaments and badges of honor, less so as money. Even today Hungarian and Slovakian museums have hundreds of these gold pieces, seemingly freshly coined and in marvelous condition, as though they had just left the mint in Antioch or Constantinople. The recipient of these treasures was above all Attila himself, whom Constantinople had made commander in chief in 449 so that it could declare at least a part of this large amount of money as a regular salary.

Now West and East feared that the Hunnic king might conquer Persia and thus wish to lay claim to the highest power in the world, indeed that he might possibly want to become emperor, *basileus*.[11] How much of this was speculation by the threatened Romans and how much Attila's real intention is hard to say. Attila, in any case, now got more involved in West Roman politics. Ravenna too had to largely meet his demand for the return of all Hunnic mercenaries and thus accept a decisive weakening of the West Roman army. Attila also made some personal, downright unreasonable sounding, demands. Eventually he came up with the idea of demanding half the western empire.

Honoria, the sister of Emperor Valentinian III, because of her dissolute lifestyle, had been forcibly betrothed to a senator. In secret she sent the Hunnic leader her ring and offered to become his wife. Ravenna seemed genuinely willing to at least contemplate handing the emperor's wayward daughter over to the Huns. But then, in July of 450, the East Roman Emperor Theodosius II, who had advised the western empire to be accommodating, died. His successor was the bellicose Marcian, who demanded an end to all humiliating negotiations and stopped payments to the Huns. This was a cause for war, but only after some hesitation did Attila decide to attack the western empire.

At the beginning of the year 451, Attila's bands marched up the Danube to the West. Alongside the Hunnic peoples marched the Gepids under King Ardaric, the Ostrogoths under Valamir, Thiudimir, and Vidimir, the Rugians, Sciri, Heruli, Danubian Suebi, and Sarmatians. Once at the Rhine, they had reason to expect that they would be joined by the Main Burgundians and the disunited Franks, who were split over a question of succession. Bringing the Gallic Alans back into the fold was another one of Attila's war aims. But the decision to attack the West was probably the work of Gaiseric, the Vandal king. Gaiseric had to fear a coalition of Visigoths and Spanish Suebi as well as the personal revenge of the king of Toulouse. Rich presents made their way from Carthage to the Tisza, and in the end they bore fruit.

The target of the attack was Gaul. The community of Romans and barbarians who lived there was seen by Attila and Gaiseric merely as a "union of discordant peoples." But the year 451 proved that this community survived its severest challenge. Its defender was Aetius, *patricius* and supreme commander of the Roman troops in the West, with whom the Huns had for decades maintained a very good relationship. Now Aetius was fighting with all his might against the former allies under the monarchical rule of Attila. The Roman force was made up of all the peoples who had found a home in fifth-century Gaul, both those who had immigrated and those who had developed into a people there. In addition to the Visigoths, we hear of Rhenish Franks, Bretons, Sarmatian and Germanic *laeti*, Burgundians, Gallic Saxons, as well as members of former Roman military districts. To these were added the Alans from Orléans under the leadership of their federate King Sangiban, a highly unreliable fellow when it came to fighting Attila. To keep the Alans from running away or switching sides, Aetius had to sandwich them between his own people and the Goths.

At first the Goths of Toulouse hesitated to join their old enemy Aetius. But eventually an envoy from the generalissimo was able to persuade them to do their duty as federates. That summer the king and his two eldest sons, Thorismund and Theodoric, marched with the Gothic army into Champagne. The great battle was fought on the Catalaunian—or more accurately, the Mauriacan—fields between Troyes and Châlons-sur-Marne. Although the battle ended in a draw, or was perhaps intentionally left undecided by Aetius, the epochal clash destroyed Attila's aura of invincibility.

Battle was joined at three o'clock in the afternoon, after the previous night had already witnessed a bloody clash between the Gepids and the Franks. In Attila's center stood the core troops of his own tribe, while the two flanks were formed by the subject peoples. The Visigothic King Theoderid commanded the right wing of the Romans. He was killed; a Gothic Amal by name of Andagis hurled the spear that struck him down. After the king's death his oldest son, Thorismund, who was commanding the engagement on the left flank and had very nearly been captured, broke off the battle: he was in a hurry to return to Toulouse to secure the kingship for himself.

This action saved Attila, who was already thinking of suicide. Still, the Huns had to return to their homeland defeated, leaving behind many dead warriors and a part of the booty. This was bound to have a negative effect on the cohesion of their kingdom. Of prime importance to Gothic tradition was the fact that Goths fought against Goths in the great Hunnic battle. Is it possible that the Hunnic Amals had a personal interest in going against the Roman Balths?[12] In any case, two generations later the Goths did not even wish to entertain such a possibility. Theodoric the Great considered the battle forced fratricide, a *parricidium.*

A military king and ruler of the Huns could not survive without victories, especially if he laid claim to monarchic power, as Attila did. That is why the campaign to Gaul was a disaster, one that would repeat itself the following year in Italy—after some great initial successes. It was not until the early summer of 452 that the Huns invaded Italy via Pannonia; they took Aquileia, Pavia, and Milan, where Attila held court in the imperial palace. But suddenly the Huns abandoned the city and began their retreat. A disease "from heaven" had struck the army of horsemen, which had begun the campaign too late in the year. Under these circumstances the mission of Leo the Great was quickly successful: the Pope went out to meet the Hunnic leader to talk him out of marching on Rome. In addition, the Romans called Attila's attention to the fate of Alaric, who had survived the capture of the city by only a few months.

> Attila's campaign was worse than a failure. He could not force the Romans to conclude another treaty with him, to pay tribute again, or to reappoint him *magister militum.* The hated Aetius remained the factual ruler of the western empire. The loot may have been considerable but it was bought at too high a price, too many Hunnic horsemen lay dead in the towns and fields of Italy. A year later Attila's kingdom collapsed.[13]

Attila's downfall was swift and hard. It fired the imagination of contemporaries and of later generations, who told many stories about him. So very recently he was said to have demonstrated in the imperial palace in Milan the pinnacle of his claim to power, as we hear from Priscus: "When he saw in a painting the Roman emperors sitting upon golden thrones and Scythians lying dead before their feet, he sought out a painter and ordered him to paint Attila upon a throne and the Roman emperors heaving sacks upon their shoulders and pouring out gold before his feet."[14] But soon after, the eastern Emperor Marcian, who feared an attack from this terrible enemy, had a most comforting vision in a dream: a divine figure showed him Attila's broken bow to announce his death. "For so terrible was Attila thought to be to great empires that the gods announced his death to rulers as a special boon."[15]

Attila's Death

Here lies Attila, the great king of the Huns,
the son of Mundzuc,
the ruler of the most courageous tribes;

enjoying such power as had been unheard of before him,
he possessed the Scythian and Germanic kingdoms alone
and also terrorized both empires of the Roman world
after conquering their cities, and
placated by their entreaties
that the rest might not be laid open to plunder
he accepted an annual tribute.
After he had achieved all this with great success
he died, not of an enemy's wound, not betrayed by friends,
but in the midst of his unscathed people,
happy and gay,
without any feeling of pain.
Who therefore would think that this was death
which nobody considers to demand revenge?

This is how the funeral dirge has come down to us, which the "best horse-men of the entire tribe of the Huns" recited as they rode around the place where Attila's body had been laid out in an open field under a tent of silk. In fact it was a "disgraceful death for a king who had gained great glory in war" but did not survive the last of his many wedding nights and died of a stroke in the arms of the "very beautiful maiden Ildico." Having mourned him in this way, "a *strava,* as they call it, was celebrated over his tomb with great reveling. They connected opposites and showed them, mixing grief over the dead with joy."[16]

4. DOWNFALL AND END

The attack on the eastern empire, planned for the middle of 453, did not take place, and soon after their father's sweet death, Attila's numerous sons, "who on account of their unbridled lust were almost a tribe in them-selves," had gambled away the Hun's power and glory. The Gepids, led by their king Ardaric, assumed the leadership of those tribes and peoples who were fighting for their independence. The decisive and last in a series of bat-tles in which the Huns and their Germanic followers were defeated took place probably in 454 (rather than 455) at the Nedao, most likely a branch of the Save River in southern Pannonia. Once again the same tribes fought on both sides; one thing is clear, though: the majority of the Hunnic Goths under Amal leadership were among the losers, while the Gepids led the vic-torious army.

After the battle the victorious tribes settled directly on the left bank of the Danube and established, between the Lower Austrian Wachau Valley and the Transylvanian Carpathians, a series of kingdoms linked as federates to Constantinople. A mighty Gepidia had taken the place of the Gothia in what had once been Trajan's Dacia. At its threshold there arose, between the Danube and the Tisza, a Scirian and a Sarmatian kingdom. West of them existed a regnum of those Suebi who had left their homeland together with the Vandals and Alans. At the Lower Austrian and Moravian march, Heruli set up a kingdom that continually grew in importance until the beginning of the sixth century. West of them settled the Lower Austrian Rugians, whose royal seat was located in the vicinity of Krems on the Danube.

Evidently the victorious barbarians of the Danube had contractually guaranteed rights to the economic prosperity of the provincials on the right bank of the Danube. To keep a rein on these claims, the defeated Goths were to be settled as federates of East Rome inside the empire, namely in Pannonia. They were lead by King Valamir and his brothers Thiudimir (the father of Theodoric the Great) and Vidimir the Elder.

These Goths, who are usually called Ostrogoths, settled in three districts. Their territory extended—like the shape of a crescent—from the southwestern tip of Lake Balaton to the river Drava, from there downstream to a point west of Osijek-Esseg, and finally to Sirmium–Sremska Mitrovica. The westernmost of the three subkingdoms was ruled by Thiudimir; the section of the youngest brother was located in the center, while King Valamir, as the oldest and strongest of the three, took over the most endangered part in the east. Valamir and his brothers probably commanded nearly eighteen thousand warriors.

The number of those Goths who did not place themselves under Valamir's leadership must have been considerable. Many of them went to Thrace and became soldiers of Constantinople; they were led by another Amal with the Latin name Triarius, who was the brother-in-law of Aspar, the highest-ranking commander of the East Roman military hierarchy. When Triarius died, probably in the second half of the 450s, his son Theodoric Strabo, "the Squinter," was able to succeed his father without problems. Yet another group of Amal Goths went to the Dobrudscha and northern Bulgaria along with Alans, Sciri, and Sarmatians. Finally, there was an Amal named Sidimund, who lived on his estates near Durazzo in Epirus. But this by no means exhausts the number of Gothic magnates who, together with their followers, had split off from the Valamir Goths; already in the early 460s, one of these dissidents must have been regarded as king.[17]

Not all of Attila's sons were ready to give up; instead, they tried to subject the Goths, whom they saw as their slaves, and to do business with Constantinople. In 467/468, Valamir was able to defeat the Huns between Belgrade and Sremska Mitrovica, after which they left the Goths in peace "for ever after." A year later the end of the Huns was at hand. A chronicle report from the year 469: "Dinzirichus [Dengezich], the son of Attila, was killed by Anagastes, general in Thrace. His head was brought to Constantinople, carried in procession through the Middle Street, and fixed on a pole at the Wooden Circus. The whole city turned out to look at it."[18]

The collapse of Attila's dominion meant that the dams that the Hun's military power had erected in central Europe against the Roman Empire had burst. Once again the Gothic and the West Germanic tribes that had either been subjugated by Attila or kept from the Roman imperial borders by Attila's rule moved against the empire from the mouth of the Rhine to the Danube. The breathing space that Attila's military might had granted the imperium had now come to an end. The western empire did not last even another twenty-five years after the death of the powerful king of the Huns. The Hunnic alternative had played itself out, and from now on the transformation of the Roman world proceeded inexorably and without any further interruptions.

But one thing that did persist in the Roman Empire was the conviction that the freedom of the individual as well as of the state was preserved and guaranteed solely by law and justice. The res publica as the concern of all citizens would always be superior to the despotism of barbarian kings and their peoples—no matter their military might. The latter did not respect the rights of people and saw them as objects, as slaves of the state, for whom they collected now eight, now twelve solidi—or, as very recently in our own day, tens of thousands, even one hundred thousand deutsche marks.

5. THE HUNNIC-GOTHIC SYMBIOSIS

During the long years of their dependency, the Hunnic Goths developed a most ambivalent relationship to their Hunnic lords. Attila had a Gothic name, as did his brother Bleda and many other magnates of the Hunnic kingdom, while Goths had Hunnic names. The Goths and other Germanic peoples, including even the Burgundians, West Germanic Thuringians, Alamanni, and Bavarians, adopted the custom of artificially deforming the skull, which was probably meant to express special status. As early as the fourth century B.C., Greek ethnography had discovered the Scythian "longheads": at the Sea of Azov, on the coast of Scythia, pressure from hands and bandages applied to the heads of newborns changed the round shape of the head and gave it a more longish appearance. Among these macrocephali, long-headed people were considered the most noble. Evidently this custom was also practiced in the Hunnic world, and was adopted even by the Germanic tribes at its borders.[19]

The subjected peoples used Hunnic tools and weapons, although they never equaled their masters' skill in the use of the composite bow. They became acquainted with the old custom—still recently practiced in "Greater Scythia"—of princes and functionaries hugging and kissing each other in public. The Goths also adopted the Hunnic notion—also until recently still prevalent in this part of the world—that emigration and separation from the main tribe were serious crimes. Thus it was said that whoever ran away from the Huns showed his contempt also for the Goths and lost his Amal identity, which was more highly regarded even than Attila's nobility. Negotiations between Romans and Huns dealt mostly with demands of the Hunnic leaders that barbarian deserters be handed over and that a sum equal to an average yearly income be paid for each Roman who had escaped slavery and wanted to keep his freedom.

The Goths were bound to the Huns on oath and remained loyal to them longer than most other Germanic tribes. But at the same time they longed for their freedom and swore sacred oaths to each other never again to serve the Huns once they had shaken off their yoke. And yet there was also a sense that there was "some kind" of kinship with the Huns, and the Goths told each other the following story: The Gutonic migration king, Filimer, expelled Gothic witches from the tribe, whereupon they had intercourse with the evil spirits of the steppe and gave birth to the Huns.

This legend combines three different chronological layers: one from around 200, when the Gutones moving into the Ukraine encountered "illicit" shamanic practices; the second from the end of the fourth century, as the Goths tried to explain the demonic nature of the new enemy; and the third from the period of subjection to the Huns, when the Goths portrayed them as descendants of their own tribe. In this way the story combines a sense of kinship with a profound loathing.

In the polylingual camp of Attila, Gothic had the rank of a lingua franca, "seeing as the Scythians, a colorful mix of peoples, speak, in addition to their own dialect, either Hunnic, Gothic, or also Latin." Bleda kept a Moorish jester whose jokes were made up, not least, of a jumble of Latin, Hunnic, and Gothic words.[20] But the basic language that the peoples of the Huns used to communicate probably didn't sound much different. Simple commands, hello and thank you, expressions of respect, questions about directions and their answers must have been familiar to all. Gothic envoys are said to have come to the imperial courts as envoys of Attila,[21] and the Turcilingus Edica was one of Attila's advisers and among the most important negotiators with Constantinople. Whether he was born a Hun or not, Edica's name is Germanic, and he went on to become the founder of the short-lived and last kingdom of the Sciri. His two sons were called Hunulf and Odovacar; the latter was the first "Gothic" king of Italy. The Gothic King Valamir and the Gepid King Ardaric were among Attila's closest advisers. They all were partners of the Huns, who were the last to command the gold of the ancient world.

One thing that remains unclear is to what extent Hunnic constitutional forms influenced the development of the hierarchical collective rule of

Valamir and his brothers. At times the Huns had two kings, who ruled jointly if over different territories and tribes. But other brothers, as for example Attila's own father or his third uncle, Oebarsius, had no dominion of their own, whereas Valamir's younger brothers were given such dominions.[22]

It is certain that the Huns did not recognize a divine kingship. Even at the height of his power, Attila was for the Huns not a divine being, no matter that some of the subject peoples feared him as the "greatest of the gods."[23] However, the Romans quite expected that Attila, once he had conquered the Persian Empire, would lay claim to world supremacy. That never happened, and we don't know if Attila ever intended to do so. What remained was the story of a sacred sword that, "holy and venerated among the Scythian kings, was dedicated to the guardian of wars." Long ago it was lost, but then an ox accidentally stepped on it while grazing and injured itself. The cowherd followed the trace of blood, found the sword, dug it up, and brought it to Attila. "The king rejoiced at this gift, and, being ambitious, thought he had been appointed ruler of the whole world, and that through the sword of Mars supremacy in all wars was assured to him."[24]

This kind of legitimation of rulership was by no means found only among the Huns. Rather, the legend of Attila merely follows the rulership tradition customary in the Scythian world, which had already been described by Herodotus. The sword incarnation is not an exclusively Altaic or Turkic phenomenon. Rather, it represents the characteristic epiphany of the Pontic war god as all the people of that area knew him. Thus the Quadi venerated their swords as gods.[25] Even a Scandinavian saga still records the name Tyrfingr-Terving as the name for both the Gothic land and the Gothic hereditary sword. This Terving was probably the manifestation of the Germanic war god Tiwaz (Gothic Tius), whom the Goths west of the Dniester considered the representative of the tribe. The possession of special weapons legitimated rulership, and they could pass from one people to another or remain peculiar to a people. Attila's tradition shows examples of both, namely the sacred sword and the sacred bow unique to the Huns.[26]

Despite his relations with Germanic princes and despite his Gothic name, which means "daddy," Attila was a Hun also in the anthropological sense. The description of Attila by an eyewitness confirms his Asian origin and is the source of our mental picture of the appearance of the Huns: "He was short of stature, with a broad chest and a large head; his eyes were small, his beard thin and sprinkled with gray; and he had a flat nose and a swarthy complexion, showing the evidences of his origin."[27] Despite his foreignness, Attila was the only non-Germanic warrior who made it into the Germanic sagas. His generosity, his courage, and his ability as a military leader made him into a kingly figure against whom all heroic kings and kingly heroes of the migration period were measured, and who was perhaps surpassed by only one other heroic figure, Theodoric the Ostrogoth.

6. THE LAST HUNS

The Huns who had remained behind at the Danube quickly lost their ethnic identity and became either Roman soldiers, members of the Gothic peoples, or Bulgarians.[28] We know the names of very few of them, and the biographies of fewer still. One exception is Mundo, a grandson of Attila and of the Gepid King Ardaric. To the Greeks Mundo described himself as a Gepid, among the Goths he was considered a Hun. Decades after the battle at the Nedao, a grandson of Attila was evidently still welcome at the court of Theodoric the Great. After 488, Mundo left the Ostrogothic king, gathered together "highwaymen, robbers, and murderers," and set up a fiefdom in Upper Moesia. Mundo was a colorful and ambiguous figure who combined in himself Hunnic, Germanic, and Roman traditions and who embodied the traditions of the Attilanic upper class. While the Gepids kept quiet after 490 and truly deserved their nickname "the lazy ones," Mundo, the Hunnic offspring of the Gepid royal family, attained some prominence. After the death of Theodoric the Great he made himself available to Justinian; he became general of Illyria and fought the Bulgarians, the Gepids, and eventually the Ostrogoths in Dalmatia, where, along with his son, he met his death in 535/536. In 534, Belisarius had captured Carthage and with it Vandal Africa. Mundo had become so popular that the old prophecy *capta Africa mundus cume prole peribit* ("after the capture of Africa the world [or Mundo] will perish with its offspring [or with his son]") was popularly applied to him. Mundo's grandson Theudimund still belonged to the barbarian military aristocracy in Roman services and fought against the Ostrogoths at Treviso in 540.[29] But the Hunnic identity had become meaningless to him and his kind; it lived on in the Bulgarians.

SIX

The Kingdom of Toulouse (418–507)

Pioneering Achievement and Failed Accommodation

1. FROM ROME TO TOULOUSE

When Alaric I died in the fall of 410 at the age of about forty, he left behind children but no son suitable to succeed him as Gothic military king. And so his brother-in-law Athaulf was made king of a people that, like the chosen people [the Israelites], was in the midst of forty years of wandering.

The precursors of the Visigoths—a name used only since the sixth century to distinguish them from their eastern brother tribe in Italy—had been the Tervingian Goths of the Danube. Up to 400 no other Germanic tribe was more Romanized than the Tervingians: the Tervingian *Gútthiuda* was more strongly territorialized, Latinized, and—despite a pagan majority—more deeply Christianized that any other Germanic polity along the Rhine and Danube.

Though the Hunnic assaults that began in 376 destroyed the Gothic land, they did all the more clearly bring about the view that the Tervingians and their peoples who had moved into the Roman Empire were *the* Roman Goths. However, so far all attempts to integrate this Gothic army, this thoroughly militarized *gens*, into the Roman Empire had failed. The Romans had concluded treaties with them that were not worth the papyrus they were written on. And so these Goths became rebels who moved about the Roman world and devastated it.

Athaulf's Goths remained in Italy until 411 and visited terrible devastation upon the land. Then Jovinus, a member of the Gallic high nobility, usurped the emperorship. He drew his backing from a coalition of Burgundians, Alans, and other Germanic tribes from the Rhine. In return the Burgundians were able to establish their first kingdom on the left bank of the Rhine. Iovinus permitted his allies to have in Gaul what the Goths in Italy had been trying in vain to obtain by force. But in Iovinus's eyes,

Athaulf also had something to offer, for if he joined the coalition the usurpation could be carried into Italy. The former Emperor Attalus brokered a short-term agreement between Iovinus and Athaulf, as a result of which the Goths left Italy, probably during 412.

Jovinus went ahead and made his brother coemperor without asking for Athaulf's consent. Evidently the Gothic king could lay claim to an actual share in the imperial rule or at least believed so. He angrily dropped Iovinus and resumed negotiations with Honorius. The Gallic representatives of the legitimate emperor promised to settle the Goths in Gaul and to secure their grain supply. Thereafter the Gallic usurpation came to a bloody end: Iovinus and his brother were captured by the Goths and handed over to their enemies. Their severed heads were publicly displayed in Ravenna.[1] But Honorius suddenly declared that he would not implement the treaty until the Visigoths handed over Placidia. The Goths' response was to lay waste to southern Gaul, though Athaulf very nearly got killed in the assault on Marseille.

In January of 414, Athaulf married Placidia, an emperor's daughter. The wedding took place in the house of a Roman nobleman. Athaulf wore the uniform of a high Roman military officer, and the ceremony too was largely Roman in nature; only at the end were Gothic songs intoned. It was at this wedding that Athaulf is said to have made the famous remarks that he had initially intended to replace Romania with Gothia, and to become for a Gothic Empire what Augustus had been to the imperium of the Romans. But once he had realized that the Goths, because of their "unbridled barbarism," would never be able to replace a res publica that lived by Roman law, he wished to become the renewer instead of the destroyer of Rome. This change of heart, he professed, had come about under the influence of Galla Placidia.

The quarrel about the authenticity of the story is fruitless since it cannot be resolved either way. We do know that after 414 Athaulf pursued a policy very much in keeping with the spirit of this story. In less than a year Galla Placidia gave birth to a son, who, for the very same reason, was given the name of the Emperor Theodosius, who had been a "friend of peace and of the Goths." But little Theodosius died soon after birth, and not long afterward his father Athaulf was murdered. Still, the forty-year wanderings of the Roman Goths came to an end. After a disgraceful intermezzo, Valia was chosen to be new Gothic king in September of 415. Already in the spring of 416 he came to an agreement with Constantius, the imperial commander in chief of the West. In return for concluding a treaty, he received sufficient grain and the task of clearing Spain of domestic and foreign enemies. Valia and his Goths went to work: in bitter fighting the Siling Vandals and the Alans who had pushed their way into Spain lost their kings and joined the Hasding Vandals. Before the Goths could turn on the Hasdingi, their old hereditary enemies, Ravenna called them back to southern Gaul. It was there that the Goths would put down roots, but Valia—like another Moses—did not live to see the founding of the kingdom of Toulouse.[2]

2. THEODERID (418–451) AND THORISMUND (451–453)

Like another Stilicho, the imperial general and *patricius* Constantius, the future third emperor of this name and father of Valentinian III, had carved out a position that made him the true master of the western empire. As such he could force Galla Placidia, Athaulf's widow, to marry him on January 1, 417, thus making Honorius his brother-in-law. Meanwhile the former Danubian Goths had become one party among others that had to be reckoned with in the struggle for the western empire. The more clearly the history of the Visigoths took shape, the more the non-Roman origin of their ancestors faded away. The Visigoths were part of the empire; in one region of the greater Gallic prefecture they were, in fact, the only Roman army at Ravenna's disposal.

On April 17, 418, Constantius arranged for the promulgation of an imperial decree reestablishing the general assembly of the seven provinces of southern Gaul. The first session took place from August 13 to September 13 in Arles, in the just recently established seat of the praetorian prefect of Gaul; Constantius probably attended. This means, in other words, that the assembly convened shortly before the Goths were recalled from Spain, and it must have also addressed the question of how they would be settled in Aquitania. We also know for certain that the Goths were assigned as federates to the valley of the Garonne from Toulouse to Bordeaux, and that they were in addition given the Atlantic coastal region, which extended from the foothills of the Pyrenees to just short of the Loire.

The settlement of the Goths in Aquitania II as well as in some urban districts of the neighboring provinces of Novempopulana and Narbonensis I, whose capital was Toulouse, was not extorted from the Romans but decreed by Constantius. Thus the Goths did not enter the land as conquerors but on orders from the imperial government and with the consent of the senatorial leadership and the *curiales* of southern Gaul. The Goths were there not so much to fight the external barbarians as preserve the existing social order against domestic enemies. The devastating passage of Vandals, Alans, and Suebi had been followed by usurpations and uprisings by the Bagaudian rebels. For more than a decade now the better part of Gaul had been all but lost. The Visigoths were needed for the effort to rebuild the country, provided they served or appeared to serve the interests of the Gallic leadership.

The first king of the kingdom of Toulouse was Theoderid, who succeeded Valia without the least problem. He could not have been very old when he ascended the throne, hardly more than twenty-five, for a full generation later he still led the Gothic army into the battle of nations in 451. Theoderid had six sons, whose names are recorded as Thorismund, Theodoric, Frideric, Eric, Retemeris (Ricimer), and Himnerith. He also had two daughters, though we don't know their names, just as we don't know the identity of the mother or mothers of these eight children. Theodoric, however, is attested as the grandson of Alaric I, and the royal clan of Toulouse is therefore described as the younger Balths. It is unclear, though, whether the conqueror of Rome was the father of Theoderid himself or—what seems more plausible—of his wife, the mother of Theodoric and his siblings. Either situation would explain well the absence of any opposition at Theoderid's elevation to the kingship as well as during his reign. The first Gothic king of Toulouse could build on the hereditary charisma of the Balths.

Of course this charisma would have been depleted very quickly as political capital if Theoderid had not been able to secure the economic preconditions for survival of his Goths. Whether or not Constantius and his advisers were contemplating a permanent Gothic settlement in Aquitaine, they did in fact establish the framework which allowed a continual and lasting solution to the Gothic problem. This model went far beyond the previous and always unsuccessful attempts to house the Roman federates inside the empire with the help of the conventional military billeting, to feed them with grain shipments, and to finance them with annual payments. To be sure, the Visigothic example was not adopted in the other Roman-barbarian kingdoms without modifications; but the Burgundians and Vandals, the Angles and Saxons of Britain, Odovacar's army, Theodoric's Ostrogoths and Italian Longobards in Italy, in fact even the Franks, all built upon the arrangement that was tried in 418 and that had proved its worth.[3]

Theoderid's kingship came to an end with his death during the battle on the Catalaunian fields in the summer of 451. Compared to this spectacular event there is little we know about his unusually long reign of thirty-three years, for the sources get lost in too much detail and in telling stories that are not very coherent. But when Theoderid was struck down by an Ostrogothic spear, he left behind a kingdom that, in terms of its institutional structure and coherence, surpassed everything that Gothic political life had hitherto produced.

There was no threat to his realm: neither from the Romans, nor from the internal and external barbarians of Gaul or Spain, nor from the princes of the kingdom. The oldest son Thorismund was recognized by all without objection as his father's successor; not even an election seemed necessary. But Thorismund had too many ambitious and powerful brothers, and neither he nor his kingship lasted very long. All that was granted him in a reign of about two years was to continue his father's rule; in 453 he was killed by his brothers Theodoric and Frideric. The older of the two became king, the younger his deputy.

3. THEODORIC (453–466)

Portrait of a King

How a Gothic king appeared to a Roman observer in the best of circumstances is revealed by the now classic portrait from the pen of Sidonius Apollinaris, a Gallic senator and contemporary of the king. The picture sketched here is the oldest detailed account of a Germanic prince. It appears in a letter addressed to a son of the same Avitus, with whom Theodoric had studied Virgil and Roman law as a young man and whom he was to make emperor in 455, to Avitus's misfortune.

Sidonius to his dear Agricola, greetings:

1. Seeing that report commends to the world the graciousness of Theodoric, king of the Goths, you have often asked me to describe to you in writing his appearance and the character of his life. I am delighted to do so, subject to the limitations of a letter, and I appreciate the honest spirit that prompts so nice a curiosity. Well, he is a man who deserves to be studied even by those who are not in close relations with him. In his build the will of God and nature's plan have joined together to endow him with a supreme perfection, and his character is such that even the jealousy that hedges a sovereign has no power to rob it of its glories.

2. Take first his appearance. His figure is well-proportioned; he is shorter than the very tall, taller and more commanding than the average man. The top of his head is round, and on it his curled hair retreats gently from his even forehead. His neck is not soft but erect and sinewy. Over each eye arches a bushy eyebrow; when his eyelids droop, the tips of the lashes reach almost halfway down the cheeks. The tips of the ears are hidden by strands of hair that are brushed back over them, as is the fashion with them. His nose is most gracefully curved; his lips are delicately molded and are not enlarged by any extension of the corners of the mouth. Every day he shaves the bristles that grow beneath his nostrils. His facial hair is heavy in the hollow of his temples, but on the lowest part of the face the barber constantly shaves it from the cheeks, which retain their youthful appearance.

3. His chin, throat, and neck suggest not fat but fullness; the skin is milk-white, but on close inspection it takes on a youthful blush, for this color is frequently produced in his case by modesty, not by ill temper. His shoulders are well-shaped, his upper arms sturdy, his forearms hard, his hands broad. The chest is prominent, the stomach receded; the surface of his back is divided by a spine that lies low between the bulging ribs; his sides swell with bulging muscles. Strength reigns in his well-girt loins. His thigh is hard as horn; the upper legs are full of manly vigor; his knees are completely free from wrinkles and full of grace; the legs are supported by sturdy calves, but the feet that bear such mighty limbs are small.

4. And now you want to know all about his everyday life, which is open to the public gaze. Before dawn he goes with a very small retinue to the service conducted by his priests, and he worships with great earnestness, though—in confidence—one can see that this devotion is a matter of routine rather than conviction. Administrative duties of the kingdom take up the rest of the morning. Nobles in armor have places near his throne; a crowd of fur-clad guards is allowed in so as to be close at hand but is excluded from the presence so as not to disturb; and so they keep up a hum of conversation by the door, outside the curtains but within the barriers. Meanwhile deputations from various peoples are introduced, and he listens to a great deal of talk but replies briefly, postponing business he intends to consider, speeding that which is to be promptly settled. The second hour comes: he rises from his throne to inspect his treasures or his stables.

5. When a hunt has been proclaimed and he rides forth, he considers it beneath his royal dignity to have his bow slung at his side; but if in the chase or on the road a bird or a beast appears within his range, he reaches back and an attendant places the bow in his hand, with the string or thong hanging loose; for he thinks it childish to carry a bow in a case and womanish to take it over ready-strung. When he takes it he either holds it straight in front of him and bends the two ends and so strings it or he rests upon his raised foot the end that has the knot and runs his finger along the loose string until he comes to the dangling loop; then he takes up the arrows, sets them in place, and lets them fly. Or he may urge you first to choose what you wish to have struck down: you choose what he is to strike and he strikes what you have chosen. If he ever misses your vision will mostly be at fault, and not the archer's skill.

6. If one joins him at the dinner table—which on all but festival days is just like that of a private household—there is no unpolished conglomeration of discolored old silver set by breathless attendants on sagging tables; the weightiest thing is the conversation, for there is either serious talk or none at all. The couches with their spreading draperies show an array sometimes of scarlet cloth, sometimes of fine linen. The food attracts by its skillful preparation, not by its costliness, the platters by their brightness, not by their weight. The goblets or wine bowls are refilled at such long intervals that there is more reason for the thirsty to complain than for the drunk to decline. To sum up: you can find there Greek elegance, Gallic plenty, Italian briskness; the dignity of state, the attentiveness of a private home, the ordered discipline of royalty. But as to the luxury of the festival days I had better hold my tongue, for even the lowest person cannot fail to note it.

7. To resume the story: after satisfying his appetite he never takes more than a short midday sleep and often goes without it. In the hours when the gaming board attracts him he is quick to pick up the dice; he examines them anxiously, spins them with skill, throws them eagerly; he addresses them jestingly and calmly awaits the result. If the throw is lucky, he says nothing; if unlucky, he smiles; in neither case does he lose his temper, in either case he is a real philosopher. As for a second throw, he is too proud either to fear it or to make it; when a chance of one is presented he disdains it, when it is used against him he ignores it. He sees his opponent's piece escape without stirring

and gets his own free without exaggerated rejoicing. You would actually think he was handling weapons when he handles the pieces on the board; his sole thought is of victory.

8. When it is time for play he lays aside for a while the stern mood of royalty and encourages fun and freedom and good-fellowship. My own opinion is that he dreads being feared. Furthermore, he is delighted at seeing his defeated rival disgruntled, and it is only his opponent's ill temper that really satisfies him that the game has not been given him. Now comes something to surprise you: the joy that overcomes him on these trivial occasions often speeds the claims of important transactions. At such times the haven of a prompt decision is thrown open to petitions that for a long time have been in distress through the foundering of their advocates. I myself at such times, if I have a favor to ask, find it fortunate to be beaten by him, for I lose my pieces to win my cause.

9. About the ninth hour the burden of royal business is taken up again. Back come the importunate petitioners, back come the marshals to drive them off; everywhere the rivalry of the disputants makes an uproar. This continues until evening; then the royal supper interrupts and the bustle fades away, distributing itself among the various courtiers whose patronage this or that party enjoys; and thus they keep watch until the night watches. It is true that occasionally (not often) the banter of low comedians is admitted during supper, though they are not allowed to assail any guest with the gall of a biting tongue. In any case no hydraulic organs are heard there, nor does any concert party under its trainer boom forth a set performance in chorus; there is no music of a lutenist, flautist, dance conductor, tambourine girls, or female guitarist; for the king finds charm only in string music that comforts the soul with virtue just as much as it soothes the ear with melody.

10. When he rises from the table, the night watch is first posted at the royal treasury and armed sentries, who will keep guard through the hours of the first sleep, are set at the entrances to the palace.

But I have already exceeded my part, for I promised to tell you a little about the king, not a long story about his rule; it is also fitting that my pen come to a stop because you desired to hear only of the tastes and personality of the great man and because I took it upon myself to write a letter, not a history. Farewell.[4]

Theodoric's Politics and Policies

Theodoric had his next younger brother, Theoderid's third son, Frideric, share his rule as vice-king. In this way he made use of Frideric's unquestionably great military abilities and at the same time kept the three younger brothers in check. We can identify as the salient feature of his kingship the intensification of the treaty of 418, which he used to expand and consolidate Visigothic rule on both sides of the Pyrenees. Moreover, as early as 455 he also acted as emperor-maker by pressuring his former tutor, Avitus, into assuming the purple. The royal brothers Theodoric and Frideric led the Gallic senator to Arles, where he was properly proclaimed emperor by Roman soldiers, but not without having first procured the consent of the senators of Gaul. The Goths made a peaceful entry into the capital of Gaul, which they had so often assaulted without success, and the Roman-barbarian community seemed to prove its viability once more.

That same year Avitus marched to Italy with the Gallic *exercitus Romanus* and with Gothic troops, but he was soon compelled to realize that the force at his disposal was not enough to win the peninsula. In Constantinople's eyes, Avitus remained a little usurper whom it owed no recognition, and the Italian army insisted that the Gallic senator who would be emperor break with his Gallic contingents. In the meantime Theodoric was waging war in Spain, where he moved against Suebi, Bagaudae, and Roman provincials "at the behest of the emperor." While Avitus—deserted by the Goths—was fighting for his survival in Italy, Toulouse proudly announced "the destruction and the end" of the Suebian kingdom in northwestern Spain. Avitus met his death soon after, but the Suebian kingdom was far from being destroyed.

In the wake of these events "abroad," meaning outside of the contractually fixed Gothic kingdom, the brothers Theodoric and Frideric had to surmount great difficulties: no less than the very existence of the kingdom of Toulouse was at stake. Avitus had been succeeded by the capable Emperor Majorian, who took vigorous measures in Gaul in 458/459. His *magister militum*, the patrician Aegidius, proved himself highly useful in the emperor's Gallic plans. Aegidius appeared to act like the successor to Aetius. But while the latter had operated in Gaul largely with the help of outside Hunnic warriors, Aegidius was the first Roman general to draw support from the Salian Franks under Clovis's father, Childeric. The Goths were defeated and remained loyal federates; at that time Saint Martin is reported to have performed his first anti-Gothic miracle.

But when Emperor Majorian next tried to attack the Vandals via Gaul and Spain, his fleet was destroyed off Cartagena. He himself fell victim in the summer of 461 to the half-Goth Ricimer, whose coup d'état in Italy very nearly resulted in Gaul's loss to the empire. Aegidius rebelled and the Goths supported the new emperor that Ricimer had installed. There was total chaos: Romans fought Romans and made deals with barbarians. A Roman general who was besieged in Narbonne by Aegidius called on Toulouse for help, and the Goths entered the coastal city in 462. In 463, Frideric was killed in the battle against Aegidius. Aegidius was now seriously planning to march against Toulouse, while encouraging Gaiseric to attack Italy, which was under Ricimer's control. Fortunately for the Visigoths, Aegidius died in 465. Theodoric launched a counteroffensive and was able to conquer some Roman territory along the Loire. This success would be Theodoric's last; deprived of his loyal vice-king Frideric, Theodoric was murdered in 466 by Theoderid's fourth son, Euric.

The new king abrogated the Roman-Gothic treaty of 416/418 and thus left the membership of his kingdom in the Roman Empire suspended for almost a decade. Up until 466 the old treaty together with the respective renewals had done what it was supposed to. In numerous battles against Bretons, Alans, and Bagaudae in Gaul, and against Bagaudae and Suebi in Spain, the Gothic kings had seen to it that their armies took booty and that the existing Roman legal and social order was retained. For the upper class of Gaul as well as for the Roman imperial government, the *exercitus Gothorum* was often the only, or at least the most important, army that kept peace internally and externally in large parts of the prefecture of Greater Gaul when it was in the Goths' interest to do so. That is also why Roman generals had to spare the often-defeated Visigoths, and woe to him who did not follow this policy.

4. EURIC (466–484) AND ALARIC II (484–507)

Theodoric had fought in Spain and Gaul as a "loyal" federate of Rome and had made the fullest possible use of the treaty with the empire. But when the imperial authority had declined to virtually nothing "because of the frequent change of Roman princes," Gothic policy had to adjust to the changed circumstances. Euric surely did not kill his brother because of the latter's pro-Roman attitude, but merely out of his own lust for power. But shortly after Euric had assumed power, the moment came to put an end to Roman rule in Gaul. All countermeasures by Ravenna and its emperors, among them those of the capable Emperor Anthemius (476–472), led to nothing. Only a few regions of the declining western empire resisted the barbarian conquest as vigorously as did the Auvergne in Aquitaine and the Tarraconensis in the Spanish Ebro Valley. In each case the fight was led by the local nobility following the withdrawal of the Roman imperial power. In the Auvergne, Burgundian federates were still available for a time; after that the locals had to rely on their own retainers.

The abrogation of the old *foedus* had put an end to the fiction that the Goths were merely serving the empire and not their own interests. The war that followed brought about a "late awakening of Roman consciousness," but in the end Euric was victorious. His war aims in Gaul were all the land between the Atlantic, the Loire, and the Rhône, and in Spain recognition of his absolute predominance. By 475 the last Ibero-Roman resistance had been broken and the Auvergne as well as all of Aquitania I had become Gothic. Both in Spain as well as in conquered Aquitaine, Euric appointed former Roman military officers as his plenipotentiaries. When Odovacar toppled the last West Roman emperor in 476 and had himself proclaimed king, Euric's troops also crossed the Rhône and occupied the entire region up to the Alps.

With the conquest of the Provence the king now commanded the most important successor state of the Roman Empire; during the first decade of his rule, he had created a Gallic-Spanish regnum that was home to about 10 million people who lived in an area encompassing three-quarters of a million square kilometers. The kingdom was more than six times the size of the old federate land. However, neither the *foedus* with Emperor Nepos in 475 nor the treaty with Odovacar in 477 (of dubious validity) disengaged this enormous territory from the Roman Empire. The often invoked autonomy of Euric's kingdom was not given any kind of foundation in terms of constitutional law. The parties merely agreed on the formula by which the emperor was henceforth content "to be called friend by the Visigothic king even though he was entitled to be called 'lord.'"

The land south of the Pyrenees did not yet serve as a settlement area of the Goths. But control of this area meant wealth and security, it provided backing to the Goths and a base to fall back on if the geopolitical situation changed. Some have seen in Euric's expansion an overextension of his people's strength, but such verdicts are based on the catastrophe of 507 and are unhistorical.

What Euric certainly did not intend was the establishment of a universal monarchy, the realization, so to speak, of Athaulf's dream. However, a consolidation of the greater Gothic kingdom would have required an appropriate ecclesiastical and legal policy, and it was only Euric's son and successor, Alaric II, who sought to pursue it to a sufficient degree. Before the end of the year 484 Euric died at Arles, of natural causes, which was a justifiably conspicuous event since no other king of Toulouse and very few of the Visigothic kings as a whole were so fortunate.

On December 28, 484, in Toulouse, Alaric succeeded to his father's place. The new king was young, about the same age as his Frankish antagonist Clovis. Alaric's reign gets only brief treatment in the sources, and what they do mention is overshadowed by his death in the battle of Vouillé and the downfall of the kingdom of Toulouse. Early on Alaric was therefore considered a weakling, an unworthy successor to his father, whose "iron rule" would have been needed to maintain the Goths' position as a great power. Quite apart from the fact that such a historical verdict is of little value today, it is also false.

Clovis's attack on the realm of the Roman King Syagrius in 486 or 487 brought the Franks for the first came dangerously close to the Gothic borders. Syagrius found refuge in Toulouse, but at a later date he was handed over to the Frankish king. After 490, at the latest, the Visigoths fought in Italy on the side of Theodoric the Great against Odovacar. Following the defeat of Odovacar, Theodoric married Clovis's sister in 493; the Gothic king of Italy was evidently interested in being on good terms with the Frankish king. At the same time Alaric II was given one of Theodoric's daughters as his wife. The disgraceful extradition of Syagrius may have occurred at that time, or possibly not until 502, when Alaric II and Clovis concluded an agreement of *amicitia* at Amboise.

For some time now Ravenna had let the Iberian Peninsula fend for itself. In the northwest were the native Basques and the kingdom of the Suebi, who had entered the land at the beginning of the fifth century together with Vandals and Alans. But by far the greatest part of the peninsula was claimed by the Visigoths, who for many decades had been plundering the Roman provincial population. It was only shortly before 500 that the policy of the kingdom of Toulouse toward the still-rich land south of the Pyrenees changed.

The years 494 and 497 witnessed the first Visigothic immigration into Spain. The Franks had already crossed the Loire by 496. In 498, shortly after the second wave of Gothic settlers had reached Spain, the Franks even occupied Bordeaux, in the process capturing the Gothic commander of the city. Prior to this, serious unrest in the Spanish Ebro Valley had been put down with indescribable brutality. It flared up a decade later in the area around Tortosa and was probably part of the Bagaudian tradition. It is possible that regional groups of the middle and lower classes were trying to defend themselves against the Gothic newcomers, for the new settlers were all great magnates—the poorer Goths remained behind in Gaul—and added to the pressure these groups were already feeling from the local owners of latifundia. Thus the hostilities around 500 provide late evidence for why the Goths had been recalled to Aquitaine in 418.

Alaric II had recognized full well that the most serious threat came from the Franks. In response he tried to mobilize the Burgundians against his northern neighbors. It would seem, however, that the king overtaxed the economic resources of his kingdom, since he had to raise revenue by issuing debased coinage. His father-in-law, Theodoric, also criticized the effectiveness of the Toulouse army on the eve of the great Visigothic-Frankish war. Alaric was aware of how difficult his situation was, but the magnates of his tribe forced him to offer resistance to the Franks in a pitched battle. The two armies, led by their respective kings, met at Vouillé near Poitiers in the later summer of 507. Alaric II was killed, supposedly meeting his death at Clovis's own hands. The troops from his father-in-law, who wanted to come to his aid, had not even been called up at this time; the Ostrogothic army was not mobilized until 508.

Alaric II's great achievement was his legal and ecclesiastical policy, to which the future belonged. His father, Euric, had never been able to integrate the territorial structure of the Gallo-Roman Church into the borders of the Visigothic kingdom. Alaric II sought to overcome this legacy. His *Breviarium,* the law code for his Roman subjects, was directly connected with the summoning of the Gothic-Gallic territorial council of Agde. Like the codification of the law, this council too was the first of its kind in the barbarian successor states of the western empire.

Today both events—the promulgation of the code and the assembly—are assessed very positively, even if—in retrospect—they may be seen as signs of a *fusion manquée*.[5] Many of the difficulties were not religious in nature at all, but arose from the fact that the various diocesans and metropolitans had their seats in the Visigothic kingdom while large parts of their jurisdictions lay in the regna of the Franks and the Burgundians. A bishop's dutiful concern for his entire bishopric could thus easily be interpreted as a betrayal of the Gothic cause. Still, roughly three-quarters of the bishops of Gaul either participated in person at the synod of Agde or sent representatives; the protocols were signed on September 10, 506. Another meeting was planned for the following year in Toulouse; this time the Spanish bishops were also to attend. In Toulouse the regional council of Gaul would have expanded into a Visigothic royal council. The Frankish invasion wrecked this plan. Nevertheless, Agde pointed the way to the future, and even the victorious Frankish King Clovis would draw his lesson from it.

5. PIONEERING ACHIEVEMENT AND FAILED ACCOMMODATION

During its hundred-year history, the kingdom of Toulouse became in many areas of political and legal life the model for the younger kingdoms of Gaul and Spain. The kings of Toulouse were the first who acted as lawgivers and whose codifications brought about the victory of Roman vulgar law and the final break with the legal development of the imperial East.

Vulgar Roman law differed from classical jurisprudence in its strong tendency toward simplification and adaptation to the realities and needs of a "smaller space." Already Theoderid had had to promulgate written statutes on inheritance and private property, statutes that his second son, Theodoric, expanded and that his fourth son may have turned into the famous *Codex Euricianus*. No matter whether it was Euric or only his son Alaric II who codified the codex, this collection of laws was still in the eighth century the model of many tribal laws, including the Alamannic and Bavarian law codes.

The law as laid down in the *Codex Euricianus* became, at the beginning of the sixth century at the latest, the personal law of the Goths. Its counterpart was the so-called *Breviarium Alaricianum,* which was promulgated by Alaric II probably on February 2, 506, and which contained the Roman law under the Goths, the *Lex Romana Visigothorum.* The *Codex Euricianus* and the *Breviarium Alaricianum* rank right alongside Ulfilas's Bible translation in terms of their importance and repercussions.

In need of regulation were disputes arising from the cohabitation of Romans and Goths, as well as questions relating to custody, loans, purchases, and gifts. The laws conveyed to the Goths such important devices as the last will, loans with interest, and the use of charters drawn up by private persons as well as the king. The form and formulas of the Visigothic royal charters are largely unknown. However, it is extremely likely that the far better attested Merovingian royal charter borrowed from the Visigothic model.[6] If this is so, the Goths of Toulouse—unlike the Vandals,[7] Odovacar, or Theodoric the Great[8]—took as their model not the imperial rescripts but the charters of the high bureaucracy of Gaul. This agrees with the fact that the display of the Roman-barbarian kingship did not imitate the imperial triumph but the way in which successful provincial generals presented themselves outwardly.[9]

Theoderid's realm encompassed several Roman urban districts, which together with the court formed its basic administrative structure. Larger units were taken over only under Euric (466–484) as successors to militarized provincial units, *ducatus*. But just as there was no Burgundian or Frankish provincial administration, there was also no Toulousan provincial administration, let alone continuation of the greater Gallic prefecture, not even when the kingdom of Euric in the seventies expanded to comprise the better part of its territory.

Already the legal sources from the period around 475—that is, about two generations after settlement—recognize only two ethnic entities, Goths and Romans, even though both were in turn composed of a multitude of religious, ethnic, and political groups. Thus we find among the Visigoths also members of the Ostrogoths who had fled before the Huns, Taifali (who had had kinship ties with the Tervingians at the Danube), Balthic Galindi, Thracian Bessi, Sarmatians, Alans, Vandals, Varni, Suebi, and even Saxons and Bretons.

From a religious perspective the Romans were differentiated into Gallic-Spanish provincials, Syrians, Greeks, and Jews. In a legal sense all four groups—including the Jews—were Romans. Only in the course of the sixth century were the Jews no longer regarded as Romans, because all non-Christians were deprived of their Romanness and because the *populus Romanus* was equated with the *populus Christianus*. The locals and the eastern Christians were grouped together as Catholic Romans and opposed to the Arian Goths. Thus a sense of alienness predominated for a long time in personal relationships between Romans and Goths.

Sidonius Apollinaris, Theodoric's biographer, once said that Sidonius avoided barbarians even when they were good people. Still, from the very beginning Romans had cooperated with the migrating Goths as well as with the kings of Toulouse. Alongside the collaborators and the profiteers were those who meekly went along and tried to support the "Gothic peace" in order to prevent worse from happening. But anyone who analyzed the situation dispassionately had to realize that he was giving himself over to an illusion if he was hoping to save the empire with Gothic help.

A person could preserve his or her Roman identity not least with, and in, the church. All too often people were faced with the choice "of losing either their hair [their lay status] or their homeland" if they did not enter service to the Gothic king. It is not surprising that the number of Roman civil servants and high military officials who acted as delegates of king Euric rose dramatically. Already in 469, the ideas of the Gallic prefect and the vice-governor of the seven provinces had caused a great stir: the two men suggested dividing up the Roman administration of Gaul and what remained of imperial Gaul between the kings of the Visigoths and Burgundians.

Of course this idea presupposed that the two barbarian kingdoms were part of the Imperium Romanum. The two high officials met with an inglorious end, but they were not political loners. In the following years at least three Roman commanders continued their careers as high-ranking and top-ranking Gothic troop commanders. And for the first time we now also hear the names of those Romans who stood at the pinnacle of the central administration that the rapidly growing state of Euric and Alaric II needed and had to develop. A Roman commanded the Goths' Atlantic fleet. To these Romans it simply made sense again to fight, for now, "under the banner of an always victorious people": they were not fighting for a lost cause.

But already in the early years of the kingdom, Toulouse had been the meeting place of Gallic magnates. It was not long after the Gothic settlement that the later Emperor Avitus began his relationship with Theoderid. The Auvergnian nobleman was permitted to call the king his friend, who had entrusted to him the Roman education of his son Theodoric. At the end of the kingdom of Toulouse, Apollinaris, son of Sidonius and grandson of Avitus, fought with his friends on the side of the Goths against the Franks. After the battle of Vouillé in 507, a son of the Merovingian king had to pay a special "visit" to the Auvergne to annex it to the Frankish kingdom.

The locals did not bow without resistance to the changing situation. Rather, they wished to remain Gothic even after the end of Gothic rule, just as once they had sought to hold high the flagpole of Rome after the last Roman soldier of Gaul had long since lowered the flag. The resistance of the Auvergne paid off also at the beginning of the Frankish period: the Auvergnians maintained their independence, as they had been accustomed to doing.[10]

SEVEN

The Vandals
(406–534)
A Unique Case

1. THE TOPIC AND ITS IDEOLOGICAL BURDEN

For those who believe that Rome did not "die a natural death but was murdered,"[1] the Goths and Vandals, the conquerors of the Eternal City, were cut of the same cloth. But unlike the Vandals, the Goths—as did the Franks, Anglo-Saxons, and Longobards—provided for their posthumous fame: they were given histories of their own that reported on the whole very favorably about them and their conversion to Christianity, a verdict that made its way into moralistic-ethnographic literature. Since the Vandals found no spokesmen for their cause, they got stuck with the notion of "vandalism" after it had started to dissociate itself from the Goths.

"Vandalism" as a word for senseless destruction arose in the eighteenth century, the same century in which "Gothic" gave its name to a cultural period in art, architecture, and writing.[2] Thus posterity created a picture of the Vandals that has about as much objectivity as an account of "the papacy of the sixteenth century based solely on Luther."[3] The peculiarities of the literary tradition alone make it unlikely that the Vandals represent a special case within the historical framework of the Germanic migration. We shall see if the historical facts bear this out.

2. THE VANDAL STORM AT THE BEGINNING
OF THE FIFTH CENTURY

The history leading up to the great Vandal assault, in which both Hasding and Siling Vandals crossed the Rhine along with other peoples and thus stepped into the bright light of history, can be reconstructed only in rough outline.

In the third decade of the fourth century, the Hasding Vandals clashed with the advancing Tervingians of the Danubian Gothic confederation in what is modern-day Transylvania. The Vandals came away the losers and are said to have asked Constantine the Great to settle them in Pannonia. In actuality there may have been, if anything, a settlement of individual Vandal groups as *subiecti*. It is quite certain that an entire Vandal tribe was not admitted into the empire at that time. Instead, the greater part of the Hasdingi remained at the upper Tisza, with the tribe's sphere of interest possibly extending to the middle reaches of the river. Until the end of the fourth century the Hasdingi were the eastern neighbors of the Suebian Quadi, whose settlement areas in eastern Moravia-Slovakia also bordered on those of the Siling Vandals in what is today Silesia.[4]

Since 380 there had existed, inside the imperial borders, the three-tribe confederation of Ostrogoths, Huns, and Alans, with strong Marcomannic-Quadian groups moving in as neighbors even before the century was out. These newcomers too were Roman federates. The Alanic element of Pannonia must have acted as a center of attraction for additional tribal comrades who had split off from the westward-moving Hunnic avalanche of peoples. To be sure, there is no secure evidence for this assumption; however, around and after 400, strong Alanic groups were operating in so many different places, and not infrequently under royal leadership, that they could not all have come from the Safrax-Alans of Pannonia, who did not have a king.

Perhaps it was the approach of the greater Hunnic dominion, most certainly the death of Emperor Theodosius I and the subsequent troubles between East and West, the example of the Alaric-Goths, and a few other reasons besides, which led to the formation, shortly before 400, of an expansive tribal coalition ready to set out for the West. Of least importance in the emergence of the coalition were the famine reported in our sources and the overpopulation in the existing settlement area. From modern-day Hungary on both sides of the imperial border came Vandals and Alans; they were joined by Roman underclasses, the "Pannonian enemies." In Gaul and Spain such native popular movements were directed against the Roman state and the property relations it protected and guaranteed; the groups involved rarely left their homeland. By contrast, the Pannonian provincials might have "become Vandals" also because they felt threatened from the outside, that is, by the Huns. Via Quadian Slovakia there were connections to the Moravian-Bohemian Marcomanni and the Siling Vandals in Silesia. From all these peoples came the most active tribal elements, in each case grouped around kings and their retainers.

The Marcomanni and the Quadi gave up their special names after crossing the Danube, in fact both the emigrants and the groups remaining in Pannonia became Suebi again. The Pannonian Suebi became subjects of the Huns. After the battle at the Nedao they set up their own kingdom, and when it fell they came, successively, under Herulian and Longobard rule, south of the Danube under Gothic rule, and eventually again under Longobard rule.

The number of Hasding and Siling Vandals who remained behind on the land must have been substantial. While the latter passed on their "Silesian" name even to the Slavic immigrants, Hasding Vandals were still attested at the Tisza more than two generations after the great westward trek.[5] However, the kings of both Vandal tribes left their homeland, and after the fall of the Hunnic Empire no Vandal kingdom was reestablished either in Silesia or at the Tisza.

By contrast, it would appear that most of the Alans left; in any case, they were strong enough to create kings for themselves, though this happened only after they were in Gaul. The other tribal splinter groups—Gepids are mentioned by name—who joined the Vandal-Alanic-Suebian trek are noted only when they all set out, after that we hear no more of them.[6]

The great trek moved at a slow pace: in Raetia, Vandals became Stilicho's federates and fought on the northern Italian battlefields against Alaric I. Alans, either directly or indirectly from Pannonia, opened the great battles of the year 402, they rode against the Goths both near Pollentia and at Verona. Shortly before, Stilicho had been successful against barbarians and domestic enemies from the Rhine to Africa. Even if troops from Gaul and Britain had to be shifted to Italy, he still seemed master of the situation, for troop redeployment was nothing new to the Roman army.

At the end of August 406, the assault of Radagaisus had been crushed near Florence, and Stilicho was at the pinnacle of his power and glory.[7] But less than four months later began the inexorable decline: on New Year's Eve 406, Vandals, Alans, and Suebi with their allies crossed the Rhine, probably between Mainz and Worms, after the federate Franks had already defeated the Hasdingi and killed their king. The Romans had succeeded in winning over an Alan king who abandoned his Vandal allies. But another Alan prince remained loyal to the Vandals, he entered the fray in the nick of time and the Franks suffered a crushing defeat. After that the floodgates were open. For more than two and a half years the barbarians crisscrossed Gaul and ravaged the land. In the fall of 409, Vandals, Alans, and Suebi pushed into Spain.[8]

3. VANDALS, ALANS, AND SUEBI IN SPAIN (409–429)

"The Spaniards now began to burn in the same flames in which the Gauls had burned."[9] While Italy had to endure Alaric's marches on Rome and eventually the conquest of the Eternal City, Spain was left to its own devices. The natives therefore tried to come to an arrangement with the invaders, to hold on to the heartland at the Ebro River and to use the enemy's tendency to split into smaller groups—a result of their tribal makeup—to get them settled separately and thus pacify them to some degree: the Hasdingi drew as their allotment eastern Gallicia, the Suebi western Gallicia, the Silings Baetica, and the Alans the provinces of Lusitania and Carthaginiensis.

For more than five hundred years nearly the entire Iberian Peninsula had been part of the Roman Empire, and for a period not much shorter the northwestern peripheral areas had also belonged to the imperium, at least nominally. The Pax Romana had guaranteed safety and order, eternal peace seemed to have descended upon the earth. Of course the reality looked far less idyllic: there were social tensions and armed resistance, robberies on land and water. But Hispania was spared larger wars against outside enemies until the first decades of the fifth century. The barbarian devastation that befell the land now was thus experienced as all the more dreadful.

It was not until 412/413 that Spain underwent division, from which the valley of the Ebro, Mediterranean-facing Tarraconensis, was excluded because of the persistent Roman resistance. The four years following the barbarian invasion saw plundering, destruction, and bloodshed nearly everywhere in the land; nevertheless, the Spaniards found the time and leisure to raise up usurpers and to fight each other as well as Ravenna.

From this time of general chaos comes a report that Emperor Honorius tried to put an end to it by concluding with the Vandals a treaty that spared the provincials. No such thing happened in real life. When the barbarians did in fact approach Ravenna to secure their conquests by treaty, the answer from the imperial government was war.

As though Spain wasn't suffering enough, the Athaulf-Goths invaded Catalonia in 415. Here their leader was murdered, and here Valia prevailed as their new king. With him generalissimo Constantius concluded the treaty of 416, which laid the groundwork for the turnaround. On the emperor's orders the Visigoths attacked the Alans and Siling Vandals encamped in Spain, defeated them in bloody battles and destroyed their independence. With the kings of the Silings and Alans dead, the defeated remnants decided to forego a kingdom of their own and joined the Hasdingi. But before Valia could move also against this Vandal tribe, Constantius withdrew the Gothic army from Spain and settled the loyal Roman federates in Aquitaine.[10]

Left over in northwestern Spain were the Suebi—Valia's daughter became the wife of a Suebian prince—and the Hasdingi, whose kings became the beneficiaries of the Gothic victories. By the time the Goths left Spain in 418, the creation of a large Vandal-Alan tribe had come to conclusion in this land. In 422 these Vandals and Alans conquered southern Spain, Baetica. Here they captured Seville and the coastal cities, among them the all-important port of Cartagena. They were soon skilled in maritime warfare and plundered the Balearic Islands.

In the meantime, the Suebi were trying to spread southward toward Lusitania. During all these expeditions the Vandals as well as the Suebi were harassed and threatened by Ravenna and the Goths who were fighting in Rome's name. The Vandal King Gunderic had died suddenly during the plundering of Seville. His successor, Gaiseric, who saw what the balance of power truly was and who was well-informed about the political developments in the western empire and its overseas provinces, decided to lead his people to Africa.[11]

4. GAISERIC (428–477)

Both in 410 and in 415 the Visigoths had entertained similar plans. However, Alaric had proved incapable of crossing the Strait of Messina in order to venture the great leap from Sicily, and it was utterly out of the question that Valia could have crossed from southern Spain the Strait of Gibraltar with its strong currents. After much longer and better preparation, after several years of training and successful warfare by sea, Gaiseric carried out what his Gothic predecessors could only dream about.

There is nothing more unrealistic than the numbers given in our historical sources; in most cases they mean merely "many," or "a great many." But if one wants to take an entire people across the sea, symbolic number games are not enough. One has to count with great precision in order to provide sufficient space on the ships. Gaiseric did just that, divided his people into eighty groups of a thousand each, and sailed from Iulia Traducta to Africa in May of 429; there were also Goths among the ships' passengers.

The Man

Gaiseric held the Vandal-Alan kingship for nearly fifty years. He was the younger son of the Vandal king who was killed in battle in 406 before the crossing of the Rhine, and successor to his half-brother Gunderic, who ruled from 406 to 428 (see Figure 3). Gaiseric's mother was of unfree status, probably of non-Vandal origin, possibly even a Roman. If the latter is the case, it would agree with the report—which, seen by itself, seems not very credible—that Gaiseric was originally Catholic and only later became Arian. For if his mother *was* Roman, she would have been a Catholic and her son would have initially professed her faith. Gaiseric is presumed to have been born around 390, which would mean that he was nearly forty when he came to power and around ninety when he died. Since his father was killed before the tribe crossed the Rhine, the future king of Roman Africa was born outside the imperial borders. If his mother was in fact Roman, she or her ancestors must have been captured during a plundering raid.

It is not impossible that Gaiseric's oldest son, Huneric, was already married to a Visigothic princess when the tribe set out for Africa in 429. The

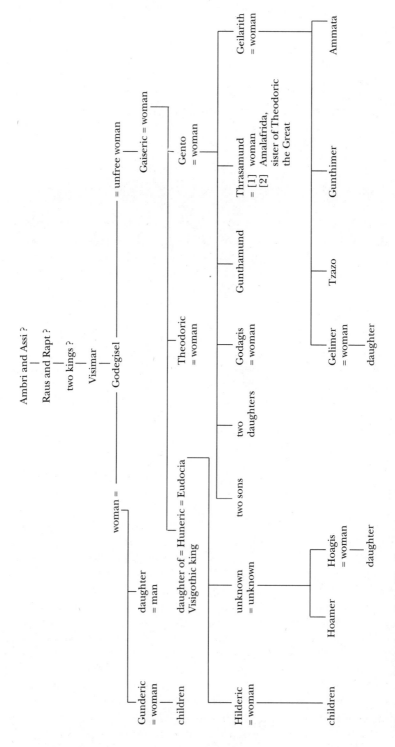

Figure 3. Genealogy of the Hasdingi

withdrawal of the Vandals to southern Spain had prompted the Visigoths as early as 422 to ally themselves—much against their habit—with the Hasdingi who were under attack from the Romans. In the 420s there was, for once, more that united Visigoths and Vandals than divided them. The purpose of their alliance was evidently to catch the Romans of Tarraconensis and the Suebi of northwestern Spain in a pincer movement. Shortly before the Vandals embarked they still beat back a Suebi thrust into Beatica; the Suebi suffered heavy losses and their king was killed.

Gaiseric succeeded his brother, even though the latter, the offspring of a full marriage, had at least one son of his own. Gaiseric's much admired succession arrangement later provided for exactly this kind of succession by seniority, by which the oldest male Hasding would accede to the kingship after the death of his predecessor. As was the case among the Merovingians, membership in the Hasding clan too would have been determined solely by the fact that the person in question had had a king as his father. However, in 428 it may have been the case that it was not a predetermined arrangement but the power of the actual situation that led the Vandals to choose the battle-tested Gaiseric over his nephew, who was still young. Based on the experience of his own accession to power, Gaiseric may have then introduced succession by seniority; to be sure, before he did so he preemptively killed his dead brother's entire family, though we know that this did not happen until the Vandals were in Africa.[12]

Gaiseric was "a man of moderate height and lame in consequence of a fall from his horse. He was a man of deep thought and few words, holding luxury in disdain, furious in his anger, greedy for gain, shrewd in winning over the barbarians and skilled in sowing the seeds of dissension to arouse enmity."[13] Gaiseric struck many as more brutal and more cruel than the brutal and cruel rulers who were his contemporaries. He and his son Huneric embodied, as it were, the "ideal of the Antichrist," Vandalism in its pure form, so to speak.

But the Greeks remembered for a long time that Gaiseric had been a superb warrior.[14] He was also regarded as an unusually impressive ruler, whom posterity very soon compared with Theodoric the Great.[15] Gaiseric was undoubtedly a spirited warrior king, as good an organizer as he was a diplomat: in short, a ruler who maneuvered himself and his relatively small tribe[16] into a seemingly unassailable position, a position from which he conducted his dealings with the entire world—Ravenna and Constantinople, Goths and Huns—as between equals.

From the Crossing to Africa in 429 to the Treaty of 435

The events that unfolded between the crossing of the Strait of Gibraltar in 429 and the capture of Carthage in 439 symbolize the testing of the Vandals in the desert; this is where, in their own tradition, they must have turned into the chosen people. Perhaps such a conviction can be inferred from their intransigent Arianism. In any case, their success seemed enormous and conceivable only with the help of God. Even without encountering any resistance, it was a superb logistical accomplishment to safely cover the two thousand kilometers between Ceuta and Carthage with eighty thousand people.

The maritime route was out of the question because the Romans dominated the sea and because of the inherent technical difficulties. And so the "long march" became a slow advance into the heartlands of Roman Africa. In June of 430, the Vandal peoples stood outside the walls of Hippo Regius (Bône-Annaba), the episcopal city of Saint Augustine, the African governor Bonifatius having earlier suffered a serious defeat against them. This same Bonifatius was said to have invited Gaiseric to Africa with traitorous intent.[17] The long-dead half-Vandal Stilicho was also blamed for the calamity. But these are the usual accusations and suspicions that fill the sources of the fifth and sixth centuries and serve to explain the almost unimaginable, the downfall of the empire. In the case of Bonifatius, however, it is conceivable that he wanted to employ the Vandals as federates to protect Africa, following the example of what Constantius had done with the Valia-Goths in Aquitaine.

Augustine died on August 28, 430, in the third month of the siege of his city; another eleven harsh months awaited the besieged and the besiegers, who lost many of their warriors. After the Vandals had temporarily withdrawn, the inhabitants left the city, and Gaiseric soon after established his residence there, despite the fact that part of it was destroyed. Carthage, however, was able to hold its own, a circumstance that did much to increase the Vandal's willingness to make peace. The first treaty between Gaiseric and the empire was concluded in Hippo Regius on February 1, 435; however, the imperial party to the treaty was not Constantinople but Ravenna, which was proper, even though since 432 the eastern empire had borne the main burden of the Vandal war.

As is so often the case, we do not know any details of the treaty, only the result, namely, that the Vandals "were assigned for settlement that part of Africa that they possessed." The diocese of Africa was made up of a relatively large number of small provinces, three of which were affected by the Vandal settlement of 435. In modern terms one would speak of their area as northeastern Algeria. Depending on one's perspective, the Vandal territory was either closed in by imperial lands to the east and the west, or it split Roman Africa like a wedge. It is highly likely that the Vandals were given an—unknown—share of the curial taxes, an arrangement that essentially must have resembled the model that had been developed for the settlement of the Visigoths.[18]

"What explains the absence of meaningful Roman resistance to Gaiseric's advance are the weakness of the troops stationed in Africa, which was hitherto regarded as safe; the serious conflicts between the *comes* Africae Bonifatius and the *magister militum praesentalis* Felix, which led to military clashes; the breakdown of the Roman border defense against the Berbers living beyond the *limes;* as well as the religious and social tensions within the provincial population."[19]

King of the Land and the Sea: The Capture of Carthage in 439

In the midst of peace, Gaiseric attacked the proconsular province, taking the capital of Africa, venerable Carthage, by surprise on October 19, 439. For a brief period the Vandals ruled all of Roman Africa and took possession of the land according to the right of the conqueror. After the conquest of Carthage, Gaiseric is said to have been given the title "king of the land and the sea";[20] true or not, a new era began on that day. The capture of Carthage in the midst of peace was no heroic military deed; however, it led to the shift of the Vandal state from Numidia to the rich provinces of Africa proconsularis and Byzacena and subsequently to the treaty of 442, which recognized the fact "that a peace was now concluded between Gaiseric and Emperor Valentinian (III) and Africa was divided between them."[21]

Razed to the ground by the Romans in 146 B.C., Carthage had been refounded as a Roman colony by Caesar and Augustus and had soon reclaimed its old position as the gateway to the Mediterranean coast of Africa. It served as the capital of the expansive and rich old province of Africa proconsularis; close to two hundred thousand people are said to have lived in the city. Contemporaries ranked Carthage second after Rome and placed the African metropolis on a par with Egyptian Alexandria. Little changed in late antiquity in this perception of Carthage: for some Carthage was the African Rome, for others it was outranked only by Constantinople. As the capital of the most important Roman territory, which produced a considerable surplus of grain and was able to export it owing to its location by the sea, Carthage may have had a population in the six figures even during the Vandal period. The total population of Roman Africa is today estimated to have been 3 million, most of which lived in the approximately five hundred cities of the land.[22] This represented a truly enormous concentration of capital and labor, which gave Gaiseric's kingdom from the very outset substantial economic clout.[23]

The new era was dated "from the taking of Carthage." For example, Carthaginian coinage was "vandalized." To be sure, the gold and silver coins continued to bear the emperor's likeness, since they served long-distance trading within the empire outside of the Vandal kingdom and thus had to respect the imperial prerogative; however, they were given the new dating by the year 439. By contrast, copper coins, which were intended for domestic Vandal trade, were used by Gaiseric and his successors to express their political theory: on these coins, not all of which record the new Carthaginian era, "the king is depicted in full figure, leaning on a spear; on either side is the legend KARTHAGO. The reverse shows a horse's head and the numerical indication of the coin's value. It has been assumed that the figure is Gaiseric and that the coins are post-439; the choice of the horse's head can be explained with the founding legend of Carthage. These coins may have been intended to appeal especially to the civilian population."[24]

Dating years according to the era of a city was not a rare practice, especially in the non-European parts of the Roman Empire. Hence Gaiseric's dating according to the capture of Carthage was nothing out of the ordinary. However, this was the first time the practice was used by a barbarian king, and on top of that in the language of the pre-Roman, indeed anti-Roman, tradition. The same holds true for the counting by regnal years, which the Vandal kings were also the first to lay claim to.

Whether Gaiseric himself already used dating according to regnal years remains an open question. Inscriptions and charters begin only with his successor Huneric. But no matter whether or not the Vandal example served as the immediate model for the practice of regnal dating in the other Roman-barbarian kingdoms, this form of a ruler's self-conception too is not entirely new nor can one read from it the kingdom's secession from the Roman Empire; after all, "in the Roman state dating was not infrequently done according to governor's years."[25] Even the depiction of the royal majesty in the "eternal victory" of the ruler, and the use of a throne as well as the imperial purple, while they certainly elevated the Vandal kings far above the highest holders of magisterial powers, in and of themselves did not make them into sovereign rulers, let alone emperors.

That said, it is true that the African kings did in fact at times trespass onto imperial prerogatives, something Byzantium took note of with much ill-humor. For example, King Huneric renamed the African coastal city of Hadrumentum after himself: Unuricopolis. After the conquest of the Vandal kingdom, Justinian quickly corrected that decision, so that the venerable old city now got its third name in two generations, Justiniana. We can see that the renaming craze of our century has imperial roots.[26]

Gaiseric probably established his residence on Byrsa Hill in Carthage. If that is indeed so, he would have taken over the residence of the former Roman proconsuls. Gaiseric's lifestyle is unlikely to have been markedly different from that of his magnates. The Vandal king was surrounded by a guard, a practice that was customary also at the court of Toulouse. The showpieces of Vandal booty that Belisarius brought back to Constantinople were golden thrones, utensils of daily life that were fashioned of precious metals and covered with jewels, and above all the state carriages for the queens; most of them came from the royal palace of Carthage. During the time of Gaiseric and his successors, Vandal troop commanders and Roman bureaucrats, with whose help the kingdom was administrated, frequented this palace. Little is known about the Vandal administration compared to that of the Ostrogothic kingdom in Italy; leaving aside spectacular isolated incidences, like the destruction of tax registers, it is likely, though, that the Roman administration continued to function unimpeded. The burned papyri simply had to be replaced with new documents that conformed to Gaiseric's ideas, for the Vandal king would not have dreamed of doing without the taxes of his Roman subjects.[27]

The Vandal-Alan Kingdom

The oldest of the preserved Germanic royal titles comes from the royal Vandal chancery. We can still read it today in two royal charters of Huneric. With respect to their transmission and their credibility, these two documents are surpassed among the royal acts of the migration period only by a donation charter of Odovacar from the year 489. The *intitulatio* of an edict of May 19, 483, and of a law of February 25, 484, reads in each case "*Rex Hunirix Vandalorum et Alanorum.*" Huneric's charters are faithful copies of imperial rescripts. Innovations over Roman imperial charters are only the dating according to regnal years and above all the title "king of the Vandals and Alans."

The connection between the two "nations" expressed in this title went back to the years between 416 and 418, when the victories of the Visigothic King Valia had led the Vandal Silings and the Spanish Alans to join the Hasdingi. In creating the African kingdom, their kings, who from that time on carried the old tribal name of the Hasdingi as their clan name, made possible a new ethnogenesis. "The names of the Alani and all the other barbarians, except the Moors, were united in the name of the Vandals."[28] This process of amalgamation did in fact diminish the special position of the Alans; however, the strength and binding force of the theory and tradition of the erstwhile joining of Vandals and Alans were not affected by it. Thus the royal titles, as attested by Huneric's charters and indicated by the epigraphic-literary evidence until 533, reflect the events of the years from 416 to 418: Gunderic was factually the first "king of the Vandals and Alans," Gelimer the last.

At least Gaiseric, the founder of the African kingdom, can safely be assumed to have actually borne this title, especially since he was the first Vandal king who performed legal acts that demanded such a documentary title.

In theory the African kingdom was the joint kingdom of the Vandals and Alans. But imperial policy interpreted the regnum Vandalicum in a more pragmatic way than the self-conception of the Vandal king and his national groups would have allowed. In Constantinople one spoke of a trinity of peoples, namely of Vandals, Alans, and Moors, when one was referring to the African kingdom. However, the relationship to the Moors, who were not mentioned in the royal title, was not always the same over the course of the one-hundred-year Vandal-African history. While the Moors initially played an important part in the rise of Gaiseric's kingdom as loyal retainers of the military king, their expansion, especially from the moment the Romans gave up Africa and their armies and fleets vanished as enemies, was directed against the Vandal kingdom itself.

The result was that a larger number of Moorish kingdoms arose, with one of the rulers even calling his realm *Regnum Maurorum et Romanorum,* which means he was taking the Vandal-Alan example as the model for his Moorish-Roman kingdom. In contrast, the title "king of the Vandals and Alans" meant that the Gothic-Suebian tribal splinters that had come along from Spain, as well as later reinforcements of Goths, were subsumed under the rule of the African two-tribe confederation, while the subjected Romans for a long time formed merely the object of Vandal policy. Hilderic's attempt to break with this hopeless policy and to build up a Vandal-Roman kingdom in Africa—provincials served in his army for the first time—was unsuccessful, not least because of his defeats against the Moors. No new beginning could succeed at a time of obvious weakness, as was the case in the fourth decade of the sixth century.[29]

The Revolt of the Nobility, or the Consequences of the Treaty of 442

To this day there persists in historical atlases and handbooks the notion that in 442 Ravenna, followed by Constantinople in 474 at the latest, recognized the Vandal kingdom as a foreign land and its king as a sovereign. This view is false, nor can it invoke Theodor Mommsen in its defense, for the latter had recognized already in the question of the Vandal regnal year that its introduction "did not, with conceptual necessity, exclude the Vandals from membership in the empire."[30] However, the treaty of 442, by which Ravenna not only formally recognized Gaiseric's state but also secured it economically, amounted to a qualitative change. Gaiseric's regnum was now transformed from a Vandal-Alan kingship of the army into the African kingdom of the Vandals and Alans. But this also meant a profound transformation of Gaiseric's position vis-à-vis those who had hitherto been the bearers of, indeed participants in, his rule. There is no other way to explain why only a short time after the Vandal conquests had been anchored in imperial law, a move that, after all, benefited economically the magnates above all, this same group of people invoked its right of resistance and proceeded to mount an armed revolt.

A contemporary chronicler—describing the situation in the language of the time—tells us that Gaiseric, because of his success, acted arrogantly toward his people, and his conduct gave birth to a conspiracy among the magnates. He adds that the Vandal king responded with indescribable cruelty to the demands of the noble opposition. The Vandals suffered more losses from his rage than from a lost war.[31] The Visigothic wife of Huneric, who was at that time living in Ravenna as a hostage, was also caught up in this opposition movement, and she was mutilated and sent back to her father, Theoderid. She would not be the last royal Gothic woman to fall victim to Vandal domestic politics.

After Gaiseric quashed the revolt of the nobility and surmounted the serious crisis of 442, his monarchic rule was uncontested. Perhaps the remarkable succession order he put in place, which aroused the astonishment of the barbarian world and won imperial recognition, was related to this decisive political success at home. In order to prevent further internal wars, the king decreed that his oldest descendants would come to power in succession. This arrangement worked until the dethronement of Huneric's son Hilderic by Gelimer in 530. To be sure, domestic peace had been bought at a heavy price. The Vandal kings after Gaiseric came to power only at an advanced age, in fact as old men, and all of them were weak rulers.[32]

Gaiseric from 442 to His Death in 477

Gaiseric showed himself faithful to the treaty and cooperated with Ravenna. Huneric was still living in the West Roman capital as a hostage and guarantor of the treaty of 442. The crown prince was let go in 445 or 446, and he returned to his homeland as the fiancé of Eudocia, one of Emperor Valentinian III's daughters and still a child. When Attila attacked Gaul and the Visigoths in 451, Gaiseric was said to have been behind this war. One reason for the Vandal intrigue was supposedly the king's fear of the Visigothic ruler Theoderid. The daughter of the Balthic king had left Carthage under disgraceful circumstances and had returned to Toulouse, and Gaiseric feared her father's revenge.

We cannot say exactly what is true about this story. By this time at least five years had passed since the mutilation and expulsion of the Visigothic princess, and those events do seem a bit belated as the motive for a Hunnic-Vandal alliance. Moreover, Attila's enemy was not so much the federate king of Toulouse but Aetius as the representative of the western empire. Gaiseric's Roman policy of the following years shows that this "family man" and proud Hasding was concerned about making good his hereditary claims as someone who was related to the Theodosian house by marriage. Like Attila, Gaiseric probably held the fundamentally un-Roman view that one could acquire the Roman Empire through marriage, as it were. The Vandals and the Huns were thus more competitors than allies, even though, or precisely because, they had enjoyed the support of female members of the Theodosian dynasty.

In any case, when Valentinian III, the last male descendant of Theodosius the Great, was murdered in 455, the new emperor married his predecessor's widow, Eudoxia, and chose her daughter Eudocia, Huneric's betrothed, for his own son. This move was so unpalatable to the champions of the Theodosian court party that a rumor was able to circulate according to which Eudoxia herself had invited Gaiseric to attack Italy in order to free herself and her daughter. Be that as it may, the Vandal fleet set to sea from Carthage, manned with Moorish landing parties, and it dropped anchor in Porto.

Without encountering any resistance the Vandals entered Rome on June 2, 455. On intervention from Pope Leo I, the residents of the Eternal City were spared life and limb, but Rome itself was plundered. It was said that large parts of the Jewish temple treasure that Titus had brought to Rome, namely, whatever Alaric's Goths had left of it, fell to the Vandals as booty. In any case, Gaiseric made off with rich human spoils: senators and artisans as well as Eudoxia and her two daughters, Eudocia and Placidia, went to Carthage as captives. Eudocia became Huneric's wife. Thereafter the Vandals established bases in Sardinia, Corsica, and the Balearic Islands, and after lengthy fighting they were also able to prevail in Sicily.

Gaiseric's rule over all of Roman Africa very soon became an unrealized claim, since more than a half dozen Berber princes were able to set themselves up in the western provinces. What Gaiseric did rule has been aptly described by Christian Courtois as the *empire du blé,* the "empire of grain." The Vandals now controlled a large part of the West Roman grain production, and they could think about choosing the ruler of Italy.

Despite minor setbacks, Gaiseric remained all but unassailable. Several Roman advances at sea—both separate and joint enterprises by West and East—led to nothing. Eventually even the largest maritime operation ever undertaken against the Vandal kingdom ended in failure. The East Roman Emperor Leo I (457–474) equipped a fleet of 1,100 ships, which in the summer of 468, with western help, sailed simultaneously against Tripolitania and Carthage.

This gigantic armada, whose strength even Belisarius's force in 533 did not come close to equaling, reached Cape Bon (Ras Addar) and dropped anchor there, only a few nautical miles from Carthage. In this critical situation Gaiseric negotiated with the East Roman General Basiliskos and got him to agree to a five-day truce, allegedly by bribing him. The Vandal king made clever use of the pause in the assault and when the winds were favorable he attacked the enemy with fire ships. The favor of the elements brought Gaiseric his greatest victory at sea; God and Gaiseric's good fortune had saved him and the Vandals.

But Emperor Leo I did not give up; he attempted another assault on Carthage in 470. Even though Roman troops were already marching toward Carthage on African soil and the fleet was approaching Gaiseric's capital, the emperor had to call off the operation because his own generalissimo, the Alan Aspar, was causing him the greatest difficulties at home. Moreover, Olybrius, the man who became emperor in the West for a short time, was Huneric's brother-in-law. In the end Gaiseric and Leo's successor, Zeno, agreed on an "eternal alliance" as early as 474. This *foedus* was to be the first transpersonal treaty that the empire concluded with one of the Roman-barbarian successor states. As late as 533/534, Emperor Justinian I still accepted the validity of the treaty of 474.

The people whom Gaiseric regarded as enemies of his regime were not so much the native provincials and their senatorial upper class—Romans willing to cooperate wore Vandal dress at the court in Carthage—as the African Catholics, and so he found it easier to take a liking to Zeno and his Monophysitist tendencies. The Vandal king now permitted the Catholics to freely exercise their religion in Carthage, though he prohibited them from appointing a bishop. Those Roman captives who belonged to the royal family were set free, and permission was granted to purchase the freedom of the others.

In 476 Gaiseric concluded an agreement with the moribund western empire, an agreement Odovacar was able to enter into a short time later. By the terms of the treaty Sicily went to Odovacar in return for a tribute, even if, by paying it, he may have recognized Gaiseric's superior status. When the Vandal king died on January 24, 477, he had outlived the fall of the western imperium by only a few months; his own regnum, however, secured by military successes and treaties, seemed built for eternity.[33]

5. GAISERIC'S LEGITIMATE SUCCESSORS (477–530)

Gaiseric was succeeded by his oldest son, Huneric (477–484), who may have already been sixty-six years old when he assumed the throne.[34] Huneric had married—possibly still in Spain—a daughter of the Visigothic king. In the mid-forties, while Huneric was living in Ravenna as a guarantor of the peace of 442, Gaiseric got rid of his son's wife in a disgraceful manner. During his stay in Ravenna between 442 and 445/446, Huneric was betrothed to Eudocia (probably born in 439), the daughter of Emperor

Valentinian III and Eudoxia. Huneric had to wait more than ten years to fi-
nalize the marriage, and before he could he had to use force to retrieve his
fiancée from Rome, where she had in the meantime married the son of her
father's successor.

The marriage was probably concluded in 456, following a precautionary
nine-month delay, and Eudocia gave birth to her oldest son, Hilderic (most
likely in 457). At least one more son was granted to the mismatched couple
(the Vandal was about twenty-eight years older than his Roman wife). In 472
the ardent Catholic Eudocia secretly left her husband, perhaps because of
his aggressive Arianism, perhaps because he was at least sixty by then, perhaps for both reasons, and fled to holy Jerusalem, where she lived to the end
of her days.

Little is known about Huneric's long life: hardly anything prior to 477 except for his marriages and his hostage period, and not much more about
his seven-year reign, the overall assessment of which is difficult because of
its contradictoriness. Huneric must have realized that under his powerful
father the Vandal kingdom had already passed its zenith. He correctly assessed the limited military and demographic capabilities of his people, and
in his dealings with the empire he showed himself willing to compromise, in
fact yielding.

At home, however, he sought to secure his rule: he went about it with
the utmost brutality but was still not convincingly successful. Thus his effort to break Gaiseric's succession arrangement in favor of his son Hilderic
failed.[35] Around 481, the king launched a purge among his brothers and
nephews as well as among the representatives of his father's regime. The
bloody action claimed many victims, but Huneric could not get his hands on
his nephews Gunthamund and Thrasamund, and both were older than his
son Hilderic.

Next Huneric launched another persecution of the Catholic Church
and used the heresy laws of the Roman emperor against it. Having issued
an anti-Catholic edict in the spring of 483, in late winter of 484 he even had
the presumption of promulgating a law of the same content, even though
the *promulgatio legis* was the sole prerogative of the emperor. The Arian patriarch of Carthage, a local provincial, supported these measures to the
fullest. Since Huneric's domestic policy was limited to a policy of persecution he was bound to fail, for this way he could not win the desired support
of the Catholic Roman bishops. It is not surprising that God punished this
ruler: the famine in the summer of 484 was followed by Huneric's death—
as horrible as it was mysterious—before the year was out.[36]

Gunthamund (484–496) was the oldest surviving son of Gaiseric's third
son, Gento, who had predeceased his father. The new king put an end to
the Catholic persecution, which had lasted only a few months, and also

permitted the reestablishment of the ecclesiastical organization by allow-ing numerous exiled bishops to return. At the same time, however, he was not willing to exercise genuine religious toleration and accept a Catholic community enjoying equal rights alongside the Arian Church. In this regard Gunthamund was no different from his predecessors or from his younger brother and successor, Thrasamund. But this opposition to the Catholic faith, which no other Roman-barbarian successor state was able to main-tain with such severity and for such a long time, also accelerated the end of the African Vandal kingdom.

During Gunthamund's reign, pressure from the Moors increased: while the Berbers had still served the great military king Gaiseric as landing troops in the capture of Rome and had been sent by him to Sardinia as mil-itary settlers to secure the island for Vandal rule, the tribes of the Aures Mountains in what is today northeastern Algeria had broken with Carthage even before Huneric's death. Now the Moors advanced against the Vandal heartland, and more principalities of Moorish-Roman identity emerged. To-ward the end of the century the Vandals were at times safe from Berber raids only in the coastal region around Carthage.

A dangerous neighbor arose for Gunthamund in the Ostrogoth Theo-doric, who in 491 very quickly dispelled Vandal hopes for a reconquest of Sicily. While Odovacar had at least paid tribute for possession of the is-land, a small Ostrogothic force was enough to destroy the Vandals who had landed. After that Gunthamund had to renounce any and all tribute payments.[37]

Gunthamund's successor, Thrasamund (496–523), is considered the most educated and peaceful, indeed the most likable, Vandal king. And still the balance sheet of his long reign was disastrous: no accommodation with the Catholic majority but adherence to an uncompromising Arianism; severe setbacks against the Berbers, whose camels struck panic in the horses of the Vandal cavalry—the result was the first catastrophic defeat of the Vandals in a pitched battle.[38]

It was probably still in the year 500, immediately after celebrating his Roman *tricennalia* (festival celebrated once in thirty years), that Theodoric the Great married his widowed sister Amalafrida to Thrasamund. In return the Vandals had to be "content with an alliance of friendship instead of yearly tribute." The Amal lady went to Carthage with a considerable retinue of one thousand elite warriors and their five thousand servants to support Theodoric's policy of a barbarian balance of power. Her success, however, was modest, even though she brought as a dowry the territory of Lilybaeum in western Sicily. Thrasamund's fleet did not set sail to aid the Goths when the imperial navy was ravaging the coast of southern Italy in 507/508 and preventing Theodoric from marching to Gaul.

In 510 and 511 the Vandal king even sided with Gesalec, the Visigothic pretender to the throne, whom the Ostrogothic expeditionary force had driven out of Spain. When Gesalec, the older son of Alaric II, sought refuge in Carthage, he was supplied with ample resources, enough for him to return home and renew the resistance to Theodoric. This lead to ill feelings between Ravenna and Carthage; however, the tensions came to a head, if at all, only in a minor conflict limited to the Sicilian border region. Thrasamund realized the weakness of his position and apologized in word and deed. The gold he offered, in atonement, as it were, was turned down, but his written apology was accepted. When Theodoric's son-in-law Eutharic held the consulship in 519, Africa, as was customary, supplied the wild animals for the hunting games in Rome. Ravenna accepted this diplomatic kindness. After that Thrasamund remained Theodoric's ally until his death.

His successor, King Hilderic (523–530), broke with Ravenna and switched to the imperial camp. Thrasamund's widow, Amalafrida—who opposed the change in policy and may have also tried to upset the Vandal succession order—and her Gothic retinue were first outmaneuvered and then killed. In response Theodoric prepared a campaign of revenge against Carthage. A hastily constructed fleet of no fewer than a thousand ships was to set sail from its bases in Italy in the summer of 526, but the Ostrogothic warships remained in their ports because Theodoric died in August of that year. His successor registered only lame protests and left the punishment of the criminals to the powers in heaven. Theodoric's reaction suggests that his sister Amalafrida and her people had been murdered the year before (525), at the latest.[39]

Hilderic too, like his father, came to power as an old man. He had sworn to his dying predecessor that he would never grant the Catholics religious freedom, and had broken that pledge as soon as he had become king. The Catholics were therefore essentially on his side. Hilderic could safely dare to challenge the Italian Ostrogoths, since the mighty neighbor did not have a fleet worthy of the name. Moreover, Hilderic could rely on the personal friendship of Justinian, who still stood behind the throne in Constantinople when the crisis began but came to power himself in 527.

The two men had probably met in 523 in Constantinople when Hilderic was in the imperial city.[40] In general Hilderic was a ruler who struck his subjects as being quite affable, "but in military matters he was a weakling and didn't even want to hear about them." He had a nephew, Hoamer, who took his place as a general so effectively that he was called the "Achilles of the Vandals." But when this nephew also suffered a serious defeat at the hands of the Moors it spelled the end to Hilderic's rule and to the other descendants of Huneric's marriage to Eudocia. The half-Roman Hilderic was accused—as was the Ostrogothic Theodahad—of planning to surrender his rule and kingdom to Justinian. At that moment a nephew once removed, who as the grandson of Gaiseric's youngest son, Gento, would in any case have been the next in line for the throne, overthrew Hilderic in a putsch.[41]

6. GELIMER (530–534) AND THE END
OF THE VANDAL KINGDOM

Gelimer was the first who dared to openly, and at first successfully, violate Gaiseric's succession order. He took Hilderic's entire clan into custody and eliminated it together with its retinue. In so doing the usurper had put in question the internal and external legitimacy of the Vandal kingdom and had broken Vandal constitutional law as well as the eternal peace of 474. No challenge could have been greater to Justinian, an emperor who wanted to restore the Roman Empire with "arms and laws"[42] and who was at the same time the personal friend of the overthrown king.

Still, open war was some time off, since bloody battles with the Persians prevented Constantinople from opening a second front. For now Belisarius, one of Justinian's favorites, was needed as a general in the East. And so Constantinople shifted to vigorous remonstrances in Carthage; Justinian reminded Gelimer that he had violated every law and should at least allow Hilderic and his people to leave. The Vandal king responded to this with haughty words and the first measures directed against the life and limb of his prisoners: Hoamer was blinded, the conditions of detention for the others were made harsher. In 532 the emperor made peace with the Persians. In June 533 the preparations for war against Carthage had been concluded, and a small but superbly equipped army set sail from Constantinople.

To be sure, the enthusiasm of the Byzantine soldiers was underwhelming: many had hoped to take home-leave after the exhausting Persian war. That is the reason Hunnic elite units wanted to switch sides and join the Vandals during the battles for Carthage; after their use in a secondary theater of the Persian war they had not been granted leave, as they had been promised on oath, but had been ordered to march against the Vandals.[43]

There was also great, if unjustified, fear of Vandal sea power, which had once inflicted so many serious defeats on Constantinople. Except for the emperor and his closest advisers almost all high functionaries were against this adventure. It was simply not thought possible to successfully attack Carthage by sea if one had to do without the bases in Ostrogothic Sicily and southern Italy. Only when an eastern bishop assured the emperor that God had told him in a dream that Justinian would become the lord of Vandal Africa in order to liberate the Catholics there, did the mood change, though this alone was not enough to create great enthusiasm for war. But how could the bishop venture to make this prophecy? Did he perhaps know from Jewish merchants that the Vandal fleet no longer posed a serious threat?[44]

While Belisarius and five thousand horsemen—who were the only force that mattered, with the ten thousand infantry troops serving merely as their support[45]—were sailing along the coasts of the eastern Mediterranean and advancing only slowly because of summertime calms, Lybian Tripolis as well as Sardinia seceded from Gelimer. A Byzantine advance force subsequently landed in Tripolis, forcing the Vandal king to abandon plans of reconquest. Sardinia, however, he was not willing to let go. He equipped one of his brothers with five thousand choice warriors and one hundred fast sailers and dispatched him with the task of retaking the island. He himself continued to give his attention to a war with the Moors, because he either expected the Byzantine sea assault at a later time or didn't take it seriously in the first place. Amalasuintha permitted Belisarius to make a logistically important stopover in Sicily. But afterward she did nothing to prevent her *comes* of Syracuse from occupying Lilybaeum, the dowry of the dead Vandal queen Amalafrida, and to keep it despite imperial remonstrances.[46]

Belisarius finally went ashore with his troops on the last day of August 533 at Caput Vada (Ras Kaboudia), about two hundred and twenty kilometers southeast of Carthage. The generalissimo had been given all powers by his emperor to operate "like a basileus." Anybody who is familiar with Procopius knows the ambiguity of that term. Had Belisarius been given royal or vice-imperial power? In Carthage he would later sit on Gelimer's throne and administer the law. His conduct gave rise to accusations that he wanted to become king, indeed that he wanted to be a usurper, a tyrant, and this would lead to his premature departure from Africa. But that day was still some time off.[47]

At sea the Roman soldiers had threatened to take to flight the instant the Vandal fleet appeared. Now they all had solid ground under their feet and were marching against the Vandal capital on the imperial road, with the horsemen on the left and the well-protected ships on the right. They were coming as liberators and their behavior toward the civilian population was to reflect that; and in fact Belisarius punished the most minor transgressions with the utmost severity. The drawn out Roman line advanced at a speed of seventeen kilometers a day, not an overwhelming pace, but the Romans wanted to play it safe.

Gelimer understood that he now had to act. He had Hilderic and those around him, but not Hilderic's children, killed in prison, asked the Visigothic King Theudis for help, and gave orders to load a fast sailer in the port of Hippo Regius with his treasure so that, if the outcome of the war went against him, it could be taken to safety in Spain, which is also where he himself intended to go.[48] Then the Vandal king joined the first battle in Decimum, at the tenth milestone or fifteen kilometers south of Carthage; it ended in a fiasco. The battle was winnable for the Vandals, had Gelimer not been abandoned by fortune and good sense: the Vandals frittered away their strength; one of the king's brothers was killed, an incident that caused Gelimer to lose his composure and give up the battle as lost before it had even begun in earnest. Carthage could no longer be defended. Belisarius entered the old capital of Africa and restored the long-neglected fortifications. He took his seat on Gelimer's throne and handed down the law.[49] In the meantime the king's brother Tzazo, having made short work of the Sardinian rebels, returned home at the head of his elite warriors. The Vandal army gathered at the border between Numidia and Mauretania and advanced on Carthage in the mistaken belief that Belisarius would accept the battle they offered before the gates of the city. The Roman general, however, would not be deprived of the initiative.

Only in the middle of December 533 did Belisarius force the battle of Tricamarum, a site about thirty kilometers from Carthage but no longer identifiable today. The clash became a catastrophe for the Vandals, since Tzazo, the victor of Sardinia, was among those killed as hostilities began. Gelimer secretly left the battlefield when the Roman troops advanced. Once again the king gave up everything for lost even before the troops came to blows.

The Vandals turned to flee and many were killed in the process. The Byzantines captured the enemy camp, including women and children and enormous treasures that nearly drove Belisarius's soldiers out of their minds. Gelimer hid with a friendly Moorish tribe and for some time defied the Roman siege of his mountain fastness. In the end he surrendered, supposedly because he saw two children, his nephew and a small Berber child, half-dead from starvation, fighting over a loaf of bread.

But this time Gelimer did not surrender unconditionally: while he was willing to be settled in the East, he demanded the allocation of rich landholdings and sufficient income as well as elevation to the patrician status. Though he did receive his lands in Asia Minor, he never became *patricius* because he would not convert to the Catholic faith. At least on the question of whether or not he would be granted this honorary title Gelimer showed a little backbone. But by the end of March or the beginning of April 534 at the latest, the downfall of the Vandal kingdom had been sealed.[50]

Belisarius set sail from Carthage at the end of spring 534, carrying with him the enormous Vandal royal treasure, Gelimer and his retinue, and Hilderic's children. Despite all his successes this was a hasty departure, much too early to really have broken the resistance of the Vandals and Moors. Belisarius urged haste because he wanted to clear himself before Justinian of accusations that had arisen as a result of the way in which he had exercised his vice-imperial power. In spite of the charges the general was graciously received by his lord, quite in contrast to the reception he would later get after what was presumed to be the final victory over the Ostrogoths. Justinian granted Belisarius a large victory procession in Constantinople, but not a triumph, even if triumphal elements may have been part of the historicizing ceremony.

Justinian himself celebrated the victory over the Vandals: "At most, Belisarius is mentioned for his role in capturing Gelimer and presenting him to the emperor at victory celebrations; at the least, his role is passed over in silence."[51] Justinian promised Belisarius the consulate for 535 and command of the next campaign of conquest, the attack against the Ostrogothic kingdom.

7. EPILOGUE

Procopius's account of the victory celebration in Constantinople that officially ended the Vandal war comes at the end of chapter nine of the second book. But the second book of the *Bellum Vandalicum* has a total of twenty-eight chapters, so even a reader with no prior knowledge must conclude that Justinian's war against the Vandals did not by any means come to an end with its official termination. Resistance came from the wives and daughters of the slain Vandal warriors, who were evidently married off in large numbers to the emperor's soldiers and who laid claim to the possessions of their dead husbands and fathers. Not surprisingly, their new husbands supported these claims and prevented the imperial administration from confiscating the conquered possessions for the emperor.[52]

Resistance came also from the Arian priests,[53] and a mutiny broke out at the island of Lesbos among the five squadrons that had been levied as "Justinian's Vandals" and dispatched to the East. A few hundred of these elite warriors sailed home again and joined the Moors.[54] And putting down the Moors was something the Romans were not able to do at all, in spite of many impressive victories.[55] Moreover, quite a few native Romans still sided with the Vandals. Whereas Gelimer, for example, had made a Roman his treasurer and had successfully called upon the peasants of the plain to kill marauding Roman soldiers and small detachments, Belisarius had a wealthy man from Carthage, whom his own secretary accused of high treason, impaled outside the gates of the city "as a warning to others." The subsequent reintroduction of the Roman tax system turned the African provincials fully against the imperial government.[56]

To this day the question is asked how it could happen that "the fourth descendant of Gaiseric, and his kingdom at the height of its wealth and military strength, were completely undone in so short a time by five thousand men coming in as invaders and having not a place to cast anchor. For such was the number of the horsemen who followed Belisarius and carried through the whole war against the Vandals."[57]

To Procopius, who penned these words, it was God and his rod Tyche ("fate") who confused Gelimer's mind in order to bring him and his people to ruin. When the captive king was handed over to the victorious Belisarius, he burst into horrible laughter, which some took as a sign of his madness but others as a response to the blows of fate.[58]

Needless to say, the "Germanic" (*teutsche*[59]) nineteenth century was not satisfied with the workings of fate as an explanation for the Vandal catastrophe. Instead, scholars believed it was apparent "that the Vandals, after settling in Africa, sank into the mire of vice. And this would not have changed even if a larger inflow of Germans had occurred, since such an inflow would have simply flowed into a swamp."[60] Procopius, too, seems to support this verdict—or rather, condemnation—when he writes: "For the Vandals, since the time when they gained possession of Libya, used to indulge in baths, all of them, every day, and enjoyed a table abounding in all things, the sweetest and best that the earth and sea produce. And they wore gold very generally, and clothed themselves in the Medic garments, which now they call "*seric*," and passed their time, thus dressed, in theaters and hippodromes and in other pleasurable pursuits, and above all else in hunting. And they had dancers and mimes and all other things to hear and see that are of a musical nature or otherwise merit attention among men. And the most of them dwelt in parks, which were well supplied with water and trees; and they had great numbers of banquets, and all manner of sexual pleasures were in great vogue among them."

In a word, they had to come to ruin because they were behaving like the Roman upper class, which, as the modern age has known since Edward Gibbon at the latest, was doomed to fall.[61] If the unbiased reader today asks why daily hygiene should render someone unfit for war, one should point out that in late-antique baths, bathing tended to be rather a secondary activity. However, it is not quite understandable why hunting, generally regarded as a preparation for real war, should have made the Vandals weak and soft. But most of all, and modern advocates of the popularized Hippocratic climate theory should take good note of this, Procopius's quote is always taken out of context.

The eyewitness and contemporary Procopius, one must realize, wrote in the dialectical tradition of an ethnography that gained its insights through comparison and contrast. While Caesar had compared the wild and utterly uncivilized Germans with the far less barbaric Gauls,[62] Procopius concerned himself with the striking contrast that existed between the Vandals and Moors. The Berbers—the word means "barbarians"—were barbarians who were unbelievably modest and easily satisfied. When they prepared for battle, they were careful "to abstain from all injustices and from all foods tending toward luxury and most of all from association with women."[63] Thus they did the exact opposite of the Vandals, but even this did not make them invincible: they won many fights and battles with the Romans, but they also lost many.

To be sure, another Greek had already noted after Gaiseric's death that Vandal striking power and enthusiasm for war had noticeably waned. But in this instance the reason lay in Huneric's decision to avoid any military entanglement with Byzantium. By contrast, there is no passage in which Procopius explained the downfall of the Vandals as the result of their dissoluteness and effeminacy. To him the responsibility simply lay with God and fate.

If this explanation is insufficient to modern ears, we can find enough "real" reasons for the disaster in the account of Procopius: the Vandals' inordinate overestimation of their own sea power, as well as their belief they could do without fortified bases and cities; Gelimer's inability to grasp the situation, his lack of determination and self-discipline, as well as the failure on his part and that of his entourage to use proper reconnaissance and intelligence services and evaluate their information. In short, the less capable general Gelimer lost to the more capable and shrewder general Belisarius. This course of events would repeat itself during the following years in Ostrogothic Italy. However, at no time did the Vandals ever pursue a unique path of development.

EIGHT

Odovacar, or the Roman Empire That Did Not End

1. ODOVACAR (476–493)

Odovacar was murdered in 493 at the age of sixty, which means that he was born in or around the year 433. Accordingly he came into the world shortly before or after the Hunnic brothers Bleda and Attila assumed power. Odovacar's father was Edica-Edekon, who would go far during the forties as servant to Attila and would become king of the Danubian Scirians after the downfall of the Hunnic Empire. The East Germanic Scirians of the migration period were only a pale reflection of their former glory. Their name means "the pure, the unmixed," which places them opposite the mixed Celtic-Germanic people of the Bastarni, who had become known to and struck terror into the Old World as early as 200 B.C. Both peoples were broken up and scattered under the onslaught from Goths and Huns. Thus the name of the Bavarian town of Scheyern probably goes back to a group of Scirians. History offered the Scirians Edica and Odovacar a last chance to gather their "old" tribe and lead it to a new life.[1]

The quarrel over whether Edica was a Hun or a Scirian is about as meaningful as the question of whether someone is a U.S. citizen or a Californian, a German or a Bavarian, an Austrian or a Tyrolean. For as long as the Hunnic Empire was flourishing there did not exist within its sphere of power any political identities of Germanic peoples—with the probable exception of the Amal Goths and possibly the Gepids. A later Greek tradition about Edica's Thuringian origins could be correct,[2] but it could just as likely be a misunderstanding that really referred to his membership in the Scirian royal family of the Turcilingi.[3] Whatever the case may be, all known members of the Edica clan had Germanic names.

The name of Odovacar's mother is not known; she is, in any case, attested to have been a Scirian. Odovacar's older brother was called Hunulf; after

469 he took up service for the eastern empire and rose to become commander in chief of Illyria. However, either unwilling or unable to continue
his career in the East, he joined his brother, the Italian king, in 479 and became his right-hand man. Odovacar's wife was Sunigilda, his son, Thela.
While his father Edica was killed in battle in 469, all other known members
of the Scirian royal clan perished in 493 along with Odovacar.[4]

After the battle at the Nedao River in 454/455, Edika had set up a
Scirian kingdom in the middle Alföld, the plain between the Danube and
the Tisza; it was to last only half a generation. In 469 a coalition of anti-
Gothic tribes lost the battle at the Pannonian Bolia River; Edika was killed
and his sons left their homeland. Hunulf headed for the eastern empire,
Odovacar went to Italy via Noricum, where he visited Saint Severin. He was
followed by numerous Rugian and Herulian bands and most of the surviving
Scirians.

At the court in Ravenna the Scirian federate Odovacar was accepted
into Emperor Anthemius's first rank of guards. In this capacity he played an
important, if not decisive role, as early as 472. At that time the conflict between Anthemius and his supreme commander, the half-Goth Ricimer,
turned into open war. Odovacar broke the oath of loyalty he had sworn to
his lord, joined the side of the patrician general, and in so doing hastened
the emperor's downfall. Ricimer carried the day, but he could not savor his
victory for long: only six weeks later he died an undeserved natural death.
The importance of the political example of Ricimer for Odovacar's later rule
must not be overlooked.

What happened next was that western emperors, some recognized by
Constantinople and some not, followed one another in rapid succession.[5]
After Nepos, the last legitimate ruler of the western empire, had given up his
cause as lost in August of 475 and had fled into his native Dalmatia, the
supreme commander and *patricius* Orestes installed his little son, Romulus,
remembered by posterity as "little emperor" (Augustulus), as imperator.

Orestes, a native of Pannonia, had begun his career as Latin secretary to
Attila and had found himself at the Hunnic royal court in opposition to
Odovacar's father, Edika. The conflict was a matter of life and death, and
Odovacar's father very nearly came to an ignominious end. Now his son
faced the old enemy in Italy: Orestes had risen to the rank of generalissimo,
while the royal son Odovacar was the noblest among the barbarian warriors serving in the Italian army.

Federate warriors had been stationed in Italy for some time, and they
were soon as numerous as the regular troops. But while the Roman army
had a vested legal claim to a third of the curial taxes, the economic security
of the federates of Italy was far less clearly established; they did not receive
"regular" pay but extraordinary monies, agreed upon by treaty, to be sure,
but revocable. In 476 the barbarians in Italy demanded to be given equal sta-

tus with the Roman army. Orestes, as the highest West Roman magistrate, rejected the demand, while Odovacar promised to fulfill it should he attain supramagisterial power. This led to rebellion: the federate warriors did the logical thing by raising the Scirian up as king on August 23, 476, and marching against Orestes and the *exercitus Romanus*. Only five days later Odovacar captured Pavia and had Orestes killed in Piacenza. On September 4, 476, at the latest, Odovacar was lord of Ravenna, where Orestes' brother Paulus met his death. Little Romulus was deposed and allowed to live as a private person. It is not impossible that he is identical with a certain Romulus who was still living around Naples with his mother in Theodoric's time.

At first glance Odovacar's seizure of power was a usurpation of unprecedented magnitude. A barbarian, a non-Roman, had deposed a Roman emperor in the original heartland of the empire. He had taken on the hated royal title and was getting ready to rule in the emperor's place, for he had taken over the imperial administration and was handing out Roman military and civilian offices. Of course, a closer look reveals a much more complex picture: in the eyes of Constantinople, which had never revoked its recognition of Nepos, Romulus had already been a usurper, which means that Odovacar, strictly speaking, had only driven out a usurper and had not deposed an emperor.

This is also why Odovacar's coinage was issued in the name of Nepos until 480, the year Nepos was murdered. Moreover, the unwritten constitution of the late Roman Empire did not know a *tyrannus quoad titulum* ("usurper as to title") but only the *tyrannus quoad executionem*. ("usurper as to fact"): that is to say, the person whose bid for power failed and who was not recognized by the other half of the empire was regarded as a usurper. While the question of de facto success was a matter of real power, settling the question of recognition seemed possible only through successful negotiation with Constantinople.

As his last official act, Romulus, under pressure from Odovacar, dispatched a senatorial delegation. The eminent lords announced in Constantinople that they renounced having an emperor of their own and described the Scirian as the man "who had been selected by them as the one suited for maintaining their state happily," since he was well versed in governing and the art of war. At the same time the senators asked that Odovacar, who was willing to give up his kingship, be appointed *patricius* and supreme commander by the emperor and entrusted with the administration of "the Italies."

However, envoys from Dalmatia also arrived at this time. They conveyed congratulations in Nepos's name on the end of the usurpation and demanded money and an army so that the legitimate western emperor could win back his dominion. Zeno, the eastern emperor, referred Odovacar's senators to Nepos, not without holding them jointly responsible for the latter's expulsion and the murder of the erstwhile emperor, Anthemius. At the same time he accepted the possibility that Nepos might appoint Odovacar a *patricius*, which would have made him the highest-ranking general of the West, and in his letter of response he already addressed the Scirian as *patricius* without inquiring first in Dalmatia.

For the moment Constantinople had gained time, while neither granting recognition nor ruling it out at some future date. That recognition might be granted was a serious concern in distant Gaul, as we learn from another delegation that the Roman King Syagrius had in all likelihood dispatched to Constantinople with the task of lodging a sharp protest against Odovacar's recognition as king of the western empire.

Odovacar, however, gave further signs of goodwill: he sent the imperial emblems (*ornamenta palatii*) to Constantinople, and he continued to date his charters by consular years and not, like the Vandal king of Africa, for example, by his own era or even regnal years. When Nepos was murdered in the spring of 480, Odovacar executed the assassin. From 480, at the latest, the consul who was chosen for the western empire was also recognized in Constantinople. In 483 this same man acted officially as Odovacar's representative in the papal elections.

However, despite attempts at a mutual rapprochement, there can be no doubt that the situation between East and West remained tense in the early eighties, and that Odovacar was never given full imperial recognition. We hear of no treaty that was ever concluded between Constantinople and Ravenna—and this in spite of the fact that Odovacar saw the legal basis of his rule as resting on Roman offices.

Men like Ricimer, his Burgundian nephew Gundobad, and eventually Orestes too had tried to rule Italy and the Regnum Hesperium in the emperor's place. Each one had been a *patricius* of the West. To be sure, the *occidentis patricius* was basically only an honorary title for the western *magister utriusque militiae*. But historical developments had, since the beginning of the fifth century, made the position of the supreme commander of the western empire, the "master of both military branches," into a function that had long since broken all bureaucratic boundaries and had made those who held it into vice-emperors of the West, endowing them with supramagisterial power. Odovacar, as king of Italy, built upon this position of power after he had abolished the regular Roman army. Constantinople could not yet reconcile itself to this situation, and for good reason.

It is generally overlooked that the East Roman imperial government had already in 475 been confronted with similar demands from a barbarian king, Theodoric Strabo. He had been far more menacing than Odovacar, since he was standing outside the walls of Constantinople. The Goth Strabo had supported a usurper against Zeno, suggesting to his candidate, interestingly enough, that he abolish the regular army, "since the Goths were sufficient." In 477 Strabo sought to arrange himself again with Zeno, who had weathered the crisis. The emperor, however, thwarted the peace negotiations not least because he aroused the opposition of the court and the army by recalling those outrageous earlier demands.

Odovacar's rule meant a dozen years of largely undisturbed development and peace in Italy. In Sicily he arrived at a compromise with the Vandals. Following the death of Nepos, Dalmatia was reunited with Italy without objection, and the alpine border was conceded to the Visigothic greater power under King Euric. Upon the advice of Roman experts, Odovacar set up the royal *patrimonium*. This newly created institution was so successful that it was not only preserved under Theodoric the Great, but was adopted by the Spanish Visigoths and even the imperial government of Constantinople. The bureaucracy administered the enormous private holdings of the ruler of Italy, to which were added the provinces of Sicily and Dalmatia, and everything conquered or reconquered within the prefecture of Italy.

The situation between Constantinople and the Italian kingdom grew markedly tense when Odovacar, like Theodoric Strabo before him, armed for open intervention in favor of the anti-Zeno party. In an effort to fend off a threatening war on two fronts, the emperor mobilized the Rugians, who since 454/455 had been setting up in northern Lower Austria a kingdom federated with Ravenna. The Rugians for their part now believed that they had the chance to fulfill an old wish and move to Italy, as so many tribal brothers had done before them. Odovacar, however, reacted swiftly. A bloody conflict within the Rugian royal family was tantamount to a breach of the treaty with Ravenna. Now the last Italian armies marched to the Danube in Noricum to chastise barbarian federates and at the same time eliminate the Roman opposition that had found a home there after 476.

Odovacar attacked the Rugian kingdom in the late fall of 487 and destroyed it. The king and his Ostrogothic wife fell into the hands of the victor and were put to death in Italy. Their son was able to escape with scattered Rugian remnants, but his attempt to reconquer the ancestral kingdom in 488 failed. This time Hunulf, Odovacar's older brother, appeared on the scene and drove off the Rugians. Those provincials whom Saint Severin had gathered in what is now central Lower Austria and placed under Rugian protection were forced by the victors to leave their homeland and emigrate to Italy.

This measure eliminated the economic basis for the formation of any other East Germanic kingdom. Driven off by Odovacar's military might, the son of the Rugian king and his followers sought refuge and help from Theodoric the Great. They had to move from Danubian Noricum to the Gothic king in modern-day Bulgaria, whom the emperor had already won over for an attack on Italy. Without going to Constantinople again,

Theodoric concluded a formal treaty with Zeno, which stipulated that "after defeating Odovacar, he shall, in return for his efforts, rule in the emperor's place until the latter shall arrive [in Italy]."

Nearly a year passed before Theodoric's Goths reached the borders of Italy. It was not until August 28, 489, that the thirty-eight-year-old Amal encountered his nearly sixty-year-old enemy for the first time. Theodoric's crossing of the Isonzo was the beginning of a "new time." Less than a month later he had reached Verona, where the king of Italy offered the historical Dietrich von Bern his second battle. Once again the Amal was victorious, but the war for Italy was not over yet. Theodoric suffered such serious setbacks that he was not able to go on the offensive again until the middle of 490.

The Visigothic King Alaric II gave one of the very rare demonstrations of Gothic solidarity and sent his warriors to Italy. The battle of Adda, probably located where the road from Lodi to Cremona crosses the river, was fought on August 11, 490. Odovacar was defeated yet again. Under these circumstances it was meaningless that he had moved to Rome in the first half of the year to have his son proclaimed Caesar. Odovacar had to withdraw to Ravenna; the "battle of Ravenna" had begun.

Odovacar's last large-scale sortie failed on the night of July 9/10, 491. But Ravenna's fall was still years away. Not until February 25, 493, did Johannes, the bishop of Ravenna, mediate a treaty by which Odovacar and Theodoric were to rule jointly over Italy. Odovacar gave his son Thela as a hostage, though he was able to obtain from Theodoric a security guarantee for his life. Theodoric had formally broken the treaty with the emperor by agreeing to the negotiated terms, but it did allow him to enter Ravenna on March 5, 493.

A short time later Odovacar was killed by Theodoric. The Scirian royal clan soon shared the fate of its leader; only Thela survived his father for a while. Many barbarian supporters of Odovacar and their families were apprehended and killed. Despite the terrible end of Odovacar and his people, Theodoric continued what the Scirian had begun. But the Amal surpassed his predecessor Odovacar not least because he had more power and more time to finish what the latter had begun. In other words, Theodoric's Italian kingdom was the more stable, richer, and stronger regnum of Odovacar, and soon after the elimination of the Scirian it won full recognition from Constantinople.[6]

2. THE ROMAN EMPIRE THAT DID NOT END (476)

There remains the question how contemporaries reacted to the events of 476. Especially in the older German historiography, this year marked an epochal change: when Romulus Augustulus was deposed the Roman Empire and antiquity came to an end and the "German" Middle Ages began.

This view was opposed by Ludwig Schmidt, and many others have subsequently followed suit. Recently, however, 476 seems to have regained importance as the year of epochal change.[7] This has been prompted by some fifth-century sources whose statements have previously been unjustly neglected. Leaving aside the exponents of Christian end-times expectations, these sources stem for the most part from East Roman authors or circles in Rome close to Constantinople. But hardly a single one of these writers declared the end of the Roman Empire as the res publica; rather, in their view the Imperium Romanum had ceased to exist regionally. There was good reason for this distinction.

The Vandals had already been defeated some time ago and the Gothic besiegers of Rome weren't getting anywhere when Justinian, on August 31, 537, decreed his important reform in the dating of official documents and ordered that counting be done by imperial years.[8] In the preamble to the law, the emperor referred primarily to the res publica, making a distinction between it and the imperium. Aeneas had founded the res publica. Its second beginning (*origo*) went back to Romulus, the founder of the city, and the first lawgiver, Numa. Only the third founding by the generals, that is to say, the imperatores Caesar and Augustus, had created the imperium on the basis of the res publica. Thus, where the "carelessness of the predecessors" had led to losses and catastrophes, one spoke of the retreat of the empire and meant by it the temporary abandonment for military reasons of either the non-Italian territories or the entire West inclusive of Rome. The fact that these profound changes were linked with the name of another Romulus, after the first Romulus had just been hailed as the second founder of the "western dominion of the Roman people," imparted an added fascination to these reflections. Moreover, this "Roman people" was no longer described as the general populus, but was seen as one particular gens among the gentes.

At the same time Constantinople would not give up an inch of the land that the res publica had possessed in the former western empire; Justinian's reconquest is sufficient proof of this. However, no tears were shed in the city of the great Constantine over the end of the western emperorship. And certain senators in Rome shared these views and may in fact have played an important part in their development.[9] This group, which clung to its opposition to the barbarian-Gothic Ravenna, included Eugippius, the author of the *Vita sancti Severini*. In his work we find the following description of the situation along the Danube in Raetia-Noricum: "At the time when the Romanum Imperium still existed, the soldiers of many cities [that is to say, fortresses (*castella*)] were paid by public funds to protect the border. Once this order had ceased to exist, the military units dissolved along with the border organization."

This passage has been rightfully related to the year 476, when Odovacar, following his seizure of power, dispensed with a military presence at the borders outside of Italy. This "narrowing of the Roman name" is also confirmed by other contemporaries. But what had happened was not that the Roman res publica (or Greek, *politeia*) had come to an end, even if in the West it had temporarily been transformed into a *tyrannis* by Odovacar's usurpation; rather, the Imperium Romanum (or Greek, *basileia*) had temporarily ceased to exist in certain areas.

Two examples from the political terminology of the Roman-barbarian regna demonstrate how accurate and important this terminological distinction is. The rulers of these regna put forth the claim they had replaced the imperium on a regional level. Thus in juxtaposing the Roman Empire and a given kingdom, it was possible very early on to speak of two regna.[10] The Germanic vernacular languages, for example, made no distinction between empire and kingdom; they have no separate words for them but have to form compound terms since both entities are the realm. At the same time the Roman-barbarian regna distinguished themselves from the res publica. As a rule no king claimed to be continuing the res publica, with the exception of Theodoric the Great and his Amal successors, who certainly did call their realm by that name.[11] But Ostrogothic Italy was not merely a federate kingdom on Roman soil; it had also remained the western half of the Roman Empire, that is to say, of the res publica. In the course of Justinian's reconquest, the western empire disappeared for a long time, and the res publica was narrowed down to the empire, whose capital was Constantinople.

And so Procopius commented on the victories of Belisarius over Vandals and Goths with the statement that the general "has brought back their wealth from the enemy and restored it once more to the res publica [*politeia*] and recovered for the empire [*basileia*] in a short space of time almost one-half of its territory on land and sea."[12] The empire existed as an eternal politeia regardless of its territorial extent; the treasures of the mighty barbarian kings Geiseric and Theodoric fell to the res publica, while the reconquest of former Roman imperial territories increased the size of the imperium, its actual military might.

Applying these observations to the problem we are examining, we see that Odovacar no longer could or wished to exercise the function of the Roman imperator along the Danube as well as on the other side of the Maritime Alps. As long as the military means were not available, the Imperium Romanum as the legitimate and properly functioning "generalship" of the emperor who embodied the res publica was no longer present here.

But two things demonstrate that Noricum ripense, especially, continued to belong to the Roman Empire in the sense of the res publica after 476: first, the activities of Severinus, who was probably sent by Constantinople, and, second, the presence of Roman opposition figures, who had fled from Odovacar's Italy to the Danube. Finally, the two Rugian wars of 487 and 488 reveal that the king of Italy was perfectly able to send armies to the Danube to ward off a real or presumed threat to Italy. But the troops did not re-establish the Imperium Romanum here; they merely fought against federate barbarians and the Roman opposition and subsequently forced the native provincials they got hold of to emigrate. It was not possible to undo such a policy everywhere. But Theodoric the Great was able to subject once more to "the Roman name" large areas abandoned by his predecessor outside of Italy but within the prefecture of Italy.

From this perspective, Odovacar's most serious mistake was his fre-quently unjustified policy of territorial abandonment. It created numer-ous political vacuums outside of the narrow borders of Italy, and whatever powers moved into them did so only to the peninsula's disadvantage. Theo-doric's revision of Odovacar's policy was not universally successful; the same holds true for Justinian's reconquest. The serious territorial losses were un-doubtedly a result of Odovacar's seizure of power; however, not all of them were suffered at a single blow in 476.

Whether the date that marks the end of the late-antique dual emperor-ship (which would not experience its medieval revival until Christmas day of 800) defines a moment when "history holds its breath" depends on the perspective of the observer. Judging from constitutional and institutional cri-teria, the year 476 brought the non-end of the Roman Empire.[13]

Of course this is not to say that the West Roman Empire did not fall. With-out doubt, the imperial Roman state was replaced by Roman-barbarian kingdoms in the two prefectures of Italy and Gaul and their neighboring lands: from Sirmium in western Illyria to Carthage in Africa, from Cadiz in southern Spain to Cologne in lower Germany and Hadrian's wall in Britain. However, there are many reasons why these epochal changes oc-curred, and though the invasion of the barbarians has for centuries been one of the most popular reasons ideologically, in actuality it tended to be of secondary importance.

Following the moralistic-ethnographic historiographers of the Middle Ages, the humanists were the ones who interpreted the fall of Rome as the result of Germanic conquests. And to this day ancient historians and their supporters in the media tend to be the ones most ready to agree with their humanist predecessors, if only for the understandable desire to have a spectacular, definitive finale to antiquity.

Recently the attempts to explain the fall of Rome were summarized into six explanatory models. There is the religious explanation, which places the blame on Christianity, regardless of whether Rome's fall is seen as a positive or negative development. The new religion supposedly promoted withdrawal and refusal, religious conflicts led to civil wars, and the members of the social classes who had hitherto been the pillars of the state became clerics and were thus lost to the state and to society.

Economic and social explanations are naturally invoked above all by Marxist historians, but their dogma of class warfare has hindered more than helped their approach. To be sure, the ancient sources are full of complaints about the miserable living conditions of the lower classes and the enormous disparity in wealth between the rich and the poor. In a situation where three Italian senators of the fifth century had a yearly income equal to the entire budget of the West Roman Empire, the res publica as the affair of all citizens had become an illusion and, within the sphere of influence of these senators, had been replaced by their personal rule. Small wonder that many non-Marxist historians and sociologists too, among them Max Weber and Ludo Moritz Hartmann, charged ancient civilization with serious systemic flaws and were and are of the opinion that "a continuation of the Imperium Romanum would have impeded the development of mankind, so that Rome had to fall for the sake of progress."

Although it may amaze us today, the scientific approach found remarkably wide support for some time. As long as it was merely a question of explaining the end of Rome as the result of exhaustion of the soil, a period of drought (measured by California's redwood trees), the dwindling of mineral resources, or the impotence of the male population due to lead poisoning (the cities drew their drinking water from lead pipes), one could easily settle the matter and move on to other issues. But when the Nazis saw the fall of Rome as an example of "racial death," they were only one step away from drawing from this explanation lessons for the present and fighting against what was falsely seen as a repetition of history with every means possible and with the most horrible consequences.

A fourth group of interpreters sees the cause of Rome's end in the failure of domestic policy, which was not able to cushion and shape the Roman-Germanic opposition in creative cooperation.

These explanatory models are transcended and discarded by the morphological idea that "cultures, like plants, grow, flourish, and pass away." The fall of Rome is presented in organic metaphors, which include the widely used term "late antiquity." Oswald Spengler and Arnold Toynbee have become known as proponents of this approach; it is probably less well known that important philosophers as well as historians, the likes of Jakob Burckhardt, Jan Huizinga, and Andreas Alföldi, preferred the morphological interpretation. "The problem of the theory of decadence lies in the fact that the basic force of a culture can be described only with metaphysical terms such as spirit of the people, soul of the culture, life force. By contrast, anyone who regards culture as merely the sum of cultural phenomena will declare the idea of a guiding cultural substance to be a chimera, so that no agreement can be compelled precisely on the central concept."[14]

The sixth and final explanatory approach accords central importance to the Germanic tribes, who play only a minor role in the other models. It was they who conquered, destroyed, indeed murdered the Roman Empire. This touches on the subject of this book and compels us to take a position. Let us assume for a moment that we know nothing about the actual events but only the approximate size of the Roman population and of the Germanic tribes who invaded the empire. The conclusion would be that about twenty thousand Visigoths conquered a Roman territory about eight hundred thousand square kilometers in size and with a population of approximately 10 million. A warrior band of the same size would have seized the prefecture of Italy, which was smaller in size but had about the same number of inhabitants. About fifteen thousand Vandals in Africa turned about 3 million Romans into their subjects. And so on.

In purely numerical terms these takeovers are thus inconceivable as conquests, and we haven't even taken into consideration yet that Germanic armies were in actuality far more preoccupied fighting each other than subjecting the Romans. Thus Theodoric the Great won his spectacular victories exclusively over Germanic competitors and was unable throughout his life to stand up to a single Roman army that was led with determination.

So what happened in 476? Did the Roman Empire perhaps not fall at all? Only a very specific circle of Roman-Italian senators seemed to have become aware at the height of Theodoric's reign, and later under different circumstances in exile in Constantinople, that a new epoch had begun in 476, that the Imperium Romanum in Rome and over the West had come to an end with the deposition of Romulus Augustulus.

Symmachus, the father-in-law of Boethius and speaker of the senate who was executed in 525 on Theodoric's orders, seems to have been the first who formulated this thought in his now lost *Historia Romana*. But it was not only a few Latin Byzantines in the middle of the sixth century who were witnesses to the notion of the end of the empire. Their Greek contemporary Procopius held the same opinion.

After the sorrow of the "true" Romans and their literary exponents had been left unconsoled and their hopes for a restoration unfulfilled by Justinian's policy, they fell silent, and the notion began to prevail that the Roman Empire could not have fallen because it had to last to the end of time and thus outlast all particularisms of the barbarians.

In our own day and age we will be wary of thinking in chiliastic dimensions or embracing false eschatological hopes and fears. The appearance of the Germanic peoples, as after them the Slavs and Arabs, must be understood not merely in terms of downfall and destruction; instead, we can see in it the transformation of the Roman world—albeit a painful one—and the emergence of early medieval Europe.[15]

NINE

Theodoric (451–526) and Clovis (466/467–511)

1. THE TOPIC AND ITS BURDEN

In 1933, a very short monograph entitled "Theoderich und Chlodwig" ("Theodoric and Clovis") was published in Germany. Its author, Wolfram von den Steinen, was a well-known German medievalist who had shortly before published a lengthy critical study of the sources, *Chlodwig's Übergang zum Christentum* (Clovis's conversion to Christianity).[1] These two works reflect the greatness and the poverty of the historical profession. The methodically superb study of the sources produced insights of timeless value; however, von Steinen's effort to apply these insights in practical terms to our time" shows him to have been captive to his own age in a way that may seem difficult for a modern reader to comprehend, all the more so since he was always opposed to National Socialism and had to publish his scholarly study in an Austrian journal. In the monograph we read that Theodoric had the sons of the senators presented to him, "and from the crowd of mongrelized or overbred weaklings his bright eye selected the true, the 'last Romans.'"[2]

Reading these words we realize with dismay how difficult it is to escape one's own age, even if one opposes its mad ideas, and it is always shocking to find that the persecutors and the persecuted speak the same language. What makes this case so poignant is, of course, the fact that it stands at the beginning of a period of incomprehensible horror. But historians must accept that this past is also part of the history of their discipline. All this lends greater justification to the attempt to free the corrupted topics from their heavy ideological burden. It is in this spirit that I undertake once again the always popular comparison between Theodoric and Clovis. The reader who weighs it against earlier studies will decide whether we know more today or are any wiser.[3]

2. CHILDHOOD AND YOUTH

The Amal Theodoric and the Merovingian Clovis were both born the sons of kings in border regions of the Roman Empire. While Clovis saw the light of day on Roman soil, Theodoric most likely was born beyond the Roman pale, though he moved to Pannonia I as a little boy. Clovis's birthplace could have been Tournai in Belgica II; his father's grave, in any case, was found in 1653 in that city, at that time located in the Hapsburg Netherlands and today in Belgium. In neither case is the year of birth securely known and each must therefore be deduced.

In 456, attacking Hun warriors caught Theodoric's uncle Valamir by complete surprise, forcing him to fight without help from his brothers Thiudimir and Vidimir. He was still able to defeat the Huns, "who were hunting renegade Goths and escaped slaves." Thiudimir's son Theodoric was supposedly born on the day the news of Valamir's victory reached him. But if he came into the world in 456, he could not have gone to Constantinople as a hostage three years later as an eight-year-old. It is not only that simple arithmetic makes this impossible; one must also consider that the parties involved would have hardly given or taken a three-year-old as a hostage, given his low life expectancy far from the family. The chronological difficulties can be avoided if Theodoric was five years older, having been born in 451. In that case the Hunnic defeat that was announced at his birth was the battle on the Catalaunian fields. But at that time three Amals were among the losers, so that Gothic tradition would have had every reason to move Theodoric's birth in order to preserve the point of the anecdote and make him a member of the Roman Empire, too.

Of Clovis we read that he died in 511 at the age of forty-five, in the thirtieth year of his reign. This means that he was born in 466/467 and was about fifteen years younger than the Goth Theodoric.

Byzantine sources, and those that depend on them, call Theodoric a son of Valamir. There are two reasons for this: Valamir was for the longest time supreme chief and king of the Pannonian Ostrogoths, while Thiudimir succeeded his older brother for only four years. In addition, Theodoric inherited the subkingdom of Valamir, who had no sons. But Theodoric's father was in fact the middle brother, Thiudimir. Theodoric's mother was called Ereleuva-Erelieva and outlived Thiudimir by decades; she followed her son to Italy, where she was regarded as queen. At this point, at the latest, she had become a Catholic and had been given the baptismal name Eusebia. Tradition calls her Thiudimir's *concubina,* which merely means that the marriage between Theodoric's parents was not fully valid. Perhaps there was a religious difference between them—Thiudimir was an Arian—or they were of different ethnic descent, which amounted to much the same thing. That Theodoric, like the Vandal King Gaiseric, had a mother of provincial Roman background is not impossible.

Clovis's parents were Childeric and Basina. His father was a Salian Merovingian, his mother probably a Thuringian of royal blood. The story soon circulated that she had left her first husband, the Thuringian king, and had gone to Childeric to be his wife. She was led to do this by the Merovingian's strength and sexual prowess (*utilitas*). According to Gregory of Tours, she told her new husband: "'You can be sure that if I knew anyone else, even far across the sea, who was more capable than you, I should have sought him out and gone to live with him instead.'"

Nothing is known about Clovis's childhood and early youth. He must have grown up in or around Tournai until 481/482, when he succeeded his father at the age of no more than sixteen. Theodoric, however, had to leave his parents and his home at the age of eight to go to Constantinople as a hostage. There he remained from about 459 to about 469; that is to say, he spent his childhood and youth up to age eighteen in the capital of a foreign empire. It requires no special knowledge of developmental psychology to gauge how much this stay must have shaped the young son of the Gothic king. Theodoric is said to have enjoyed the emperor's favor. This piece of information from Gothic tradition may well be true, though it is also in keeping with that tradition's overall bias.

At the imperial court the growing Gothic child must have witnessed many events known to us from history. The peace of 459/460, which the little Theodoric was guaranteeing, held for a remarkably long time; the Gothic hostage experienced the time abroad as learning years. Later, as king of Italy, Theodoric wrote to Constantinople that "he had, with God's help, learned in the state of the emperors how to rule justly over Romans."

"Sensing what was to come, Greece raised you in the bosom of public life protected by law, *in gremio civilitatis*"—thus the king was reminded of his youth, and he enjoyed hearing it.[4] Little Theodoric was surely not educated into a perfect rhetorician in Constantinople, but he must have learned at least how to read, write, and do arithmetic, thus acquiring the basics of classical administrative practice. That he was illiterate and used a stencil with the four letters *legi* ("I read") as his signature is nothing other than a repetition of the charge of illiteracy that was leveled against Justinus, the Illyrian peasant on the imperial throne of Constantinople.

Following Theodoric's death, Gothic princes wanted to force a change in the upbringing of his grandson and successor, Athalaric. To that end they invoked a saying by the king that was critical of education: the Goths should stay away from school lest "the straps of the schoolmasters beat the courage out of them." At a time of political strife, with the old order breaking down, a personality as deep and complex as Theodoric's could "disintegrate" after his death and serve as justification for contrary policies. Greek tradition, in any case, established a causal link between Theodoric's stay in Constantinople and his literary education.[5]

In the imperial city the young Theodoric witnessed the imperial General Aspar at the peak of his power and glory. Aspar was of Alanic-Gothic descent; his personal power was made up mostly of Gothic warriors (*buccellarii*), among whom another Theodoric held the highest rank. This was Theodoric Strabo, "the Squinter," Aspar's brother-in-law and subcommander. His father, of whom we know only his Roman surname, Triarius ("elite soldier"), had not moved to Pannonia with the Goths Valamir, Thiudimir, and Vidimir after the end of the Hunnic Empire. In spite of, or precisely because of, the fact that Triarius was probably also an Amal, he had not placed himself under the leadership of the three royal brothers, but had gone to Thrace with his people.

At the imperial court, little Theodoric from Pannonia enjoyed the pro-Gothic atmosphere that Aspar and his people were creating and upholding. The example of the Alan General Aspar made a lasting impression on Theodoric; when he was Gothic king of Italy, Theodoric still remembered the words with which the Arian Aspar had justified to the eastern senate his refusal to be elevated to the emperorship. But in Constantinople, Theodoric son of Thiudimir must have also learned to fear and hate the competing Amal family of Triarius and Theodoric "the Squinter." As long as these two had the say in Constantinople, all that was left for his people back in Pannonia was the role of the poor relatives, tolerated and spared, to be sure, but kept from the levers of power.

At the end of his stay in Constantinople, Theodoric, now about seventeen years old, witnessed Aspar and his clan pass the apex of their power. In the spring of 467, Constantinople sent the successful General Anthemius to the West to be proclaimed emperor there. Evidently Byzantium felt strong enough to release Anthemius, who had defeated Goths and other barbarians in the Balkans, to the western empire, where he was to give a similar demonstration of military strength. Almost at the same time Constantinople was setting out to eradicate private soldiering with the full severity of the law, a measure that was aimed directly against Aspar's retainers. And finally, a large fleet set sail against Vandal Carthage, against the wishes and advice of the imperial general.

In this situation it was weak consolation that Aspar's son Patricius was elevated to the rank of Caesar and made one of the emperor's sons-in-law. For the other son-in-law was the Isaurian Tarasicodissa, the future emperor, who was already calling himself Zeno. The disastrous outcome of the Vandal war kept everything up in the air for a while and prevented the outbreak of open conflict between the "Gothic party" and the Isaurians. Then came the year 469: once more against Aspar's will, a great war was launched in the East and the West against the Goths, the "poison of the state." But the Balthic Goths in Toulouse as well as the Amal Goths in Pannonia were not merely able to ward of the offensive, they triumphed over the imperial armies and their barbarian allies. As a sign of his willingness to make peace, the emperor let the young Theodoric go home, probably still in 469. The year 471 witnessed Aspar's downfall and murder.[6]

His time as hostage having come to an end, young Theodoric returned to Pannonia at the age of eighteen. Equipped with the prestige of a stay in Constantinople, and possibly on the basis of a testamentary disposition by Valamir, he was given his uncle's part of the kingdom in eastern Slavonia. Supreme authority over the three Pannonian subkingdoms was now in the hands of Theodoric's father, Thiudimir. As early as 470, Theodoric launched his first successful military expedition with his Gothic warriors, without his father's knowledge and probably against his wishes. A king of the Tisza-Sarmatians had wrested the city of Singidunum-Belgrade from Constantinople's control. Theodoric crossed the Danube with six thousand men, the military force of his subkingdom, attacked the main Sarmatian army and defeated and killed the king, whereupon Singidunum too surrendered.

This war, begun in the name of the emperor, ended with the last expansion of the Pannonian Goths. Theodoric retained Singidunum, which lay in Upper Moesia outside of the territory contractually assigned to the Goths; the victorious army acknowledged his skill as a general. Whether or not he was acclaimed king at that time, Theodoric celebrated the thirtieth anniversary of his rule in 500, which means that—at least in retrospect—he traced the beginning of his kingship to the success in 470. With this victory he had demonstrated that he was now a player in the game of power without regard for anyone, be it his own father, brother, or another Amal.[7]

When Childeric died in the faraway Frankish West in 481/482, his son Clovis was barely sixteen years old. His father's funeral must have been quite an event: as a Merovingian king and Roman general, he was laid in his grave richly attired and fully armed, "as was the custom of pagan men."[8] Clovis probably inherited from his father the sexual power that was generally attributed to the Merovingians: thirty years later the king had a grandson (from his son Theuderic) who was not much younger than Clovis himself had been when his reign began. This means that Theuderic, Clovis's son from a *concubina,* must have already been born when his grandfather died in 481/482.[9]

Clovis must have enjoyed a certain measure of Roman education, which also included knowledge of civilian administrative practice. How else could we explain that Bishop Remigius of Reims so evidently welcomed the fact that the young Frankish king—like his ancestors before him—had taken over the "administration of Belgica II."

During Childeric's last years, peace—if a forced one—had prevailed. Visigothic superiority left the Franks in the north of Gaul no choice but to keep quiet. And so "the peoples who long flourished in peace under your ancestors" were also able to enjoy this pleasant state of affairs during the initial years of the new king's reign. But in 484 the Visigothic King Euric died, and Clovis set out to challenge the rule of the Roman King Syagrius in northern Gaul.[10] The victory over Syagrius in 486/487 began Clovis's unstoppable rise.

3. WITH THE EMPIRE AND AGAINST IT

Theodoric

Theodoric was a little child when his family, which invoked Amal-Gothic traditions, ruled over those Goths who lived as Roman federates along the middle Danube. In the months prior to February 457, three Amal brothers had concluded a treaty with Constantinople that allowed their people to settle in southern Pannonia. The Ostrogothic settlement areas extended in a crescent shape from the southern shores of Lake Balaton to the environs of modern-day Belgrade.

Theodoric's uncle Valamir and his two brothers probably controlled about eighteen thousand warriors. A dozen years later, in 469, it was touch and go whether the Pannonian Ostrogoths would be able to hold their own against a coalition of Roman troops and barbarian tribal warriors. Though the Goths lost their King Valamir, they triumphed over their enemies and for another half a decade remained faithful to the treaty of 456/457. In the second half of 473, the Amals and their people left Pannonia: the younger brother Vidimir went to Italy with his son of the same name; the older, King Thiudimir, and his son Theodoric moved their federate kingdom from the Danube to Macedonia, where Thiudimir died in 474. His Goths followed his choice of a designated successor and elevated Theodoric to the kingship. A younger brother was passed over and we don't hear much about him later.

Soon after 474, in any case prior to 476, Theodoric gave up his Macedonian bases and marched back to the Danube with his people, this time to Lower Moesia. The center of this second attempt at establishing a kingdom became the city of Novae-Svistov (Bulgaria), favorably located in strategic terms. Here Theodoric remained, with interruptions, until 488, when he and his Goths set out for Italy.

In January of 475, Emperor Zeno had been driven out of Constantinople by a usurper. Theodoric Strabo had been deeply involved in the events. At this time, at the latest, "the Squinter" became the supreme commander of the imperial army and thus also the superior of Theodoric son of Thiudimir. It is therefore possible that Strabo gave his "poor cousin" the order to come to Thrace and cover his back from the Danubian side. The younger Gothic king freed himself from this subordinate and dependent position only by allying himself with Zeno. The emperor returned, the usurper and "the Squinter" fell, and Theodoric son of Thiudimir inherited all of his namesake's honors and titles. Thirty years later King Theodoric, who had risen to become the master of Italy, celebrated in these words the support he had given to Zeno: "Let us look through the history books, let us ask the annals! Where is it written that a king by birth ever bought back with his own blood the rule of a man driven from power?" "For this you can name an emperor clad in purple as a witness of your loyalty and services."[11]

After his reentry into Constantinople, Emperor Zeno went on the offensive against "the Squinter," who was operating in Thrace. Sometime during the second half of 476, Zeno, following barbarian custom, adopted Theodoric son of Thiudimir as his "son in arms"; he called him his "friend," made him commander in chief of the East Roman troops, and bestowed on him the title of *patricius*. At the same time, Constantinople recognized the federate kingdom in Lower Moesia and promised to subsidize it with annual payments. But as long as a federate kingdom was dependent on yearly payments, its economic problems remained unsolved; its existence was subject to recall, so to speak. The Ostrogoths had learned this painful truth in Pannonia and Macedonia, and soon they would learn it again in Lower Moesia.

The threat to their ethnic identity was further heightened by the fact that Theodoric Strabo, king of the Thracian Goths, had no intention of giving up without a fight. The years that followed were full of chaos and fighting, of seemingly pointless campaigns across the entire Balkan Peninsula, of empty promises and broken treaties. The end of the seventies found Theodoric—defeated several times by the imperial army but not destroyed—in Epirus. Around 479/480 he had only six thousand warriors at his command, as many as he had had at the beginning of his career, while his enemy Theodoric Strabo received pay from the imperial government for more than twice that number.

Theodoric son of Thiudimir had moved into modern-day Albania. Sidimund, an Amal and blood relative who was considered a friend of the Romans and held in high esteem, had claimed he had an order from Zeno to clear the area for Gothic settlement. The ruse worked. A majority of the population along with two thousand soldiers did in fact leave. After the land had been vacated, Sidimund invited the son of Thiudimir, who was encamped at Bitola, to come and set up his fourth federate kingdom.

The Roman military leadership was not willing to accept the seizure of the coastal area of Epirus along with the capital, Durazzo. Though the Romans began negotiations, they also made preparations for a military response. But the Illyrian units under Odovacar's older brother Hunulf took no action, and neither did the soldiers of his superior Sabinianus. The punitive expedition the Romans had for some time threatened to launch collapsed completely when Sabinianus dropped out of the picture in 481 and

Theodoric Strabo died suddenly that same year. Strabo's death meant the end of the Ostrogothic dual kingship; Theodoric son of Thiudimir had survived the most serious crisis of his career.

Freed from his most dangerous enemy and rival, Theodoric began an offensive against Greece in 482. Terrible devastation finally forced Zeno in 483 to conclude a treaty favorable to the Goths: the Amal was returned to his post as commander in chief and *patricius,* he was even designated consul for 484, and was given Dacia ripensis and parts of Lower Moesia.

Theodoric returned to Novae in 483, but he appears to have been in Constantinople on January 1, 484, to begin his consulship. From that time on, at the latest, he also possessed Roman citizenship, through which his Amals were given the surname commonly used for new citizens since the time of Constantine and were called Flavians. As consul, the Gothic king received the usual honors; apparently the Amal had been given this high honor at the age of thirty-three—that is to say, *suo anno* ("in his year"), as though he were from one of the leading Roman families. Theodoric the barbarian and Theodoric the Roman are not two successive and separable phases in the life of the same man, but had been, ever since his childhood, two aspects of a single personality.

In his year as consul, Theodoric was to take strong measures against a rebellion in Asia Minor. But then, we are told, "it occurred to the Roman emperor that he could become disloyal," and he had him replaced under humiliating circumstances. To save what he could of the relationship, Zeno gave the Gothic king permission for a magnificent entry into Constantinople, which must have surpassed even that of Clovis into Tours in 508, and allowed him to set up an equestrian statue in the capital. Still, a genuine peace could not be ensured this way. During the renewed outbreak of hostilities in Thrace, the emperor conceived of the plan to send the Goths to Italy. The reasons for Theodoric's departure from the Balkan Peninsula would be easy to guess if they weren't explicitly recorded. The Gothic king realized that in the long run he was no match for the imperial power. Time, Zeno's ally, was working against him. If Theodoric had no success to show, or if he proved unable to secure the rank and status of his people, which amounted to much the same thing, they would leave him and he was certain to meet a disgraceful end.

By marching against Odovacar at the emperor's request, Theodoric put himself in the service of Zeno's vacillating policy, but at the same time he was finally given a chance to become independent of the imperial treasury. After at least four unsuccessful attempts at establishing a regnum, the possibility of setting up a lasting kingdom seemed within reach for the very first time.[12] From now on Theodoric could claim that the situation of *praeregnare* that he had negotiated with Zeno in the treaty was in effect. The *foedus* contained the provision that "following the defeat of Odovacar,

Theodoric, in return for his efforts, is to rule [Italy] in place of the emperor until he arrives there in person."[13] Thus the Amal king had to exercise the regnum for a legitimate emperor—during his absence—and with his recognition. But this also meant that the rule of the Amal Flavians ranked above the other barbarian kingdoms in the same way in which the imperium ranked above the Italian kingdom. Later, in 508, probably as a reaction to Constantinople's recognition of Clovis, Theodoric tried to present his Italian regnum to the emperor as a part of the unified Roman Empire, as independent as it was subordinate. To the same degree that Theodoric ranked below the emperor he surpassed the other gentes and their kings.

This was the thinking behind the statues erected for Theodoric. The Romans acclaimed him their lord, at times even called him augustus, and compared him to the emperors Trajan or Valentinian. The Gothic king was thus "in fact a real emperor,"[14] a *princeps Romanus* who called the Roman *imperatores* his predecessors. But for that reason he had to have his rule recognized by Constantinople lest it be considered a *praesumptio regni*, an act of usurpation.[15] In 497 Theodoric finally received imperial recognition in a form that left nothing to be desired during his own lifetime.

Even when Belisarius was attacking the Gothic kingdom of Italy, his secretary Procopius penned this very pre-Justinian verdict of the dead Theodoric: having slain Odovacar and "after gaining the adherence of such of the hostile barbarians as chanced to survive, he himself secured the supremacy over both Goths and Italians. And though he did not claim the right to assume either the garb or the name of emperor of the Romans, but was called 'rex' to the end of his life, for thus the barbarians are accustomed to call their leaders, still, in governing his own subjects, he invested himself with all the qualities that appropriately belong to one who is by birth an emperor. For he was exceedingly careful to observe justice, he preserved the laws on a sure basis, he protected the land and kept it safe from the barbarians dwelling round about, and he attained the highest possible degree of wisdom and manliness. And he himself committed scarcely a single act of injustice against his subjects, nor would he brook such conduct on the part of anyone else who attempted it, except, indeed, that the Goths distributed among themselves the portion of the lands [taxes] which Odovacar had given to his own partisans. And although in name Theodoric was a usurper, yet in fact he was as truly an emperor as any who have distinguished themselves in this office from the beginning; and love for him among both Goths and Italians grew to be great, and that, too, contrary to the ordinary habits of men. . . . But Theodoric reigned for thirty-seven years, and when he died, he had not only made himself an object of terror to all his enemies, but he also left to his subjects a keen sense of bereavement at his loss."[16]

The core of Theodoric's rule in Italy continued to be the kingship he had entered into in 474 as his father's successor. Two decades later, in 493 in Ravenna, Theodoric was elevated to the kingship once again. This time the act was not merely that of raising an Amal up as Gothic king; Theodoric's federate warriors also acted as the imperially legitimated army of the West. Theodoric was made monarchical ruler of Italy and consequently carried the Latin royal title *rex*.[17] After Justinus had assumed the emperorship in Constantinople in 518, he too recognized the treaties with Theodoric and was also willing to guarantee a succession arrangement based on the principle of Amal legitimacy. Justinus adopted Eutharic, an Amal and son-in-law of the king, as his son-in-arms "according to barbarian custom"; he granted him Roman citizenship; and in 519 he assumed the consulship jointly with Flavius Eutharicus Cilliga. The emperor even had the name of the Gothic pretender to the throne precede his own. The legitimation of succession was thus made in a decision that was as clear to the Goths as it was to the Romans. It comprised all the elements of Theodoric's own kingship, namely, designation by the predecessor, adoption by the emperor, the granting of citizenship, and the holding of the consulship.[18]

Clovis

Clovis's father had died a Roman general. More than two hundred solidi lay in his grave; they bore the coinage stamps of the emperors of the West and the East from Valentinian III (425–455) to Zeno (476–491). Clovis took over from his father, Childeric, not only the kingdom of Tournai but also the administration of all of Belgica II. The latter was at first more a claim than reality, for there were at least two rivals in the south of the province, the Salian king of Cambrai and Syagrius of Soissons. Syagrius had followed in the footsteps of his father (the military chief of Gaul, Aegidius, who was so important to the Salian Franks) more as a Roman king than a magisterial official of Rome; the area he controlled was able to maintain itself as a buffer state between the greater Gothic Empire and the Frankish kingdom until 486. Clovis reached an agreement with his cousin and conquered the kingdom of Syagrius, who fled from Soissons to the Visigoths. At first the Visigoths gave him refuge, but later—we are not sure exactly when—he was handed over to Clovis, who had him executed.

Neither Ravenna nor Constantinople showed any irritation at the attack on Soissons. The Italian King Odovacar didn't care much for Syagrius, since his envoys, as the only ones from the entire western empire, had gone to Constantinople in 476 to protest Odovacar's seizure of power. Byzantium, for its part, regarded the Romans from Soissons as highly irksome warners at a time when it was necessary to get along with Odovacar and pay off Childeric. But the events surrounding Clovis's great Gothic war showed that the imperial government of the East was constantly watching the events in Gaul, and that it intervened with diplomatic means even more so than with money.

4. *ORIGO ET RELIGIO*

One could entitle this section "origin and religion," but the literal translation captures only a shadow of the original meaning. The *origo* is not a common biological descent of a given group nor is it only the traditional account of the origins of a single person or group; it also proclaims the heroic-divine origins of a gens and its kings, origins that have to be continually renewed in the cult and thereby kept alive. This belief outlasted even the conversion to Christianity without any major problems: what remained of the belief in divine descent was the belief in a nobility that was sanctified by Christ and his church.

Racial madness and führer-ideology have caused so much pain and suffering in our century that it is difficult today to speak freely of the charisma (*Heil*) and splendor of clan or blood. It thus comes as no surprise when we find that a scholar who experienced firsthand the crimes of those neopagan cults and ideologies is deeply opposed to the notion of the sacred kingship and royal charisma of the Germanic tribes. After all, the exponents of modern irrationalism, too, invoked the manifestations of a rule long past and tried to legitimize in that way their own mad ideas and crimes.[19] But distortions of history do not relieve us of the obligation to deal with the abused traditions. Precisely because the topic is so heavily burdened, it is indispensable that we undertake the tightrope walk between the dangerous glorification and the equally dangerous disregard of the archaic tradition.

For if we listen to the sources, it is clear that both Theodoric and Clovis were convinced that they were raised in some "superhuman" way above ordinary mortals. As part of their nonliterate education they were told about their heroic and divine ancestors and were obliged to follow their example. Certain families, among them especially those of royal descent, invoked divine ancestors and derived from this lineage a special charisma, a royal fortune, for themselves and their retainers.

Critics of such explanations argue that the tradition of these genealogies was developed only after the fact, whereas the original tradition declared that the entire tribe was of divine descent. This observation is true, but it does not negate the importance of divine genealogies of kings. Thus the author of the history of the Goths conceived of his work as the "origin of the Goths, the noble line of the Amali, and the deeds of brave men."[20]

In defiance of the catastrophes of the fifth century and notwithstanding the brilliant eschatology of Augustine, the Ambrosian-Eusebian imperial theology dominated also the official policy of the successor states of the western Roman Empire. People remained loyal to the notion that Roman history was occurring on two levels: as profane history and the goal of every *origo gentis* within the framework of time; and as redemptive history beyond all time. These ideas shaped the way in which tribal traditions were codified.

The authors of the tribal origins, who used the language of the ancients to write the history of their own tribe or of a foreign gens, had honed their style and skill at historical explanation by working on classical traditions. Not infrequently the authors were excellent Latinists who made the object of their works dependent on Latin literature. Added to this was the example of the Bible, which prefigured current events and the motivations behind them. Therefore an origo could and should refer to both classical Roman and Biblical models.

Cassiodorus, for example, reckoned seventeen Amal generations, or about 430 years, from the origins of the lineage to 526, the year Athalaric assumed the kingship. This span of time corresponded to a not very old Roman tradition, with which Cassiodorus was familiar, according to which Romulus, the founding hero of Rome, had ruled as the seventeenth king of the Albans after Aeneas. Moreover, in ancient mythography the number seventeen takes us back not only to the Trojan War but to many generations before that. Dionysius of Halicarnassus reported that Oinotros had led the aborigines from Arcadia to Italy seventeen generations before the fall of Troy.[21]

Then again, seventeen peoples witnessed the Pentecostal miracle in Jerusalem. According to Augustine, the Ten Commandments were held in the power of the sevenfold Spirit. The apostles, who became fishers of men and were to teach all peoples, netted 153 fish in a miraculous catch, a number that is made up of the triangular number seventeen. The total length of the Amal generations, 430 years, corresponds to the knowledge that Moses led the Chosen People from Egypt in the 430th year of God's promise. As late as the ninth century, a pope would use this argument to oppose the claims of the Bavarian Church in Pannonia.

After receiving the Law at Mount Sinai, the Israelites remained in the desert for forty years. In the work of Jordanes-Cassiodorus we find the statement that Amal rule was interrupted once by a forty-year-long interregnum.[22] All this does not mean that the authors invented things or produced deliberate fabrications; rather, they chose selectively from the genuine tradition before shaping it into final literary form.

As king of Italy, Theodoric the Great had his family tradition put down in writing. He decided who belonged to the Amal clan, and—logically consistent—he presented his marriage policy as the emanation of the splendor of the Amal clan. But the most consummate mastery of late-antique political language could only lend outward form to the meaning "splendor of the

Amals." The royal clan had already professed the Amal tradition at a time when Theodoric had not yet entered Italy.

After he had become lord of Ravenna, Theodoric proclaimed the Amals to be the legitimate royal lineage of the Ostrogoths from time immemorial, and the Balths their Visigothic counterpart. The origins of this arrangement coincided, we learn, with the time the Goths migrated into the region of the Black Sea and divided into these two tribes. The Amals and the Balths were the families of "kings and heroes"; each of the two clans represented its Gothic people. Thus the Amals were the "family of the Ostrogoths" and the Balths the "family of the Visigoths." The latter were of "wonderful descent," their name *baltha* meant "bold." However, their nobility ranked only second, since membership in the Amal clan was regarded "the highest honor among the [barbarian] peoples." For when the Goths, in times long past, had realized that they were being victorious with the help of the royal *fortuna* of the Amals, they acclaimed them as Aesir and realized that in this way the divine, "by no means purely human," origin of the clan had been established. Amal, too, the eponymous hero of the lineage, "stood out by his *fortuna*."[23]

Theodoric combined this knowledge concerning his forefathers with an Arian Christianity his father had already known. Young Theodoric must have learned in Constantinople how important this Christianity was for the Gothic upper class in proximity to power. The Gothic-Arian religion and constitution, the *Lex Gothica,* saw its greatest flowering in the Italian kingdom of Theodoric the Great. But it is unthinkable without its Latin and Greek roots and without its opposition to Catholic Roman Christianity.

This dialectical relationship allowed the switch from one confession to another. This switch was not only in one direction, from Arianism to Catholicism, though Goths tended to take this step more often than did Romans. Theodoric professed the Arian faith and worked on its behalf without making a big to-do about it: "Though he was an adherent of the Arian sect, he did not take any steps against the Catholic faith."[24] On the occasion of his visit to Rome in 500, Theodoric, we are told, "honored the apostolic prince Peter with the greatest reverence, as though he himself were a Catholic."[25]

The Ecumenical Council of Chalcedon in 451 had not settled the doctrinal controversies within the early church. On the surface the quarrel concerned the nature of Christ, with the West accusing the East of advocating Monophysitism, the doctrine that the Savior had a single divine nature. Above all, however, Rome opposed the primacy of the patriarch of Constantinople. Moreover, the men on the throne of Saint Peter, like the mighty Pope Gelasius, challenged the emperor's right to be the final authority in questions of the faith. Only under the influence of the future Justinian I did

Justinus seek compromise and accommodation with Rome, its senatorial nobility, and the papacy.

Until then, the majority of the Catholic ruling class of Italy had supported the Gothic ruler of Ravenna. The toleration that the Arian Gothic king extended to the Catholic faith, willingly or not, was preferred to Constantinople's imperial rule over the church. With the reconciliation of East and West the Gothic alternative fell by the wayside—and this even though Theodoric had always taken the papal side and had accepted as well the fact that this delayed his recognition by the emperor. The king must have been aware of the opportunity the conflict between the two Catholic powers offered him, and yet he supported all efforts to settle the quarrel.

Religious unrest was part of public life in the late-antique state; it was the safety valve for the multifarious pressures to which the broad mass of the population was exposed. But this kind of unrest could easily get out of hand. It disturbed the domestic peace and usually affected the innocent, as the Jews of Rome and Ravenna discovered. And between 499 and 514, schism held even Rome in its grip and intensified the already existing split in the church. On one occasion even Saint Benedict did not know when he should celebrate Easter.[26]

Theodoric proceeded with the utmost caution in this difficult conflict. He invoked Aspar's refusal to be declared emperor as an Arian in order to protect himself against the demand that he intervene as an arbiter. In 501 in Rome, Theodoric spoke these words to the assembled Fathers, indirectly also emphasizing that Catholic and Arian bishops were of equal rank: "If you ask for my opinion—whatever God commands in the Gospels you should do." "It is alone your task to pacify the senate, the clergy, and the people. Write what you decide. We will confirm that you are doing a good thing by giving peace to the people, the senate, and the clergy. If you cannot accomplish that, you demonstrate that you are only supporting one party. You must not fear me, since you must answer in the presence of God. And if someone wants to coerce you by force to commit an injustice, you must defend not your estates and prejudices but what is right. For many bishops of both your faith and mine have risked their office and possessions for the cause of God and yet they are alive."[27]

The king was, of course, the heart of the Arian Church. The artistic fruits of his efforts still today rank among the most beautiful and valuable accomplishments of the European mind. Theodoric's capital of Ravenna witnessed a splendid building activity: the Arian baptistry, the modern-day day Oratorium Santa Maria in Cosmedin, followed the example of the orthodox baptistry San Giovanni in Fonte near the cathedral. The court church, on the other hand, today San Apollinare Nuovo, is probably the most magnificent example of sacred Arian architecture, a generation older than the Catholic church of San Apollinare in Classe. Ravenna was also home to the Arian churches of San Andrea dei Goti, Saint George, Saint Anastasia, as well as the Eusebius church, whose builder is said to have been a certain Bishop Unimund. On the road to Classe, where an Arian church of Saint Zeno was located, the Goths built a church dedicated to Saint Sergius in Caesarea, the third city of Ravenna. Arian bishops resided at all three sites. In Ravenna proper, the church of Theodorus (still standing but robbed of its mosaic decoration) served as the seat of a Gothic bishop; we know that it was built by Theodoric. It is also certain that there were two Arian churches in Rome, and evidence points to what may have been an Episcopal church and a baptistry in Salona in Dalmatia, near modern-day Dubrovnik.

Among the most splendid artifacts of Ostrogothic Arianism is also the famous Codex Argenteus, which contains the Gothic Bible. This magnificent manuscript is today in the university library of Uppsala in Sweden. Ulfilas's Gothic translation of the Bible was written down in silver letters on purple-dyed parchment made from the skin of young or unborn calves. Details such as the names of the evangelists are highlighted in golden ink. The letters themselves are conspicuously regular, as if traced from a stencil. The layout of the text is done according to the golden mean; the canon tables, which serve the purpose of concordance, are reminiscent of Ravennese church architecture.

Although this silver Bible with its 336 pages, 188 of which still exist, is not the only extant text in the Gothic language, it is by far the most comprehensive. Most of the other surviving Gothic Bibles are also from Theodoric's Italy. In all probability the Codex Argenteus was originally part of the royal treasure and was taken to safety in Pavia before 540, from where Totila moved it to Cumae in southern Italy. When Cumae surrendered to Justinian's forces in 553, the Bible did not fall into the hands of the imperial troops but, for reasons unknown, remained in the south until it eventually made its way to Carolingian Germany. The subsequent fate of the Codex Argenteus is well known and among the most fascinating chapters in the history of books.[28]

Clovis's background was much the same as Theodoric's, though with the significant difference that he grew up a pagan and thus "knew"—in a more immediate way than Theodoric—that his ancestors were a "race of gods," *genus deorum*. One major reason for his hesitation to undergo baptism was the fact that Christ evidently could not boast of a comparable descent.[29] But while Theodoric could invoke fourteen Ansic and eleven Amal ancestors, Merovech, the eponymous hero of the Merovingians, was already of the second generation before Clovis, no matter whether or not he was Clovis's grandfather. We have to go back no farther than Clovis's real or supposed great-grandfather to find a figure wearing horns, perhaps because he was a bull god or perhaps because some other god had bestowed this kind of head ornament on him.

Two Frankish historians tells us about the beginnings of the Merovingians. The older of the two, Gregory of Tours, reports that "some say that Merovech, the father of Childeric, was descended from Clodio." But the younger chronicle by the so-called Fredegar records a "sacred wedding" and goes on to say: "This race [the Merovingians] was celebrated in pagan feasts. It is said that one summer Clodio went to the sea with his wife; when she waded out into the waters at midday to bathe, she was attacked by a monster of Neptune, similar to the Minotaur. It is not clear whether she conceived of the monster or her husband, in any case she gave birth to a son with the name Merovechus, after whom the kings of Franks were later called Merovingians."[30]

The Merovingian "sacred marriage" was the object of religious celebrations, which in eternal return kept alive the divine origins of the lineage and the tribe. A golden bull's head was sent to the grave alongside Clovis's father, Childeric, bull's heads decorated the belted outfit of a Frankish queen, and even Einhard, the biographer of Charlemagne, knew of the ox-driven wagon of the Merovingian kings, even if he did make fun of the old-fashioned and pitiful vehicle.[31]

As a pagan, Clovis had the choice of which Christian faith he and his people would convert to. The abandonment of the traditional faith, the *origo et religio*, was, after all, only a matter of time once the tribe was on Roman imperial soil. No matter how tenaciously the Franks might cling to their traditions, they and especially their kings could not remain pagans west of the Rhine if they wanted to govern Romans and take over their institutions in good order.

However, it was important not to act too hastily: the faith in the divine origins of the "long-haired kings" (*reges criniti*) legitimated their rule and was rooted in paganism. If the king abjured this faith without first ensuring for himself the consent of "his people and his tribe," he himself gave up the foundation of his kingship.[32] But once the king and his magnates had made the decision in favor of Christianity, it still made a lot more sense around 500 to convert to the Arianism of the Latin-Germanic kings than to adopt the faith of the Romans and their distant emperor who resided in "Greece."

In fact, all "Gothic peoples," including the Burgundians and Lombards, professed the "Gothic law," Arianism. The Gothic faith took the place, as it were, of the abandoned tribal religion, even if it never quite fulfilled the function intended for it. The old tribal religion was dominated by the idea of a community of law and faith of the living and the dead that was constantly renewed in the cult and from which outsiders were excluded. This is why Gothic Arianism preserved the feeling of foreignness between Romans and barbarians, though it was also part of its nature that it allowed a certain measure of religious tolerance or indifference toward followers of a different faith. As late as the sixth century, for example, it was considered "Gothic" to show respect to Christian houses of worship as well as to pagan temples.

Of course such an attitude did not preclude conflict with the Catholic Roman majority. For example, the Goths repeatedly confiscated Catholic churches to conduct their own services in them. There were also zealots who baptized the children of Catholic parents or wanted to rebaptize them. At the same time, Goths who split off from the two main tribes were easily converted to Catholicism, whereas the army of the emperor continued for a long time to have Arian Gothic soldiers.

Arian bishops strike a noticeably unassuming posture in the sources. When one of them ordered a Catholic church destroyed, he had overstepped the bounds of his authority. Arian Gothic bishops were members of their tribe and subject to its laws; their lord was the king who appointed them, whom they had to obey, and whom they barely dared to resist.[33]

By contrast, Catholic bishops, owing to their background and office, had very different status. During the fifth century they had been the heads and leaders of their *civitates* and had thus become partners both of "barbarian kings wrapped in furs and emperors clad in purple."[34] Of course, the emperors were far away, and dealings with the kings were among the bishop's day-to-day duties.

The occasion for Clovis's baptism is believed to have been an unexpected victory in the battle the king fought against the Alamanni either in 496 or 497. If we accept the second date we end up with the chronology I have used, otherwise everything moves up one year. The conversion experience may well have been historically true, but this did not prevent Clovis from preparing his conversion in protracted negotiations with bishops and Frankish magnates. At the same time the candidate for baptism (the catechumen) underwent instruction, which took some time. It was probably in the spring of 498 that the assembled army approved the king's intention by acclamation. The following summer the Franks advanced across the Loire deep into the Aquitanian south. The invaders withdrew ahead of the Gothic counterattack, but Clovis was able to make his baptismal promises on November 11 (Saint Martin's Day) in Tours, still on Gothic soil.

Clovis probably had himself baptized on Christmas Day 498 in Reims; the ceremony was conducted by Bishop Remigius, to whom are attributed the famous words: "Bow your head in meekness, Sicamber [Frank]. Worship what you have burnt, burn what you have been wont to worship."[35] Only two generations later Clovis was seen as a "new Constantine," his conversion was seen as the repetition of the example given in the legend of the great emperor. Clovis was joined in baptism by his oldest sister, who was still a pagan, and by another Salian king, named Chararic, and his son. In addition, three thousand, or six thousand, Franks followed the example of their king. The number three thousand had a venerable model in connection with baptism: three thousand Jews had themselves baptized after the Pentecostal preaching of the apostles. In secular texts this number is tantamount to a tribal army.[36] Last, an Arian sister of Clovis's converted to Catholicism.[37]

Clovis's decision to adopt the faith of the Roman majority of his realm had repercussions far beyond his kingdom and assumed—though only in the centuries following his death—world-historical importance. To be sure, the conversion of Clovis was no more than a promissory note, but his contemporary Avitus, metropolitan of Vienne, already realized the potential inherent in the king's decision: "Your faith is our victory." "Greece no longer has only one Catholic ruler"—these were the prophetic words of the first bishop in the kingdom of the somewhat Arian Burgundians.[38]

It is not entirely clear why Clovis decided to convert. It was often assumed that in so doing the Merovingian king wanted to stake out an anti-Gothic position, that he wanted to present himself as *the* alternative, as it were, to the Arian kings. But until 498 Clovis had not even consolidated the Merovingian kingship in his hands, let alone won a decisive victory against the great Gothic powers of his time. To be sure, for at least two generations the Franks in the north of Gaul had already been a force to reckon with, but around 500 no observer would have seriously expected them to have enough military power to establish a great Catholic realm.

The Gothic peoples, as we read especially in the Greek ethnographers, all had a common origin, the same Arian faith, and the same language. That was true for the Ostrogoths, the Vandals, the Visigoths, the Gepids, the Rugians, the Scirians, and the Burgundians, indeed even the Alans.[39] However, linguists maintain that while Marbod and Arminius could still understand each other, "it is doubtful whether that was the case for Theodoric and Clovis."[40]

Was it the possible difference in language that prevented Clovis from professing the *lex Gothica*? This could not have been the reason, for among his sisters it was not only the one who married Theodoric the Great in 493 who converted to Arianism, but also the youngest, who had remained in close proximity to her brother. Moreover, we know that Clovis gathered detailed information about Arianism and its possibilities as he was carefully considering the question of his baptism.[41]

We are far more reliably informed about Clovis's father, Childeric, than about his mythical ancestors. As a federate king of the empire Childeric had fought against Visigoths and Saxons. The integration of the Frankish forces into the army of northern Gaul, indeed its subordination to its commanders, must have been so pronounced that Frankish tradition fashioned it into a very peculiar story: Childeric's sexual promiscuity and bull-like energy, we are told, was too much even for the Franks, and so they sent him into exile for some time and in his place elevated the Gallic commander Aegidius to the kingship.[42]

However one may chose to interpret this story, it does reflect a striking openness on the part of the Childeric Franks toward the Romans and their institutions and beliefs. It is not impossible that this attitude laid the groundwork for Clovis's decision, a decision that was excluded by the political constitution of the Goths. Thus while Goths who lived far from their tribes converted to Catholicism with no problem, the members or even kings of an Arian kingdom on Italian or Gallic soil never took that step at all or—as in the case of a Burgundian king—did so in secret.[43]

A king who changed his faith was not acting as a private person. Historians have therefore asked, with good reason, about the general preconditions—the public reasons, as it were—for Clovis's step. If we refuse to cling to ahistorical laws, lay aside our belief that we understand the cynical and power-hungry Clovis, and avoid overstretching the motivations that drove him by attributing to him an nonhuman farsightedness, we can come up with an answer: the very personal influence of Clotild must have decisively influenced, if not actually caused, Clovis's conversion. This answer may not please proponents of a "history without names," but that does not make it any less likely.

The Burgundian Princess Clotild came from a Catholic branch of the royal house and had married Clovis sometime between 492 and 494.[44] Two generations later Gregory of Tours put their story down on parchment. The couple's firstborn son was named Ingomer. The pagan father had given the child a name that linked it to the pagan god Ing. Half a millennium earlier, the uncle of Arminius had borne the name Ingomer. However, the queen was not content with just the naming by the father and insisted, against Clovis's will, that her son be baptized. But no sooner had Ingomer been baptized than he died. An angry Clovis blamed this tragedy on the weakness of the Christian God. But this obvious divine verdict did not deter Clotild, and she demanded that her second son also be baptized. And in spite of what had happened, Clovis let the queen have her way. Soon the very thing Clovis had feared seemed to happen: little Chlodomer seemed so close to death that his father gave up on him. The child survived, however, and Clotild attributed his recovery to her prayers.[45]

There is no reason to doubt that the queen's first two sons were baptized. But this is not the only story that attests that Clotild was an unusual woman with a striking degree of willpower, something she showed also after Clovis's death.[46] I am not arguing for an uncritical acceptance of the tradition, but the conversion of Clovis must be attributed above all to the persuasiveness of his queen, Clotild. The victory over the Alamanni may have acted as the triggering event.

Clovis did not need the example of the Goths and Burgundians to enforce his authority over the church against the Catholic bishops of the Frankish kingdom. Just as five years earlier Alaric II had summoned the first Gothic-Gallic council, in 511 the first Frankish synod assembled on orders of the Frankish king. The Catholic bishops of the Frankish realm gathered in Orléans. At that time there were already negotiations regarding Arian clergy who had converted to Catholicism after the Frankish conquest of Aquitaine.[47] In theory bishops were installed by the respective metropolitan "with the king's will and in accordance with the election by the clergy and the people." However, in a number of episcopal appointments, Clovis found that his will was quite enough.

Clovis built the Church of the Apostles in Paris, already called Saint Geneviève in the time of Gregory of Tours, which was to be the final resting place for him and his wife.

We have no reports that Clovis supported monasticism in any way; however, his sister Albofledis, who converted with him, died a nun, and the king also gave rich presents to Saint Martin of Tours, the "national saint" of Gaul, to whom he felt indebted for his victory over the Goths.[48] Following that victory Clovis established his royal residence in Paris. Whether this decision, made largely for strategic reasons, triggered an extensive building activity in the still-small town is not reported and is also unlikely.[49]

5. POLITICAL CAREERS

"To understand how the prince of a German tribe that had come from the north could take control of the better part of Gaul, let us imagine that a few battalions of Frankophile Zouaves or Spahis [former Berber troops in the Frankish army], against the backdrop of a serious political crisis, set up one of their commanders as the leader of the state. This commander wears a turban but is covered with French insignia, speaks Arabic but has abjured Islam in order to be accepted by the Christian world in which he lives. To be sure, such a comparison—taken literally—is pointless; but if we bear in mind the magnitudes involved, we can gain a better understanding of the extraordinary gamble that Germanic tribal groups took by forming themselves into standing armies [of Rome] and then taking possession of a civilization whose only way of dealing with conflicts was to bring them to court and settle them there."[50]

Such intellectual musings on the rise of Clovis are meant to illustrate the unusual; their point is not the comparison—inevitably incongruous—between Islam, a sophisticated religion, and a Frankish paganism that had long since lost its inner strength and credibility on Roman imperial soil. Moreover, the political and military starting positions of Clovis were by no means so insignificant that his rise to the top was unique. Well over a dozen other army chiefs were in a similar position: Theodoric son of Thiudimir was not much stronger when he set out "to lead the entire Gothic people, that is to say, those who had given him their consent, into the western [Roman] empire."[51] Like Clovis, he had to prevail not only within the Roman state but also against a host of Germanic rivals before he could become Theodoric the Great; both men, Clovis and Theodoric, began their careers at the fringe of the Roman world.

The Elimination of Barbarian Rivals

Just as Dietrich von Bern in the heroic saga did not fight Romans or Huns but Germans, the historical Theodoric too waged his fiercest struggles against his own tribesmen and clansmen. While the tradition of the Amali celebrated their unity as the highest good, the history of Theodoric teaches us that only one Amal, namely the most violent and ruthless, could assert and continue the tradition of the clan.

The Amal Goths had split while still in Pannonia. Young Theodoric's success in 470 posed the greatest threat to his uncle and cousin, the two Vidimirs. His brother Thiudimund had to withdraw after giving proof in the "gorges of the Balkans" how little royal fortune he possessed. For more than a decade Theodoric "the Squinter" had prevented his namesake from expanding, eventually even challenging the Ostrogothic kingship from his base in Thrace.

Only after Theodoric Strabo had died in 481 was Theodoric son of Thiudimir able to enter upon the inheritance of his dead namesake. To be sure, "the Squinter" left behind a wife, two brothers, and a son, Rekitach, but none of the Thracian Goths were a danger to the Pannonian-Moesian relative. Rekitach had soon gambled away his father's position. First he killed his uncles, then he lost Strabo's army. In 484, Rekitach was murdered in Constantinople by the consul of that year, Flavius (Amalus) Theodoricus, with the emperor's knowledge. This spectacular deed, committed in bright daylight, would not be the only one of its kind in the life of Theodoric the Great. And the motive too, blood vengeance (probably for Rekitach's uncles), was not unique to this deed.

Nine years later, on March 5, 493, Theodoric was able to enter Ravenna, having concluded with his enemy Odovacar a treaty by which the two would jointly possess the royal city and share the rule over Italy. Ten days later Odovacar was dead, slain by the hand of his coregent during a common meal.[52] Two contradictory motives were circulated as justification for the crime: first, Odovacar's death was blood vengeance for his killing of the Rugian relatives (evidently it didn't matter for this version that the son of the Rugian royal couple was at this very moment in open rebellion against Theodoric); second, the Gothic king had merely preempted an ambush by his rival.

In actuality the Amal broke the treaty out of the blue and committed open murder. Not even the words put into Theodoric's mouth can change this: when Odovacar's asked, "Where is God?" Theodoric answered, "This is what you have done to my people." While two of Theodoric's men who were pretending to be suppliants grabbed Odovacar's hands, the Gothic king ran his treaty partner through with his sword and is even said to have spoken these words over Odovacar's slain body: "The wretch doesn't even have bones in his body."

The events following Odovacar's murder clearly reveal that the deed was carefully planned. Odovacar was refused a Christian burial, his wife was starved to death. His older brother Hunulf sought refuge in a church, where Gothic archers killed him from outside. Odovacar's son Thela survived; he was sent into exile to Visigothic Gaul, but he, too, was eliminated when he made efforts to return to Italy. On the very day of Odovacar's murder, his barbarian supporters and their families were attacked: the Goths cut down everybody they could lay their hands on.

But even for Theodoric, now lord of Italy, the struggle for the monarchical kingship was far from over. In 504, Theodoric turned on the Gepids at the lower Save to drive the king of the sister tribe from Roman imperial territory. Three years later, after Alaric II had been killed at the battle of Vouillé, a inner-Gothic war broke out and lasted until 511. Only when it ended was Theodoric the Great also king of the Visigoths. Alaric's premarital son, the Balth Gesalec, was eliminated, and the "genuine" son, the Amal-Balth Amalaric, was kept from exercising an independent rule during his grandfather's lifetime, even after he had come of age.

Theodoric proceeded much the same way against his sister's son, Theodahad. Even though Theodahad was, apart from Theodoric, the only male Amal among Thiudimir's progeny, he was step-by-step deprived of power. While his mother had become queen of the Vandals and his sister queen of the Thuringians, Theodahad himself was still stuck in Tuscany, and all he could do was expand his possessions at the expense of his neighbors.

When it became clear that Theodoric would not have any male offspring, the king put Eutharic, Vidimir's grandson from Gaul, in place of his nephew. In 515 he married this Amal he had "found" among the Visigoths to his daughter Amalasuintha and designated him his successor. Even when Eutharic died a few years later (522/523), his son Athalaric and Amalasuintha were once again given preference over Theodahad, and they were to become the rulers of the Amal clan. Until Athalaric's death, Theodoric's decision kept the Amal "philosopher" from power: only then did Theodahad reach the kingship, though it was an inglorious one and ended with his death after only two years.[53]

To follow Theodoric's struggle for power we must work our way through many sources. By contrast, Clovis's rise to power is much easier to track. The outrage over the crimes he committed in the process still echoes fifteen hundred years later. "Our Merovingians were in no way inferior to African tyrants when it comes to their frenzy and cruelty"—a French journalist recently commented on the three chapters in which Gregory of Tours describes Clovis's brutality.[54] It does indeed remind us of the raging of African despots and self-appointed emperors, and may even be compared to crimes far worse.

The barbarians of the migration period, however, were nothing other than Rome's able students when they turned defeated enemies into unlawful rulers and proceeded to liquidate them in this horrifyingly automatic fashion. And so it was only cold-blooded logic when Clovis, immediately after the victory over the Visigoths, more than twenty years after his conquest of the kingdom of Syagrius and more than a decade after the decisive victory over the Alamanni, eliminated the other Frankish kings.

Clovis moved from the external to the internal situation. He prepared his absolute seizure of power within the Salian kingdoms by acquiring the kingdom of the Rhine Franks. The kings of Cologne—father and son, recent allies against the Alamanni and Goths—were first turned against each other and then destroyed. Next Clovis moved against the Salian King Chararic and his son, both of whom had been baptized with him. To justify his actions, word was put out that Chararic had refused to aid Clovis when the latter had attacked the Roman King Syagrius of Soissons; this, however, was an event that had occurred twenty years before. After Chararic's downfall, the Salians of Cambrai were next: Ragnachar—who did support Clovis against Syagrius—and his own brothers.

> In the same way he encompassed the death of many other kings and blood relations of his whom he suspected of conspiring against his kingdom. By doing this he spread his dominion over the whole of Gaul. One day when he had called a general assembly of his subjects, he is said to have made the following remark about the relatives whom he had destroyed: "How sad a thing it is that I live among strangers like some solitary pilgrim, and that I have none of my own relations left to help me when disaster threatens!" He said this not because he grieved for their deaths, but because in his cunning way he hoped to find some relative still alive in the land of the living whom he could kill.[55]

6. PERSONAL QUALITIES

The insincere lament about the dead relatives is not the only example of words Gregory of Tours puts into the mouth of the Frankish king. But in every passage the author draws the same picture of Clovis as a power-hungry man as successful as he was cynical and brutal, and whose piety and faith in God can all too easily strike us today as hypocrisy. The same misunderstanding also dominates the interpretation of the famous story that is said to have transpired at the yearly gathering of the army after Clovis's victory over Syagrius. Gregory of Tours recounts that Clovis, desirous of returning a precious liturgical vessel to a bishop, had asked his warriors during the distribution of the booty in Soissons to grant him the vessel even though it was not part of his share. All agreed to do so except one, who insisted on his rights, smashed the vessel with his battle-ax and departed unmolested. The following year the king assembled the entire army on the parade ground to inspect in person the weapons of his warriors. Eventually he came to the man who had smashed the liturgical vessel. In typical soldier's jargon he criticized the deplorable condition of the man's weapons. Then he seized the warrior's ax and threw it on the ground, and when the latter bent down to pick it up Clovis raised his own battle-ax and split open his skull.[56]

The picture of Clovis could hardly be any bleaker, one would think. But the picture of Theodoric would appear in the same hues were we to draw it based only on the accounts relating the story of the king's struggle to obtain and maintain power. But in contrast to Clovis, Theodoric found a discriminating observer, Ennodius, who wrote also about the king's brighter side: "Italy's ruler reconciles in friendship the two greatest opposites: in anger he is as lightning and like nobody else, in joy he is of unclouded beauty."[57]

Theodoric must have fought his battles in person and at the front lines until he was past middle age. At the lower Danube the king still defeated a khan of the Bulgars in a duel; he did not kill the defeated enemy but let him live and evidently concluded a treaty with him.

Ennodius tells us that Theodoric hurled himself into the Gepid battle at the Vuka in 488 with the words: "Whoever seeks a path through the enemy's ranks follow me; whoever seeks an example for battle look at me and no one else! Bravery does not ask about numbers; few must take the burdens of war upon themselves, many enjoy its fruits. The Gothic army will be judged by what I do, and the tribe will triumph in my deeds. Raise up my battle standard that I may be visible to all; let every enemy know whom he is attacking or by whose blow he perishes. He who clashes with me will win honor only by his death."

Before the battle of Verona in late summer of 489, Theodoric, then thirty-eight years old, bid farewell to his mother and is said by Ennodius to have addressed her in these words:

> Mother, known to all peoples through your son's honor, you know that you have given birth to a man. Today is the day when the battlefield will prove the manhood of your son. With arms I must show that the fame of my ancestors does not come to an end with me. Without reason would we invoke the deeds of our ancestors if we had none of our own to show. Before my eyes stands my [dead] father, whom never a fickle fortune made a fool of in battle, who always won his victories himself by virtue of his own strength." . . . "Fetch the noble

robes and precious clothes! The battle line shall behold me more festively attired than feast days are accustomed to doing. Whoever does not recognize me
from my attack shall surmise me from my radiant splendor. Let the honor of
the dress invite the eyes of those eager for it; let my appearance, so much more
splendid, bring me enemies to defeat. He to whom you, O Fortuna, give my
life shall have a consolation for his efforts! Then may those stare at the splendor of him killed in battle to whom it was not given to see him alive in battle.[58]

The rhetorically elevated language of the panegyrist Ennodius may strike
some as empty words and remind others of the false pathos of a so-called
great age. It does show, however, what impression Theodoric made on a well-
informed Roman contemporary. No matter how much he exaggerated, a
panegyrist could not leave the ground of reality for otherwise he would
turn the object of his praise into a laughingstock.[59] Moreover, Ennodius,
bishop of the royal city of Pavia, proves quite credible in one important, verifiable detail. Two extant portraits show Theodoric with long hair and no
headdress, and Ennodius says: "Let no one give ill-timed praise to magnificence and splendor; what the crown does for other rulers, God-guided nature has done for my king." And further: "It is the tall stature that distin-
guishes the king. The snow of the cheeks is combined with a healthy red
color; the eyes radiate with youthful freshness in eternal cheerfulness. The
well-formed hands distribute doom to rebels and requested honor to the
subjected."[60]

7. THE CONFRONTATION

It all began when Theodoric the Great, in 504, launched the only offensive
war he would conduct as lord of the western empire. While things were
mostly quiet along the Dalmatian rivers Drina and Neretva, which had for
decades formed the border between the Italian kingdom and the empire,
the situation at the estuary of the Drina near the old Pannonian imperial
city of Sirmium was far less stable.

A Gepid subtribe had settled in Pannonia II (present lower Slavonia) following the departure of the Goths in 473; as early as 488 it had obstructed
Theodoric's trek to Italy. This area, however, was the "old home of the
Goths," the territory of the Amal high king Valamir and of Theodoric's first
small kingdom. If Theodoric wanted to follow in the footsteps of "his ancestors," the western Roman emperors, he had to conquer Sirmium for two
reasons. First, he had to liberate Roman imperial territory from the barbarians; second, he had to reconquer from Constantinople a province that had
always belonged to the western empire. Theodoric's eastern policy was thus
in the tradition of the centuries-old quarrel between the western and eastern
emperors over the boundaries of their respective imperia.

A Gothic army, not overly large but powerful, drove out the Gepids, who withdrew via the Tisza to Transylvania, and quickly conquered Pannonia II. However, the victorious Goths pushed ahead and penetrated into the valley of the Moesian Margus River, today the Serbian Morava, which was a violation of Byzantine territory. Since Theodoric would not give up any of his conquests, he was automatically in a state of undeclared war with Anastasius I. Even though the emperor did not take any direct military countermeasures, the quick successes in the Pannonian war cost the Gothic king dearly. Imperial diplomacy more than made up for the territorial losses by wrecking Theodoric's policy toward the other tribes. During the five years between 505 and 510, when Theodoric reached a peace treaty by giving up his conquests in Moesia as well as southern Pannonia, the emperor prevented the Ostrogoths in every instance from coming to the aid of their allies or from doing so in a timely fashion. The greatest beneficiary of the Gothic stalemate was the Frankish King Clovis.

Theodoric launched his famous marriage and alliance policy after the murder of Odovacar in March of 493. That same year, or in 494, the Amal king of the Ostrogoths took the Merovingian Audofleda, Clovis's sister, as his wife. Audofleda gave birth to Amalasuintha and was to seal the friendship between the two rulers, at that time already the mightiest of the Roman-barbarian kings.

In fact the two rulers avoided any direct confrontation, though they did cause each other enough trouble.[61] After Theodoric's last marriage, his daughter Thiudigotho married the Balth and Visigothic King Alaric II. His other daughter, Ostrogotho, had already been betrothed to the Burgundian Crown Prince Sigismund while Theodoric was still fighting for Italy, but the marriage was probably not formalized until 497, the year Emperor Anastasius recognized Theodoric. Following his Roman tricennial in 500, Theodoric's sister Amalafrida married the Vandal King Thrasamund; about ten years later, around 510, their daughter Amalaberga became the wife of the Thuringian King Herminafrid.[62]

Theodoric, who had organized the Raetian hill country into the "bulwark and locking bolt of Italy," took the threatened Alamanni under his protection. In addition, Ravenna demanded in 506 that the Frankish king cease pursuing the defeated enemy, in return for which it guaranteed a secure border and the prevention of any further Alamannic attacks against Frankish territory. In order to fulfill that promise, Alamannic groups were accepted into Raetia I, but above all they were marched via Noricum ripense and settled in Northern Italy and the upper Save River.

The Alamannic crisis was not serious enough, however, for Theodoric to entirely cut off friendly relations with the Frankish royal court. The delegation that was to negotiate the Alamannic question with Clovis was accompanied by a citharist, "an Orpheus, who was to tame the wild hearts of a foreign people with his sweet sounds."

No less a man than Boethius, philosopher and member of the high nobility, had been instructed by the Gothic king to give proof of his expertise
by selecting a suitable musician. The accompanying letter itself was one
of the first accomplishments of the new quaestor Cassiodorus, one of the
most important men in the administration of the Ostrogothic kingdom. At
the same time Boethius began constructing a device to measure the hours
for the Burgundian king, and Cassiodorus wrote the explanatory remarks:
the Gothic kingdom of Italy had the duty and ability to bring culture to the
barbarian kings of Gaul.

Of course this cultural export could not hide the fact that the trans-
alpine peace was seriously endangered. Despite vigorous diplomatic activities, Theodoric was not able to break up the Frankish-Burgundian alliance
and prevent its attack on the Visigothic kingdom. Nor was the appeasement policy Theodoric had recommended to his son-in-law Alaric II of any
avail; without any provocation, Clovis struck with full force at the beginning
of the campaigning season in 507.

These events caught Theodoric completely by surprise; not until the
summer of 508 did he order his army to be called up. To be sure, an imperial fleet had ravaged the southern coast of Italy shortly before. Theodoric's
calculation that his brother-in-law, the allied Vandal king, would keep his
back clear proved wrong; the ships of the Vandals remained in their har-
bors, and Theodoric couldn't even begin to think of intervening in Gaul. As
a result Alaric was left to his own devices, and he lost the battle, his kingship,
and his life.

Now the Ostrogoths had no choice but to march to Gaul, where they
were involved in ever new battles from the middle of 508 until 511. The
two brothers-in-law of the Amal king, the Vandal king of Carthage and the
Frank Clovis, made a concerted effort to prevent Theodoric from becoming king of the Visigoths as well. Only after the Ostrogothic armies had
thwarted all attempts by one of Alaric's premarital sons to gain the Visigothic
kingship did Clovis suspend any further support for Theodoric's Visigothic
enemies.

Committing his forces in the West prevented Theodoric from saving
his son-in-arms, Rudolf, king of the March Heruli, when he was attacked by
the Longobards, the Heruli's former slaves, and crushingly defeated. Theodoric's attempt to use the Danubian Heruli to thwart the Franco-Lombard
rapprochement failed, much as the attempted mobilization of anti-Frankish
Germanic tribes along the Rhine had failed earlier. The protective circle that Theodoric had drawn around the borders of Italy, constructed of
friendly and dependent peoples, broke in the years 506–508. What caused
the breakdown was the first Franco-Byzantine coalition.

Theodoric was still able to prevent the worst: with his newfound Thu-

ringian friends in central Germany he was able to close off the area between the Danube and the Alps to the Franks. As long as his relationship
with the Thuringians held, there was no direct contact between the Franks,
the Longobards, and Byzantium. Only when Theodoric the Great was dead
was this bulwark broken, and now the perennially vacillating Burgundians
were no longer able to hold their own against the powerful Franks, their
erstwhile allies. The goal of Justinian's reconquest was to recapture as much
of the western empire as possible, but it merely ended up destroying what
the Byzantines wanted to conquer.

The Franks became lords not only of Gaul but also of the region of the
eastern Alps and the Thuringian kingdom. Unlike the Romans, they were
also able to subject territory in central Germany over the long term from
their base on Roman soil. Justinian's victory over the Vandals merely returned a severely weakened Africa to the Roman fold, while the conquests in
southern Spain could be defended against a resurgent Visigothic kingdom
for barely two generations. But it was Italy, more than any other place, that
turned into a battlefield on which the Gothic war raged for eighteen years.
It was followed by the division of the peninsula, on which Constantinople's
erstwhile allies, Franks and Longobards, established themselves. Justinian's
policy of reconquest at any price was so enduring that the division of Italy
lasted into the nineteenth century. Italy, however, had forever lost the Alpine and Danubian provinces of Raetia, Noricum, and Pannonia—leaving
aside the never implemented Carolingian plan announced in 806.[63]

What was new about Justinian's western policy was not its anti-Gothic
tendency—from which the Franks profited—but the resolute use of the empire's military means in Africa, Italy, and Spain. Anastasius I had already
supported the non-Gothic barbarians of Gaul. The Burgundians held a relatively strong position as long they had to deal only with the pre-Euric Visigoths and the Romans. With the beginning of Euric's expansionary policy,
the rise of Frankish power, and the establishment of the Italian-Gothic kingdom, they fell increasingly behind and thus took the initiative in seeking
the emperor's help. As early as 474, when Zeno and Geiseric concluded an
eternal—that is to say, transpersonal—peace, the Burgundians renewed an
old-style treaty, as a result of which their kings once again took over Roman
military offices. The monarchs saw themselves as commanders of Gaul,
kings of imperial federates, and bearers of Roman official titles and designations of rank.

While the Burgundians had requested Roman legitimation on their own,
in the case of the Merovingian king legitimation was the result of both a
diplomatic offensive on the part of Constantinople and Clovis's own efforts.
After his great victory over the Goths in 507, and having captured Toulouse
and then Angoulême at the beginning of 508 together with his Burgundian

allies, Clovis came to Tours, probably in the middle of 508, to hold a victory celebration. There he met Byzantine envoys who presented to him the decree naming him an honorary consul.

These events, which took place prior to Theodoric's intervention in Gaul, have remained to this day the subject of many interpretations. Some have even seen them as the "first German coronation of an emperor." More recently a much more sober and far more convincing explanation has been put forth. According to Gregory of Tours, the ceremony began outside the walls of Saint Martin. In the cathedral church Clovis donned a purple tunic and chlamys, a vestment that was part of the usual uniform of imperial officials. He added a diadem, mounted a horse, and rode in procession into the city up to the cathedral, tossing gold and silver to the inhabitants who lined the streets. Michael McCormick has argued that "the triumph parade on horseback, the conclusion of the procession at a local sanctuary, even the festive *sparsio* of cash to win the hearts and minds of a newly subjugated town all recall the victory celebrations not of Constantinople, but of imperial commanders operating in the provinces."

Before the beginning of the parade, the Catholic Merovingian king had made an offering of part of the Arian-Gothic booty to the local saint, Saint Martin. "At Tours, the founder of the Merovingian kingdom utilized the traditional Roman ritual forms derived, at least in part, from provincial victory celebrations to build a new political consensus, to win the approval of the foreign majority he hoped to govern." All this took place with Constantinople's blessings and had received the emperor's recognition, a recognition that was visible to all.[64]

8. THE OUTCOME: FRANKISH REALITY AND GOTHIC MYTH

Theodoric and Clovis embody two designs for a Roman-Germanic synthesis. The future belonged to Clovis's design; his Frankish kingdom did not fall and it provided Charlemagne the foundation for the reestablishment of a western empire, which some have even seen as the prefiguration of modern Europe. Clovis converted to the Catholic faith and established his kingdom in what was, from the Byzantine view, distant Gaul. Theodoric's kingdom of Arian Goths was too close to be tolerated as an alternative, either in religious terms or as a res publica divided into barbarians and Romans and thus paradoxical in its very nature.[65]

The architecture of Theodoric's royal tomb, the famous mausoleum in Ravenna, symbolizes even beyond his death his program for a union of West and East, of *Romanitas* and *gentilitas*. Is that why the tomb has been empty for so long? We cannot blame the medieval monks of the monastery of Saint Mary (erected next to the tomb) for having no use for the bones of the heretic king. But in all likelihood the monks were never put into a position of having to dispose of the dreadful memorial: already in the ninth century the porphyry sarcophagus next to the monastery's gate stood empty. Nobody knows who removed Theodoric from his final resting place or when.

There were many rumors and stories about Theodoric's death. In one version the spirits of the senators he had persecuted and killed, hurled him into the crater of the volcano on the island of Lipara. In another version, Theodoric was taken off by demonic horses. Procopius has him die of typhoid fever brought on by fear and remorse at his misdeeds:

> And he died in the following manner. Symmachus and his son-in-law Boethius were men of noble and ancient lineage, and both had been leading men in the Roman senate and had been consuls. But because they practiced philosophy and were mindful of justice in a manner surpassed by no other men, relieving the destitution of both citizens and strangers by generous gifts of money, they attained great fame and thus led men of the basest sort to envy them. Now such persons slandered them to Theodoric, and he, believing their slanders, put these two men to death, on the ground that they were setting about a revolution, and confiscated their property for the public treasury. And a few days later, while he was dining, their servants set before him the head of a great fish. This seemed to Theodoric the head of Symmachus newly slain. Indeed, with its teeth set in its lower lip and its eyes looking at him with a grim and insane stare, it did resemble exceedingly a person threatening him. And becoming greatly frightened at the extraordinary prodigy and shivering excessively, he retired running to his own chamber, and bidding them place many covers upon him, remained quiet. But afterward he disclosed to his physician, Elpidius, all that had happened and wept for the wrong he had done Symmachus and Boethius. Then, having lamented and grieved exceedingly over the unfortunate occurrence, he died not long afterward. This was the first and last act of injustice that he committed toward his subjects, and the cause of it was that he had not made a thorough investigation, as he was accustomed to do, before passing judgment on the two men.[66]

In the eyes of the barbarians, of course, the Gothic king had not died. He sat on his charger armed, ready to lead the demonic army of the dead or, as the god of war, to receive the consecration of the warriors. The Germanic peoples of Italy, and the Longobards as the last of them, told stories that were no less dramatic about a certain Dietrich von Bern (Verona) who had had to flee into exile among the Huns and had not been able to return to his homeland for thirty years, an entire generation. When he finally did return, Hildebrand, Dietrich's loyal armorer, had to kill Dietrich's own son because the young hero would not accept the old warrior as his father, thus "robbing him of his honor."

Compared to the Frankish reality, the Amal tradition had become a vague myth, which, strangely enough can still touch us today.

TEN

A Battle for Rome
(526/535–552/555)

Theodoric's succession arrangement failed: his Visigothic son-in-law Eutharic died in 522/523, and the Roman opposition had its own ideas about the future of Italy. It was probably still in 523 that Albinus, the ex-consul and representative of the Roman inhabitants of Rome, corresponded directly with the emperor about the question of Amal succession, bypassing Theodoric. The letters were intercepted by the Roman opposition faction and taken to Ravenna, where Theodoric summoned the *consistorium,* the highest court responsible for Roman affairs.[1]

Boethius, recently appointed *magister officiorum* and thus ex officio a member of this court, tried to exonerate Albinus, but the Roman Cyprianus, a friend of the Goths and enemy of the Romans from the city, insisted on a charge of high treason. Boethius's reaction was imprudent: "The accusation brought by Cyprianus is false," he declared. "If Albinus did anything wrong, I myself and the entire senate are also guilty." Now the court party of Ravenna gained the upper hand over the Roman senators; Boethius not only failed to save his friend but became entangled in the affair himself.

From the fall of 523, Boethius spent more than a year in prison in Pavia, where he wrote his famous work *The Consolation of Philosophy.* Without a chance to be heard by the king, Boethius was sentenced to die in the summer of 524 as a criminal, his property was confiscated, and he was bludgeoned to death. In 525 Symmachus, the leader of the senate, shared the fate of his son-in-law Boethius. Theodoric, however, was still not satisfied, and he became increasingly caught up in an excessively harsh course against the circles he regarded as the Roman opposition. When he even went so far as to throw in prison the pope, who died there in the spring of 526, the break with Rome and Constantinople was complete.

Though the Gothic king was able to promote his candidate to the apostolic seat, it was clear that a storm was brewing. When the king died on August 30, 526, from dysentery—like Arius before him—most Catholics were sure that the Gothic king had gone to hell.

Athalaric, born in 516, was only ten years old when his grandfather Theodoric died. The seventy-five-year-old king had had enough time to arrange the succession with the Gothic magnates, "the *comites* and the first of the people," but had not been able to obtain the approval of Byzantium. Amalasuintha was to exercise the regency for the child Athalaric and carry out the political testament of the dead king, namely, to seek accommodation with the senate and to live in peace with the emperor. Agents sent from Ravenna put Romans as well as Goths under oath to the new king, promising in return the continuation, or rather the renewal, of harmonious relations between the two peoples. Special pledges of protection were offered to the senate and it received once again the right to mint copper coins. In a letter to the emperor, Amalasuintha dissociated herself from the harsh course of her father. At the same time the families of Symmachus and Boethius were given back their confiscated property.

The death of Theodoric also put an end to the personal union of the two Gothic kingdoms. His Visigothic grandson Amalaric assumed independent rule for the next five years. This entailed a diminution of Ravenna's power. The Visigothic royal treasure was returned from Italy. Now that the Rhône formed a real border, Gothic Gaul was no longer jointly defended, which meant an added burden for Ravenna. In addition, the Ostrogothic army was seriously weakened by the agreement that every Goth could chose one of the two Gothic kingdoms: since far more Ostrogoths were stationed in western garrisons than vice versa, a large Ostrogothic group once again joined the Visigoths.

Nevertheless, in the first years after Theodoric's death there was peace at home and abroad. Territorial violations were vigorously punished: for example, the attempt by the Gepids and Heruli in 530 to conquer Gothic Pannonia Sirmiensis failed. While the Ostrogothic troops were victorious along the northeastern frontier, Amalasuintha was striving to improve relations with the Burgundians: she ceded the territory north of the Durance and entered into a full-fledged alliance with her Burgundian neighbors in southern Gaul.

But every time it came to marching against the Franks, Ravenna could not muster the courage to do so. The Ostrogothic troops did not come to the aid of the Thuringians in 531 and 534, nor did they leave their own territory in 532/533 to support the Burgundians against the Franks. As a result the two allied neighboring kingdoms lost their independence, and what had been a short Frankish-Gothic border at Theodoric's time became a border nearly one thousand miles long. Every additional expansion along this line by the Franks was an immediate threat to Ostrogothic territory.

Amalasuintha's rule did not go unchallenged for long. To be sure, contemporaries praised her manly courage and sagacity, as evidence of which one might mention her early attempt to improve relations with her cousin Theodahad. The fortune of Theodahad's mother had been confiscated after her death. Amalasuintha agreed to a partial restitution and held out the prospect of the remainder provided Theodahad acted loyally in the future. But precisely that was what Theodahad was not willing to do: after a temporary setback, the intransigent court party surrounding the brothers Cyprianus and Opilio was able to regain its old role as early as 527/528, and there can be no doubt that both Theodahad and outstanding Gothic generals openly or secretly belonged to this faction.

In late 532 or early 533, this group believed the time had come to take over power. To that end they had to get Athalaric on their side, for the king had just turned sixteen and was approaching his majority. The pretext for this intervention was the young Amal's upbringing and education, which they charged was un-Gothic and violated the principles laid down by Theodoric.

The regent gave in and changed her son's teachers, though this merely precipitated a full-fledged crisis. Amalasuintha asked the emperor for political asylum and sent a clipper with the state treasure on it to Durazzo, where Justinian had assigned her a palace. At the same time the emperor invited the Gothic queen to come to Constantinople. The ship dropped anchor in its port of destination; it was filled with forty thousands pounds of gold, equivalent to roughly twice the annual budget of the western empire.

Amalasuintha herself, however, remained in Ravenna and fought back. Things soon got too hot for her cousin Theodahad: he too wanted to emigrate to Constantinople and sell all of Tuscany to the emperor. As for the three leading generals who were her enemies, with the Franks having attacked the Burgundians in 532, in the process even taking the Gothic city of Arles, Amalasuintha did not need to invent a pretext for sending them to the front, where they were killed on orders from the queen. The opposition collapsed, and Amalasuintha could recall her golden ship from across the Adriatic.

The crisis of 533 had been mastered, but that didn't mean that Athalaric had become a man, and it seemed that there was little hope he ever would. When he died in 534, Amalasuintha showed that she was not unprepared. Even though the victory over her domestic enemies was barely a year old, she appointed her hostile relative Theodahad coregent and officially declared herself queen. Her cousin had to swear that he recognized her as the actual ruler and would serve merely as the figurehead of the Gothic kingdom.

Theodahad, who had been made king and coruler in November of 534, strove, with Amalasuintha's support, to gain Constantinople's recognition.

But soon after, during the last weeks of 534, he arrested his cousin, removed her from Ravenna, and confined her on an island in Lake Bolsena. By April 30, 535, at the latest, the Gothic queen was no longer alive; her personal enemies, the survivors of the faction of nobles she had defeated in 532/533, had murdered her in revenge.

A delegation dispatched to Constantinople by Theodahad prior to the murder to reassure Justinian collapsed in the process of carrying out its mission: when the murder of the Gothic queen became known in the spring of 535, neither further assuagements nor letters from Theodahad to the emperor and the empress were of any avail. Amalasuintha's violent death constituted a casus belli: it meant the declaration of "a war that ruled out any negotiated peace."

With Italy in turmoil, with Romans and Goths turning against the new regime and the Gothic army fighting to preserve peace at home instead of rallying against an attack from outside, Justinian launched his war of reconquest on land and sea. He opened his offensive in Dalmatia, whose capital, Salona, was captured even before the year 535 was out. Belisarius, the general who had vanquished the Vandals, was sent into action to establish a second front.

Belisarius was given orders to attack Sicily with a small but powerful army of about nine thousand men. The emperor's instructions to his general reveal caution and uncertainty about the expected resistance and the extent of Italo-Roman cooperation. Belisarius's naval mission was therefore declared to be a reinforcement for the Carthaginian garrison. When the ships of Belisarius were approaching Catania in Sicily in June of 535, it was still possible to call off the attack and explain it away as a stopover on the way to Africa.

The great concern on the part of the Byzantines proved unfounded, however. The Roman militias of Sicily opened the gates of their cities, and even Syracuse, the seat of the Gothic *comes,* surrendered without a fight. Only the garrison of Palermo refused to give in, but because the city's fortifications were weak it was quickly taken. On the last day of the year 535, at the end of his consulship, Belisarius entered Syracuse in triumph, showering gold coins on the inhabitants. The Roman general had been remarkably successful.

Theodahad wanted peace and negotiated with the emperor over the price for abdicating and handing Italy over to Justinian. The negotiations were in full swing when, on Easter 536, the imperial troops in Carthage rebelled and the Goths simultaneously won their first victories in Dalmatia. This gave Theodahad new courage: he broke off all talks and forgot about the agreements already made.

However, when Belisarius crossed the Strait of Messina, he encountered Theodahad's son-in-law, who immediately surrendered. Thereafter Belisarius marched unopposed as far as Naples, where he met the first fierce resistance. The city could not be saved; however, Theodahad no longer hid in Ravenna but advanced toward the imperial general as far as Rome, in the vicinity of which he concentrated the greater part of the Gothic army. But a revolt took place among the Gothic troops at the end of November 536, and Vitigis was raised up as king. Theodahad tried to escape to Ravenna, but he was murdered en route on orders from the new king.

In the five years between 531 and 536, the last three kings who can be attested as members of the Amal clan died. All had been closely related: two grandsons of Theodoric and their uncle. All three were done in by their own people. Athalaric fell victim to the excesses of the Gothic lifestyle. Amalaric and Theodahad were deserted by their Gothic peoples and killed because they failed in the struggle to preserve their gens. No *idoneus,* no Amal suitable for ruling was alive, and the non-Amal nobility could not fill the gap. The Gothic leading stratum had suffered severe losses during the last years. And so the proven commander Vitigis was raised on the shield, and while he was not from an "illustrious family," he and his relatives belonged to the Gothic military "establishment": both the uncle and the nephew of the new Gothic king had been high-ranking commanders and sword bearers.

1. VITIGIS (536–540)

Vitigis made it abundantly clear that his rule was that of a king of the army: he is the first Gothic king known for certain to have been raised on the shield and "with [his warriors'] swords drawn according to ancestral custom." Vitigis saw himself as a relative of Theodoric, whose deeds he was imitating. This plan of association to the Amal clan on the basis of personal suitability also demanded that as the new king he give up his advantageous position in Rome and move to Ravenna, seize the royal city, and marry Matasuntha, Theodoric's granddaughter. Vitigis presented his rule as an Amal kingship not only for the benefit of the Goths; he was also hoping that in this way he could obtain imperial recognition along with peace.

In Ravenna, Vitigis concluded the long-overdue treaty with the Franks. The Ostrogoths paid an indemnity of two thousand pounds in return for which the Franks refrained from an attack on Italy, handed over to the Franks their protectorate over the Alamanni and the other eastern Alpine peoples, and relinquished Gaul, from which the Ostrogoths could now recall their troops. With the addition of the Gallic army, Vitigis's force was numerically superior to that of his Roman adversary. Retreating to Ravenna, gathering the Gothic forces in northern Italy and carefully rearming them with offensive weapons and armor: these well-planned moves—alongside the constitutional measures to secure the kingship—show a seasoned general at work. Moreover, Vitigis proceeded to attack the Romans in Dalmatia.

Between the end of November 536 and February 537, Vitigis led the Gothic army from Terracina south of Rome to Ravenna and back to Rome. To be sure, during this time the Eternal City was lost, contrary to the Gothic war plan, a loss even the senatorial hostages whom the Goths had taken along could not prevent. But Vitigis had strengthened his army, he had prevented a war on two fronts with the help of a timely treaty, he had won the royal city and had taken Matasuntha as his wife. The young woman, about eighteen years of age, showed that she however was not pleased with the situation, though her displeasure probably had less to do with Vitigis's age—he was born around 500—than with his birth. Perhaps she was also bothered by the fact that her royal consort had repudiated his first wife to marry her.

In the meantime Belisarius had entered Rome on December 9 or 10, 536. He had about five thousand imperial troops at his command, not counting the city militia. When Belisarius, in a dispatch to the emperor, lamented the thirtyfold superiority of the enemy he was greatly exaggerating, but it was time for Constantinople to realize that the situation had changed since the death of Theodahad. Byzantium's *drôle de guerre* of the first eighteen months had turned into a full-scale Gothic war.

The situation of the Roman army was soon so desperate that Vitigis was actually afraid he might not be able to force Belisarius to accept battle. But in this war too there was no danger of arriving too late at the front line. Since Vitigis made a detour around Belisarius's advanced strongholds at Spoleto and Perugia, he reached the city on the Tiber sooner than anticipated. On February 21, 537, the Goths stood before the gates of Rome, and even though the city had lost much of its population, which had once come close to a million, it offered a home and protection to what was still a very large number of people.[2] The first act in a battle for Rome had begun.

For more than a year the Goths assaulted the city's walls, suffering defeats and winning victories in splendid cavalry attacks. The Goths hurled themselves at the walls with no regard for losses, and the defenders' heavy artillery and the mounted and armored archers wrought havoc among the Gothic lancers and foot soldiers. In addition, the arrival of Roman reinforcements soon brought to an end Gothic superiority in numbers. To be sure, the large-scale Gothic assault on the eighteenth day of the siege nearly succeeded, and this seemed to justify the decision of those who had deserted to the Goths at the very outset because they had given up Belisarius's cause as lost. But they were all proved wrong.

Though hunger and epidemics were raging in the city, Belisarius managed to hold out. In the meantime, the Gothic attack on Dalmatia had failed, and the Gothic king's efforts to make peace met with no response whatsoever from Constantinople. The imperial general also refused to entertain the offer to divide Italy along the lines of the status quo. *Fortuna* now deserted Vitigis. The Gothic king concluded an armistice from which only Belisarius profited. It gave the imperial general plenty of time to reprovision Rome and gather enough forces to break the armistice at the next best opportunity and resume hostilities.

In the first months of the winter of 538, a Roman cavalry force crossed the Apennines, laid waste Gothic Picenum, enslaved the women and children of the Gothic warriors besieging Rome, and finally advanced as far as Rimini, where it entrenched itself dangerously close to Ravenna. Vitigis hastily lifted the siege of Rome at the beginning of March 538 and returned to his royal city. The mountain fortress Auximum-Osimo south of Ancona was to stop the advance of the imperial army: the "key to Ravenna" was placed into the hands of its strong Gothic garrison.

Belisarius advanced northward at a slow pace, too slow in Constantinople's view. A Byzantine fleet landed an army in Genoa and opened a second front in Liguria. Milan was lost, though with the help of Burgundian "volunteers," who behaved barbarically, the Goths recaptured it at great cost to the inhabitants. Vitigis's nephew Uraias eventually succeeded in expelling the imperial troops from Liguria, but the king's uncle was killed in battle outside of Rimini.

As though this weren't enough, Alamannic raiders now swept through upper Italy, and Vitigis decided to enter into an alliance with the Franks. Perhaps now the Goths could get along with their northern neighbors after all, enter into treaties with them and use their support. In 538 starvation ravaged the land, afflicting friend and foe alike. Its horrors, suffered especially by the peasants in the lowlands, went hand in hand with an increasingly brutal warfare, for which Belisarius's cavalry commanders bear much of the responsibility.

Belisarius had not set out from Rome until June 21, 538. Shortly after his departure, Narses went ashore in Picenum, probably at the port of Fermo, with seven thousand men. The numerical superiority of the Goths was now once and for all a thing of the past. They could only hope that rivalries and disagreements among the Roman generals would prevent the successful operation of the imperial forces. In fact this hope materialized as soon as the two armies united at Fermo. At times the quarrels between Narses and Belisarius completely paralyzed the imperial forces. While Narses advocated a combined action and wanted to destroy the Gothic army in a head-on attack—a strategy with which he did in fact put an end to the Gothic war more than a decade later—Belisarius intended to split the Gothic army into smaller units and defeat them one by one. By forcing them to defend strategically important sites the imperial forces would deprive the Goths of any mobility, and the end result would be the eventual siege and capture of Ravenna.

As early as the summer of 539 Uraias had to expect the arrival of a reinforced imperial army in Liguria. When it did arrive it thwarted all his attempts to leave the Po Valley to relieve Gothic-held Fiesole. As a result the garrison of this protective barrier to central Italy was soon in great distress. But the main theater of war was on the Adriatic coast, where Belisarius, with eleven thousand men, was assaulting the fortress of Osimo, defended by four thousand elite Gothic warriors.

Vitigis, in the meantime, sat in Ravenna and no longer intervened actively in the fighting. But he was not completely inactive either, nor as helpless as Procopius makes him out to be. It is more likely that the Gothic king had correctly recognized Belisarius's strategic superiority and tried to act accordingly by exchanging the role of the hapless general for that of the statesman with broad vision and grand strategy. Gothic envoys approached the Longobards, but they turned down the request for help by pointing to their own alliance with the empire. Next Vitigis dispatched two Persian-speaking clerics to try and mobilize the Persians against the empire. This threat was taken so seriously by Justinian that the Gothic delegation Vitigis had sent to Constantinople at the beginning of his reign was immediately sent back with promises of peace. Belisarius, however, detained the envoys for some time, eventually exchanging them for a Roman delegation seized during the days of Theodahad.

On top of everything else, King Theudebert led his Franks on a sudden raid into northern Italy in 539. Like an all-destroying whirlwind the barbarians fell upon the Goths and then upon the imperial army. But the Frankish advance was soon stopped in its tracks by food shortages and the outbreak of an epidemic. Theudebert turned back and vacated a large section of Italy, but he had lost all credibility with the Goths: from now on they wanted nothing to do with the Franks.

After the Frankish storm had blown over, Fiesole and Osimo fell, and at the end of 539 Belisarius united the main Roman army outside of Ravenna. Thus began the siege of the royal city, which Vitigis was to leave only as a captive. At this time his nephew still commanded a considerable force of four thousand men, but it was not put to use. The Gothic garrisons north of Genoa surrendered, which freed up the rear of the imperial forces. At the same time the families of most of Uraias's warriors were helplessly exposed to the enemy. His army dissolved, his people went home and submitted to the emperor. Uraias had no choice but to shut himself up in Pavia with his remaining loyal followers: exactly half a century earlier Theodoric the Great had done the same.

In the spring of 540, at the latest, another offer of assistance from Theudebert arrived in Ravenna: the Frankish king asked for half of Italy in return for driving out Belisarius. Vitigis declined, in part no doubt because the imperial general was eagerly negotiating with him and was holding out the prospects of an agreement acceptable to both sides.

In the meantime the reports from the Persian border worried the emperor, so much so that he was genuinely willing to make peace with the Goths. Suddenly their offer to divide Italy between a Gothic kingdom and the empire seemed a desirable solution. But the situation had changed so decisively in the emperor's favor since December of 537 that he could now demand much more, namely, half of the rich royal treasure and all the land up to the Po River. Although this would essentially have confined the Gothic kingdom to the two Italian provinces of Liguria and Venetia-Istria, from our point of view this solution would have been almost ideal for all parties concerned. Italy would have been spared the truly destructive phase of the Gothic war, and a small but compact Gothic kingdom north of the Po would have been the best protection for the peninsula. The Gothic kingdom and imperial Italy could have found a peaceful accommodation that would by no means have lead to the actual division of the land.

Vitigis and his Goths as well as the advisers around the imperial general were in favor of accepting the peace offer from Constantinople. But Belisarius was a general, and generals fight until they have forced the enemy's unconditional surrender. He refused to sign the treaty, whereupon the Goths withdrew their support for the agreement.

It is also possible that the Goths misinterpreted the hesitation of the Roman *patricius* and supreme commander because it suited their own wishful thinking. Belisarius's appointment by the legitimate Roman authorities as well as his success over the Italian Gothic army had made him almost "automatically" king of the army and *rex* of the western empire. Vitigis no longer dared wage the decisive battle and fight for the existence of the gens. The unsuccessful leader of the gens now offered the kingship to the victorious enemy.

However, there must have been earlier negotiations concerning Belisarius's elevation to the emperorship to the West. Such negotiations are clearly mentioned before the offer of the kingship. Furthermore, Belisarius made a peculiar and, in light of the numerical superiority of the Goths, nonsensical decision before marching into Ravenna: he sent away four commanders and their units to distant places because these officers "had behaved in a very hostile manner toward him." He did the same with the new praetorian prefect who had just arrived from Byzantium with an appointment for Italy. Only then did Belisarius enter the capital of the western empire with the few contingents loyal and faithful to him. But in principle this army, as the *exercitus Romanus*, had the right of proclaiming an emperor; mutatis mutandis Belisarius's soldiers would have taken over the role the Gallic army had played at the elevation of Avitus, while the Vitigis Goths would have taken on the part played by the Visigothic army.

Whether Belisarius was seriously thinking about accepting the elevation to the emperorship—his removal of the unreliable Roman troops and his cool reception by Justinian upon his return to Constantinople lend weight to such a notion—or whether he merely wanted to create the impression that he was prepared to do so is not something we can decide. He did, however, use the theory of the barbarian kingship and the traditional policy of the regnum Hesperium with such skill that he maneuvered Vitigis and his Goths into a position where they had no choice but to surrender, since they were already suffering from a terrible famine. The imperial army entered Ravenna unopposed, took captive the Gothic king and his army, and thus seemed to have ended the conquest of the western empire in May 540. Procopius describes the scorn and horror of the Gothic women when they realized to whom their men had surrendered. But the war was not over; as usual, a war fought with the aim of "total victory" had gambled away peace.

Wars are not won by declaring that they have ended in victory. But that is precisely what Belisarius had done in Carthage in 534, and he repeated the mistake on imperial orders when he left Ravenna prematurely in 540 in order to bring his emperor the Gothic royal treasure together with the king and queen, the court nobles, and a band of Gothic elite warriors. Among the deportees were also the son and daughter of the former Thuringian queen Amalaberga, allegedly a son of Vitigis from his first marriage, as well as children of a Gothic magnate who was encamped north of the Po with his people and had had himself declared king that same year. Belisarius, however, sailed away, and the war began anew.

Immediately after Belisarius's departure, the Italian army of the emperor suffered severely from desertions. Disagreements among the imperial generals as well as a rigorous, indeed ruinous, collection of taxes eroded the morale of the civilian population; at the same time the imperial treasury reduced the pay to the troops, if it did not stop it outright. The Goths, "undefeated in the field," could thus afford bloody clashes between two Gothic candidates for the kingship, followed by the murder of the new king and the elevation of a Rugian as king without having the Romans intervene.

In this situation a Gothic kingdom north of the Po, which had originally been intended for Vitigis, was able to hold its own for more than a year, with no imperial generals crossing the river during this time. Eventually the Gothic army decided to offer the kingship to the successful commander of Treviso. This commander demanded that the king from outside the tribe be killed, and his demand was met. In October of 541, at the latest, he became the new king of the Goths: his name was Totila.

2. TOTILA (541–552)

Along with Valamir and Theodoric, Totila was undoubtedly one of the three most capable commanders of the Ostrogoths. To be sure, in the long run even Totila was no match for a general like Narses, and the catastrophe at Busta Gallorum, which decided the fate of the Gothic kingdom in the summer of 552, does not show him in the best light. But he was king for nearly eleven years before that fateful battle, the second-longest reign of a Gothic king in Italy, after that of Theodoric.

Like Alaric I, the "heroic youth" Totila is among the favorite figures in German historiography. As late as 1949 even Ern(e)st Stein, who stood above all indulgence in Germanomania, shared the "real admiration" his Viennese teacher Ludo Moritz Hartmann had felt for Totila. However, some authors to this day follow the judgment of Totila's contemporaries who felt that his "elevation was a disaster for Italy." Neither interpretation does justice to the sort of motivations that drove Totila and the age in which he lived. The Goths declared him king so that he would recover for them the "dominion over the Italians." He thus had no choice but to enter upon his kingship with all his powers, lest he shared the fate of his predecessors.

Totila's history is the story of eleven years of war in Italy, on the Italian islands, and along the coast of Dalmatia and Epirus. The details of military operations—advances and retreats, which cities were besieged and for how long, whether the besiegers took a city by assault, starvation, or treachery—are the concern of specialists. Military historians may be intrigued by these details, for at times a comparison between Procopius's *De bello Gothico* and events of World War II in Italy forces itself even upon the layman. The accounts concerning the cities and regions of the peninsula are full of destruction, decline, and misery. They are therefore of great interest also to local historians investigating the fate of a particular Italian region during the transition from antiquity to the Middle Ages. But the general historian can condense the era of Totila into three phases.

The first phase of the war encompasses only the time from the elevation of Totila in the fall of 541 to the spring of 543. The second phase is the longest, stretching from the capture of Naples in 543 to the year 550, when Germanus was appointed supreme commander for Italy and Justinian at the same time made possible the quick and successful conclusion of the war through a large-scale military effort. The third and last phase of Totila's reign begins in the spring of 550 and ends in the summer of 552 with the battle at Busta Gallorum, to which we can add Teja's kingship in October of the same year as an epilogue.

Eleven Years of War

Phase I. Already in the spring of 542, Totila won his great victory at Faenza. With a skillful pincer movement, in which three hundred Gothic lancers played a decisive role, he routed a large Roman army more than twice the size of his own. Soon the Gothic army amounted once again to twenty thousand men. Next it tried to open up the Via Cassia to Rome, and the Romans suffered another crushing defeat, this time north of Florence. While the Roman army, shattered into small groups, was hiding behind the walls of the cities of northern and central Italy, Totila broke through to southern Italy, where the imperial generals least expected him.

Phase II.   In the spring of 543 Totila was able to enter Naples, and his lenient treatment of the Roman garrison and the civilian population caused a tremendous stir. Here it became clear, as it would later in Sicily, that the Gothic king had a long memory. The Italians would be rewarded or punished depending on whether they had remained loyal to the Gothic cause since 535 or had in Totila's eyes betrayed it. If these were the criteria, the Neopolitans, in particular, had nothing to fear from the Gothic king.

During the seven years from 543 to 550, a war of attrition in the most terrible sense of the word raged on Italian soil. Land and people suffered terribly. In November or December of 544, Belisarius, who was crossing from Pola, went ashore at Ravenna, but his appeal to Romans and Goths to desert Totila and rejoin the emperor met with no response whatsoever. In fact, Totila was able to capture numerous cities in central Italy, thus cutting the link between Rome and Ravenna.

In December of 545 Totila began his first siege of the Eternal City; this time, it seemed, the battle for Rome would end in victory. In 546 Totila's diplomacy eliminated the Frankish threat. King Theudebert was given most of Venetia; this allowed him to secure his conquest of the Alpine regions, and thereafter he took a stance of friendly neutrality. On December 17, 546, Totila entered Rome: the Isaurian soldiers, who had not received any pay for some time, opened the gates to the Goths.

Once again the vanquished enemies were treated very well, especially because there was still enough booty to be had in Rome. The wealth of the Thracian Goth Bessas, in particular, was plundered. This tough senior officer of Belisarius's had taken advantage of the food shortage in the city to enrich himself shamelessly. While he himself narrowly escaped to Belisarius in Porto, his treasures fell into the hands of the Goths.

Totila opened negotiations with Constantinople from what he considered a position of strength. He wanted peace, but if his offer was refused he threatened to destroy Rome, kill the captive senators, and attack Illyria. The emperor, however, was not ready to talk. And now Totila committed— or was he compelled to commit?—the momentous mistake of giving up Rome, even though the imperial general, who had just suffered a severe case of typhus, was encamped in Porto.

By April 547, while the Gothic army was marching to Ravenna, Belisarius had already regained his foothold in Rome. While it is not true that Totila abandoned the city carelessly, all attempts to secure Rome even after the departure of the Goths failed, either because of the sheer size of the city or because it was impossible to implement the contemplated measures. Thus Totila lost his first battle for Rome and with it much of his standing in the world of the *gentes*. As late as 549/550, just prior to his second capture of the city, his suit for the hand of one of the daughters of a Frankish king was rejected with reference to this very debacle. This shows that Rome still enjoyed undiminished prestige among the peoples outside of Italy.

Totila returned to Latium in the spring of 547, probably in May, but his attempts to recapture Rome were in vain. As a result of this setback the Gothic king was severely criticized by his leading nobles, even though the military situation of the Goths had, on the whole, not deteriorated appreciably; still, a great victory had been gambled away. The year 547 had much worse in store for Totila's Visigothic great-uncle. King Theudis sought to benefit from the success of his nephew by gaining a foothold on the other side of the Strait of Gibraltar in Septem-Ceuta, just as he had tried to do during the Vandal war. His troops attacked the Romans in Mauritania, but the king suffered such a crushing defeat that he lost the throne and his life in 548. Meanwhile the war in Italy dragged on, and in the summer of 549 it was carried also to Dalmatia and Illyria.

From the summer of 549 to January 16, 550, Totila besieged Rome once again. For the second time the city fell because of the treachery of Isaurian soldiers who had not been paid. This time the losses of the vanquished were more serious, and the survivors joined the Gothic army. Totila now saw himself as the ruler of Rome, whose old mint resumed operations. Its coins competed with those from Pavia, Ravenna's successor as royal city of the Goths. The design of the coins shows a frontal portrait of the Gothic king wearing an imperial diadem. A new senate was created from Romans and Goths, and for this purpose Totila also brought back the surviving senators from Campania. Eventually another embassy was sent to Constantinople. It was the third since Totila's elevation to the kingship, but the first authorized to engage in serious negotiations. The embassy was instructed to renounce Sicily and Dalmatia and simultaneously offer an annual tribute and a contingent of troops. Upon their arrival in Constantinople the envoys were neither received by the emperor nor allowed to return home. Justinian's answer was "total war."

Phase III.   In the spring of 550, Justinian appointed his nephew Germanus, Matasuntha's second husband, as the new supreme commander of the Italian army. Belisarius had been recalled by the emperor as early as the fall of 548, soon after the death of his great patroness, Theodora. The appointment of Germanus was preceded by imperial propaganda for Amal legitimacy; aimed at Italy, it also influenced the Italian émigrés in Constantinople itself. It is not impossible that Jordanes wrote his extract of

Cassiodorus's history of the Goths at this time to win over Goths and to support the hopes of the refugee senators that Germanus would renew the western empire. While Justinian had no intention of reestablishing an independent western empire, he did use the nostalgic ideology to win over Goths and Italians.

Germanus, however, died in the summer of 550 in Serdica-Sofia, where he was preparing the invasion of Italy. It was thus probably his idea "to put the boot on from the top," that is, to conquer Italy with strong land forces via the Isonzo. In any case, it formed the basic idea behind the strategy of Narses, an Armenian eunuch who, like Belisarius, was a favorite of Theodora's and who had had plenty of opportunity to prove himself as a general. In April of 551 Narses, now supreme commander and successor of Germanus, hastened to the army and arrived at Salona in Dalmatia in the summer. By this time the Roman fleet had won a naval victory at Senigallia near Ancona. In spite of this, Narses did not go by boat across the Adriatic when he left Salona for Italy in April of 552, but marched via Dalmatia and Istria to the Isonzo.

Once there the Romans discovered, however, that the interior of Venetia was blocked by the Franks, and Teja, the *comes* of Verona, had flooded the Via Postumia and made all roads unusable. But neither the Franks nor the Goths paid any attention to the coastline, which seemed impassable owing to its many estuaries and marshes. Yet the unimaginable happened: led by superb guides, Narses moved with a gigantic army of nearly thirty thousand men along the coast to Ravenna.[3] While the Franco-Gothic "northeast wall" became useless, the Gothic position in southern Italy collapsed. Constantinople's strength at sea allowed the temporary transfer of the permanent garrison at Thermopylae to Calabria, where the Goths suffered a serious defeat.

Narses entered Ravenna on June 6, 552. Only nine days later he departed again and set out on the march to Rome with all available troops. Before Narses could rejoin the Via Flaminia at Gualdo Tadina, a memorable battle was fought at the end of June or beginning of July 552 on the plateau of Busta Gallorum ("the tomb of the Gauls"), a battle that put an end to the kingship of Totila and the kingdom of the Ostrogoths.

Narses had arranged no less than eight thousand archers in a crescent-shaped formation well adapted to the broken ground. Behind them stood the "phalanx," the "flower of the Roman army": the general with his officers, surrounded by their *buccellarii* on the wings, with dismounted barbarians, primarily Longobards and Heruli, in the center. The strongly reduced cavalry force of fifteen hundred men was to act as a tactical reserve: one-third to back up retreating troops, and two-thirds to attack the Gothic infantry in the rear.

Totila was aware of the fact that his army was numerically inferior. He therefore had to try to confuse the enemy and, if possible, find a moment to strike unexpectedly. Finally a last reinforcement of two thousand horsemen arrived, which Teja was bringing to his king from northern Italy. Totila signaled the attack, ordering that "no other weapon but the lance be used": the plan was to ride down the Romans. But the cavalry charge at the "tomb of the Gauls" collapsed in a shower of arrows unleashed by the imperial archers and the battlefield became the "tomb of the Goths." Six thousand warriors are said to have been killed, a credible figure and one that signaled the end of the Ostrogothic kingship.

There are two accounts about the death of Totila himself: one relates that he was struck and killed by an arrow at the outset of the battle, the other that during his flight he was killed by the leader of the Gepids in the army of Narses. Be that as it may, Totila's death brought to a close the third phase of the war he had waged against the emperor.

3. THE EPILOGUE: TEJA (552)

After the catastrophe at Busta Gallorum, Teja hastened to the royal city of Pavia. Declared king, he took possession of the treasure and made a pact with the Franks. Under Teja began the final struggle of the Goths, with all the horrors of a lost war in its final convulsions: the murder of hostages, reprisals against innocent Romans, the march to the south and the withdrawal to the area around Naples, and finally the treason of the Gothic naval commander that rendered Teja's position untenable. The last battle of the war was fought between the Mons Lactarius (the "Milk Mountain") and the Sarno River. After the death of their king, the Goths fought on until Narses guaranteed their return to their "own land" if they promised to become loyal subjects of the emperor. On this assurance the remnant of the Gothic army at the Mons Lactarius surrendered, all except a band of a thousand warriors whom a deserter, a former *buccellarius* of Belisarius, freed from the Roman pincer and led across Italy to Pavia. But once they had reached their royal city, these Goths did not, in the end, raise a new king, in spite of several attempts to do so. With this admission of weakness, half a millennium of Gothic history came to an end.

What followed was a belated act of heroism that individual Gothic commanders kept up for three years in the hope of resurrecting their gens. The last bastion to capitulate was Compsa–Conza della Campania in 555, located at the Ofanto River northeast of Salerno. But only some of the seven thousand men penned up in this town were Goths. Many had been recruited from the "wreckage" of the Franco-Alamannic invasion in 553/554, which had continued the Gothic war and at the same time put an end to it.

The epilogue of the Roman war against the Goths led to a split among the Goths: some decided against a Franco-Gothic Italy, others for it. The barbarian invaders and those who supported them perished.[4] The others, freed from the constraints of tribal tradition, became Catholics, though they did remain a legal community and a military and political factor with which the emperor had to reckon, as after 568 the Longobards did as well.

Pope Pelagius II (579–590), Gregory the Great's predecessor, was the son of the Goth Hunigild. But even as late as the eleventh century, there were still people in Italy who "professed" the Gothic law; that is, they lived by Gothic personal law. Thus the "last" Italian Goths were by no means the last, even if their battle for Rome had long since been lost.[5]

ELEVEN

Britain Too Was Not Conquered

The Making of England in the Fifth and Sixth Centuries

1. THE NATIVES

Under pressure from the barbarians who were coming across the Rhine, the inhabitants of the island of Britannia and some of the tribes of Gaul had broken away from Roman rule. Henceforth they lived independently, no longer obedient to Roman laws. The Britons took up arms and freed their cities from the invading barbarians by taking the hazards of war upon themselves. Aremorica [modern-day Bretagne] and other provinces of Gaul followed the example of the Britons. They freed themselves in the same way by driving out the Roman officials and setting up their own administration, one answerable to them.[1]

This passage from the *New History* was written by the Greek historian Zosimus around the year 500, or by 540, at the latest. For a long time it was taken to mean that the Britons had used the occasion of the Vandal storm, which swept across Gaul in 407 and temporarily destroyed Roman statehood there, to free themselves from centuries of foreign Roman rule, organize their own defense against the Picts and Scots—the northern barbarians—and eventually proclaim a somewhat premature declaration of independence.

However, recent research on both sides of the channel has shown that the Britons, who were as Roman as all other provincials of the empire, neither liberated themselves of themselves nor initiated a separate development in the diocese of Britannia. Rather, the transformation of the Roman world during the fifth and sixth centuries took place here, as elsewhere, within a framework determined by Roman constitutional law and the constraints of real life. A Roman diocese with four or five provinces was transformed into the lands of native and foreign kings and tribes.

Ravenna's inability to defend its overseas provinces became only too clear around 400. In response the affected provincials and military organized their own defense and supported native usurpers. But while the African revolt was bloodily quashed, Honorius agreed that the Britons could take their fate into their own hands. In 410, the legitimate western emperor told the cities in Britain that henceforth they were to defend themselves against domestic and foreign enemies.

And so it was the urban upper class of the *curiales* who, with its bureaucratic and military personnel, tried to fill the vacuum left by the withdrawal of the regular Roman troops and the absence of civil governors and diocesan vicars, or perhaps their expulsion as a result of many usurpations. Whenever fifth century sources name a Briton dignitary, he always has something to do with city governance, so much so that one of them is even called Curialis.

Germanus of Auxerre, a former general and bishop in Gaul, came to Britain in 429 and again around 435 in order to enforce the imperial legislation against the Pelagian heresy. These missions show very clearly that Britannia was considered part of the empire. On both visits *curiales* acted as partners of the bishop of Auxerre. The year 429 witnessed the first invasion of Britain by a coalition of Picts and Saxons. Germanus assumed command at the head of the urban levies and won the famous alleluia victory: the cruel pagan enemies were defeated without weapons and merely with calls of alleluia.[2] As long as the cities were functioning, the traditional Roman tax system, which earmarked part of the revenue for military matters, was also functioning. Just as the cities in the contemporaneous Gallic kingdoms of the Visigoths and Burgundians formed the basic administrative units and the curial tax was used to maintain the federate warriors, the Britons basically made use of the same organizational forms. In addition, like the Gauls, the Britons too took those barbarians under contract who had hitherto given them the most trouble and with whom they were consequently most familiar. Thus the Saxons in Britannia seem like the Goths of Aquitaine.

To be sure, there were differences between the island and the continent, but they must not be exaggerated. In Britannia it was not Roman generalissimi, like Constantius and Aetius, who directly ordered the settlement of royal federates and carried it out in conjunction with Ravenna and the local *curiales*. Rather, the British *curiales*, legitimized by the emperor's order, took the initiative themselves: some called federate warriors into the land, other eminent *curiales* took advantage of the chance to transform their office into a dominion and at times even make themselves kings.

This development too was not unique to Britannia. In fifth- and sixth-century Spain, many dominions were formed by native potentates, both from the senatorial class proper and the circle of *curiales*, who may have also regarded themselves as senators and described themselves as such.[3] And the

Roman King Syagrius of Soissons and Riothamus, king of the Loire-Britons, were in Gaul what Ambrosius Aurelianus, Vortigern, and maybe even "King" Arthur were in Britain.

In the eastern part of the island, the Saxon federates soon made themselves the masters over their treaty partners. This development too parallels events on the continent and took place in much the same way in the Kingdom of Toulouse. It had nothing to do with the fact that in Britain only lower-ranking, and thus apparently even less powerful, *curiales* had concluded the treaties. The same sort of thing happened to Aetius as well.

"The Alans, whom the *patricius* Aetius had given the land in the other part of Gaul to divide with the native inhabitants, rose up in armed rebellion, drove out the land-owning lords, and took possession of the land by force." Thus reports a Gallic chronicle immediately following its account of the Saxon breach of the treaty in 442 and the establishment of the first Germanic lordships on the soil of Britain.[4]

Under the influence of Justinian's reconquest, however, voices were raised—both in the emperor's entourage and in Britain itself—that called any form of Roman kingship a tyrannis and condemned those who held it as usurpers. In 414, Saint Jerome had spoken of *Britannia fertilis provincia tyrannorum,* "the province of Britannia fertile for usurpers."[5] In the sixth century this theme was picked up again by the Greek Procopius and the Briton Gildas. Now we read: "Britain has kings, but they are tyrants."

A usurper is a nonruler, a perversion of human and cosmic order. Such a monstrosity had to embody all the vices that existed: tyrants are greedy, unjust, incompetent, and arrogant; they hate God and humankind and engage in terror and violence.[6] Gildas finds confirmation for this politico-theological verdict of the false rulers of his day in the fact that it was a usurper who had called the foreigners into the land, that is to say, those barbarians who had now become masters over large stretches of Britain. But Gildas's verdict, conditioned by contemporary events, was based on good fifth-century accounts that gave an accurate depiction of the situation and can still be made out clearly even in the author's flaming accusation:

> Then all the members of the council, together with the proud tyrant, were struck blind: the guard [*praesidium*]—or rather the method of destruction—they devised for our land was that the ferocious Saxons (name not to be spoken!), hated by man and God, should be let into the island like wolves into the fold, to beat back the people of the north. . . . Then a pack of cubs burst forth from the lair of the barbarian lioness, coming in three *keels,* as they call warships in their language. The winds were favorable; favorable too the omens and auguries, which prophesied, according to a sure portent among them, that they would live for three hundred years in the land toward which their prows were directed, and that for half the time, a hundred and fifty years, they would repeatedly lay it waste.

On the orders of the ill-fated tyrant, they first of all fixed their dreadful claws on the east side of the island, ostensibly to fight for our country, in fact to fight against it.

When the barbarians who had stayed behind found out how successful their advance party had been, new hordes arrived: "The barbarians who had been admitted to the island asked to be given supplies [*annonae*], falsely representing themselves as soldiers [*milites*] ready to undergo extreme dangers for their excellent hosts [*boni hospites*]. The supplies were granted, and for a long time 'shut the dog's mouth.' Then they again complained that their monthly allowance [*epimenia*] was insufficient, purposely giving a false color to individual incidents, and swore that they would break their agreement [*foedus*] and plunder the whole island unless more lavish payment were heaped on them. There was no delay: they put their threats into immediate effect."[7]

Leaving aside the author's understandable despair, his language clearly reveals that the Saxons were settled according to the modalities customary on the continent. Gildas reports the same about the Britons and Saxons that a Greek rhetorician tells us about the settlement of the Visigoths following the treaty of 382, namely, that Romans and foreigners lived under the same roof. The Saxons, we hear from Gildas, served as *milites*, and as such they were undoubtedly entitled to the *annonae*.

In Ostrogothic Italy, federate warriors were called *milites* (like the regular Roman soldiers) and allotted the *annonae* only if they served in combat or were permanently stationed in barracks.[8] Perhaps this was also the arrangement envisaged by the first federate bands brought into Britain by the *curiales*. Later, of course, these lords of the cities appeared as "hosts," *hospites*, a term that stands for the actual settlement "under the same roof." There can thus be no doubt that the foreign warriors, who were all considered Saxons in spite of their diverse backgrounds, had initially come to the island not as conquerors but at the invitation of the Britons.

Gildas did not care much about chronology, but he links the arrival of the Saxons with a date that can be attached to a specific year. We are told that prior to contacting the Saxons, the Britons had sent a plea to Aetius, asking him for help against the Picts and Scots. This had happened when the lord of the western empire held the consulship for the third time, which was the case in 446. However, a Gallic chronicle noted that in the year 442 "the provinces of Britain, following a series of serious defeats, fell under the lordship of the Saxons." Another author reported: "The British provinces have been abandoned by the Romans and have been turned over to the rule of the Saxons."[9]

These brief comments from observers on the continent depict conditions that prevailed for parts of Britain at a specific time. Unlike Gildas, they do not report the victories and defeats of the invaders and say nothing about the successes and failures of the native kings. There is one aspect, however, that the historiography of the fifth and sixth centuries on both sides of the channel had in common: the authors—in keeping with traditional Roman ethnography—were not interested in who these Saxons were, where they came from, and what motivated their actions. Only the learned Anglo-Saxon Bede (who died in 735) showed that he had information on all these questions.

2. THE FOREIGNERS

It was surely not a single, one-time decision that brought the Germanic peoples to Britain. Long before the island declared—or was forced to declare—that it no longer belonged to the Roman Empire, Germanic soldiers had been serving there in the regular armies as well as in all kinds of irregular units. In particular, Saxon seafarers had become such a threat to the coasts of Gaul and Britain during the fourth century that the system of the *litus Saxonicum,* the (fortified) "Saxon coast," had been set up on both sides of the channel. During and after their first expeditions, Saxons groups had gained a foothold at the mouths of the great rivers of Gaul from the Seine to the Loire.

It is difficult to answer the question of whether the Saxon migration went from Gaul to Britain or the other way around. However, it is likely that more than a few of the foreign barbarians came to Britain not from across the distant North Sea but from the other side of the channel only. That holds true not least for the Franks who were tagging along and who sought out the bridgehead of Kent, and for the Frisians.[10] The majority of the foreign Germanic peoples, however, were Angles, Saxons, and Jutes from what is today northern Germany and mainland Denmark. The Saxons tended to be the vanguard, particularly so where the invaders appeared without kings. By contrast, the Angles, who were surely organized around a king, had an easier time prevailing and spreading even in areas where they were latecomers. Thus the mighty royal house of Mercia traced its descent from the Anglian kings of the old homeland.[11]

> From the Jutes are descended the people of Kent and the Isle of Wight, and those in the province of the West Saxons opposite the Isle of Wight who are called Jutes to this day. From the Saxons—that is, the country now known as the land of the Old Saxons—came the East, South and West Saxons. And from the Angles—that is, the country known as Angulus, which lies between the provinces of the Jutes and the Saxons and is said to remain unpopulated to this day—are descended the East and Middle Angles, the Mercians, all the Northumbrian stock (that is, those people living north of the river Humber), and the other English peoples. Their first chieftains are said to have been

the brothers Hengist and Horsa. The latter was subsequently killed in battle against the Britons, and was buried in east Kent, where a monument bearing his name still stands. They were the sons of Wictgisl, whose father was Witta, whose father was Wecta, son of Wodan, from whose stock sprang the royal houses of many provinces.[12]

Thus reads the account of Bede, who at the beginning of the eighth century tried to clarify old traditions to himself and his listeners and to set the record straight. He no longer knew very much about the onetime, surely minor, difference between the Angles and the Saxons, and he knew even less about the Jutes. But the great Anglo-Saxon scholar also had reports about peoples who were involved in the English tribal genesis.[13] Not least he knew—probably from the venerable episcopal see of Canterbury—about pagan tribal traditions.

The brothers Hengist and Horsa, "stallion and horse," the grandsons of the warrior god Wodan, had been the military kings of those tribes who were allegedly the first to set foot in Kent. This dual monarchy strikes us as highly archaic and, like the Greek Dioskouroi, seems to have been linked to some kind of horse totemism.[14]

The protective or helper gods who appear as pairs of horses or other animals belong to the Vanir world of gods and, in terms of the history of religion, predate Wodan and his Aesir.

The story of Longobard origins preserved this chronology more faithfully: here the Vinnili who were lead by a Dioscourian pair of chieftains became the Longobards only at the moment Wodan—overcome by cunning—was forced to take them on as his charges, grant them a victory, and give them a new name.[15] By comparison, the Anglo-Saxon tradition seems smoothed out in that it removes the contradictions by reversing the tradition and making the representatives of the older *memoria* into descendants of the younger high god Wodan. Wodan, the leader of warrior bands, stands at the top of all Anglo-Saxon royal genealogies, with the exception of the royal clan of Essex, which traced itself back to the older Géat-Gaut, the same Scandinavian god with whom the Gauts and Goths had already associated themselves. But since the Dioscourian element appears in the wrong place, as it were, Horsa must die without descendants. The Oiscings, however, the venerable royal house of the Kentish folk, revered Oisc-Aesc as their ancestor, but his father was Hengist, "who was the first to enter Britain with his son."[16]

In this case Bede's source preserved the traditional system as faithfully as the Longobard tradition: one of the brothers who appear in the role of nonroyal *duces* had a son with whom the royal lineage of the tribe begins. There is only one minor difference: in Kent it was the older brother, among the Longobards the younger.

Gildas's belief that new barbarians were continually coming to Britain from the lands across the sea is confirmed by archaeology. For example, while the inhabitants of East Anglia during the fifth century were Angles and Saxons, the sixth-century kingdom of the same name was in all likelihood created by immigrant Scandinavians. The magnificent royal burial of Sutton Hoo, near Woodbridge in Suffolk and which dates to the seventh century, is ample testimony to that effect.

While there was no great difference between British Britain and Saxon Britain in institutional terms, since numerous kingdoms existed on both sides, the difference could not have been more pronounced in the religious-cultic sphere: the Britons were Christians; the Angles, Saxons, Jutes, and other barbarians, however, were pagan lords of the subjugated "Welsh" population, *wealh*,[17] whose Christianity suffered heavy and even disastrous losses.

In July of 598—early by East Rhenish standards, late enough for the native Britons under foreign rule—Pope Gregory I wrote to the patriarch of Alexandria: "We have heard that last Christmas more than ten thousand Angles were baptized." Led by the sainted monk Augustine, numerous missionaries had fulfilled the pope's wish and undertaken the conversion of the Anglo-Saxons. Gregory's decision to dispatch these missionaries can be seen as further proof that Rome had not written off Britain but continued to count it as part of the empire.

The principles of missionary work that the great pope formulated for his brother after his installation as bishop of Canterbury reflect deep wisdom and humanity, and they are thus as relevant today as they were back then:

> We have been giving careful thought to the affairs of the English, and have come to the conclusion that the temples of the idols among that people should on no account be destroyed. The idols are to be destroyed, but the temples themselves are to be aspersed with holy water, altars set up in them, and relics deposited there. For if these temples are well built, they must be purified from the worship of demons and dedicated to the service of the true god. In this way, we hope that the people, seeing that their temples are not destroyed, may abandon their error and, flocking more readily to their accustomed resorts, may come to know and adore the true God. And since they have a custom of sacrificing many oxen to demons, let some other solemnity be substituted in its place, such as a day of Dedication or the Festivals of the holy martyrs whose relics are enshrined there. On such occasions they might well construct shelters of boughs for themselves around the churches that were once temples, and celebrate the solemnity with devout feasting. They are no longer to sacrifice beasts to the Devil, but they may kill them for food to the praise of God, and give thanks to the Giver of all gifts for the plenty they enjoy. If the people are allowed some worldly pleasures in this way, they will more readily come to desire the joys of the spirit. For it is certainly impossible to eradicate all errors from obstinate minds at one stroke, and whoever wishes to climb to a mountain top climbs gradually step by step, and not in one

leap. It was in this way that the Lord revealed Himself to the Israelite people in Egypt, permitting the sacrifices formerly offered to the Devil to be offered thenceforward to Himself instead. So He bade them sacrifice beasts to Him, so that, once they became enlightened, they might abandon one element of sacrifice and retain another. For, while they were to offer the same beasts as before, they were to offer them to God instead of to idols, so that they would no longer be offering the same sacrifices.[18]

Ethelbert of Kent (560–616), who knew himself to be the great-grandson of Hengist,[19] was the first king to be baptized and gave permission for the establishment of the first bishopric in Canterbury; still today, the bishop on the seat of Canterbury is the head of the Anglican Church. The year 604 saw both the establishment of the Kentish bishopric of Rochester and—again with the active involvement of Ethelbert—the conversion of the kings of Essex and the creation of a bishopric in that kingdom's capital, London. To be sure, the missionary endeavor that had thus begun so auspiciously would suffer severe and even disastrous setbacks; but the next generation would witness, as early as the middle of the seventh century, the conversion and baptism of most of the kings of England.

Not the least of the forces behind this great achievement were Irish missionaries, the Celtic sons of Saint Patrick who had become Christians outside the boundaries of the empire, but to whom many parts of the empire that had been re-barbarized or had slid back into paganism owed so much. For the Irish and Anglo-Saxons did not stay on their islands; instead, with the Celts leading the way, they set out for the continent, to the Frankish realm and Germania across the Rhine, in order to bring Christendom to those parts, to internalize the new religion or to revive it. I will mention one for all of them: Winfrid-Bonifatius, the mighty saint from Wessex. Though he was not the "apostle of the Germans," as he is often called, he was in fact the organizer and reorganizer of the Germanic Church, the founder of Fulda and Mainz who consecrated Pippin King of the Franks in 751 and met a martyr's death among the Frisians in 754.[20]

Thus things came full circle: Ethelbert of Kent, the great-grandson of Hengist, himself the great-grandson of Wodan, became the first Christian king of England, and Winfrid-Bonifatius, like many of his countrymen, sought to bring Christianity above all to those tribes on the continent from whom the Anglo-Saxons traced their descent. For the English said of the Old Saxons: "We are of the same bone and blood."[21]

Of course the causality of the events is made up of chains of interconnected motifs and effects, not of demonstrable facts. In short, it is a story but not history—and yet it became history. Bonifatius was in truth one of the fathers of Europe; we simply cannot imagine the history of the creation of the "new" Carolingian Empire without his work in Gallia and Germania, as he himself called the large Frankish realms in classical fashion.

TWELVE

The Burgundians

Weakness and Resilience

(407/413–534)

1. WHAT IS BURGUNDY?

"Many marvels we have been told in ancient tales"—thus begins the *Nibelungenlied*. As late as 1200 its subject matter still so enthralled an unknown author along the Austrian Danube that he cast the "old, marvelous tales" of the Nibelungs into epic form. In the second stanza we read: "In the land of the Burgundians there grew up a maiden of high lineage. . . . Her name was Kriemhild."

By the time the poem was written, nearly seven centuries had passed since the last Burgundian king fell victim to the Frankish power, and nearly eight centuries since the royal family of the Gibikungs (Nibelungs?) had met its end. And yet Burgundy had not become merely a name in the saga. Instead, it had persisted in real life, and around 1200 there was no telling when it might end.

In 534, Burgundy became part of the Merovingian kingdom; shortly thereafter it formed—alongside Neustria and Austrasia—one of the "three kingdoms" to which the Merovingian dominion had been progressively reduced in the seventh century, and it remained one of these three heartlands that provided the stage for the rise of the Carolingians to the kingship. Burgundy would contribute its share to the successful attempt by the new dynasty to reestablish and expand the Frankish kingdom, which would culminate in Charlemagne's coronation as emperor.

When the late Carolingians themselves went the way of their Merovingian predecessors and were forced to yield rule to stronger contenders, the Carolingian imperium was divided, and with it Burgundian territory: the duchy of Burgundy with the capital of Dijon formed one of the "territorial principalities" (the *principautés territoriales*) that made up the West Frankish—

French kingdom. Along the Rhône and the Saône, meanwhile, a kingdom of Burgundy took shape, and between 888 and 1032 it sought—as an independent regnum—to continue to expand its statehood as an alternative between East and West. In 933 it united with the realm of Arles. Henceforth one speaks of Upper Burgundy along the upper reaches of the Rhône and of Lower Burgundy along the lower reaches. This kingdom in the middle also included Arles, the last Roman imperial city of Gaul. When it became the third regnum of the medieval empire under Conrad II in 1032, the high medieval kingdom of Burgundy stretched from the bend of the Rhine at Basel to where the Rhône flowed into the Gulf of Lyon.

The "German" empire was not able to hold Burgundy against the French crown, and larger and larger areas were lost to the West. But this did not mean that Burgundy's splendor was fading. On the contrary. In the fourteenth century its star shone over the French Duchy of Burgundy, which the younger Valois had made their center. Though it was a fief to the empire as well as the French crown, the duchy combined the Burgundian tradition with that of the middle kingdom of Lotharingia. Burgundy now shifted its center of gravity from the Rhône to the Rhine, from the Gulf of Lyon to the North Sea.

Burgundy: the name stood for economic progress and wealth as well as a vacillating policy in the Hundred Years' War between France and England, for glorious knighthood and its downfall in the battles of Crécy in 1346 and Agincourt in 1415, for the Golden Fleece and the surrender of the "witch" Jeanne d'Arc to the English. But Burgundy was also the dreamland to which the young *Weißkunig* Maximilian still journeyed to woo his bride, Maria, the daughter of Charles the Bold, the last of the Burgundian Valois, and protect her against the (French) "forces of darkness." And Burgundy determined, not least, the policy of Maximilian's grandson Charles V, who in four long wars broke Flanders loose from French suzerainty, thus winning by force of arms the creation of a *Germania inferior*, the Habsburg Netherlands, which would live on in the Benelux states.

Like few other things, Burgundy was both a dream and a reality of European history. The power political basis of its own history, however, strikes me as astonishingly weak. Three generations of independent statehood, almost continuously threatened by setbacks and even destruction, is all that was granted to the Burgundians from the time they crossed the Rhine. Perhaps the resilience of the Burgundian tradition lay precisely in the fact that those who embodied it within Gaul had to represent a credible alternative to resist the powerful kingdoms in East and West. And so it may be more than a coincidence that the splendid material artifacts of the later Burgundy today grace the treasury of the Wiener Kunsthistorisches Museum, in the capital of a country whose people have learned to chose the third option when confronted by two alternatives.

2. THE BURGUNDIAN KINGDOM OF WORMS
ALONG THE MIDDLE RHINE (413–436)

In 407, a Roman usurper had concluded a treaty with the Alamanni and the Burgundians to enlist these two peoples in the protection of the Rhine border. Four years later Jovinus, a member of the Gallic high nobility, usurped the emperorship; a tribal coalition under Burgundian-Alamannic leadership in 411 gave him the political power to do so.

The monarchical king of the Burgundians who was involved in this coalition was Gundahar (see Figure 4), the Gunther of the Nibelungen saga. In 413, Jovinus gave Gundahar's Burgundians permission to found a kingdom on the left bank of the Rhine, the center of which probably lay in Worms or farther downstream. Gundahar was the first Burgundian king of his clan who did things we know to be historical. However, a tribal *memoria* a hundred years later mentions Gundahar as only the fourth in a line of kings whose kinship is not only suggested by the alliteration and variation in their names, but who are also explicitly identified as relatives. The tribes' progenitor was Gibica, whom the saga also remembered as the ancestor of the Gibikungs. The list also contains a certain Gundomar and a Gislahar, the Giselher of the *Nibelungenlied*.

Gundahar and his Burgundians retained their status as federates after the downfall of the usurper. Only when they were threatening, at the beginning of the 430s, to strike out from the province of Germania superior, which had been allotted to them, into Belgica I, did the Roman General Aetius attack them in 435 and prepare their destruction. In 436, Aetius's Hunnic mercenaries, who may have been trying to make up for something, attacked the Burgundians: Gundahar and nearly his entire tribe were wiped out; thousands of Burgundians were killed.[1]

The downfall of Gundahar and his people in the battle against the Huns formed the historical core of the *Nibelungenlied*. Of course it was not the Roman General Aetius but the Hunnic King Attila who became the Etzel of the saga. As catastrophic as the historical defeat was, Burgundian history continued in real life, unlike in the saga. To be sure, the name of no Burgundian king has come down to us in the two decades after 436, but the Gundioc-Gundovech who is mentioned in 456 may well have been related to Gundahar. However, the evidence seems to point less to a direct kinship than to the passing of the royal power from the immediate descendants of Gibica to a side branch with strong Gothic connections. As late as the mid-sixth century in Gaul, the story was told that this Gundioc was descended from the lineage of Athanaric, the judge of the Danubian Goths and persecutor of the Christians. In fact, in 457 it was even claimed that the Burgundians were dependent on the Goths of Toulouse.

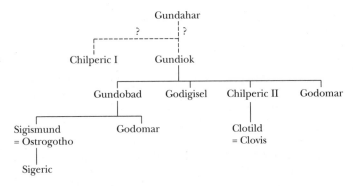

Figure 4. Genealogy of the Burgundians

3. THE KINGDOM ALONG THE RHÔNE (443–534)

In the year 443, Aetius arranged for the resettlement of the severely defeated Burgundians from the Rhine to eastern Maxima Sequanorum or Sapaudia, that is to say, to the region south of Lake Geneva and on its northern shore as far as Lausanne. "[This province] is handed over to the remnants of the Burgundians to share with the natives."[2] What this refers to is settlement on the same conditions under which the Visigoths had been given large parts of southern France in 418: two-thirds of the regular tax revenue went to the newcomers, to whom was assigned the defense of the border against the Alamanni in a threatened part of Gaul.

Aetius was able to call upon his Burgundian federates as early as 451 for the battle against the Huns on the Catalaunian fields. They suffered serious casualties, and, like the Goths, had to fight against fellow tribesmen who had joined Attila's army. The Vandal assault in 406 had led to the split up of the Burgundians, as a result of which only the later founders of the kingdom along the middle Rhine had crossed the river in 407. But large numbers of Burgundians must have remained east of the Rhine until well past the middle of the fifth century. This Burgundian community appears to have gradually dissolved only after the defeat of Attila, when an undetermined number of Burgundians from the right side of the Rhine slowly moved into the kingdom along the Rhône.

In the year 456, King Gundioc (before 456 to around 470) and his brother, the underking Chilperic I, fought alongside the Visigoths against the Suebi of Spain as loyal federates of the "Gallic" Emperor Avitus. When Avitus lost the throne and his life soon after, and another treaty had thus been terminated, the Goths and the Burgundians expanded their dominions with the consent of the Gallic senators. The Burgundians pushed down the Rhône and were able to take Lyon for the first time.

Avitus was followed by the capable Emperor Majorian, who came to Gaul in the winter of 458/459 and took strong measures. His actions had to be all the more surprising, since the Goths, the Burgundians, and the aristocracy of southern Gaul all agreed not to recognize a "foreign," that is, Italian, emperor. But Aegidius joined his friend Majorian. Appointed commander in chief and *patricius*, Aegidius for a while played the role in which Aetius had been cast until his murder in 454. Aegidius marched out of northern Gaul down the Rhône, killing and burning. He recaptured Lyon for the empire in 458 and energetically pushed back the Burgundians and the Visigoths. Following these successes, Majorian intended to attack the African Vandals via Spain. But the emperor lost his fleet and his *fortuna* off Cartagena; by 461 he was dead.

The master of Italy at the time was Ricimer, a half-Goth and brother-in-law of Gundioc. The Burgundians were now able to move their capital permanently from Geneva to Lyon, and to expand their sphere of power to the Drôme in the following years. Gundioc became the supreme commander in Gaul. The power of his kingdom had grown enormously compared to its modest beginnings around Lake Geneva and had assumed nearly Gothic dimensions. And so it happened that in 469 the prefect of Gaul, Arvandus, suggested to Euric not to make peace with the imperial government in Italy and to instead divide Gaul between the Goths and the Burgundians. The reason for this "treason of Arvandus" was the fact that in the same year Constantinople sent the proven general Anthemius to the West to be proclaimed emperor there. Arvandus, however, represented the party of the Gallic aristocracy, which rejected the foreign "Greek emperor" and preferred to make pacts with the local Goths and Burgundians.

Gundioc died around 470, and his brother Chilperic I succeeded him. When the Visigoths triumphed over the last imperial troops in 471 and were getting ready to conquer the lower Rhône Valley, Chilperic remembered his duty as federate and pushed the attackers back. This first Burgundian-Gothic conflict left behind a broad strip of scorched earth and led to severe famine among the Roman population. But in the Auvergne, until around 475 the Burgundians continued to support the local senators in their fight against the Visigothic King Euric. After that the Burgundians got involved in fierce fighting against the Alamanni, the struggle being waged above all over Langres, Besançon, and the Jura. The end result was that a large part of Lugdunensis I fell under Burgundian control, along with the entire province of Maxima Sequanorum.

Gundobad (ca. 480–516)

Chilperic died around 480 without any offspring, and his brother's sons became his successors: Gundobad, Godigisel, Chilperic II, and Godomar. The oldest brother, Gundobad, became head king and took up residence in the capital of Lyon; Godigisel resided in Geneva, while the other brothers probably resided in Vienne and Valence.

Prior to becoming king of the Burgundians, Gundobad had supported his uncle Ricimer in Italy and had briefly followed in his footsteps after his death. Even if his Italian glory did not last long, Gundobad did signal that the Burgundian royal house, unlike those of the Goths and Vandals, was still willing to take on high and top-ranking Roman military offices as well as remain federates in the conventional sense. Even before Euric was ready to negotiate a new kind of treaty with Ravenna, Chilperic I had already renewed the old *foedus* in 474, thus recognizing the *militiae tituli*—as Gundobad's son Sigismund would still call them—as the Burgundian obligation. The Burgundian kings always understood themselves to be Gallic generals and rulers over imperial federates in the old style.

From 472 to 474 Gundobad had also briefly held the office of the commander in chief of the western empire. Prior to that the Burgundian prince, as second *magister militum praesentalis,* had fought alongside his uncle against Emperor Anthemius, even killing him with his own hands when the emperor, abandoned by all, had sought refuge in a church in Rome. This had occurred on July 11, 472. The following month Ricimer died, whereupon Gundobad became commander in chief. Confirmed in this position by the next emperor, the Burgundian prince acted as emperor-maker as early as the late winter of 473 and stayed on in Italy until June of 474. Then a new emperor came to the throne, and Gundobad had to make way; his withdrawal to his homeland was like a desperate flight. Around 480 Gundobad succeeded his uncle Chilperic I as king of the Burgundians.

The first decade of his rule seems to have been relatively quiet. Gundobad divided the kingship—though not the kingdom—with his three brothers. This Burgundian peculiarity, too, is mentioned by the *Nibelungenlied.* It is likely that both Godomar and Chilperic II—the father of Clotild, the future wife of Clovis—died natural deaths around 490. In the early nineties, however, the events became rapidly more and more dramatic. While Theodoric and Odovacar were fighting over control of Italy, the Visigoths as well as the Burgundians marched into northern Italy in 490, the former to show their Gothic solidarity, the latter to claim what appears to have been a contractually guaranteed indemnification in neighboring Liguria. In any case, years later the Burgundian King Gundobad could still argue that he had compensated himself at the expense of the Ligurian civilian population for the breach of the treaty on the part of a ruler of Italy.

The tradition is obscure; probably it was deliberately obfuscated since the truth would have compromised Theodoric the Great. But both the military help of the Visigoths and the Burgundian invasion were the occasion for Theodoric and his allies and opponents to establish an extensive system of peace secured by marriage ties and treaties. The newly rising star in northern Gaul, the Frankish Merovingian King Clovis, was also to be integrated into this system.

Four marriages of great political importance were concluded during these years: Theodoric married his daughter Thiudogotho to the helpful Visigothic King Alaric II, and his daughter Ostrogotho-Areagni to Gundobad's son Sigismund. He himself took Clovis's sister Audofleda as his wife, while the Frankish king married the Burgundian Princess Clotild. The sources do not allow us to establish a clear chronological sequence of the marriages, though it is likely that the marriages of the kings Theodoric and Clovis took place before those of Theodoric's daughters, with the Burgundian-Gothic liaison possibly finalized only in 496 following a lengthy engagement, though in any case before 497.[3]

Nevertheless, relations between the Ostrogoths and the Burgundians remained almost always tense. We know of two friendly gestures only from the period between 501 and prior to 507. At Gundobad's request, Theodoric had a specially made water clock and sundial sent to the Burgundian kingdom along with the personnel to operate it. The chronometrical marvel had been constructed by none other than Boethius. On another occasion permission was given to the Catholic convert Sigismund to travel to the apostles' graves in Rome and visit Pope Symmachus along the way.

The conversion of his Burgundian son-in-law was of some concern to Theodoric, but the presence of Catholics within the Burgundian royal clan was something one had to reckon with at all times. The same was true for their missionary zeal, as the example of Clovis's wife, Clotild, shows. It was this Burgundian princess who converted her husband to Catholicism, and his way of thanking her, so to speak, was to attack Arian Burgundy in the year 500.

What made the first Frankish-Burgundian war possible was the fact that Clovis had concluded a secret treaty with the subking Godigisel in Geneva; Godigisel, his wife's uncle, was to become independent vis-à-vis her other uncle Gundobad and in return would hand over Burgundian territory. The Frankish army under Clovis and the Burgundian army under its King Gundobad met near Dijon. During the battle, Godigisel and his men switched sides and joined Clovis, as had been agreed, whereupon Gundobad suffered a serious defeat. He was barely able to escape to the far south of his realm, where he holed up in Avignon, a city impregnable to the Franks.

Clovis, believing the issue was decided, left behind a few thousand Frankish warriors to support Godigisel and returned home. However, this serious disturbance in the political balance brought the third Gallic kingdom—the Visigoths—onto the stage. Alaric II gave his support to the legitimate party. Godigisel and his Frankish reinforcements were overpowered in Vienne; Godigisel himself was killed, his Burgundian and Roman advisers were tortured to death. Frankish prisoners were taken to Toulouse, and the victorious Burgundian King Gundobad ceded Avignon to the Goths in 501. After the end of the serious crisis of 500/501, Sigismund no doubt succeeded his disloyal uncle in Geneva.

Clovis himself had suffered a setback, at worst, and it had done nothing to dismiss the danger he posed to the Visigoths and the Burgundians. In 502, Alaric II sought to peacefully accommodate the Frankish king, and soon after, Gundobad himself switched over to Clovis's camp. The outbreak of the Alamannic crisis might have caused—or at least given an impetus to—this *renversement des alliances*. For many generations Burgundians and Alamanni had been sworn enemies, a situation that had prevailed when the Burgundians had still stood in the Alamanni's backyard along the Main in Germania. The Burgundian settlement along the middle Rhine and its shift to Lake Geneva had also been motivated by the desire to fight and fend off the old enemy. In the 470s, Chilperic I was still waging a successful war against the Alamanni, and from the very beginning the imperial government had also been using the Burgundian hatred of the Alamanni to safeguard its own security.

Clovis had won the great victory over the Alamanni in 496, but it was not possible to say that even in name it had been won for the Roman Empire. A decade after the battle of Zülpich the Alamanni had regained enough strength to rise up against the Franks once more. The result was disastrous, the second defeat was far worse even than the first: if Theodoric had not intervened, the Alamanni may well have disappeared from history. The Burgundians, however, were able to expand their territory as far as Vindonissa-Windisch; the alliance with the Franks was paying off. That is also why Theodoric's urgent warning to the Burgundian King Gundobad against the suicidal alliance with Clovis fell on deaf ears. The Frankish king was able to hold his Burgundian allies and in the following year push deep into Visigothic territory. Thus the Burgundian Gundobad entered the great Gothic war as the junior partner of the more powerful Frankish king, and he would return from the conflict a scapegoat and whipping boy.

Between 507 and 509 the Burgundians suffered serious losses; they were the real victims of the Ostrogothic intervention in 508/509. They lost all their conquests in southern France; and not only did they have to abandon Arles and Avignon, they also had to stand by and watch the devastation of their lands as far as Orange and Valence. Theodoric, however, forswore any further offensive policy and had the Durance line fortified as the permanent border of his realm.

Sigismund (501/516–523)

Sigismund had followed in the footsteps of Godigisel, the underking of Geneva, and in 516 he succeeded his father Gundobad. Wedged between the aggressive Frankish kingdoms and the unified Gothic superpower, Sigismund sought support in Byzantium. The king of the Burgundians emphasized once again the status of his kingdom as an old-style federated regnum. In response to his overtures to Byzantium, Sigismund was honored with the title of *patricius* even before he assumed the throne.

In view of the fact that the relationship between Byzantium and Ravenna had noticeably deteriorated, the Burgundian leader's pro-imperial policy meant that he was lining himself up against Theodoric, and the latter therefore tried to cut off the diplomatic traffic between Lyon and Constantinople. A number of letters, which were probably all written by the great Bishop Avitus of Vienne at the king's request, have come down to us. The letter in which Sigismund tried to outdo himself with his protestations of deference and obedience toward the emperor was among those intercepted. It culminated in the declaration, "My people are yours, and it is a greater honor to me to be subject to you than to rule over them."[4]

In actuality, though, the Burgundians did not have sufficient military strength to undertake any action against the Goths. The fact that the reigning Burgundian king was a *patricius* and general was only a latent and implicit threat. And so it was no more than a pleasant memory that many years ago Gundobad, as the successor and nephew of Ricimer, had held the military authority in Italy. It was likewise meaningless that the Burgundian kings past and present regarded themselves as "soldiers of the emperor."

In spite of the difficulties between Theodoric and his Burgundian son-in-law, peace prevailed along their mutual border for nearly fifteen years. Then Theodoric's daughter died, and in 522 Sigismund had his son Sigeric, born of his Ostrogothic wife, killed. The end of the Burgundian pro-Gothic faction put an end to Theodoric's defensive policy regarding Burgundy. The Goths and the Franks invaded Burgundy simultaneously, catching Sigismund's army between two fronts. The Goths were out to revenge a dead Amal, the Merovingians a dead relative, explanations that may well have been intended merely to veil hard power politics. Be that as it may, following a Burgundian defeat in battle, Sigismund and his family were abandoned by their own people and handed over to the Franks. After about two years of captivity, one of the Merovingian kings killed the prisoners by having them hurled into a well.

Godomar (524–534)

In the meantime, after the Franks had withdrawn, Gundobad's other son, Godomar, had succeeded in 524 in establishing himself as king in the greater part of the Burgundian realm. For now only the territory between the Durance and the Drône, and most likely as far as the Isère, which the

Ostrogoths had occupied, was lost. In 524 two Merovingian kings and their Franks launched another attack on Burgundy. A battle took place east of Vienne, in which one of the enemy kings was killed. Thereupon the Franks left, and Godomar was king of the Burgundians for another decade.

In 530 Amalasuintha renounced the territory north of the Durance in her son's name and on this occasion concluded a Burgundian-Ostrogothic pact of mutual assistance. But when the Franks attacked the Burgundians once again in 532, in the process occupying even Ostrogothic territory, the Gothic army, "the terror of the barbarians," swung into action, but only to restore the violated borders. And in 534, as well, when the Burgundian kingdom and Gundobad, the partner in the mutual aid pact, met their fate, the Ostrogothic army in Gaul remained in its garrisons. In that year the victorious Merovingian kings divided up the Burgundian kingdom. The last piece of news from the history of the Burgundians concerns Godomar's serious defeat. Then there is silence.[5]

4. BURGUNDIAN PECULIARITIES

Neither in the *Nibelungenlied* nor in the actual political constitution of the Burgundians[6] did the younger brothers, who *were* regarded as kings, share in the rule of their oldest brother, who held the rank and power of a high king. According to legend the latter resided in Worms; in actual fact his seat was in Lyon. The younger sons were given certain territories with residences— Geneva is repeatedly attested, Vienne and Valence can be inferred—though this practice did not lead to an actual division of the realm, as it did among the Merovingians. This kind of political constitution is visible among the Visigoths only in rudimentary form, if at all; among the Ostrogoths a similar setup—in which the younger brothers were not kings—is detectable only in the generation of Theodoric the Great's father. If this setup did in fact go back to Hunnic influences,[7] it was subsequently substantially modified. To be sure, the Gallic Burgundians of the first generation were the only Germanic peoples west of the Rhine who were familiar with the Hunnic custom of artificially deforming the head.[8]

Two legal codifications appeared among the Burgundians, quite a bit later than the law codes of the Visigoths. Before or around 500, King Gundobad decreed the Law of the Burgundians, which has made its way into tradition as the *Lex Gundobada*. The redaction of this tribal law, which is extant today, was drawn up under King Sigismund in 517/518; it combined Germanic and Roman elements. At about the same time there appeared the *Lex Romana Burgundionum*, the counterpart to the Visigothic Roman law.

In spite of what appears to have been a clear separation of the two peoples, Burgundians and Romans lived side by side as equals, they had the same amount of wergild and were subject to the same punishments, they both served in the king's army, and neither was prohibited from intermarriage. Thus in the Burgundian kingdom the usual social differentiation was not burdened by an ethnic element. On the Burgundian side there was the threefold group of freemen, who as *faramani* constituted those who had been "participants in the military campaign that had led the conquest of land." This group was made up of the nobility (*optimates*), the upper stratum of warriors (*mediocres personae*), and the simple people (*leudes*). The half-free and the unfree naturally made up the greater part of the population. The Roman senators held the same rank as the Burgundian nobility, and the lower classes of Romans had as much standing as the Burgundians of comparable rank.

Like the kingdoms of the Goths, the Burgundian kingdom was made up of *civitates,* though little distinguished them from the way the rural area, the *pagi,* was structured. These *civitates* were identical with the episcopal dioceses and the spheres of authority of a Burgundian and a Roman *comes.*[9] No other contemporary administrative structure had such a pronounced Roman-barbarian parity. And the same holds true for the role Catholic Christianity played as an equal to Burgundian Arianism. The Burgundians on the right bank of the Rhine supposedly all turned Catholic to successfully fend off the Hunnic threat.[10] In Gaul, however, the majority of the tribe along with the ruling line of the royal house professed the "Gothic faith," Arianism.[11] Sigismund was the first high king who turned Catholic.[12]

It is difficult to say how much of his conversion was a response to Clovis's conversion and how much was genuine conviction. In all likelihood contemporaries too would have been unable to answer this question. Sigismund's death turned him into a Catholic martyr and the object of religious veneration. In any case, the king summoned a royal synod at the beginning of his reign (517), and there is evidence that several provincial synods were held. In 499 Bishop Avitus of Vienne, with the help of King Gundobad, had obtained a papal privilege by which the Burgundian metropolitan attained primacy in Gaul over the bishop of Gothic Arles, even if only for a short time.

In the seventies, Sidonius Apollinaris, a native of the Auvergne, had made fun of the Burgundians and their language, and had lamented how greatly annoyed he was by the oversized and gluttonous allies who reeked of garlic, onions, and rancid butter. Who could possibly write hexameter verses, he complained, when these seven-foot-tall fellows started to sing. In another letter he mocked his friend Syagrius-Burgundio, who had such an excellent command of the Burgundian language that the barbarians were afraid of committing a barbarism in their own language. To be sure, this Syagrius of Lyon, a "new Solon of the Burgundians," had been able, as a Roman jurist and expert in Barbarian customary law, to familiarize them with the Latin language and attitudes that prevailed in the region and, in a sense, to implant a "Latin heart" in the Burgundians.[13]

For a long time linguists considered the Burgundians to be an East Germanic people, but today they are no longer so sure. It is true that the Burgundians were occasionally counted among the "Gothic peoples," probably because most of them were Arians for a long time. But in the eyes of the Gaul Sidonius Apollinaris they came from the land east of the Rhine and were therefore a Germanic people, a classification that no ethnographer of late antiquity would have applied to the Gothic peoples.[14]

The small size of their tribe and their desire to establish a home for themselves in Gaul impelled the Burgundians to form a completely open society as an alternative to the Gallic kingdoms. As early as the fourth century, when they were still far from the Rhine, the Burgundians had already been certain that they were related to the Romans.[15] Regardless of what we wish to make of this story, the Burgundians acted accordingly once they had set up their kingdom in southern Gaul, bestowing their name on the Roman provinces that made up this regnum. And though the Burgundians, together with the native magnates, were able to defend their independence for only three generations, the Burgundian identity was not destroyed, and the Burgundian name lives on to this day in the region of Burgundy.[16]

THIRTEEN

The Spanish Kingdom of the Visigoths (507/568–711/725)

The First Nation of Europe

1. THE LONG CRISIS (507–568)

The death of Alaric II turned the serious Visigothic defeat at Vouillé into a catastrophe. To be sure, the victorious armies of the Franks and Burgundians were not able to conquer Gothic Gaul with one stroke and divide it up between them. On the contrary, the Burgundians went away empty handed, and even the Franks needed almost another quarter of a century before they had de facto control of Aquitaine. And the Visigoths were able to hang on to the Mediterranean coast of Narbonensis, the area of Septimania rich in cities. Still, the lost battle at Vouillé triggered a long period of crisis that lasted from 507 to 568, interrupted by periods of relative stability.

From 418 to 507, nearly ninety years, the younger Balths had held the Visigothic kingdom without encountering internal opposition and resistance from the nobility. During this time the magnates of the kingdom of Toulouse had to put up with quite a bit, if we recall the fratricides that accompanied two changes of ruler or the filling of top-level command positions with former Roman military officers. But as long as a son or grandson of Theoderid's was on the throne, all great lords remained loyal until 507; there was no stirring of opposition, no hint of a movement comparable to the revolt of the Vandal nobility in 442. Still, things must have been seething under the surface when the magnates forced their king in 507 to battle the Franks against his better judgment and without awaiting the arrival of Ostrogothic help. Great unrest was building up, and the defeat and death of the king caused the dam to burst, so to speak. After the battle at the Catalaunian fields the Gothic army had also returned without a king, but it had defeated Attila and was led by the son of the dead monarch, who had seized the reigns with a strong hand. Nothing like this happened in 507 and the following years.

Alaric II, about forty years old at the time of his death, had made no provisions for his succession. He left behind two sons: Amalaric, about five years old, born to him of Thiudigotho, the daughter of Theodoric the Great, and the already grown Gesalec, who came from a marriage that was not fully valid. At first Ravenna was willing to accept that the Visigoths elevated the older son to the kingship in Narbonne in 507 or 508; after all, Theodoric's or Geiseric's descent had not been much better.

Gesalec, however, was unable to hold the ersatz capital of Narbonne against the Burgundians and made no serious effort to defend Carcassonne, where the greater part of the Visigothic royal treasure and his half-brother Amalaric had been taken to safety. The new king seemed to give no thought at all to a reconquest of Toulouse, and he did not have unconditional support from the Visigothic ruling class. Gesalec's lack of ability as king was soon evident. In the summer of 508 Amalaric's grandfather in Ravenna mobilized the Ostrogothic army, which Theodoric's General Ibba led against the Gallic "barbarians" with great success. At least that is how the situation was perceived in Ostrogothic Italy, where Franks, Burgundians, and the fraternal Visigoths too were counted among the barbarians. "Ibba" is a shortened name form, and in its full length it could have read Hildebrand. Was Theodoric's loyal general and governor the historical model for Hildebrand, Dietrich von Bern's armorer?

Even before the year 508 was out, the Ostrogoths had driven back the Franks and the Burgundians who were besieging Arles, and they had liberated Carcassonne and begun the siege of Narbonne, which fell in 509. Thereafter the Franks withdrew from the coast of the Mediterranean, and the Burgundians had no choice but to do the same. But the Ostrogoths had not come to the aid of their hapless brothers in order to prop up the luckless Gesalec, who was obviously willing to conclude a peace with the Franks and Burgundians that involved giving up territory;[1] rather, he had to fall to allow for an Amal solution to Alaric II's succession.

In 510, Ostrogoths and Visigoths fought against each other for the first time since 451. This time the victors of the Catalaunian fields were defeated; Gesalec lost, fled, and began to pose a prime security risk. First he solicited help from the Vandals, and with Thrasamund's money he then went to Aquitaine, where he stayed for one year and raised a Gothic army. The fact that Clovis, or his successors, tolerated or had to tolerate Gesalec's activities indicates, first, that the Frankish conquest of Aquitaine was incomplete, and, second, that Goths were still settled in the heartlands of the former kingdom of Toulouse.

One last time, in 511/512 or 513/514, Gesalec tried his luck against the Ostrogoths. He lost the battle on what is today Catalan territory and then played his last card, the Burgundians. But on the way to the Burgundian King Gundobad, he was captured by the Ostrogoths "on the other side of the Durance" and was executed as a rebel. In the meantime, by 511 at the latest, Theodoric the Great had been made king also of the Visigoths; it was at least his third elevation to kingship. The Amal had the Visigothic lands governed first by Ibba and then by his sword bearer and lieutenant, Theudis. The territory lost to the Franks remained lost; any attempt at recapturing it was written off when Theodoric made peace with Clovis's heirs in 512/513 or 514/515. While expulsions of Goths took place in the regions of Angoulême, Saintes, and probably also Bordeaux, Toulouse and its environs probably became Gothic once again and remained so until 531.

By then, of course, Theodoric the Great was long dead, and his grandson, Amalaric, who had held the Visigothic kingship for five years, was also no longer alive. But even this brief reign was made possible only by the death of his grandfather. What, then, was Theodoric's Amal solution to the Visigothic question? There is hardly any doubt that there had been no room for Amalaric in Theodoric's original plans. Evidently the royal court in Ravenna had put the word out that Theodoric was exercising the regency for his Visigothic grandson. But if that was so, Amalaric, and not his Ostrogothic grandfather, would have been the legitimate Visigothic king, and from about 517 on, the claim of regency would in any case have become meaningless, as Amalaric attained the age of majority and thus became qualified to rule. No, the Amal solution appears to have been headed in a different direction, one Theodoric had already taken when Amalaric was still underage.

Since about 427, there had been living among the Visigoths a branch of the greater Amal clan that traced its descent from Ermanaric, the "noblest of the Amals," and counted kings among its ancestors, that had tried to obtain the Visigothic kingship in the third and fourth decades of the fifth century. In 515 the Ostrogothic king chose the husband for his daughter Amalasuintha from among these Amals. This man was called Eutharic, and soon after the wedding his father-in-law designated him his successor.

Though it took some time before Constantinople accepted Theodoric's ideas, when recognition came in 519, the Amal succession arrangement contained all the elements of Theodoric's own kingship: from designation by the predecessor to imperial adoption to the granting of citizenship to the holding of the consulship. Of course this decision by the emperor applied not only to Italy and its neighboring lands but also to the Visigothic kingdom, which comprised the greater part of the prefecture of Gaul. Just as Theodoric did not wish to draw a distinction between the two kingdoms, Constantinople too did not make one.

It was probably "a long-range goal of Theodoric's policy to create a greater Gothic dominion and to reverse the separation into East Goths and West Goths. And in fact the two tribes grew together at that time."[2] Ostrogothic troops went to the West, Visigothic contingents were stationed in Italy. The portion of the Visigothic royal treasure that had been saved was taken to Ravenna. However, great dissatisfaction soon arose among the Spanish provincials over Theodoric's ecclesiastical and tax policies; a restoration of the conditions as they had existed under Alaric II and Euric was vehemently demanded and forced through. Moreover, Ravenna did take measures that were contrary to the policy of amalgamation. In 509/510, for example, Euric's last conquest, the land between the Alps and the Rhône, taken in 476, was detached from the Visigothic kingdom and set up as the Gallic prefecture of the Ostrogothic kingdom with its capital in Arles.

The prefecture of Gaul, a late Roman large-scale territorial organizational institution, had once comprised all of Gaul, Britain, Spain, and the African western province of Tingitana. In the fifth century its capital was moved from Trier to Arles. The revival of the prefecture for Provence was an expression of a politics of pawns, one which Theodoric did not give up even after 511, when he officially became king of the Visigoths. Ravenna celebrated this step as the liberation of the territory from the barbarians and its integration into the Roman Empire, even though the Visigothic kingdom was legally part of the empire.

Theodoric appointed as praetorian prefect of Gaul the seasoned Liberius, who held the office from 510 to 534; the last two years he spent also as commander in chief of the Gothic-Gallic troops, with the rank of *patricius praesentalis*. Even before his appointment Liberius was considered a military man, and he had been "wounded" in action. North of the Durance River near Arles, that is, close to where the river flows into the Rhône, Liberius got caught in an ambush sometime between 512 and 513. What probably happened was that Visigothic warriors, in the midst of peace, attacked the new Gallic prefecture via Burgundian territory and nearly killed the head of the Ostrogothic administration who had been installed by the very man who was also their king. This casts a revealing light on the stability and harmony of the united Gothic kingdoms. Still, much was done to reestablish Gothic unity during the fifteen years that Theodoric ruled over both realms. In spite of Ravenna's propaganda the two Gothic peoples became strongly interwoven. When Theodoric died in 526 and his two grandsons assumed independent reigns, many Goths were forced to choose one or the other of the two kingdoms. At the same time Athalaric returned the royal treasure to his cousin Amalaric; for the next eleven years the Rhône formed the border between the two Gothic regna.

Ostrogothic help was never given selflessly, but as long as Ravenna offered it the Visigoths were able to hold not only the Mediterranean coast but also large stretches in the interior of southern Aquitaine. The uncertain situation following the death of Theodoric led Amalaric to pursue an alliance with the Franks, a policy that had little success, to be sure. He asked for the hand of Clotild, the daughter of Clovis and the deeply religious Clotild. Her Merovingian brothers consented, and Amalaric married the

Frankish woman. But by the fall of 531 this marriage served as a pretext for the Merovingians to declare war on the Visigoths. The fanatical Arian Amalaric allegedly maltreated his wife because of her Catholic faith, whereupon her brother Childebert played the avenger and invaded Septimania. In the fall of 531 a battle took place near Narbonne, and Amalaric lost. The luckless king fled to Barcelona, where a Frank named Besso, who may have been one of the queen's men, killed him. Childebert took his sister along as he set out for their homeland, which she never saw again, as she died on the way. What the Franks did bring home was the rich booty they had made in the land of the Goths.[3]

Following the inglorious end of the Balthic royal clan, those Ostrogoths who had remained in the Visigothic kingdom asserted themselves and raised Theudis, Theodoric's former sword bearer and until 526 his Visigothic governor, as king. Theudis, who probably did his part to hasten Amalaric's end, had married a rich woman of the Roman senatorial class; his wife brought so much wealth into the marriage that he was able to equip and maintain no fewer than two thousand private soldiers, that is, nearly an entire tribal army. Theudis immediately took up the fight against the Franks, and in a very short time he made such a good name for himself that he was measured against Theodoric.

For example, Theudis was probably the first Visigothic king who, following the example of the great Theodoric, called himself *Flavius rex,* thus making the imperial praenomen part of his name.[4] By as early as 533, Gelimer expected that Theudis and his Goths would come to his aid against Belisarius or at least take him in as a refugee. The Visigothic king declined the former, the need for the latter never materialized. But when the Ostrogoths, after the catastrophe of Vitigis in 540, raised up Hildebad as his successor, they did so not least because he was a nephew of the Visigothic king and they therefore expected help from the latter in their struggle against the emperor. Once again Theudis kept the peace, even though the Byzantines had moved a strong garrison to Septem-Ceuta and had occupied the Balearic Islands, hitherto under Vandal control. Hildebad's indirect successor was his nephew Totila; he too expected help from his royal relatives. It was probably in 547, a year after Totila had reached the height of his power, that his great-uncle Theudis sent his troops to cross the Strait of Gibraltar and attack Ceuta and the small imperial province of Tingitana. The expedition ended in a catastrophe, in part, no doubt, because the Catholic Byzantines attacked the unsuspecting Arian Visigoths on a Sunday. The constellation of the battle of Pollentia in 402 had repeated itself. But Theudis's defeat was far more severe than that of Alaric I; it was one of the reasons the king lost his throne and his life in 548. However, it is also possible that he fell victim to a blood feud.

Under King Theudis the focus of the kingdom shifted from its northern border to southern Spain, and it was increasingly menaced by a victorious Byzantine Empire. To fend off the external dangers, the hitherto largely independent region of Baetica was far more strongly integrated into the Visigothic kingdom. Theudis's successor, Theudegisil, is sometimes believed to have been identical with the Ostrogothic Amal and nephew of Amalaric of the same name. If that was indeed the case, it remained unknown to the Amal *Origo Gothica* and to Isidor's *Historia vel Origo Gothorum* or was considered to be inconsequential. Of no importance, at any rate, was Theudegisel's brief reign, as he was murdered in 549 during a banquet in Seville.

The *morbus Gothicus*, the "Gothic disease," was raging: as if in a fit of madness the Goths eliminated kings by deposition or murder. Beginning with Alaric I there were just under forty kings and anti-kings of the Visigoths; barely half died a natural death or without having been deposed.[5]

Theudegisel's successors too were not able to hold their own, and in 552 an East Roman army under the command of the aged Liberius, the "inventor" of the Ostrogothic settlement in Italy and loyal helper of Theodoric and his daughter,[6] occupied the southern coast of Spain. Athanagild (551/555–568) had called the imperial troops into the land to support his rebellion against Theudegisel's designated successor. Liberius is said to have been ninety years old at the time, and yet Justinian believed that he could not do without this eminent man, who had turned his back on Italy and had entered into imperial service only after the murder of Amalasuintha. In any case, the Visigoths knew who and what Liberius was.

The landing of East Roman troops initially reduced inter-Gothic tensions. The then-reigning king, Athanagild, resumed the marriage policy with the Franks, as a result of which the famous and infamous Brunhilde came to the Franks and dominated their politics until her death in the year 613. But when Athanagild died in 568, the Visigothic kingdom stood on the brink of disaster; its survival was hanging from a thread, its final collapse seemed only a question of time.[7]

2. LEOVIGILD (568/569–586) AND RECCARED I (573/586–601); OR THE CREATION OF THE KINGDOM OF TOLEDO

After the death of Athanagild, Liuva I (568/569) was elevated to the kingship. Once again the ceremony took place in Narbonne; the kingship and its electors had withdrawn from Spain and considered Septimania the last bastion of Visigothic rule. And there, in Narbonne, a historic moment occurred. Liuva had a younger brother, Leovigild, whose abilities he recognized and appreciated. He made Leovigild coruler, assigned him Spain, and probably also arranged for him to become his successor in Septimania, which he did only four years later. Leovigild was an exceedingly successful ruler, and his son Reccared I followed in his footsteps. The generation of their rule seems as though cast of one mold, even though, or perhaps because, the son broke with his father's religious policy. But essentially Reccared did not change course, only ship.

"Leovigild restored the land of the Goths, which had been reduced by many small rebellions, to its old boundaries." That was the verdict of a contemporary, and we wonder how the king accomplished this. Apparently he was able to make the regnum attractive once again and to win larger numbers of the most active warriors to his side, thereby not only turning the regional and local potentates (the "tyrants") into unlawful rulers, but also reducing their numbers substantially.

Almost every year the king marched out at the head of the army against Byzantines, Suebi, Basques, and enemies at home. In 578, he proclaimed the founding of a new city northeast of Toledo, naming it Reccopolis after his second son. Prior to this only Theodoric the Great and the Vandal King Huneric had had the nerve to present themselves as imperial founders of cities. Reccopolis, located inside of Spain, was probably intended to become the capital of the Visigoths. In 573, Leovigild had made his two sons Hermenegild and Reccared coregents, *consortes regni,* a measure that was probably also intended to restrict the electoral right of the Goths and to establish a new dynasty. It is likely that for this move, as well, the king took imperial constitutional law as his model. It is also noteworthy that Reccopolis was named after his second son, even though the great crisis between Leovigild and his firstborn son could not yet have broken out in 578.

In the year 579, the Merovingian Ingunde journeyed to Spain to become the wife of Hermenegild. Her reception in Toledo left nothing to be desired. But the young lady—she was only twelve at the time—was strong enough to cast the Visigothic kingdom once again into a serious crisis. She had no intention of becoming Arian, and she got her husband to sympathize with Catholicism. The scandal was greatly exacerbated when Leovigild's second wife, the widow of his predecessor Athanagild and stepmother of his coregents, tried to force conversion upon her daughter-in-law. To calm the situation down a bit, Leovigild removed the young couple from court and made Hermenegild governor in southern Spain. There the young king came under the influence of the monk Leander, the older brother of Isidor of Seville, and did in fact convert to Catholicism. This amounted to an open break with his father; an alliance with the Byzantines seems to have been merely the result of his conversion.

Leovigild's reaction to this situation was both logical and consistent: he tried to exhaust every possible way of unifying Spain religiously in favor of Arianism. An Arian council met in Toldeo in 580, and it made an effort—interesting also on theological grounds—to win over the Catholic Roman majority to Arianism. For example, the Catholic sacrament of baptism was recognized and rebaptism for converts, previously obligatory, was abolished.

Conciliatory positions were adopted toward the veneration of relics and saints, which was foreign to the Arians. Most especially, however, the doctrine of Christ's subordination to the Father was softened. Thus, Leovigild thought it possible "to describe Christ as equal, *aequalis*, to the Father, whereas hitherto he had been only similar, *similis*, in relation to God the Father."[8]

The king consistently pursued his goal of unifying the kingdom under the banner of Arianism, but his anti-Catholic measures did not turn into outright persecution. While some bishops were in fact banished, vacant dioceses were filled with new appointees. Above all, Leovigild promoted conversion, a step taken even by some Catholic bishops.

All in all, Leovigild did not attain his goal: Arianism had fallen so far behind Roman orthodoxy intellectually as well as in terms of popular religion that Leovigild was doomed to failure. Arianism was too weak to bring about the unity Leovigild desired and to replace the Spanish gentes with the unified national people, the *populus*. Reccared, however, drew lessons from his father's failure: if he wanted to unify the Visigoths in terms of religious policy he had only one choice, that of converting to Catholicism. But a decade of vigorous and clarifying debates and controversies took place before he would take that step.

After breaking with his father in 579, Hermenegild tried to present himself as the victim of persecution and to forge alliances against his father and his kingdom in the name of Catholicism. He found allies among the Byzantines; among local potentates, whose independence Leovigild had so recently curtailed; among the Suebi of northwestern Spain, who had become Catholic nearly a generation earlier; and among his wife's Frankish relatives. However, this obvious policy of trying to encircle his father was unsuccessful: Leovigild took advantage of the discord among the Merovingians and established contacts with the king of Neustria, contacts that were to be consolidated with a marriage. Even though the marriage did not happen, Leovigild had reason to be pleased with his Neustrian ally. Not least, Leovigild had the advantage of the internal line of communication, which he knew to make use of. Thus Leovigild had time to pursue his religious policies, time, in 581, to fight the Basques once again and to negotiate with Hermenegild.

Hermenegild had sent his godfather to Constantinople, where he struck up a friendship with the later Pope Gregory I. But the emperor could not be prevailed upon to intervene actively in Spain. There were too many military clashes and threats that were much closer to the capital: Avars and Slavs in the Balkans, the Longobards in Italy, and the Persians on the eastern frontier. The alliance with Byzantium would thus provide only as much help as the regional imperial commander in southern Spain was able to muster, and that was not very much. Effective help could be expected only from the

Suebians, whose King Miro wanted to make up for the defeat he had suffered in 576 at the hands of Leovigild.

In 582, the Visigothic king launched a war against his son and his son's supporters, which he carried on very harshly until 584. Mérida fell in the first year of the war, and its loss all but cut off the lines between Hermenegild and the Suebians; nevertheless, the Suebians launched an attack in 583 and paid the price, suffering a thorough defeat. Lured into an ambush, Miro was forced to capitulate and to recognize Leovigild's suzerainty. Hermenegild for his part had withdrawn to Seville. The city did not fall until 584, after a lengthy siege, and shortly before it did, Hermenegild and his wife found refuge in Córdoba, which was once again in Byzantine hands. But all hopes of persuading the imperial troops to get involved, after all, were dashed. The Byzantine commander concluded a treaty with the Visigothic king, returning the city of Córdoba and probably the other territory occupied since 579 in return for thirty thousand gold solidi. Hermenegild was not even mentioned in the treaty.

While the Byzantines departed with Hermenegild's wife and young son, Athanagild, Hermenegild himself sought refuge in a church, from where he intended to negotiate with his father. In return for guarantees that his life would be spared, he submitted, laid down the insignia of power, and was taken to Toledo, where he officially renounced his royal position. At first he was banished to Valencia. Later he came to Tarragona, where he was murdered in 585, though we cannot say anything certain about the killer and his motives.

Pope Gregory the Great wrote that Hermenegild died because of his faith, thus making Leovigild responsible for his death. Back home, however, the rebellious son was by no means regarded as a martyr. Even though all contemporary and near contemporary reporters were Catholics, and some—like Leander and his younger brother Isidor—were personally affected by the events, they were unanimous in condemning the step that Hermenegild had taken.

Although Gregory's *Dialogi* made its way to Spain quickly, the story of Hermenegild's martyrdom that was found in it was either quietly ignored or at times spectacularly altered. For example, we read that when Reccared I became Catholic he "did not follow his unbelieving father but Christ the Lord." Gregory the Great, however, had written that the king "did not follow his unbelieving father but his brother and martyr."[9] For in the eyes of the Spaniards, it had been merely ambition and a desire for power that had driven Prince Hermenegild to rebel against his father, which is why Leovigild's harsh response seemed quite justified.

Gregory of Tours, the author of the *History of the Franks*, was truly no friend of the Spaniards and Goths. Nevertheless, he too came to the conclusion: "Poor prince, he did not realize that the judgment of God hangs over anyone who makes such plans against his own father, even if that father be a heretic."[10] After Hermenegild's downfall, the Visigothic troops pushed ahead. Though Byzantine southern Spain continued to exist on a smaller scale until 625, the independence of the Suebian kingdom came to an end in 585, after 150 years of separate history. It was only a question of time before the Iberian Peninsula would form a single political entity.

Leovigild had not only restored the Visigothic kingdom internally and externally, but had also imparted an imperial style to its rise to new great power status. It is not possible to determine to what extent such things as the court, ceremonies, the elevation of his sons as coregents, the minting of gold coins in his own name, the mention of victories in the legends, and finally the comprehensive amendment of Gothic law were directly copied from Byzantium. In any case, the reshaping of the Visigothic kingdom in the image of the empire dispensed with any universalism. Thus the elevation of the sons as coregents had, above all, the practical goal of both eliminating the nobility's right of election and establishing a new dynasty. Renewing the laws was likewise a very practical concern, since the large Visigothic codifications were two generations old. With the exception of the law on court costs passed in 546, no Visigothic king since Alaric II had found time to amend or adapt the law. Leovigild's law code, the Antiqua, exists today only in partial form in a later redaction. Nevertheless, the king's legal policy can be clearly made out. Leovigild sought an accommodation between Romans and Goths, to which end the special status of the Goths, already curtailed in 546, was to be entirely eliminated. The prohibition on intermarriage between Romans and Goths was abolished; this was, as the king explicitly said, for the benefit of the entire people (*populus*), not of a particular gens. In all likelihood, Leovigild also abolished the entire *Breviarium Alaricianum,* the *Lex Romana Visigothorum.* In any case, he based his code on the *Codex Euricianus,* which was easy to do since this "Gothic" law too was essentially Roman vulgar law. Leovigild's Antiqua no doubt had territorial validity, and one-third of it contained Roman law, which served to consolidate the monarch's power.

Although an *intitulatio,* an official royal title, is attested only for his son Reccared I, Leovigild, too, must have presented himself as *Flavius rex.* His enthronement has an imperial flavor: "as the first among his people he sat on the throne in royal robes; before his time the kings wore the same dress and took care to wear the same accouterments as the other Goths also when sitting on the throne."[11]

Even before Leovigild, the Visigothic king had presented himself to his non-Gothic subjects as lord and ruler; now the king was also singled out from among his own people and was, literally, "set apart." The throne occupied an elevated place. Ascending the throne was tantamount to acceding to power, and it was an act of such importance that a portable throne was carried along on campaigns. We can get some idea about the king's vestments from the images on the coins. Like the emperor, the king wore a chlamys, a *paludamentum,* which was derived from the Roman general's cloak. In Constantinople, purple-dyed cloth was used for making these vestments, in keeping with Roman tradition and in deference to the emperor's exclusive privilege of wearing this color.

Since neither Visigothic grandees, nor laymen, nor even clerics respected this imperial privilege, it is unlikely that the king paid much attention to it, either. Following his usurpation, Hermenegild had the same sort of coins minted, which means that his royal mantle too must have resembled that of his father. Of course, after his capture, the prince was ceremoniously stripped of his vestments. Paulus, another usurper who reached for power in 673, also took off his royal garb as a sign of his surrender.

The king's festive regalia also included crown and scepter. We know for certain that Leovigild's son Reccared was crowned, and he also gave a crown as a votive offering to a church. Crowns of this sort from the seventh century in the name of Recceswinth (653–672) have been preserved among the treasure found in Guarrazar. The significance of this emblem of rule is also revealed by the mocking use to which it was put when King Wamba had the defeated usurper Paulus enter Toledo wearing a crown of disgrace. Like the throne, the scepter was considered a sign of lordship. During military campaigns, the king carried along a standard (the "banner") that was reserved for his exclusive use; this too had Roman precedents. To demonstrate his rulership, the king thus possessed insignia that symbolized the regnum, insignia one could assume legally, usurp, return voluntarily, or be forced to renounce.

The *comites* of the realm, who strike me as so very Roman and who in many cases can be attested only around the middle of the seventh century in the entourage of the kings of Toledo, may well go back to the time of Leovigild or even farther. For instance, the marshal (*comes stabuli*), the cupbearer (*comes scanciarum*), and the treasurer (*comes thesaurorum*) were probably active already at the royal court in Toulouse. The overseer of the royal private estates, the *comes patrimonii,* could go back to Theodoric the Great, who in turn had put this "invention" of Odovacar's to such successful use that Emperor Anastasius adopted it for Constantinople. The arms bearer of Toulouse (*comes armiger*) turned into the *comes spat(h)ariorum* in the Visigothic kingdom of Spain, probably on the Byzantine model, though without being a eunuch like his counterpart in Constantinople.

The office of chamberlain (*comes cubiculariorum*), the overseer of the king's private quarters, could have been taken over from Byzantium or—more likely—from Ostrogothic Italy. In Italy, the *praepositus cubiculi* was always a Goth. As head of the "royal bedchamber" he supervised the court chamberlains and court eunuchs, though he also administered the royal treasury. When Theodoric was king of the Visigothic realm from 511 to 526, the taxes of Spain officially went to the treasury and thus to the *cubiculum*, even though the money itself may well have stayed in the land.

By contrast, the thoroughly Roman office of the chief notary of Toledo, the *comes notariorum*, had no counterpart in any other Roman-barbarian successor state, and Byzantium too had no such position. And while the other court offices frequently had multiple officeholders and thus atrophied to mere honorary titles, the acts of the councils of Toledo were always signed by a single *comes notariorum* who therefore did in fact exercise his office.

That the Visigoths drew on antiquated Roman traditions and models that had been preserved in Spain is also revealed by the fact that Leovigild immortalized his successes on coins, which was good old imperial custom, to be sure, but long since given up in Byzantium. The same holds true for adoption of the imperial epithets *pius* and *felix*, which Visigothic minting introduced after older Roman models; from about the middle of the fifth century, Constantinople had been using *pius* and *perpetuus* for this purpose.

It is possible that Leovigild, who, like his sons, demonstrably strove to create larger administrative units as subdivisions of the empire, also reestablished the late-antique provincial structure, at least partially. The kingdom of Toledo was basically divided into *civitates* (city districts) from which *comites* at times administered entire duchies, militarized former provinces. But unlike their Ostrogothic counterparts, these *comites* had no superiors other than the king. However, in the seventh-century kingdom of Toledo, at the latest, there were also *duces* who were placed above *comites*, and correspondingly we find several *ducatus* as territorial entities; Septimanian Languedoc is attested as a *ducatus* in the year 694.[12]

Leovigild died in 586, and his son Reccared I succeeded him without the least difficulty. As early as 587, the new king converted to Catholicism, thus in his own way carrying out his father's policy of establishing the confessional unity of the Visigothic kingdom. Opposition came, not least, from the Arian episcopate, which found vigorous support at the royal court in the person of the king's stepmother, Gosvintha, who had now outlived two Visigothic kings. Only Septimania witnessed an armed rebellion, though it soon collapsed.

Leovigild had used every one of many opportunities to cut the Visigothic nobility down to size: "He was, however, quite dangerous to many of his own: for when he saw that someone acted excessively noble or powerful, he either had his head cut off or sent him into exile after confiscating his property."[13] Now the son reaped the benefit of this policy, especially since he was quite willing to put the nobility in its place with acts that demonstrated his intent with unmistakable clarity. When a high-ranking lord conspired against him, he was captured, subjected to *decalvatio* (he either had his hair

shorn or was scalped; the meaning of the word has not been fully determined), had his right hand—the oath-taking hand—chopped off, and was
led through Toledo on a donkey to let everyone know what fate "awaited
servants who pridefully rise up against their lord."[14]

After thorough preparations and negotiations, the Third Council of Toledo convened in 589. All five metropolitans of the kingdom came, as did
nearly fifty Catholic and all eight former Arian bishops. In addition, a large
number of Arian clerics and Gothic grandees made their appearance. Following the solemn conversion of the Visigoths, the converted Arian bishops
retained their titles, even though it meant that double occupants had to be
accepted on some episcopal seats, contrary to canon law. The bishops next
professed the Nicene Creed and signed it along with the Gothic grandees,
whose education must therefore have still been based on a command of the
written language. King Reccared, who had brought about this conversion,
was considered by contemporaries to be "the most holy prince," "filled by
the spirit of God," deserving of "apostolic merit since he had fulfilled the
apostolic duty." With these and similar words the assembly acclaimed the
king, hailing Reccared as the apostle-like basileus. If the ruler of East Rome
was called the "orthodox emperor," the man who ruled in Toledo was the
"orthodox king."[15]

In keeping with such a depiction of the kingship was the king's actual
rule over the church, which resembled the position of the emperor in the
church of his empire. Thus Reccared could explain in a letter to Pope Gregory the Great that after God, he was the highest lord of his subjects. The
principle articulated in late medieval France that "the king is emperor in
his land" seems to have been anticipated here. Finally, Reccared was also
fortunate enough to win one of the greatest victories that a Gothic army
ever won against its Frankish neighbors. His campaigns against the Basques,
though, were the usual actions without any significant successes. In fact,
to this day no foreign power has been able to completely subjugate the
Basques.

When Reccared I died in 601, his son Liuva II succeeded him as though
it were a matter of course. However, the eighteen-year-old new king was not
able to preserve the great legacy of his father and grandfather and at age
twenty already fell victim to a conspiracy.

3. THE KINGDOM OF TOLEDO (603–710):
AN OVERVIEW

Leovigild's dynasty came to an end in 603, and the Visigoths returned to the
elective monarchy with all its murderous mechanisms. Thus there were no
fewer than seventeen Visigothic kings in the seventh century, ten of whom
were definitely or in all probability either deposed or murdered.[16]

None of this, however, seriously jeopardized Leovigild's and Reccared's work of unifying the kingdom. The religiously sanctified kingship and the power of the landowning nobility linked up with a strong Roman tradition and initiated a social, legal, and economic development that anticipated the medieval feudal state. The accommodation between Goths and Romans set in motion a process that seemed to realize the creation of a medieval nation outside of and earlier than the Carolingian Empire, though at the same time it put the unity of the Visigothic kingdom in question. Those who saw themselves as Gauls, that is, the inhabitants of Visigothic Septimania, mocked the Spaniards; the Spaniards looked down on the Gauls as barbarians and subhumans and denied that they were Visigoths.[17] The sources tell us this in connection with, of all things, the first evidence of the royal unction, the highest expression of divine right.

In 673, Septimania rebelled. The *dux* Paulus, whom King Wamba (672–680) sent out to bring Gothic Gaul to heel, joined the Septimanians and usurped power. After his usurpation, Paulus wrote a jeering letter to his former lord, which opened with the words: *Flavius Paulus unctus rex orientalis Wambani regi austro,* "Flavius Paulus, anointed king of the East, to the southern King Wamba." Two things Paulus wanted to express with this salutation: first, that the Visigothic kingdom was to be divided along the prenational faultlines and Septimania recognized as a separate kingdom; second, that there was only one Flavian and one anointed king, and he was the one. It was, of course, the height of provocation to invoke the anointing and address Wamba as the unanointed king, for Wamba, in particular, placed great stock in sacramental matters.[18]

The Visigothic king accepted the challenge on both levels. Since the campaign was against the despised Gauls, it was fairly easy for him to assemble a large Spanish army, and as the true anointed of the Lord he was eager to bring about a favorable divine verdict. But not all who marched in the Spanish army were as pure of heart as the king. While still in Spain itself they began to plunder and to rape the village women. Quoting the Old Testament, the king is said first to have publicly declared: "If only we keep ourselves unsullied by crimes, we shall undoubtedly triumph over our enemies." Thereafter he made a clean break with the perpetrators.

The anti-Jewish legislation that had begun immediately after the conversion of the Visigoths and had been passed by every royal council of Toledo under the auspices of the king, is among the most terrible and senseless codifications of hatred of which the Middle Ages was capable. But precisely against this background we can make sense of the punishment that Wamba inflicted on those who were endangering his holy war: the king had the rapists circumcised, thus expelling them from the army, making them into non-Christians, into Jews.[19]

King Wamba had assumed the reins of power one year before the usurpation of Paulus. He is the first Visigothic king whose anointing after Old

Testament models is described in the sources unequivocally, in detail, and as though it were a matter of course. The sacramental act had no legally constitutive force, only election possessed that. But anointing legitimated a kingship that lacked dynastic charisma. This religious act was, however, not necessarily "invented" only for Wamba. In all likelihood, a Visigothic king was anointed as early as 631, and he too was not necessarily the first.

It would seem that this sacramental act was at first not very important to contemporaries, since the Visigothic king lists do not indicate the date of the anointing until 680, that is, beginning with Wamba's successor. However, the growing interest in the ceremony reveals that its importance grew steadily. When Boniface anointed the former majordomo Pippin III, King of the Franks, in 751, and Pope Stephan II repeated the sacred act three years later, it fulfilled the same function it once did in Spain. Spain had never had a royal clan in the Frankish sense. No dynasty could lay claim to a right of blood that would have even come close to the claim of the Merovingians. This lack of political continuity was probably remedied by the royal anointing as an ecclesiastical act that was borrowed from the episcopal consecration and comparable to it. But whether this example came to the Franks directly or indirectly via insular strands of tradition is a question of interest to specialists. We can note that the Visigoths were the first to anoint one of their own kings, and this makes the ceremony a model for European kingship.

In its strengths as in its weaknesses, the seventh-century Visigothic kingdom was the most perfect successor state to the Roman Empire. Italy's disunity and the weakness both of the Merovingians and of the Byzantines who were threatened from all sides soon made it appear that Toledo was without competition. But the absence of an external challenge led the kingdom of Toledo into splendid isolation; the Toledans lost interest in the rest of the world. Latin literacy flourished in the Visigothic kingdom like nowhere else in Europe, where writing was being relearned laboriously, if at all.[20] Though most of the buildings from the Visigothic period have disappeared, a few northern Spanish churches from the seventh century have survived. Here the ecclesiastical sculpture shows both Byzantine and oriental influence, and even in small objets d'art, Germanic traditions, which had still been alive in the sixth century, were given up.

The Visigothic economic system seems to have arranged itself within an area that was now reduced in size though by contemporary standards still large. A flourishing foreign trade was neither pursued nor missed, otherwise the Visigoths could not have afforded to conduct such a persistent persecution of Jews. Wealth was seen to lie in agriculture, as had been the custom since time immemorial. The late antique system of latifundia is unlikely to have changed in any way. In fact, a process of concentration seems to have begun, one that increased wealth in the hands of some and led to a rise in the number of dependents, both free and unfree. The grandees who were obligated to render military service did so by heading their own warriors, a situation that shows feudal traits. However, the statements in the normative sources should not be misinterpreted to mean that a small group of grandees lorded it over an amorphous mass of servants, and that the downfall of the Visigothic kingdom was thus almost predestined for social reasons.[21]

4. THE FALL OF THE VISIGOTHIC KINGDOM

In 625, King Suinthila (621–631) had taken Cartagena, the capital of the Byzantine province, thereby becoming the first Visigothic king who "possessed the dominion over all of Spain (on this side of the Strait of Gibraltar)."[22] Thereafter Spain would not have to tolerate foreign troops on its soil for decades, leaving aside the usual fighting with the Basques in the north and the attacks by Mediterranean pirates. However, a new element did appear among the pirates between 672 and 680 when an Arab fleet ravaged the coastal towns of Spain.

The Seventeenth Council of Toledo, held in 694 in the capital with the king presiding, saw the height of anti-Jewish legislation: all Jews were to be deprived of their property and their freedom; they were to lose their right of residence and their children once they had reached the age of seven; in addition, the king had the right to give the Jews away as he saw fit. The king declared that it had always been his intention to convert the Jews, and now, by the command of God, the time had come to eradicate Judaism from his realm.

Not the least of the justifications for the measures was the accusation that the Jews of Spain were in contact with their fellow Jews abroad in order to conspire against the Visigothic kingdom. To this day, isolationist political systems consider contact with foreign countries a crime, and a cosmopolitan quality has always been part of the essence of Judaism. Through their foreign contacts the persecuted Spanish Jews knew that their fellow believers were tolerated under Arab rule; for them, change could thus only be for the better.

While the acts of the council of 694—the last to be preserved by posterity—reveal all too clearly that the king and the magnates took the impending threat to the kingdom seriously, the intensification of the permanent persecution of the Jews was surely the least suitable measure for warding it off. What was really needed was a radical improvement in the structure of the army and an accommodation between the leading families of the Visigoths.

The only thing that the Visigothic army had in common with the Roman federates who had defeated Attila and with the army that had clashed with

Franks and Byzantines with varying fortunes was the name. What the king could muster was primarily the nobility, who heeded the call with their free and especially unfree dependents if they believed that doing so was in their own interest. Generally the great lords thought it was quite enough to take one out of every twenty slaves along on a campaign, or to excuse themselves entirely on grounds of illness and to send only their unfree dependents. Even this would have been acceptable to the king if at least one out of every ten slaves had followed his lord into battle.[23]

Qualitatively the most important units of the Visigothic army were, of course, the mounted noblemen and those of their dependents who could afford a horseman's equipment or to whom their lords furnished it. But since the number of unfree who marched along, and who were the sole responsibility of their lords, grew steadily, there were more and more lightly armed foot soldiers. No source reports that any Gothic infantry after 500 had much military value.[24]

The elective monarchy had changed considerably since the middle of the seventh century. Wamba (in 672) and Roderic (in 710) were elected kings. The other kings attained the throne through designation or appointment as coregents. However, the number of families qualified for the kingship had been reduced to two competing branches of a single clan. Both traced their descent from Chindaswinth (642–653) but were mortal enemies. Thus their common ancestor, who had reigned as king from age seventy-nine to age ninety, had, as a great legislator, creative reorganizer, and ruthless persecutor of the nobility, created the most important preconditions for a situation in which only his descendants were eligible for the kingship.[25]

In 693–694 and 707–709, terrible plague epidemics swept through the Visigothic kingdom. Between 698 and 701, a Byzantine fleet, following the temporary reconquest of Carthage, must have landed on the eastern coast of Spain, probably in the area of Alicante, but it was driven off.

Despite their isolation, the Spanish upper class knew that the Arabs were threatening the Roman Empire. The empire would fall, but, Spanish contemporaries consoled themselves, the Visigothic kingdom would carry on its traditions.[26] But now, in 709 or 710, the Arabs had reached Tanger and Ceuta. Probably as early as 709, but definitely in the summer of 710, small units had crossed the Strait of Gibraltar, engaging in armed reconnaissance and extensive plundering. Meanwhile the Arab propaganda mill went into high gear. While the invasion army was assembling at Tanger, the mints put out copper coins that proclaimed the jihad, Holy War, and "payment in the path of Allah." Then the caliph gave the order, and the well-planned expedition got under way in the summer of 711 under the leadership of Tarik.

In the spring of 710, the Visigoths had elected Roderic king, following the death of his predecessor Vitiza from the other branch of the royal family. But the relatives of the dead king, whose son or sons were probably still too young to be designated by their father, were unwilling to accept the election of Roderic. And so the Visigoths indulged in the luxury of a serious quarrel between their two leading families while preparations for a Holy War were in full swing across the Strait of Gibraltar.

When Tarik set foot on Spanish soil with an army composed largely of Berbers, Roderic was off on the seasonal campaign against the Basques in the north. A memorable battle took place on July 23, 711, at the small river Guadalete south of Arcos de la Frontera in the province of Cádiz. Roderic and his Visigothic enemies joined forces in the battle against the invaders, and they perished together; the legend of the stab-in-the-back, the treason committed by the supporters of the dead King Vitiza, goes back to a later attempt to explain the catastrophe. Tarik had about twelve thousand men, and the Gothic army was probably about the same size.

This defeat did not by any means spell the end of the Visigothic kingdom, and especially not of the Visigothic resistance both south and north of the Pyrenees. It would be another fourteen years before the Arabs had truly secured the victory of 711. The Visigothic grandees, in particular, showed that in their own regions they were quite able and willing to put their men in the field and offer tough and not always unsuccessful resistance. Regardless of whether or not the Visigoths converted, the Arabs considered them brave enemies and treated them with magnanimity. In the long run, however, the Gothic tradition departed for the realms of myth and legend. Much the same happened to the kingship. To be sure, its tradition did not disappear completely after 725 even on the Iberian Peninsula; however, it moved northward to the mountainous regions of Asturia, which had been distant from the king "during the time of the Goths" and had been only loosely associated with the kingdom. Spanish Gothicism was thus in its very origins the result of a deliberate renaissance, though this does not mean that one should underestimate its historical significance.

For instance, in 974 the title *Ranimirus Flavius princeps magnus basileus unctus* was used when the kingdom of León went through a period of a relative increase in power. The royal title of Ramiros III (965–984) shows that the universal claim that the Gothic name Flavius had preserved over centuries and the invocation of anointing could give rise to a unique Spanish imperial title.[27] And when the realm of Charles V in the sixteenth century had grown to such size that the sun never set on it, the court historian of his younger brother Ferdinand, Wolfgang Lazius, sought to prove that the Gothic migration across all of Europe had made the regions from the Black Sea to Cádiz into a kind of nation-state, so that "these countries are now with full right once more united under the dominion of the Habsburgs."

The Goths had in fact unified Spain; the *gens vel patria Gothorum* was the country in which the people had begun to form the first nation of the Middle Ages. The events between 711 and 725 put an abrupt stop to this process, and we have good reason to ask how much of this was able to continue during the long centuries of Arab rule or even influence and shape it.

In all likelihood, Gothic Spain was not more than a memory that later generations could use, forget, change (whether they wanted to or not), and correct. It could and can also be distorted: today one can read *fuero godos* ("Goths go home") on some houses in the Canary Islands, a slogan calling for the expulsion of the mainland Spaniards, not of the *Alemans* and their hard currency.[28]

FOURTEEN

The Longobard Epilogue (488–643/652)

1. REFLECTIONS ON A TRUISM

In the year 568, the Longobards left their homeland in Pannonia and pushed into northern Italy. To this day the truism persists that this event marked the end of the migration period. And in fact the Longobards were the last people who went on to establish a lasting kingdom on Roman soil, in the ancient heartland of Italy, no less.[1]

The Longobards unite in themselves the experience made by nearly all tribes—of Germanic as well as non-Germanic origins—who participated in the migrations. As Germanic peoples of the Elbe River, they were classified by linguists as members of the West Germanic peoples. The story of their descent begins with a Scandinavian-Northern Germanic origin saga. On the plains of Pannonia they became so thoroughly acculturated to the customs of the Gothic-Sarmatian horsemen that Ludwig Schmidt had good reason for admitting them into his group of "East Germanic peoples." Finally, there is no doubt that after 568 the period of the spectacular large-scale migrations did come to an end for the Germanic peoples on the continent. Truisms, we can see, are not without truth.

2. THE LONGOBARDS AT THE MIDDLE DANUBE (488–568)

Following the disappearance of the federate kingdoms of the Suebians, the Scirians, the Pannonian Goths, and that of the Rugians in 488, the Heruli took advantage of the tribal vacuum and expanded their power in all directions. The peoples they subjected included the Longobards, who had fallen under the power of the Heruli in their settlement areas in Bohemia (and present-day Moravia). Soon after 488, the Heruli moved parts of this

Elbgermanic-Suebian tribe to the former Rugiland to secure the western flank of the Herulian realm against the barbarian peoples along the upper Danube. In actuality, the oldest archaeological finds attributed to the Longobards in their new home appear only in the eastern Waldviertel and the western Weinviertel (that is, northwest of Vienna), or, precisely where the Rugians had lived. This archaeological material corresponds to that from Bohemia and central Germany and reveals Thuringian elements.

It was probably around 505 that the Longobards crossed the middle Danube for the first time. They occupied the Lower Austrian Tullner Feld south of the river, site of the Roman cities that had become tributary to the Rugians after 480. Perhaps the arrival of more Bohemian-Thuringian tribal elements led to the expansion. In keeping with the Exodus theme of ethnography, tribal migratory movements are usually depicted as the winning of new land and the simultaneous abandonment of the old settlement areas. In actuality, Longobards also remained behind north of the Danube after 505.

Until recently, scholars identified the *feld* ("field") to which Longobard tradition has the tribe move after the alleged abandonment of the Rugiland with areas located at some greater or lesser distance from the latter. While locating the *feld* in the Marchfeld of Lower Austria or even in the interfluve of the Danube and Tisza Rivers provides more impressive "fields" than the Tullner Feld, all these locations have the drawback that they not only lack Longobard remains but contain virtually no remains whatsoever. The Tullner Feld, by contrast, overflows with Longobard finds. The great turning point in the history of the Longobards, which led to the downfall of the Herulian kingdom (probably in 508), must therefore have originated in central Lower Austria and southern Moravia, possibly also in Bohemia.

The Italian Longobards told the story that their ancestors had moved into the Rugiland under a king whom they reckoned as the fifth in their line of rulers. This king, Gudeoc, and his son Claffo belonged to the Longobard royal family of the venerable Lethingi. It was probably in 508 that Tato, Claffo's son and the seventh king, successfully stood up to the challenge of the Herulians. Most likely the battle took place at the Lower Austrian or southern Moravian March, and it changed the ethnic composition of the victors.

As a dependent tribe of peasants, the Longobards and their servants (*Aldiones*) had lived well in the Rugiland, which a short time later seemed to the Herulians an unfruitful desert when they themselves moved to the land vacated by their former slaves. Now the Longobards became the heirs of the Herulian masters and their kingdom. They took over the helmet and the banner of the slain Herulian king, whose daughter Silinga was later queen of the Longobards for a time. Against all tribal logic, the man who took advantage of this new opportunity was not the victorious military king Tato, but his nephew Wacho, who succeeded in 510 in killing his uncle and displacing the ruling line.

Wacho (ca. 510–540)

In Longobard tradition, Wacho was considered a usurper, and the conflict with Tato's grandson Hildigis dragged on for decades. Nevertheless, the tribal memory always remained conscious of Wacho's great accomplishments. His residence, probably the conquered capital of the Herulian kingdom, lay in southern Moravia. From here, as well as from the Lower Austrian heartland, the Longobard king expanded his dominion over present-day eastern Austria and western Hungary, with the Danubian Suebians being the first tribe he subjected.

Until the death of Theodoric the Great, Wacho respectfully kept his distance from the Gothic borders. Only after 526 did the Longobards advance into Pannonia, though without threatening the borders of the Gothic realm from Noricum ripense to Pannonia Sirmiensis. And this is where matters stood until the great Gothic war, for no source reports any entanglements between Goths and Longobards as long as Ravenna ruled over its provinces in western Illyria. However, it must have been quite soon after Theodoric's death that Wacho concluded the first Longobard alliance with Constantinople in order to secure his territorial acquisitions in eastern Noricum ripense and in Pannonia south of the river Drau. He remained faithful to this treaty in 539 when the Gothic envoys of King Vitigis asked him for help.

The ever deeper penetration of the Longobards into Pannonia necessitated a reorientation of their policies, reflected in Wacho's three marriages. Around 510 he married Ranigunda, the daughter of the Thuringian royal couple Bisin and Menia. The Thuringians had been the Longobards' neighbors in Bohemia. Moreover, at that very time Theodoric the Great had impressively strengthened his friendship with the new Thuringian King Herminafrid and had given him his niece Amalaberga as his wife. But once Wacho was firmly in power, he could do without the goodwill of the Thuringians and Goths, and so Ranigunda was not queen of the Longobards for very long.

As early as 512, Wacho sought to establish a bond of kinship with the royal house of the Gepids and married the Princess Austrigusa-Ostrogotho. Ravenna was surely not happy about this decision, but it was actually defensive in character, an expression of a trend to protect the kingdoms of the Longobards and Gepids jointly against the Gothic superpower. The shift of focus of Longobard interests from the Thuringian northwest to the Gepidic east allowed Wacho during the next decade or two to make pacts with the western Franks. As a result, the Longobards remained neutral in the

Frankish-Thuringian wars of 531 and also tolerated Frankish expansion in 536/537 into the Gothic-Italian provinces of Raetia and Noricum.

Several intended and actual marriages consolidated the young Longobard-Frankish friendship. During the lifetime of Theuderic I (511–533), the victor over the Thuringians, Wacho betrothed his older daughter Wisigarda, born to him of his Gepid wife, to Theuderic's son and future Frankish king Theudebert (533–547/548). This first Longobard-Frankish treaty was probably concluded in 532/533.

To be sure, the Merovingian groom, unwilling to get rid of his concubine Deoteria, let his Longobard bride wait for seven years and had to be forced by his Franks into concluding the marriage in 539, when he was already king. At that very time Theudebert also wanted to win over the Longobards and the Gepids for a planned campaign against Byzantium. And so he did finally make the Longobard-Gepid princess his wife. After that Wacho did not hesitate to marry another daughter to the Merovingians. Theudebert's son Theudebald (547/548–555), born to him by the Roman concubine Deoteria, married Walderada, his stepmother's sister or half sister. Wisigarda died shortly after marrying Theudebert, while Walderada solidified the Frankish-Longobard ties with varying success beyond her father's death.

We don't know when Wacho's Gepid wife, Austrigusa, died. However, her death did not disturb relations with the Gepids or the Franks, even though Wacho took a third wife, this time the Herulian Silinga. As the daughter of the Herulian king killed in 508, she legitimated once again Wacho's claim that the Herulian kingship was being carried on by the Longobards.

Audoin (540/541–560/561)

During his reign of about thirty years, Wacho had maintained neutrality in the conflicts between the great powers of the time, subjugated isolated groups like the Pannonian Sarmatians and the Danubian Suebians, and made his Longobards *foederati* of Constantinople. The expansion of his power had made especially Pannonia I into Longobard territory. Wacho's successor was Audoin, from Gautic descent, who acted first as regent for Walthari, last of the Lethingi and the minor son of Wacho's Herulian wife, and about seven years later as king. "Soon after," Paulus Diaconus tells us, "he led the Longobards to Pannonia."

What does this statement by Paulus Diaconus mean, and what had happened? The initial beneficiary of the battle for Rome between the Byzantine emperor and the Goths had been the Merovingian King Theudebert. Having taken possession of the eastern Alpine lands in 536/537, he also got control of Venetia in 545. The Ostrogothic King Totila had ceded the province to him in order to free his rear. As a result, Theudebert and his Franks stood at the borders of Pannonia, and his language even toward Justinian I was more than arrogant.

In its countermove, Constantinople took advantage of the willingness of Audoin's Longobards to be deployed against the Franks. In 547/548 the emperor concluded a treaty with the Longobard king, giving him "the city of Noricum as well as the fortifications of Pannonia, many other places, and a large amount of money." Only now did the Longobards leave their home and settle south of the Danube.[2] Apparently at the same time the emperor gave the daughter of Herminafrid and Amalaberga as a wife to King Audoin. In this way the daughter of the Thuringian king and great-niece of Theodoric, who had come to Constantinople in 545, brought the "splendor of the Amal blood"[3] to the Longobards. There was no reaction from the Franks, for Theudebert died and his weak successor Theudebald was no danger.

However, what the emperor gave the Longobards in 547/548 was not the territory south of the Danube, but Gothic Pannonia and that portion of Norican territory south of the Drau that was still under his control. Noricum itself—with the likely exception of the *civitas* of Poetovio-Pettau, the "city of Noricum"—had been for a decade in Frankish hands. Thus Audoin did in fact lead the Longobards to Pannonia: to Pannonia south of the Drau, that is, a territory that had been given the old provincial name since the time of Theodoric the Great, which the emperor had nominally regained for the empire and now transferred to the *foederati*. The Franks, by contrast, were occupying Venetia "without right," and the Gepids too had broken the treaty with Constantinople by taking possession of Sirmium.

In this way the Longobards became the "mortal enemies" of the Franks. The imperial army that General Narses led to Italy via Istria in the spring of 552 included no fewer than fifty-five hundred Longobards. For that reason the Franks refused the Romans passage through Venetia, whereupon Narses did the unthinkable and marched his troops to Ravenna along the coast. And fate—or, rather, Roman tactics—would have it that in the battle of Busta Gallorum in the summer of 552, the Longobards, together with Herulian units, formed the center of the line of battle and played a decisive role in the disastrous defeat that spelled the end of Totila and his Ostrogothic kingdom.

That same year Audoin had been able to inflict a heavy defeat on the Gepids with the help of his brother-in-law Amalafridas, the son of the Thuringian king who was in the emperor's service. The conflict between these two peoples seems to have broken out once before under Wacho.[4] Imperial diplomacy did its best to stoke the fires of this enmity. For example, in 549 imperial troops showed up in support of the Longobards, but the latter were quick to enter into a truce with the Gepids.[5] A year later a panic that broke out in both armies led to the same result.[6]

It was not until 552 that the conflict was put to the test of arms. Audoin had levied what was for tribal standards a huge army of *foederati* and placed it at the disposal of the Romans in their war against the Goths. In return,

Constantinople had promised to send imperial troops should Audoin attack the Gepids. When the king did just that, Amalafrida was the only imperial officer who came to his aid with his troops; on orders from the emperor, the other Byzantine commanders stayed put in the interior of the empire. Once again the Longobards discovered how little they could rely on an alliance with Constantinople. But the year 552 had shown that the Longobards were no longer a small people: the fact that they were able to wage and win two wars at the same time means that they now constituted a considerable military power.

Both the institutional possibility of mass emancipation and the openness of the tribal tradition toward outsiders characterize Longobard history and were the reasons why the ethnogenesis begun by Wacho had turned Audoin's Longobards into a large people. In the forties, at the latest, they had been joined by provincials from Noricum and Pannonia as well as by Sarmatians.

Alboin in Pannonia (560/561–568)

Frankish-Longobard relations improved in the middle fifties, and this is reflected in the resumption of the policy of intermarriage. Following the early death of Theudebald in 555, his widow, Walderada, was supposed to become the wife of his great-uncle Chlothar I (511–561). But that same year the Merovingian had to separate from her because they were too closely related, and he passed her on to the Bavarian Agilolfing Duke Garibald I. At the same time, Chlothar I did all he could not to disgruntle the Longobards. As early as 552, the son of the Longobard King Alboin, had distinguished himself in the fight against the Gepids; in fact, the "saga" even reported that he slew the enemy king's son with his own hands. In 555, Alboin was honored with marriage to the Frankish Princess Chlodoswintha, the daughter of Chlothar I. When Audoin died in 560/561, there was no doubt that his son would succeed him.

Still, the Longobards—in a departure from Lethingian tradition—proceeded to elect the new king, whose name, of course, was Alboin. At first, Alboin continued his open policy toward the Franks and Constantinople. Although the Gepids had repeatedly hurt Byzantine interests, the imperial government supported them, and in 565 they won a victory over the Longobards. Following the defeat, Alboin called upon the Avars for help, while the Gepids tried in vain to prevail upon Emperor Justinus II, who had succeeded Justinian in 565, to continue this policy of support. The conflict between the Longobards and the Gepids flared up again in 567, and Alboin won a great victory: "The tribe of the Gepids," Paul the Deacon tells us, "went into such decline that henceforth they didn't even have their own king."

The following year, Alboin began the well-planned and orderly departure of the Longobards from their homeland. The Longobards were joined in 568 by provincials from Pannonia and Noricum, among them no doubt a few high-ranking clergymen, by Suebians from the Danube, by Sarmatians, Bulgarians, Herulians, and Gepids, as well as by large Thuringian-Saxon contingents.[7]

It did not take long for the saga to grip the person of Alboin: even Bavarian and Saxon heroic songs celebrated his weapons, his fortunes of war, and his bravery. Still during the lifetime of Paul the Deacon, who died at the end of the eighth century, the Longobard *dux* of Verona went down into the tomb of Alboin to take his sword and other grave goods; and legend has it that he saw Alboin in the tomb.

The Longobards were able to defeat their Gepid enemies so decisively because they had won the "new" people of the Avars as their allies. Alboin's victory confirmed his ability as military king and expanded the power of the Longobards. As the story goes, he was the son-in-arms of his opponent Kunimund, whom he supposedly killed in battle and whose daughter Rosamund he married after his victory. Still, in spite of all successes, being neighbors to the Avars eventually cost the Longobards their settlements. Constantinople's continuously vacillating policy of playing off one tribe against the other and preventing any stability along its northern border for the sake of short-term gains undoubtedly played a role in Alboin's decision to leave. Moreover, warriors returning from the Gothic war probably praised still-rich Italy in glowing terms. And it was probably more than just a legend that Narses, offended by Constantinople, invited the Longobards to Italy.

Be that as it may, the imperial government repeated the old mistake of surrendering barbarians who were part of the empire and largely assimilated, and who carried on the tradition of the Roman state, to peoples who had either broken with the Roman tradition or made no effort to even try and continue it. Just as Justinian had mobilized the Franks and Longobards against Gothic Italy, his successor Justinus II (565–578) did much the same by tolerating, indeed promoting, the downfall of the Gepids. Their place was taken by the Avars and their Slavic subjects; and with the departure of the Longobards from Pannonia, the emperor had at the same time gambled away Italy's peace and unity for many centuries to come.[8]

3. THE LONGOBARDS IN ITALY (568–643/652)

Alboin (568–572)

Alboin's warriors set foot on Italy's soil almost exactly eighty years after Theodoric the Great's Goths, either at the same site or not far from it. The successful military leader was king of the Longobards, but he could just as readily be seen as a representative and continuator of the Gepid as well as

Herulian kingships. This threefold nucleus of tradition became a great attractor, not only for threatened barbarians and provincials of Pannonia and Noricum, but also for peoples inside Germania, such as the Thuringians and Saxons; it is said that of the latter no fewer than "20,000 men with women and children" joined him.[9] It is not impossible that Alboin's army surpassed even that of Theodoric the Great in numerical strength and consisted perhaps of 150,000 people or more.[10]

Given the size of the army, it is all the more remarkable that Alboin and his leaders were able to create the necessary organizational and logistical requirements for the orderly departure of such masses of people. The trek was set to begin right after Easter of 568, and for the last time an immense migratory column, with women and children, household goods and animals, departed the Pannonian homeland in carts, on horses, and on foot. The timing was unusually early; normally tribes set out in the fall, after the harvest had been brought in and sufficient stores had been laid.

Apparently haste was of the essence this time, and the long march began before the Avar horsemen, who depended on the availability of sufficient grass for their horses, could begin their campaign season. Evidently Alboin wanted to protect himself against unpleasant surprises, even though the had ceded Pannonia to the dangerous enemies by treaty. He had even imposed certain conditions on them: thus the Longobards were not to forfeit their rights of possession to their homeland for two hundred years. During the same period the Avars should come to their aid in Italy if they needed it. One source even claimed that this Longobard-Avar treaty was put down in writing.[11]

As befits the genre of a history of origins, the arrival of the Longobard in Italy was depicted as the arrival of a chosen people in its promised land: Alboin climbed up on a hill, since then known as "the king's mountain," and just as Moses was allowed to see from the top of Mount Nebo the land promised to his descendants, the king beheld the "land of Italy flowing with milk and honey."[12] As justification for their conquest, however, the invaders invoked not only the Bible but also Roman ideas: "The entire time when they were settled in Pannonia the Longobards helped the Roman Empire against its enemies."[13]

With these words, Paul the Deacon reminded his readers of the fact that the Pannonian Longobards had been at all times loyal *foederati* who had "done their duty" in Constantinople's wars against the Goths, the Heruli, the Gepids, and even the Persians. And now, one could carry the thought further; a "minor" unauthorized action had taken place: Alboin had been forced by military necessity to move the "Roman" Longobard army from the middle Danube to the rivers Isonzo and Po. All that had really happened had been a change of the imperial garrison, nothing more. Needless to say, Constantinople had little sympathy for such notions, and it let the unusually long period of four generations pass before peace and a new treaty were concluded between the empire and the Longobards.

In May of 568, the column of the Longobard army reached the province of Venetia, whose easternmost *civitas* was Cividale, located at the Nisone River. Here, in Forum Iulii (from which Friaul took its name), Alboin established the first duchy, which would remain extremely important in the future. He handed the duchy of Friaul over to his kinsman and marshal (*marpahis*), Gisulf I. This step reveals how open Alboin was to adopting late-antique institutions. Prior to this the Longobards had had neither a *dux* nor a duchy. Nor do we later find vernacular equivalents to these two political terms, even though the Longobards had a rich vocabulary to describe tribal institutions. The *dux* who was responsible for a city and its surrounding territory, a *civitas*, was the late Roman-Byzantine continuation of the *comes civitatis*, who even in the Ostrogothic kingdom of Italy had been the king's most important official.[14] Alboin thus had no qualms about adopting a Roman-Gothic institution and structuring the *exercitus Langobardorum* on this model. The designation of this institution as duchy (*ducatus*) and no longer as county (*comitatus*) reflected the progressive militarization of all territorial units; in other words, now the border was everywhere, and those in command along any borders were *duces*.

With the *ducatus* the king combined the traditional order of the Longobard *farae*, which had hitherto made up the army. Very revealing in this context is the report that Gisulf was given permission by the king to chose a number of these units as his troops. The word *farae* is obviously related to German *fahren* (to travel) and means a fighting and traveling community that saw itself, however, as a community of descent. In this sense the Longobard *farae* can be compared to the Gothic *kuni*, which likewise comprised the family members in the narrower sense as well as other household members and retainers.[15]

How literally we should take the story of Gisulf choosing his *farae* is not a question we can decide, but it teaches us two things: first, the *farae* who followed him had previously been linked to him by bonds of kingship as well as lordship, otherwise he would not have insisted that he be given the right to choose them. Second, his *ducatus* was considered an institutional innovation, since *dux* and *farae* had first to be joined by the primordial acts, so to speak, of Alboin and Gisulf. From then on these two political entities belonged together: Longobard law, for example, guaranteed every freeman that he could enter the services of a lord—usually the duke—with his *farae*, and leave again with the king's permission. Friaul, in particular, has many place names that are derived from *fara*, and they remind us to this day of the Longobard units that had been transformed from traveling bands into settlement communities.[16]

In Italy it was not individual tribal groups who would have made Gisulf their dux, as is reported by the tribal *memoria* for the first *duces* Ibor and Aio. Instead, an Italian *dux civitatis* was installed by the king and was given, with the king's permission, a number of *farae*, which allowed him to impart to this Roman-Gothic office new meaning and new possibilities of exercising power. The holders of the duchies created in this way therefore differed little or not at all from the imperial *duces*, the military leaders of imperial Italy. And it was soon entirely up to the *duces Langobardorum* whether they gave allegiance to a king, left the kingship vacant, or offered their services by contractual arrangement to the exarch in Ravenna. Alboin's proud military power was consequently soon put to a severe test, one in which Longobard identity threatened to dissolve.

In the same way that the great victory over the Heruli had, against all tribal logic, once cost the victorious military king his rule and life, Alboin too was not able to enjoy for very long the fruits of his great achievement. "Alboin left Pannonia in the first year; in the second year [the Longobards] began to plunder in Italy; in the third year, however, he became the lord of Italy."[17] By one method of reckoning, the new year began on September 1. Hence it was already the third year when Alboin entered Milan in September of 569. Thus the tribal tradition has the Longobard royal rule over Italy begin with the conquest of the former imperial city.[18]

Reality, of course, was different. After capturing Aquileia, the Longobards did control the most important road junction in northeastern Italy. However, they could advance westward only on the northern route—the Via Postumia—by way of Treviso, Vicenza, Verona, Brescia, and Bergamo. Oderzo, however, resisted the attackers and had to be bypassed; in fact, the city remained in Byzantine hands for another two generations. The cities located along the southern route (the Via Annia)—Altino, Padua, Monselice, Mantua, and Cremona—also resisted the Longobard assault, as did the fortresses along the southern slopes of the Alps from the valley of the Aosta to Lake Como. And we are not even talking about the lagoons from Grado to Venice, which the Longobards never managed to get under their control.

The Longobards and the Roman Bishops

The two metropolitans of northern Italy, the archbishop of Aquileia and his colleague in Milan, fled before the advancing Longobards; the former went to Grado, the latter to Genoa. Most of their suffragans, however, quickly reached an accommodation with the Longobards. As early as 569, a certain Felix of Treviso accorded Alboin the *occursus regius*[19] by going out as far as the Piave River to meet him, thus recognizing the Longobard ruler as king and receiving in return the confirmation of his ecclesiastical possessions. But

in the two metropolitan seats, as well, some of the clerics remained behind
to preserve continuity, while the refugee bishops continued to call themselves by their original *sedes*. Even where the foreigners, "mired in pagan
error,"[20] helped themselves to the church's wealth, they did not confiscate
the entire episcopal patrimony.

For more than a hundred years, the bishops had been acting also as the
political representatives of their fellow citizens whenever the Roman population sought to find a modus vivendi with barbarian armies and lords.[21] The
same situation now existed once again in Italy, in fact to a heightened degree, since not a few pagans were marching along in the *exercitus Langobardorum* and the majority of the Christians were Arians. But the necessity to get
along with the foreigners was not infrequently coupled with a certain willingness to join them as a safeguard against the emperor and the pope. The
decision to take this peculiar step was given added incentive by an ecclesiastical quarrel, the controversy of the "Three Chapters."

For the sake of peace and harmony, the Ecumenical Council of Chalcedon in 451 had explicitly accepted three propositions ("chapters") of the
Nestorian faith. The Persian monk Nestorius had been called from Antioch
to Constantinople in the year 428. As the new bishop of Constantinople, he
made a distinction between the two natures of Christ and maintained that
Mary had given birth only to Christ's human, not his divine nature; she had
therefore become the mother of Christ, Christotokos, but not the mother of
God, Theotokos. The Nestorian teachings were diametrically opposed to the
doctrine of Monophysitism, which had originated in Alexandria, Antioch's
old rival. That doctrine asserted "that the divine nature of Christ had absorbed his human nature into itself, so that only one nature, namely, the divine one, remained."[22]

Emperor Justinian I, believing that he had to win over the Monophysites
to the imperial church, passed an edict in 543/545 condemning the three
Nestorian propositions. A little later the emperor forced the pope to do the
same. What followed was a string of retractions and renewed condemna-
tions; in the end, Rome and those bishops Ravenna could reach gave in,
while the north of Italy remained firm in its refusal to permit any imperial
meddling in internal church affairs. The first bishops the Longobards encountered had thus become alienated from the Roman central authority
and its protecting power in Constantinople. We can say this even though the
two metropolitan bishops had gone into exile to await further developments.

Milan gave up the schism in 571, during Alboin's lifetime, but in Aquileia
the split in the church was to last until about 700. That split was further exacerbated when the patriarch, who resided in Grado, gave in to Byzantine
pressure in 606/607 and sought union with Rome, while the Longobard
king and the duke of Friaul established the seat of the mainland patriarch

of Aquileia in Cormons, south of Cividale. And even after the quarrel over the "Three Chapters" had ended, the schism continued for as long as Byzantium was able to hold on to the coastal strip of Grado.

Nevertheless, in January of 591 a number of bishops from the Longobard part of Aquileia asked the emperor for help. Gregory the Great had just assumed the papal throne and was planning to take strong measures in the schism; Constantinople had given him the green light to go ahead and the exarch of Ravenna had pledged his support. The suffragans of Aquileia were opposed to such a move, and the bishops under Longobard rule were emphatic in making the following point: a victory by the pope would remove the last institutional bond that linked the Longobard region with Grado and the Roman Empire.

The bishops invoked the oath they had sworn at their ordination to remain loyal to the imperium. They were now the "church outside of the empire among the peoples," *ecclesia in gentibus.* They were hoping for a restoration, but until then Constantinople could exert through them its influence beyond the narrower boundaries of the empire. But if the emperor chose to decide against them, they would procure their ordination from the bishops in the neighboring Frankish kingdom. This had already happened once before in the case of Virunum, Teurnia, and Aguntum. Had Emperor Justinian at that time not given appropriate orders, only Frankish priests would have been installed there by Frankish bishops. Less than a year before the first clash between Bavarians and Slavs in the valley of the Drau, the mainland suffragans were conscious only of the Frankish threat; the Slavs were not yet on anyone's mind. The emperor, however, relented.[23]

The Concentration and Dissolution
of the Longobard Army (569–572/574)

After taking Milan, Alboin turned his attention to Pavia, "where Theodoric had erected a palace." The imperial troops in the old royal city not far from the estuary of the Ticino in the Po Valley put up a determined resistance, which took Alboin nearly three years of siege to break.[24] The fact that the army was pinned down so long outside the walls of the city created considerable tensions. As early as 569 or 570, devastating raids were launched into Frankish Burgundy with or without Alboin's toleration, though surely not at his command; until 574/575, the Longobards and their Saxon allies ravaged this region on several occasions.[25] And although it is unlikely that the Longobards established themselves permanently in Tuscany earlier than 578/579,[26] it is likely that plundering bands had already crossed the Apennines during the siege of Pavia.

Even by the standards of tribal armies, the *exercitus Langobardorum* was composed of an unusually large number of tribal groups. This makeup of the army created conflicts that even a successful military king like Alboin was unable to contain, let alone smooth out. Alboin belonged to an eminent group, the Gaui-Gauti, which embodied Scandinavian traditions. The same was true of other groups: the Harudi, for example, from whom was descended the future King Rothari (636–652), who could name no fewer than ten Harudi ancestors. And there were plenty of other families and clans who were the equals of these two large Longobard families or small tribes. One example is the Lethingian traditions: these were Thuringian traditions— among them were those of the Anawas and of the Agilolfings who would become so prominent north and south of the Alps—which largely shaped the Longobard kingdom even as late as the seventh century.

It comes as no surprise that all these bands of the high nobility seized the duchies with and without Alboin's consent and, as largely independent *duces*, demonstrated impressively that they were qualified to be kings. But while the Gausi and Harudi had joined the Longobards long before, though without relinquishing their own tribal memory, the Gepids were a fairly recent addition, a problematic situation heightened by the fact that they were so numerous.

In the middle of 572, Alboin was assassinated; the band of conspirators included above all his foster brother and arms bearer, Helmichis, his wife, Rosamund, as well as the exarch of Ravenna, Longinus. Paul the Deacon tells us that he had seen with his own eyes a cup that came from the royal treasure and was shown to guests on festive occasions. It was said that Alboin had fashioned this cup from the skull of his father-in-law, the Gepid King Kunimund, which he would have done, of course, while still in Pannonia. That cup would play a role in Alboin's death. Alboin put on a feast in Verona. During the banquet, and undoubtedly while drunk, Alboin called for this cup, commanded that "the queen be served wine, and urged her to gaily drink with her father." This mocking challenge reminded Rosamund of her duty to revenge her father. She teamed up with Helmichis and another one of Alboin's confidants, whom she craftily seduced, and eventually secured the help of the exarch of Ravenna. One day, when Alboin had withdrawn to his chamber in the palace of Verona for his noontime nap, the door remained open and unguarded; the royal sword had been put out of commission for this occasion, and the murderer, Helmichis, easily slew the king. After this deed he married the queen, seized the royal treasure and Alboin's daughter, and intended to succeed Alboin to the throne.

The usurpation failed; the murderous couple fled to Ravenna, where they met a shameful end. For now Rosamund wanted to marry the exarch and therefore tried to poison Helmichis. After he had drunk from the fatal cup, Helmichis realized what had happened and forced Rosamund to drink as well. "And so the infamous murderers died within an hour through the judgment of Almighty God."[27]

The story of Rosamund is the best known among the many legends concerning Alboin. It represents typical narrative material that personalizes broader and highly explosive events to make it easier for them to be received into the tribal memory. We must therefore ask what historical facts we can deduce from this tale.

A man who had enjoyed Alboin's confidence since childhood offered himself to the Gepids—who in Queen Rosamund had a member of their tribe at the top—as an alternative to the very ruler who had destroyed the glorious dominion of the Gepids. To this we must add disgruntled Longobards and the exarch's realization that he could not control the Longobard avalanche by open resistance but only by breaking it into smaller pieces..As it was, the Longobard enterprise was increasingly in danger of getting completely out of control; all the more reason for the exarch to bring the individual *duces* into his camp with money and honors.

We can distinguish three acts in the Helmichis episode: act one, Alboin's assassination; act two, attempted usurpation; act three, flight and entry into Byzantine services, with strong Gepid-Longobard units accompanying the regicides. Of course the various acts were separated by longer intervals of time. Two months after Alboin's death, the Longobards in Pavia elevated Clef, a *dux* of the highest nobility, to the kingship. The expected confrontation between the two pretenders to the throne did not take place, since Helmichis evidently believed he had no chance to begin with and gave up his cause as lost. He must have escaped to Ravenna by ship on the Po River, since the land route was no longer safe. What actually happened in Ravenna is difficult to say. The marriage proposal from the exarch could be historical, however, for it seemed possible to get one's hands on the Longobard kingship by marrying the queen, as was later demonstrated on several occasions. Moreover, such a plan may have been in line with Byzantine ideas.[28]

Clef's kingship lasted all of eighteen months: the king met his death at the hands of a slave, and we have no idea what lay behind the assassination. Alboin's death had also terminated a treaty that the king had concluded with a Saxon group to win them over for the trek to Italy. Now the Longobards were no longer willing to tolerate the contractually guaranteed autonomy of the Saxons; like the other Longobard peoples, they wanted to divide them up among the various *duces*. In response the Saxons left northern Italy and returned to their old homeland via the Frankish kingdoms. However, what prompted their departure was not the Longobard demand that the Saxons give up their own law (*leges, iura*), but the threat that they would lose their independence and no longer be allowed to live *in proprio iure*.[29]

The Rule of the Dukes (574–584)

After Clef's death no king was elected for ten years. The Longobard army dissolved into at least thirty-five units which were led by *duces*. The oppression of the native inhabitants that had begun under Clef worsened during the kingless period. However, the Longobards must have retained some centralized form of exercising power, even if under collective leadership, since even before the restoration of the kingship a step was taken that was of great importance for institutional history: the settlement of the Longobards proceeded essentially under the same model that had been developed for the Ostrogoths.[30] At the same time, the united Longobard *duces* were quite able to beat back a larger Byzantine attack in 575/576.[31]

Still, odd contradictions emerged during the reign of the *duces*. The conquest of Italy progressed: Tuscany, Spoleto, and Beneventum fell into the hands of the Longobards, who, probably in 578, took Monte Cassino, the venerable foundation of Saint Benedict. In the summer of 579, Rome was so completely cut off from the outside world that a new pope had to be installed without imperial consent. But the siege of the Eternal City failed, as did the attempt by the Longobards to take Naples in 581.

On the other hand, many *duces Langobardorum* were willing to ally themselves with the exarch of Ravenna, indeed, to be integrated, at least nominally, into the imperial army with their *farae*. Moreover, the kingless period had a not unexpected consequence: while the bishops of northern Italy had found ways and means of reaching some kind of accommodation with the Longobards under royal leadership, the organization of the Catholic Church in Tuscany, Spoleto, and above all Beneventum, was driven to the brink of extinction when Longobard dukes established themselves there. Arians, and indeed pagans, were still very strongly represented among the followers of the dukes; in fact, "the rule of the dukes led to a lasting division of the tribe into pagans, Arians, 'Three Chapter' schismatics, and Catholics."[32]

While the Longobard advances into central and southern Italy were a time of sorrows for the Roman civilian population and posed a challenge to Constantinople, the concurrent devastation of Burgundy, which had been launched by various *duces* already during the royal period, took on almost suicidal dimensions. After bands of Longobard raiders had suffered crushing defeats in 574 and 575, the counteroffensive of the Frankish Burgundians took them across the western Alps into northern Italy, where they occupied the valleys of Susa and Aosta. It was at that time that these parts of Italy became Frankish, and to this day the people there speak French, not Italian.

The constant Longobard challenge to the Franks and the Byzantines invariably led to a joining of these two powers. The emperor made enormous sums of money available, and in 584 the Franks invaded the valley of the Po once again. The Longobards withdrew into their fortified cities and put up virtually no resistance of any kind. About two-thirds of their *duces* submitted to the Frankish king and asked for peace in return for large annual payments of tribute. Further territory was also given up between Susa and Aosta. The remaining twelve *duces* tried their luck with Byzantium.[33] Now the end of the Longobard state seemed at hand, the downfall of the barbarians only a matter of time.

The Restoration of the Kingship in 584 and the Establishment of a Three-Partite Longobard State

Finding themselves in a very difficult situation, those *duces* who had drawn closer to the Franks proceeded to elect a new king. Apparently the only candidate was Authari, the son of Clef, who had been murdered in 574. Authari, duke of an unknown city, was elected king "on the joint resolution" of the *duces* and those qualified to make political decisions; "because of the honor" of the office, he was given the name Flavius, "which henceforth all Longobard kings carried with great good fortune."[34] The title used in Longobard royal documents does in fact read *Flavius N. vir excellentissimus rex.* Its immediate model was the Gothic royal title first used by Theodoric the Great. Evidently the assembly of the army in 584 wanted to furnish their king with a political statement that would win him recognition from as many groups as possible.

For nearly a century, the Flavian royal title had been a significant political element of the kingdom of Italy; it was familiar to the Goths and other barbarians who lived there as well as to the politically important stratum of Roman bishops and landowners. If the king of the "nation" wanted to present himself to all of these groups in such a way that they would "look favorably upon him,"[35] the adoption of the Flavian title and its use in royal charters and on insignia guaranteed that he would be very successful. Usage of the title in charters and on insignia corresponded to the traditional Roman-Gothic politics of the peninsula. On the other hand, the fact that the Longobard king could not merely be a supratribal *Flavius rex* reflects the odd split of Longobard policy in Italy and forms a parallel, as it were, to the division of the peninsula after 568. Evidently those who codified the tribal law beginning in 643, could conceive only of a separate tribal king who addressed his fellow tribesmen and the other Italian barbarians as *vir excellentissimus rex gentis Langobardorum.*[36]

In 584, the main issue was making the kingship viable in economic terms; and since the initiative for its restoration had come from the *duces,* it was up to them to make the necessary sacrifices. It would seem that at the beginning of the kingless period, the *duces* had laid claim to two-thirds of the regular taxes, while one-third remained for local self-government. Now the *duces* gave up half their tax share, so that the king and the territorial rulers were entitled to one-third each. Of course neither the dukes of Beneventum and Spoleto nor those who had joined the Byzantines participated in the economic restoration of the kingship. While Authari left the south to its own devices, even though the saga celebrated him as the founder of the great duchies, he moved successfully against the renegade dukes of northern Italy and some pockets of Byzantine resistance. After that the king tried to conclude a three-year truce with Ravenna.[37]

It seemed that Authari was quickly fulfilling all hopes and expectations placed in him. However, the process of consolidation called back onto the scene the Franks, who had an old score to settle. After carrying out plundering raids beyond the Alps for years, the Longobards had themselves become the targets of attacks since 575; the Frankish counterattack, however, had come not from Provence or Burgundy but from the north. The Merovingian eastern kingdom had allied itself with Byzantium and was sending its armies across the passes of Raetia into Italy. Fighting took place especially in the valley of the Etsch in Tyrol, from Meran right up to the gates of Trient.

After some initial successes of the Franks, the duke of Trient, Eoin, was able to crush the invaders near Salurn. Perhaps as early as 575, or not until 578, the duke had married a daughter of the duke of Bavaria, Garibald I, and his Lethingian Longobard wife, Walderada. Regardless of whether this liaison between the Bavarian duke and his Tridentine son-in-law came about before or after the latter's victory, which changed the whole situation, it was clearly aimed against the Franks.

When in 584 the Franks marched to Italy once again, now in Byzantine employ, the Longobards not only moved quickly to reestablish the kingship in the person of Authari, they were also able to beat back the enemies quite easily, since the latter were not united. The next Frankish advance in 588 turned into a total fiasco, in part because this time the Bavarian Duke Garibald was unequivocally on the side of the Longobards.

On May 15, 589, outside the gates of Verona, Authari celebrated his marriage to Theudelinde, who was probably the younger daughter of Garibald and Walderada. However, at that time the Bavarian princess was already fleeing from the Franks, who had attacked her father because of his support for the Longobards the previous year and had put an end—how exactly we don't know—to the rule of the Bavarian duke. As a result, Garibald's son Gundobald, the brother of the future queen and duchess of Trient, had fled to the Longobards together with Theudelinde; his royal brother-in-law, Authari, made him duke of Asti.

The following year, 590, witnessed a large-scale campaign of revenge by the Franks. Once again they advanced from Raetia down the Etsch River, seizing numerous Longobard-Roman fortresses above and below where the Eisack flows into the Etsch. Even though the Franks pushed deep into the Po Valley, their attack once again petered out very soon. It is indicative of Duke Eoin's undiminished power that he was able, in 591, to arrange a lasting peace between Longobards, Franks, and probably the Bavarians as well.

The chronology of the Longobard tradition often leaves much to be desired. But if, despite these misgivings, we accept the relative chronology of events, the duchy of Beneventum was established prior to Authari's elevation to the kingship and the duchy of Spoleto after 584.[38] These two duchies, whose holders did not participate in the reestablishment of the kingship, maintained their independence vis-à-vis the *regnum gentis Langobardorum* until Charlemagne conquered it.

While Spoleto became part of Frankish-Longobard Italy in 774, Beneventum, now elevated to a principality, survived the empire of the Carolingian conquerors, the Ottonians, and much of the rule of the Salians in Italy. In 1077, the last bearer of its tradition died, and the Normans of southern Italy displaced the Longobard princes for good. Not only Authari, but the kings of the seventh and eighth centuries as well, whose power was ever increasing, had to give up the idea of permanently unifying the multiple bases of Longobard statehood. These two "greater dukes," *maiores duces,* carried on the political legacy of the Longobard dukes and forced a division of Longobard rule in Italy into three parts, a division the emperor, the pope, and most of the kings had to recognize de facto.[39]

Agilulf (591–615/616)

The Longobard-Frankish peace of 591 worked to the benefit of Agilulf, the former duke of Turin who succeeded Authari both as king and as Theudelinde's husband. Agilulf hailed from the clan of the Anawas, who had preserved their Thuringian identity under the Longobards and embodied the old ties between the two peoples. However, the name of the Bavarian ducal family of the Agilolfings presupposes a founding ancestor Agilulf. In actual fact, the Longobards and the Thuringians were probably those "Bohemian men" from whom the Bavarians derived their name.[40]

The Longobard kingship was still on shaky feet. Theudelinde guaranteed in her person the widest recognition and legitimacy. As a result, she was given free hand in choosing her second husband, but in so doing she was really only exercising a right that every Longobard widow possessed by tribal law. "Constitutive for Agilulf's kingship was only the elevation by the tribal assembly in Milan in May of 591."[41] The "eternal peace" with the Franks, which Eoin of Trient had negotiated, had not been cheap. Only Agilulf's successor was able to replace the yearly tribute due since 584 with a one-time payment. To be sure, this king, Adaloald, was the son-in-law of a Frankish Merovingian. At the beginning of his reign, Agilulf was able to conclude also the first of a series of peace treaties with the Avars, which turned into another "eternal peace" in 602.[42] Together with the Avars and Slavs of the khagan, Agilulf's Longobards fought against the Byzantines in Istria and against the imperial troops in Cremona. But the khagan hurried to the aid of the Longobard king also when the latter set out to punish the renegade duke of Friuli.

The strengthening of the position of the Longobard kinship internally and externally found expression not least in the fact that in 609/610 an exchange of envoys between Constantinople and the Longobards became possible. Previously the Longobards had negotiated only with the exarch of Ravenna, and even if the emperor was not yet willing to conclude a peace treaty, the first step in that direction was taken. At the same time, Agilulf, who was granted a reign of twenty-six years, consolidated his kingship "over all of Italy" as a divinely inspired rule. A crown that is no longer extant bore the inscription: "Agilulf, glorious man by the grace of God, King over all of Italy."[43] Together with Theudelinde's consecration crown it was kept in the queen's treasury in Monza.

Authari had not tolerated any non-Arians in his entourage, and toward the end of his reign he had forbidden the Longobards to baptize their children in the Catholic faith. Still, he had married the Catholic princess from Bavaria. Even though Theudelinde supported the position of the church of Aquileia and of the bishops of northern Italy in the "Three Chapters" controversy, she was nevertheless a Catholic and thus the hope of the Romans and Catholic Longobards. In her second marriage the queen was even more forceful in advocating her religious conviction. Although Agilulf, too, remained Arian, he did allow his second son, Adaloald, born in 602, to undergo Catholic baptism. Only two years later, Adaloald was designated and elevated to the kingship in the presence of his father.

Previously, Catholic baptism and a very early arrangement of succession had been unknown in the Longobard royal families. The succession arrangement of 604 was undoubtedly introduced on the Visigothic model, and it would be used repeatedly until the end of the independent Longobard kingdom.

Agilulf's successful restoration policy has been justifiably compared to that of Leovigild, the savior of the Visigothic kingdom. It is likely that the Byzantine institution of coregency too reached the Longobards via Toledo. Both the Longobards and the Visigoths used this institution as an instrument to contain the nobility, which was seeking to insist on its right of election in the face of the dynastic principle.

After this there would be no resistance of any kind from the nobility in the Longobard realm. Through a clever maneuver, Agilulf probably prevented the imminent revolt of the nobility. At the same time that Adaloald was designated the successor and elevated to the kingship, he was betrothed to the daughter of the Frankish King Theudebert II (596–612). King Theudebert, to whom the Longobards were tributary, thus became the guarantor of this institutional innovation favoring his future son-in-law.

In 616, feeling that the end was near, Agilulf installed Theudelinde as regent for his minor son and coregent. This unusual arrangement, as well, met with no opposition: we can undoubtedly look for institutional parallels or even models for this, and point for instance to the example of Amalasuintha or the Frankish regent Brunhilde. But the decisive factor was surely Theudelinde's prestige and actual power; Theudelinde was queen for about thirty-five years, and even after Adaloald attained majority, she ruled jointly with him until his downfall in 626.

His Frankish wife notwithstanding, Adaloald lost the kingship and his life after a decade because he proved "unsuitable"—it was even said that he had gone mad—but primarily because the policy of Catholicization pursued by mother and son ran into opposition from the Arian Longobards. Evidently the latter still clung to the old "Gothic" belief that the loss of the Arian tribal church would mean at the same time the loss of the ethnic identity. The successful counterexample of the Spanish Visigoths, who had converted to Catholicism in 589, was apparently not enough to convince them otherwise. Adaloald's successor married his sister Gundberga, who during the following decades would play a role similar to that of her mother, Theudelinde.

Gundberga's first husband, Arioald, was a compromise candidate of the three religious "parties," the Arians, the schismatic Catholics, and the supporters of Rome. Until the end of the seventh century, when the last Arian bishop put his signature under the Nicene Creed, an event soon followed by the end of the "Three Chapters" controversy, Longobard politics depended in two ways on the preservation of a balance in religious policy: first, if this delicate balance was upset there was open resistance, which at times could bring down the king; second, the policy initiated by Authari formed the precondition that allowed the *regnum gentis Langobardorum* to assert itself successfully against the empire and the Franks.[44]

Rothari (636–652)

As it is described, Gundberga's role in the transfer of power to Rothari is so reminiscent of that of her mother that the historical veracity of her actions seems questionable, at the least. Frankish historiography, which sees in Gundberga a relative of the Frankish royal house, seems to exaggerate her importance considerably, whereas Longobard tradition hints at a conflict between Rothari and his queen. In any case, it is clear that the new king continued his successor's policies toward the aristocratic opposition as well as toward Byzantium and his own Roman subjects. The high point of his reign occurred in the year 643: not only did Rothari conquer the coast of Liguria, he also launched a successful drive against Ravenna, while the dukes of far-off Beneventum followed his example and continued their attacks against imperial Italy at the same time. Fighting lasted until 652 and was stopped by another truce. Even if this agreement was still not a full-fledged peace treaty, peace was secured for half a century.

In the same year in which Rothari proved himself as a military king, 643, he also fulfilled the old obligation of a ruler—"weapons and laws," *arma et leges*[45]—and published his famous *Edictus Rothari*. Apparently the legal code "was written down in a short period of time following the questioning of legal experts, and was accepted and affirmed at the assembly of the victorious army on November 22, 643, near the capital city of Pavia, through the ancient rite of "spear assembly," *gairethinx*.

In Dilcher's words "the edict advocates the legal theory of a cooperation between the king and the people: the legal code is accepted by the tribal army and the council of the magnates. However, it is the king who initiates and improves the legal traditions, for which role he invokes—in classical topoi—Christian and Roman-Byzantine legal ideas, the right of the Germanic tribal and military kings, and the ancestral fortuna of his own clan."[46]

The contradictory nature of Longobard policy lay not least in its relationship to the empire and its subjects. Kings and dukes fought against the imperial Romans; at the same time, however, they tried to conquer as much of imperial Italy as possible and to preserve the line of continuity to both Romans and Goths. Even Paul the Deacon still reflected this contradiction when he portrayed the Longobards as loyal federates of the empire before their arrival in Italy, but then turned around and took their side unequivocally in the battle against the imperium and the "Greeklings."

The situation was much the same in the sphere of practical politics. The Longobard kings had undoubtedly the best chancery officials and jurists of the time, most of whom must have been Romans. The preambles of imperial laws provided the model for the prologues of the *Edictus Rothari* and his novels, which were decreed by a "king of the Longobard people"; however, a royal charter in which a *Flavius rex* invokes Roman-Gothic tradition does not carry on the tradition either of imperial charters or of late Roman official charters, but follows the "private" style of Roman bishops and landowners, *curiales*.

This contrast is manifested most clearly by the royal title that Rothari created for his edict. In it, Longobard traditions were to be put into a form that the Gothic kingship had already fashioned on the model of its legendary Roman predecessor. Thus Rothari was the only bearer of the tribal royal title who indicated his place within the line of Longobard kings. He counted himself the "seventeenth king of the Longobard people." The number seventeen, however, is the result of deliberate selection, which the king and his advisers probably made only when they sought to shape their own tradition after Roman-Gothic models. Both Athalaric, the nephew of Theodoric the Great, and Romulus, the founder of Rome, had been seventeenth kings after the primordial deed of a heroic or divine founding king: Athalaric in line from the Scandinavian god Gaut and the Asic conquerors of the Romans, Romulus in line from Aeneas. By adopting this model to himself, Rothari juxtaposed himself as the founder of the law (*conditor legis*) to Romulus, the founder of Rome (*conditor urbis*). In founding Rome, the seventeenth king of the Romans renewed the regnum established by the mythical ancestor Aeneas. The seventeenth king of the Longobard people gave an improved law purged of everything superfluous, decreeing it after a great victory over the Romans as a new basis for peace internally and as a sign of strength externally. In so doing, Rothari consciously placed his kingdom alongside those of his Roman-Gothic precursors. However, since Longobard tradition forbade following the Gothic and Roman example and claiming a single royal family in a line of seventeen successors, Rothari, in an appendix to the king list, named a respectable number of his own Harudian ancestors.

4. A LOOK AHEAD

The Longobard kingdom was not unified either politically or religiously under Rothari and his immediate successors. But even when King Liutprand (712–744) became a "Christian and Catholic king of the exceedingly fortunate and Catholic people of the Longobards beloved by God," when he seemed to wield power even over the dukes of Spoleto and Beneventum, the division of Italy was not healed. And yet, it was the kingdom of the Longobards that prepared the ground for creation of a medieval Italian nation; to be sure, it was not a nation that united Italy, but the Longobards did preserve it as a political entity notwithstanding all territorial losses and secessions.

None of this was altered by the fact that Charlemagne became "king of the Franks and Longobards" on June 5, 774. The often-invoked and decried subjugation of the Longobards by the Franks would not have been accomplished in purely military terms; it was only by a treaty that the Longobards joined the Franks and retained their independence. And that did not change when Charlemagne became emperor of the West, when the emperorship passed from the Franks to the Germans and the Longobard kingdom transformed itself into the dominion of the Italians and eventually into the regnum Italiae. The center of the Longobard kingdom had been located from the outset between Milan and Pavia. Still today, when we speak of this region, one of the preeminent regions of Europe, we do not call it Liguria or cisalpine Gaul, as the Romans did, but Lombardy.[47]

FIFTEEN

The Transformation
of the Roman World

1. THE TOPIC OF THE PRESENT BOOK

The purpose of this book is to describe and explain the most important non-Frankish successor states on Roman soil. Its topic is the creation, duration, and historical impact of kingdoms that are called Germanic and that simultaneously transformed, dissolved, and continued the western empire. Hence the primary question that needed to be answered was how it was possible for the Germanic military kings and their warrior bands to win political-military recognition from the relevant imperial governments in Ravenna and Constantinople, and to be integrated into the empire socially and economically.

While writing a history of the Goths a number of years ago, I discovered to my frequent surprise that the history of these kingdoms, their putative splendor and tragic end, has captured the imagination not only of Germans but also of many other Europeans and North Americans.[1] And the historical understanding of a broad public also encompasses the fact that the "transformation of the Roman world"[2] was not, and could never have been, the work solely of the Germanic kings.

2. THE ARABS

In fact, there were two extraordinarily successful counterexamples to the Roman-barbarian regna, the reason for their success being that they presented radical alternatives to the Pax Gothica.[3] Men like Theodoric, Geiseric, and Clovis competed with the late Roman state for the distribution of wealth produced by the Mediterranean economy, and they succeeded in gaining control over the traditional apparatus of power.[4] To be sure, religion did not play an insignificant role in the whole process, especially since the

majority of the barbarian rulers were Arians; but sooner or later they all
agreed on the Catholic-Roman creed, and most of them didn't have to become Christians do to so. There were, in any case, no religious wars. That
changed, however, when the Arabs, in the name of Allah, conquered the
entire southern half of the Roman Empire and—following defeats and victories—established themselves as its successor for a long time to come.

3. THE SLAV ALTERNATIVE

The story of the second counterexample, the conquests of the Slavs east of
the Elbe, the Enns, and the Adriatic Sea, was very different.[5] We cannot describe the phenomenon of Slav expansion in conventional historical categories, let alone explain it. A silent revolution took place from the end of the
fifth century to the beginning of the seventh century in large parts of eastern and central Europe between the Baltic Sea and the Aegean, and nobody
can really say how half of Europe could become Slavic in such a short period
of time. After the end of the tribal migrations, Germania was, if anything,
smaller than before, if we subtract the losses in the east from the gains in the
west and south. Over the period of half a millennium, the empire was able
to Romanize only part of the land under its rule. By contrast, in only a few
generations Slavicization had a much more lasting success, which was more
than the result of a mere migration and also far exceeded any imperial policy, let alone military conquest

The decline of the Roman order and the waning or departure of those
groups who had taken it as their model made room not only for immigrants but also for new social and economic developments. Many of those
developments would not be understood as progress in the modern sense, for
example, the marked decline in the social division of labor. But what happened was not merely a "relapse into barbarism." For instance, it was only
after the disappearance of Roman rule that use of the lighter, soil-turning
plow, which made possible economical cultivation in smaller units, became
established in southeastern Europe.

However, the model of tribal genesis, which has been developed using
most of the Germanic migrating peoples, is hardly applicable to the early
Slavs. Prominent nuclei of tradition are missing; where rulership developed, it was often "imported"; attempts at reconstructing an original, "pan-
Slavic" constitution can start only below the royal level with a segmented social and legal order. Perhaps the "obscure progression of the Slavs"[6] can best
be characterized as follows: the Germanic bearers of tradition and their
warrior bands departed from the region east of the Elbe, and a Slavic identity seems to have emerged among the Germanic-Sarmatian peasant population left behind. However, this did not take place in a continuous sweep

from east to west, as certain areas were passed by and became Slavic only at a later time.[7]

Soon after 500, Roman writers took note of the Slavs, and we have evidence that Slavic groups came into contact with Gepids and Lombards around 550. The rightful heir of the Longobard kingdom was driven out, and he fought his way to Italy with a huge army. Apart from his personal retinue of three hundred Longobards, about seven thousand Gepids and Slavs were among his followers. At the same time, Slavic "mountain infantry" fought in the Roman army against the Goths.[8]

The first description of the Slavs comes to us from Procopius, the chronicler of the Gothic war: "They live in pitiful hovels which they set up far apart from one another, but, as a general thing, every man is constantly changing his place of abode. When they enter battle, the majority of them go against their enemy on foot carrying little shields and javelins in their hands, but they never wear corselets. Indeed, some of them do not wear a shirt or a cloak, but gathering their trews up as far as to their private parts they enter into battle with their opponents. And both the two peoples [the Sclaveni and Antae] have also the same language, an utterly barbarous tongue. Nay further, they do not differ at all from one another in appearance. . . . And they live a hard life, giving no heed to bodily comforts, just as the Massagetae do, and, like them, they are continually and at all times covered with filth; however, they are in no respect base or evildoers, but they preserve the Hunnic character in all its simplicity."[9] At times, of course, they forgot all about their peaceful simplicity and skinned Roman captives, impaled them, beat them to death with clubs, or burned them in their houses.[10]

When the Avars arrived, Slavic groups were found in a wide arch outside of the Carpathians, from the Elbe River all the way to the lower Danube; at a few points they might have even crossed the Carpathians. But with the exception of the Antes, who were originally not Slavs, no uniform larger groups had formed. Many groups did not limit their activities to the tranquil pursuits of peasant life; the myth of the Slavs, which goes back to Herder, has little to do with historical reality. Wherever Slavs appear in the sources prior to 568, they do so as warriors and plunderers, who at times also formed bands organized in retinues, though these did not stay together very long.[11]

The old question of whether the Slavs thrust across the Danube all the way to the Elbe because they were ordered to do so by the Avars or were fleeing from them, or whether they did so on their own initiative, can hardly be posed in this way. Our sources do not even allow us to say anything very specific about the nature and chronology of this expansion. The movement of Slavic expansion predates the invasion of the Avars, but it was fundamentally changed by the completely new political situation after 568, following the departure of the Longobards from Pannonia.

It is striking that the same or similar names occur among the Slavs on both flanks of the Avar kingdom. The name of the Croats appears here and there from Saxony to Athens; as a tribal designation it was used in the northwestern Balkans as well as in Carinthia and on both sides of the Carpathians. The ninth century knew of Abodrites both in Mecklenburg and east of Belgrade. We could be dealing with old Slavic tribes that broke apart under Avar rule, or were perhaps even purposely resettled. This explanation has been widely used, but it is not necessarily correct. It is quite possible that Slavic groups in various places fell back on the same pre-Slavic name tradition, or that outsider designations by the Avars were involved. In any case, Avar influence declined noticeably toward the Baltic Sea. The Slavicization of the land "between Hradcin and Vineta"[12] can therefore hardly be attributed to the Avars.[13] But precisely in this region lay Germania Slavica, which, to use a formulation by Walter Schlesinger, together with Germania Germania and Germania Romana formed the foundation of a history of the Germans. But who were the Avars?

4. THE AVARS

Whether it was Juan-Juan or Wu-huan, dissident Turks or scattered Hepthalites, Hungarians or Uigurs who gave impetus to the Avar migration, these names alone are of little use to the historian of the Avars, a steppe people in central Europe. What is beyond doubt is that the Avar migration was connected with the expansion of the Turks, who always looked upon the Avars as runaway slaves. In fact, the Juan-Juan kingdom was destroyed by the Turks in 552.

The first Avar embassy arrived in Constantinople in 558/559, during the reign of Justinian I. A short time later the Avars had subjected the peoples of the Black Sea steppe zone. As early as 562 they stood at the lower Danube and demanded the Roman province of Scythia minor, modern-day Dobrudja. Justinian offered them instead lower Slavonia west of Belgrade. For a moment it looked as though there would be war, but then the Avars attacked the Frankish kingdom in 562 and again in 566. What gave the Khagan Baian this idea was probably not Byzantine diplomacy, but his desire to prove himself as a monarchical military king, and for that he needed an appropriate military success. The Longobard allies had destroyed the Gepid kingdom in 567/568, and had soon thereafter set out for Italy. Now there was no competing power left along the middle Danube. The settling of the Avars in Pannonia was completed when Baian captured the old Illyrian capital of Sirmium in 582.

The Avars comprised many peoples and formed a federation that was open to a continual stream of new immigrants: Gepids, Bulgars, Kutriguri, and above all Slavs belonged to the Danubian Khaganat. As early as 600, a successful offensive by the East Roman Emperor Maurice had revealed the internal conflicts of the Avar dominion. Nevertheless, in 602 Byzantium had to withdraw completely from the Danube. The large-scale Avar-Persian siege of Constantinople in 626 failed, however, and the Danubian kingdom of the Avars seemed near the end. The decades following the catastrophe of 626, which was greatly exacerbated by the Samo uprising, saw the beginnings of the formation of Slavic tribes, which led to the creation of the Carantanians of the eastern Alps, the Croats, and the Serbs.

It may have been in 711/712 that the Avars crossed the Enns and destroyed Lorch and its surrounding region. A Bavarian chronicler saw this as an unexpected attack that broke trust and good faith. Following this thrust across the Enns, the Avars tried around 740 to break the independence of the Carantanians in present-day southern Austria and suffered a decisive defeat at the hands of a united army of Bavarians and alpine Slavs. After that they ceased being aggressors. In the end they themselves fell victim to the Carolingian aggression in the years 788 to 796, until the old Russian proverb finally came true: "They vanished like the Obor-Avars, who know neither clans nor offspring."[14]

Few of the peoples who determined the fate of Europe during the transition from antiquity to the Middle Ages have remained as unknown as the Avars. For nearly a quarter of a millennium, from 558 to 796, they ruled from the Hungarian steppes over large parts of central and eastern Europe. At its height, the Avar Khaganate drove Byzantines and Franks onto the defensive, maintained contacts with the Persian Sassanids and the Turks of Central Asia, and shaped the movement of Slavic expansion between the Sudetes and the Aegean. And when the Avar kingdom fell, Charlemagne's court marveled at the treasures that had been accumulated in the "ring" of the khagans between the Danube and the Tisza.

Still, the Avars have remained foreigners in European history. Even the Huns, who were able to maintain their power for only a few decades, had a far greater impact on the consciousness of posterity. The *Nibelungenlied* and frescoes in the Vatican tell of Attila; every schoolchild learns his name. The Khagan Baian, however, who established the great Avar power in the second half of the sixth century, is mentioned in few scholarly handbooks.[15]

The Avars introduced to Europe an important innovation in the technology of warfare: the iron stirrup, which improved the steadiness of the Hunnic long-distance fighters and gave the lance-wielding horseman a whole new level of support. While the West was slow in adopting the innovation, the stirrup was part of the standard equipment of Byzantine horsemen as early as 600.

The Huns had reestablished the Scythian composite bow in eastern

Europe, and the Avars had followed their example. This miracle weapon was composed of several layers of wood, sinew, and horn glued together and frequently reinforced with bone plates, all of which greatly increased the bow's penetrating power. This bow was definitely a long-distance weapon: the arrows, tipped with heavy, three-winged heads, had a reach of nearly fifteen hundred feet. In addition, the composite bow was between twenty-four and sixty-three inches and thus shorter than most simple bows, which made it much easier to handle in the saddle. Huns or Avars could fire up to twenty arrows per minute forward or backward while in full gallop. However, the complicated process of making such bows, which could take up to ten years, and their vulnerability to wet climates, probably prevented the composite bow from coming into general use in central and western Europe; it remained a typical feature of the mounted peoples of the East.[16]

5. THE YEAR 626: PERSIANS, AVARS, AND SLAVS AT THE GATES OF CONSTANTINOPLE, TURKS AT THE GATES OF CHINA'S CAPITAL

The Persians too played a role in the transformation of the Roman world. Unlike the Avar Khaganate, Persia still exists; the current western border of Iran is located approximately where the Imperium Romanum had its eastern frontier at the height of its power. Roman-Persian relations formed a very durable system, with the help of which—in spite of military clashes and contradictions—the world was ruled.[17] In the year 540, when the Ostrogothic King Vitigis capitulated to Belisarius, the situation along Rome's eastern border began to change. Persia's western policy became more aggressive, with the armies of the Great King pushing toward the Mediterranean. After the fighting along the Danube had cost Emperor Maurice the throne and his life, things got steadily worse. The richest provinces of the East Roman Empire fell into Persian hands: Syria was taken in 613/614, Jerusalem fell in 614, and Egypt was conquered by 619. Subsequently, Emperor Heraclius I (610–641) won his first victories against the Persians, who now wagered everything on a large-scale assault on Constantinople itself.[18] Let us briefly compare this to what was happening at the other end of the world.

On September 23, 626, the Turks, supposedly one hundred thousand men strong, appeared before the gates of the Chinese capital. The emperor, who had just ascended to the throne, met the challenge successfully. This would prove the last large-scale enterprise by the Turkish Khaganate, from which the Avars had once fled to the West: a few years later it was forced to submit to the Chinese. The parallel to the siege of Constantinople in the same year may be merely coincidental, but it does reveal something about the rhythm that political entities of the steppe were subject to.

Barbarian armies had appeared outside Constantinople with hostile intent on numerous prior occasions: in 378, for instance, the Gothic victors in the battle of Adrianople had pushed onward to the very walls of the city, where they experienced some strange things. Theodoric the Great showed up to put pressure on Zeno, and even the veteran General Belisarius still had to chase the Kutriguri from the suburbs of the city. And though the Frankish King Theudebert I boasted that he would march on Constantinople with the Longobards and the Gepids, never before had barbarians undertaken a serious siege of the city. Not so in 626: simultaneously with Avars and Slavs, a newly levied Persian army marched from Syria to Chalcedon on the Asian banks of the Bosporus.

The operation was a miserable failure. The deadly shower of arrows that had decided so many pitched battles could not bring down the ramparts of the imperial city, and the Avar siege engines were, in the end, no match for the superior military technology of the Byzantines. Evidently the Persians had done nothing that would have allowed them to attack the city from the sea. Consequently, and on this point all the sources agree, the outcome was in the hands of the Slavic boatmen.

But the "naked Slavs" did not fight with the utmost effort. They jumped into the water, hid under their overturned boats, or tried to save themselves by swimming away. The defeat of the khagan could not be averted. Many centuries later the Byzantines still remembered August 7, 626, as the day of their liberation from the barbarian danger. By Friday the eighth, only a few horsemen of the Avar rearguard could still be seen outside the walls of Constantinople. Slav refugees reported that the khagan had to force the Slavs to go with him.

The Danubian Khaganate teetered, but it did not fall; by contrast, within a few years the Arabs brought the glory of the Sassanids to an end. In 661, the last shah died a refugee at the Chinese imperial court.[19]

There is no question that the siege of Constantinople by the combined forces of the Avars, Slavs, and Persians was an event of world-historical significance, but the consequences and lasting impact were not very far-reaching. What did last were the "naked Slavs," who established their small-scale, multicentered forms of social and political organization from the Peloponnese to the Baltic island of Rügen. Still today, historians are impressed—as contemporaries were back then—by politics on a grand scale, the kind pursued by Goths, Longobards, or Avars. But precisely their successes, and the social polarization it caused, eroded over time the foundations of their achievement. The Slavs of the sixth and seventh centuries "did not produce a Theodoric, but neither had they to suffer a Teja." The many small entities they created were no match for tribal or imperial competitors in a direct confrontation, but they had a good chance of outliving all of them.[20]

6. THE LONG-LIVED CONSEQUENCES
OF SHORT-LIVED POLITIES

The splendor of the great names faded away; what lasted was the successful mastery of day-to-day life. This holds true also for many Germanic traditions—though revealingly enough not for the Goths and Vandals: the Roman province Liguria became Lombardy, Lugdunensis I became the French region of Burgundy, the *agri decumates* and the adjoining regions on the left bank of the Rhine became Alamannia, Raetia and parts of Noricum turned into the land of the Bavarians, France and England replaced Gaul and Britain. By contrast, all that remained in Europe of the dromedary nomads so often invoked by Franz Altheim were a few scattered camels in zoological gardens and circus menageries, even if the Franks may have tried from time to time to use these undemanding animals as means of transport.

While daily life withdrew into the small regional space and the formerly international ruling stratum was economically and culturally provincialized, the invasion of Germanic and non-Germanic migratory tribes did expand the geographical and ethnographic horizon of the Old World beyond anything previously imagined. To be sure, the foreigners had not studied geography but knew it from experience and suffering. Yet early on we find Germanic kings and scholars who took an interest in the distant lands of northern and eastern Europe, since they traced their origins from there. And so migration and settlement on Roman soil had a lasting impact on late-antique and early medieval description of land and peoples, with the newcomers either furnishing merely the material, as they had done before, or participating themselves in geographic and ethnographic research.[21]

The Germanic peoples could neither conquer the more advanced Roman world nor restore—let alone maintain—it as a political and economic entity. Instead, the universalism of the empire had to give way to a tribal particularism, which joined hands with the late Roman trend toward territorialization and the appearance of a regional patriotism. In a similar way, the Germanic element also strengthened all the developments and tendencies that had alienated the Roman provinces from the central government.

At the same time, the Germanic kings tried to take over the traditional administration, even if in a reduced form, and to preserve the existing socioeconomic conditions. Not even the Vandals interfered in any substantial way with the Roman administrative apparatus. In any case, the Germans left the Roman tax system and practice of slavery intact, and they made no consistent efforts to turn the population of their territories into Arians, let alone pagans. With the exception of the Longobards, by 600 all Germanic peoples had become Catholics, and the days of Longobard Arianism too were numbered.

7. CHRISTIANITY AND ITS CONFESSIONS

Splinter groups, heresies, and sectarian beliefs existed already in early Christianity. Greek intellectualism and Greek philosophy strengthened the trend toward the formation of deviating beliefs and religious creeds. But as long as the Roman state was persecuting the church, these disagreements and divergences hardly reached the surface. However, when Constantine the Great not only tolerated Christianity but emphatically favored it, the problem of orthodoxy became a political factor that was urgent and public as never before. And as far as the formation of Germanic kingdoms on Roman soil is concerned, none among the large number of heretical teachings and creeds played a role comparable to Arianism.

Arianism goes back to Arius, a presbyter of Alexandria (about 260 to 336), who taught that Christ was only similar to God. What he meant was that the Son of God had not existed from before the beginning of time; rather, he had been conceived and created in time, so that the other humans too could attain similarity to God. The conflict between Arius and his opponents took such dangerous forms that Emperor Constantine in 325 called the First Ecumenical Council to the small town of Nicaea in Asia Minor. The council condemned Arianism and formulated the Nicaeanum, the creed which has substantially remained the same to this day. But at the end of his life, the emperor fell increasingly under the influence of Arian bishops, and he not only pardoned Arius but was baptized by an Arian bishop in 337, the year of his death.

In the course of the fourth century, the doctrine of Arius won many followers, especially in the East, among them top secular and clerical notables and even emperors. The creed adopted at the Imperial Council in 360 formed the basis also of Germanic Arianism. But with the elevation of the Spaniard Theodosius to the imperial throne, the Nicaean position, never relinquished in the West, won out also in the East, which soon returned to the Catholic doctrine.

Of course, at the end of the fourth century the vast majority of Christian Germans stood on the soil of the eastern empire, and even during the following century the emperor did not dare touch their Arian creed. The unique position and resilience of the tradition of Ulfilas rested not least on the fact that it was formulated in the vernacular language. Scattered attempts by Catholic bishops to win Gothic souls through sermons in the vernacular could do very little against this tradition.

The Gothic-Vandal peoples who wandered westward in the fifth century took their faith with them, but they were too weak to reverse the decision that had long since been made in the West in favor of Catholicism. It is therefore not surprising that the Merovingian Clovis, who as a Frank was further removed from the religious tradition and the language of Ulfilas, chose the Catholicism of the Roman majority. Many have seen in his case, as in many others, a good deal of power-political reasoning and cold calculation. Without wishing to deny that the most diverse, even contradictory, motives can flow into human actions, it should be said that the creeds of people at all times—and thus during the transition from antiquity to the Middle Ages, as well—were fundamentally shaped by the desire to save one's soul and find salvation.[22]

8. THE TRANSFORMATION OF THE GERMANIC WORLD

Under the influence of the Roman state, the constitutional structures of the Germanic peoples were fundamentally reshaped: the kingship took on a monarchical, even vice-imperial, form; the gentes who followed the leadership of the kings combined into new, polyethnic formations in which the old divisions and units either disappeared or took on new meaning. The element of retainership was superimposed upon what had once been communities of descent, altering them, with the result that in many cases even the clan now appeared only as a traditional community of law.

The change can be traced, for instance, in the practice of blood feud: the obligation to seek blood vengeance could be transferred from the clan members to the members of the band of retainers who were bound to each other by oath. A man stood up for the lord and the lord for his retainer. In fact, the lord, in the place of the dead man's clan, could demand the wergild for his slain retainer. However, the old ideas did persist. For example, it was not rare for political murders to be cast as cases of blood vengeance, something even Theodoric the Great did at least twice during his life.

To this day, Christian late antiquity has left the Romance languages the legacy that the heathen is called a *paganus,* a country yokel. In like manner, Germanic paganism (*Heidentum* in modern German) became the faith of the lower classes (those who lived in the *Heide,* the countryside). Origins and religion were, if not Christianized, at least given an ecclesiastical imprint: in the lines of ancestors of kings and magnates, saints took the place of the old gods.

The existence of Roman legal codes and the forms they took provided the models during the transformation of Germanic legal customs into tribal laws fixed in writing. These tribal laws consisted of statutes that the king, with the consent of an eligible public, had "found"—in reality, decreed—as God-given law. Writing continued to be in Latin; leaving aside the Gothic-Arian language of the religious cult, the vernacular languages were only of marginal importance. Non-Roman tribal traditions were preserved in artistic work, in the cult of the dead, and in sagas of origins that survived in most cases only in fragments. Moreover, the tribal traditions were assimilated to the Christian-classical models at least in their form, if not content.

9. HENRI PIRENNE, OR THE END OF THE UNITY OF THE MEDITERRANEAN WORLD

Needless to say, the dissolution, indeed the destruction, of the unity of the Mediterranean world went hand in hand with the establishment of the Roman-barbarian regna. It must be said, though, that the general crisis of the third century and false economic measures by the late Roman state had already made the building of large ships so unattractive that they eventually disappeared altogether. For instance, in the second century the state used for official transport services only boats with a capacity of fifty thousand *modii* or more, while the imperial government in the fifth century had to conscript even tubs of two thousand *modii* capacity.[23] To this we can add other factors: the shift of production and consumption to the provinces and the countryside furthered the de-urbanization of the Roman world; most large cities lost their function and shrank, many small cities disappeared altogether, not least because demand and supply declined. Whereas in 480 it was perfectly ordinary for the inhabitants of the episcopal town of Lauriacum in Noricum ripense to cook and light their rooms with olive oil,[24] it was not long before the plant oil from the Mediterranean region had to be replaced with butter and wax. When exactly this happened and to what extent is unknown; in all likelihood, oil imports and elections of bishops along the Danube came to an end along with urban life.

In general, we lack the sort of reliable figures on demographic, economic, and social developments that modern scholars are accustomed to analyzing. For instance, Procopius claims in his *Secret History* that Justinian's African war had cost 5 million dead, and the Gothic war in Italy three times that number, namely, 15 million.[25] Modern estimates, by contrast, assume a total population for the African provinces minus Egypt of 3 million, for Italy 8 to 10 million.

At the same time, even modern estimates can diverge so much that they occasionally become useless and can convey at best approximate ideas. Anyone who seeks absolute numbers will invariably be disappointed. Scholars do agree, however, that the transition from late antiquity to the early Middle Ages was marked by a strong decline in population. This drop in West and East is attributed to epidemics, famines, natural catastrophes, and the ravages of war. Metropolises with a population of several hundred thousand or, in the case of Rome, perhaps as much as a million, declined within a few generations to a fraction of their former size and lost their political and economic importance.[26]

Other centers arose to take the place of the old metropolises. As early as the beginning of the fifth century, Ravenna replaced Milan as the capital of the West Roman Empire because this city on the Adria was more defensible and more easily supplied by sea.

In Gaul and Spain, none of the old imperial cities and metropolises retained their function: Trier's role was first taken over by Arles, a city on the Rhône, but neither the kings of the Goths nor the kings of the Burgundians established their central royal seat there. Toulouse was chosen for practical reasons, and though it remained the eponymous center of the Westgothic kingdom until the loss of Aquitania to the Franks, it was a rather modest town of perhaps fifteen thousand inhabitants. Still, its size and division of labor was sufficient to satisfy the needs of the royal court and the seat of the royal administration.

After 507 it took two generations before the Visigoths—following the intermezzi in Narbonne and Barcelona—had found another permanent capital in Toledo. But this town had not been an old metropolis, and it now became a kind of royal castle located in the less populated and less Romanized interior. Toledo was well-situated strategically and thus the ideal center for the Gothic settlement. But in spite of its humble beginnings, the importance of Toledo as the royal city of Visigothic Spain cannot be exaggerated. Much the same is true of Pavia for the Longobard kingdom and of the Merovingian residences for the Frankish kingdom.[27]

To explain the processes of shrinkages and shifts, which are so difficult to determine in detail, Henri Pirenne tried in 1922 to show "that the progressive decline of Mediterranean trade had a decisive influence on the political, economic, and social changes in western Europe." The great Belgian historian brought his observations together in his work *Mohammed and Charlemagne,* published posthumously in 1937, where he formulated the thesis that it was only the Arab conquest of a large part of the Mediterranean region that provided the Franks with the opportunity to establish a European continental kingdom and reestablish the western emperorship in the person of Charlemagne.

To this day, the "Pirenne-thesis" has found many critics and supporters. Some of the arguments in the debate strike the neutral observer more like passionate creeds and ideological polemics than scholarly statements. Sober historians will thus turn with relief to Dietrich Claude's excellent study on trade in the western Mediterranean during the Early Middle Ages, which closes with this observation:

> Given the divergent developments in the Mediterranean region, particularly in the spheres of politics, the church, and cultural life, it would be presumptuous to burden overseas trade and traffic with the decisive function it allegedly played in maintaining the unity of the Mediterranean region. At least the

boats in the western basin of the Mediterranean—not very numerous, of low carrying capacity, and slow even during the summer season—were entirely unsuited for such a role. We would be hopelessly overloading these sailing ships by asking them to take on the burden of evidence in this question.

While the emperor of Constantinople was not dependent on merchant ships, the correspondence of Gregory the Great shows the outstanding importance that shipping played for papal activities outside of Italy. We cannot be sure that England could have been missionized under papal leadership without ships that were sailing between Italy and Gaul. The fact that the papacy was able to act—at least to a modest degree—as the highest ecclesiastical authority in the West was due also to merchant ships, on which its envoys reached the kingdoms of the Franks and Visigoths and kept alive among their bishops the memory of the *vicarius sancti Petri*. The effectiveness of the alliance between the pope and the Frankish king, which was of world-historical significance, depended at times on the precarious sea links between Italy and the Provence. To that extent, shipping played an immediate role in the transition from the imperial unity of the ancient Mediterranean to the Christian Catholic unity of the Carolingian Empire.[28]

10. *TRANSLATIO IMPERII*—THE TRANSFER OF THE EMPIRE

The Germanic peoples neither destroyed the Roman world nor restored it; instead, they made a home for themselves within it, just as the Spaniards, Gauls, and Illyrians had done before them. In contrast to their predecessors, however, they gave up the western empire and the universality of its social order and way of life: the one emperor in Constantinople was "enough" for them—that was the gist of Odovacar's message to Zeno.[29] And the royal heirs of the western empire honored the Byzantine emperor as their lord and father in the same way that they accepted the primacy of the model of Byzantium unquestioningly for many centuries.

Only the success of Charlemagne—king of the Franks (a people "orthodox since time immemorial") and the Longobards (a people long since "very Catholic") and *Patricius Romanorum* recognized by the emperor and the pope[30]—made possible the reestablishment of the western Roman Empire as an imperium that now took its place as equal to—though not of the same rank as—the *basileia* of the Romaioi. Thus the imperial coronation on Christmas Day in the year 800 established, via the Frankish kingdom of the Merovingians and Carolingians, the link between the Imperium Romanum and "its" Germanic peoples and the high medieval Holy Roman Empire of the Germans.

Medieval people themselves were aware of this connection and developed the notion of the *translatio imperii*, the "transfer of the empire": according to this idea, the imperium was transferred from the Romans to the Greeks, from the Greeks to the Franks, from the Franks to the Longobards, and from the Longobards to the Saxons and Germans, that it might last to the end of time.[31] Such an interpretation found its justification both in the prophecy of Daniel and in Sallust, who had recognized, in the prologue to his work on the conspiracy of Cataline, that this political crisis had been the result of political-moral decline: "And so the imperium is always transferred to the best from those who are not so good."[32] It is not surprising that such paradoxical, vague, and deterministic prophecies have ever since linked the dream of the Reich with a positive and even aggressive identification with the Germanic peoples.

The dream of the Reich and the identification with the Germanic peoples have become set pieces in history's chamber of horrors. Too many people have suffered from them, too many have paid for them with their lives. Europeans today must no longer seek to create identities with backward-looking hopes and vague images. But this does not mean that we should or can afford to forget the past. The "distant mirror" of history, to use Barbara Tuchman's phrase, always gives insight into the present, provided we use it wisely. For our topic that means: we must know the Germanic past as well as the history of the empire in order to accept the European continuity in its totality, preserving what is good about it while simultaneously protecting ourselves against becoming victims of its terrible dreams, false beliefs, and horrible deeds. In short: we must do this to stand up to history, and if need be to resist it.

ABBREVIATIONS

ALMA	*Archivum Latinitatis Medii Aevii*
CC Ser. Lat.	*Corpus Christianorum: Series Latina*. Turnhout, 1953 ff.
CFHB	*Corpus fontium historiae Byzantinae*
CIL	*Corpus inscriptionum Latinarum*
CSEL	*Corpus Scriptorum Ecclesiasticorum Latinorum*
CTh	*Codex Theodosianus*
DsÖAW	*Denkschriften der Österreichischen Akademie der Wissenschaften, philosophisch-historische Klasse*
FHG	*Fragmenta Historicorum Graecorum*
FMSt	*Frühmittelalterliche Studien*
HRG	*Handwörterbuch zur deutschen Rechtsgeschichte*
JE	Philipp Jaffé, *Regesta Pontificum Romanorum ab condita ecclesia ad annum post Christum natum* MCXCVIII. Bd. 2 (Leipzig, 1888)
MGH	*Monumenta Germaniae historica*
MIÖG	*Mitteilungen des Instituts für Österreichische Geschichts-forschung*
PG	Migne, *Patrologia Graeca*
PLRE 1	Jones, *Prosopography*
PLRE 2	Martindale, *Prosopography*
RE	*Realencyclopädie der classischen Altertumswissenschaften*
RGA	*Reallexikon der germanischen Altertumskunde*
VIÖG	*Veröffentlichungen des Instituts für österreichische Geschichtsforschung*
WG	Wolfram, *History of the Goths*

NOTES

INTRODUCTION

1. Demandt, *Spätantike*, 34.
2. Ibid., 224 and 417 f.; Augustine, *De civitate Dei* III.10, Engl. translated by Henry Bettenson (Penguin Books, 1972).
3. Demandt, *Spätantike*, 34 ff.
4. Virgil, *Aeneid*, 6.853.
5. Ammianus Marcellinus, *Rerum*, XVI 6.3; Demandt, *Der Fall Roms*, 44–77, esp. 62.
6. Birkhan, *Germanen*, esp. 181 ff.; Dobesch, "Germanennamens," 77 ff.; Heinrich Beck, ed., *Germanenprobleme aus heutiger Sicht*.
7. Wenskus, *Stammesbildung*, 152 with notes 41 f.
8. Ibid., 113 ff. (Gustav Kossinna).
9. Much, *Germania*, 356 ff. and 526, on Tacitus, *Germania*, chaps. 28 and 46.
10. Ammianus Marcellinus, *Rerum*, XXXI 2.17.
11. Wenskus, *Stammesbildung*, 57 ff.; Much, *Germania*, 528.
12. Wenskus, *Stammesbildung*, 234.
13. Tacitus, *Germania*, chap. 2.
14. Birkhan, *Germanen*, 181 ff.; Wenskus, *Stammesbildung*, 640 f.
15. CIL III.1 no. 4453 (Aistomodius). Schmidt, *Ostgermanen*, 40 ff.; Wenskus, *Stammesbildung*, 30, 249 ff., and 267 f. (sense of unity), 654 (Veneti), and 655 (Volcae). Birkhan, *Germanen*, 62 (vowel shift).
16. WG 19 ff., 28 ff., 36 ff. (Gutones), and 44 with note 9; Tacitus, *Germania*, chap. 44 (Suiones); Jordanes, *Getica*, 21–24 (Scandinavians). Sidonius Apollinaris, *Epistulae*, V 5.1–3 (Burgundians).
17. Caesar, *De bello Gallico*, I.47; Dobesch, "Germanennamens," 87.
18. Caesar, *De bello Gallico*, VI 11–20 (Gauls), 21–28 (Germans; some scholars claim that chaps. 25–28 are a later interpolation). See Zeitler, "Germanenbegriff," 41 ff., and Lund, "Germanenbegriff," 87.
19. Helbling, *Goten und Wandalen*, 86.

20. Compare Livy, *Ab urbe condita*, V 34.1–5; Wenskus, *Stammesbildung*, 654 s.v.
21. Andronikos, *Museum Thessaloniki*, esp. 14 ff.
22. Strabo, *Geographica*, VII.292 ff., rejects the explanation of the migratory movements as the result of natural catastrophes.
23. Wenskus, *Stammesbildung*, 305 ff. and 409 ff.
24. See below note 23.
25. WG 11 ff.
26. WG 19 f.
27. Geary, *Before France and Germany*, 6.
28. Gollwitzer, "Germanismus," 284 f. and 306.
29. WG 21 with note 61 f.
30. WG 1–3 with notes 1–17; Messmer, *Gotenmythos*, 49. Compare Gollwitzer, "Germanismus," 282 ff., as well as Öhlinger, "'Unser sind der Goten, Vandalen und Franken Triumphe,'" 124 ff. Helbling, *Goten und Wandalen*, 73 ff.
31. Gollwitzer, "Germanismus," 356. Compare 322 ff.
32. Wolfram, *Mitteleuropa*, 125 with note 1; Willibald, *Vita Bonifatii*, chap. 5.
33. Wolfram, *Mitteleuropa*, 195 f. and 347 with note I; Wolfram, *Intitulatio* II, 133 f.
34. See Graus, *Vergangenheit*, 220 ff.
35. Wolfram, "Zisterziensergründung," 19 ff.

1. KINGS, HEROES, AND TRIBAL ORIGINS

1. Snorri Sturlson, preface to *Heimskringla*, translated by Samuel Laing and Peter Foote, 4th ed. (London and New York, 1968), 3 f.
2. Wenskus, *Stammesbildung*, 305 ff. and 409 ff.
3. Tacitus, *Annals*, II 88.
4. WG 75 and 112 ff.
5. Procopius, *De bello Gothico*, I (V) 1.25 ff.; Wolfram, *Intitulatio*, I, 79 ff.
6. Tacitus, *Annals*, II 45 f. and 88.
7. Wenskus, *Stammesbildung*, 409 ff.; Wolfram, "Gotische Studien I," 20 ff., and II, 293 ff.; Wolfram, "Early Medieval Kingdom," 1ff.; Tacitus, *Germania*, chap. 7. On the Burgundian kingships see Ammianus Marcellinus, *Rerum*, XXVIII 5.9–14, and Wenskus, *Stammesbildung*, 575 ff.; *Rigthula* (edition Thule 2, new ed. 1963), 113 ff.
8. Pohl, *Awaren*, 164 ff.
9. Wolfram, "Early Medieval Kingdom," 4 f.
10. von See, "Heldendichtung," 37; Wenskus, *Stammesbildung*, 370 f.; Wolfram, *Geburt Mitteleuropas*, 381 with note 16.
11. Cassiodorus, *Variae*, XI 1.14. See Wolfram, "Origo gentis," 24 with notes 37 f.
12. *Beowulf*, 2208 ff. (final deed); 2579 and 3086 (*theodcyning*).
13. Höfler, *Sakralkönigtum*, 189 f.
14. Wolfram, "Fortuna," 29 with note 73.
15. von See, "Heldendichtung," 38.
16. WG 26 f.
17. *Bjarki-Lied* 32 (Thule 1 [1934], 186). Cf. L. M. Hollander, *Old Norse Poems* (1936); Snorri Sturlson, *Heimskringla*, 360 f.
18. von See, "Heldendichtung," 38.

19. WG 102.

20. Weber, "Jüngere Edda," 401 ff.

21. Rainer Maria Rilke, *Duino Elegies,* trans. David Young. New York, 1978; *Beowulf,* verses 2900–3027: the death of Beowulf means the end of the Géats, which is why the royal treasury is to be burned with his slayer (Wiglaf's prophecy).

22. Dove, "Studien," 25 with note 2, after Cassiodorus, *Expositio psalmorum* XCV v. 7; and Dove, "Studien," 38 f. (a people in arms).

23. Tacitus, *Germania,* chaps. 2 and 39. Compare Wenskus, *Stammesbildung,* 411.

24. WG 30 f. with note 104 and 112 with note 484; Wenskus, *Stammesbildung,* 504; Kuhn, "Asen," 458.

25. WG 40 f. and 112; Much, "Wandalische Götter," 21 f; Dove, "Studien," 25 with note 3 (*gens* for princely families) and 44 (Burgundians).

26. WG 30 ff., 85 ff., 111 f., and 115 f.; Wolfram, *Mitteleuropa,* 326 with note 45.

27. Gildas, *De excidio,* 23.3; Campbell, ed., *The Anglo-Saxons,* 26.

28. Hauck, "Lebensnormen," 206 ff., esp. 208 note 126 (Frea as Vanir); and Much, "Wandalische Götter," on the Origo gentis Langobardorum chaps. 1 ff.; Paulus Diaconus, *Historia Langobardorum,* I 1 ff.; compare Fredegar, Chronicon, III 65; Snorri Sturlson, *Heimskringla:* "Hakon the Good," chap. 32, 109: the obligation of bestowing a gift when giving a name.

29. Compare Wenskus, *Stammesbildung,* 489.

30. Tacitus, *Germania,* chap. 43.

31. Hauck, "Lebensnormen," 186 ff.

32. Tacitus, *Germania,* chap. 2; Much, *Germania,* 71 ff., esp. 85 ff.

33. WG 20 ff.; Hauck, "Lebensnormen," 210 with note 139.

34. Jordanes, *Getica,* 78 f.

35. Tacitus, *Germania,* chap. 40.1.

36. Wolfram, "Origo gentis," 31; WG 29 ff., 36 ff., and 324 ff.

2. THE EMPIRE AND THE "NEW" PEOPLES

1. Bannert, "Tod," 459 ff.

2. Schmidt, *Westgermanen,* 162–177; Wolfram, *Mitteleuropa,* 323 and 440 (Regensburg) as well as 57 and 263 (Lauriacum).

3. Tacitus, *Germania,* chap. 37; Lund, "Germanenbegriff," 53 ff.

4. Dobesch, "Germanennamens," 77 ff.

5. Zeitler, "Germanenbegriff," 41 ff., esp. 50 ff.; Lund, "Germanenbegriff," 61 with note 57 and 71 f.; compare, for example, the contradiction in Tacitus between *Germania* chap. 5 and *Annals* II.62.

6. Much, *Germania,* 441 ff.

7. Schmidt, *Ostgermanen,* 571 f.

8. WG 43 f.

9. Ibid.

10. Wolfram, "Ethnogenesen," 98 f.; Themistius, *Orationes,* X 131 b–c.

11. WG 43 f.; Waas, *Germanen,* 5 f.; Staufenberg, "Macht und Geist," 303 ff.

12. Symmachus, *Epistulae,* III 47; Matthews, *Aristocracies,* 8 f.; Straub, "Niederlage," 195 ff.; and Straub, "Christliche Geschichtsapologetik," 240 ff.

13. Procopius, *De bello Vandalico*, I (III) 2.25 f.; Demandt, *Spätantike*, 146; Matthews, *Aristocracies*, 300 ff.

14. Much, *Germania*, 375 ff.

15. Alföldi, *Weltkrise*, 400; Hoffmann, *Bewegungsheer*, 1, 1 ff.

16. Dirlmeier et al., *Quellen der Alamannen* I, 9 ff.; Castritius, "Vielfalt," 73 ff., opposes, for good reasons, the notion that Cassius Dio already attested the Alamanni in 213; WG 43 f.; Ewig, *Civitas*, 475; *Die Germanen*, 2, 16 ff.

17. Wenskus, *Stammesbildung*, 521 f.; Ewig, "Civitas," 475.

18. Agathias, *Historiarum*, I 6.3; Castritius, "Vielfalt," 76 f. sees the name of the Alamanni as a *nomen antiquum*, in the sense for example of "all humans, humanity as a whole," as is expressed, for instance, in the word *Suomi*, used by the Fins for their own country. Even though Castritius offers an explanation worth considering, and one that would have great historical significance, I have chosen to adhere, with all due caution, to the interpretation given in the text. See below note 19.

19. WG 20 and 28.

20. WG 14 f. and 324; Wagner, *Getica*, 28 f.

21. Geuenich and Keller, "Alamannen," 137 ff.; Castritius, "Vielfalt" (see note 16); Wenskus, *Stammesbildung*, 255 ff., and esp. 501 ff.; Schmidt, *Westgermanen*, 237 ff. and 253; Wolfram, *Mitteleuropa*, 331; Ammianus Marcellinus, *Rerum*, XVI 10.20 (sole mention of the Suevi by the author; he probably means the Juthungi) and XVII 6.1 (first mention of the Juthungi as *gens Alamannica*). Kuhn and Jänichen, "Alemannen," 137 f.

22. Schmidt, *Westgermanen*, 320 f.; Wenskus, *Stammesbildung*, 553 ff.

23. Kuhn and Jänichen, "Alemannen," 138 f.

24. Wenskus, *Stammesbildung*, 110 and 502.

25. Werner, *Ursprünge*, 226; Wenskus, *Stammesbildung*, 513 ff.; Zöllner, *Franken*, 1 ff.; WG 29; Wolfram, "Donau," 27 (primordial deed).

26. Schmidt, *Westgermanen*, 37 ff.; Wenskus, *Stammesbildung*, 547 f.

27. Tacitus, *Germania*, chap. 2.

28. Cassius Dio, *Historia Romana*, 55.1.3.

29. Wolfram, "Gotische Studien," I.7; Wenskus, *Stammesbildung*, 321; Miltner, "Vandalen," cols. 300 ff.

30. Wenskus, *Stammesbildung*, 504; WG 111; Kuhn, "Asen," 458.

31. WG 45 with note 61.

32. Schmidt, *Ostgermanen*, 132.

33. Orosius, *Historiarum*, VII 32.11.

34. Ammianus Marcellinus, *Rerum*, XXVIII 5.9–14; Isidor of Seville, *Etymologiae* IX 2.99; IV.28.

35. Ammianus Marcellinus, *Rerum*, XXXI 5.17.

36. WG 43–57.

37. Castritius, "Vielfalt," 74 with note 26.

38. Alföldi, *Weltkrise*, 349 ff., and 361 ff.; Dirlmeier et al., *Quellen der Alamannen* 6, 102 ff.; Hoffmann, *Bewegungsheer* 1, 1 ff. and 247–257.

39. WG 34 f. and 56–58; Dirlmeier et al., *Quellen der Alamannen* 6 (104 ff.).

40. Wolfram, *Mitteleuropa*, esp. 342 f. (Slavs).

41. Geuenich and Keller, "Alamannen," 142.

42. Ammianus Marcellinus, *Rerum,* XV 4.1 ff.

43. Ibid., XXIX 4.7.

44. Geuenich and Keller, "Alamannen," 141 with note 38; Hoffmann, *Bewegungsheer* 1, 165 ff.

45. Geuenich and Keller, "Alamannen," 141 f.

46. Dirlmeier et al., *Quellen der Alamannen* I, 22 f. (quote about the successes of Maximian).

47. Zöllner, *Franken,* 8–12; Ennodius, *Panegyricus,* XI 5.3 f.; WG 268 with note 144 and 305 with notes 319–326 ("seaworthiness-unseaworthiness").

48. WG 49 ("canonical letter"), 56 f.; Zöllner, *Franken,* 12.

3. THE GERMANIC PEOPLES AS ENEMIES AND SERVANTS OF THE EMPIRE IN THE FOURTH CENTURY

1. Isidor of Seville, *Etymologiae,* II 29.14.

2. *Digestae,* I 3.31.

3. Isaac, "*Limes* and *Limitanei,*" 125 ff., esp. 146 f., regarding CTh XII 1.56 (a. 363).

4. WG 441 f. note 293; Demandt, *Spätantike,* 257, is misleading in this regard.

5. Demandt, *Spätantike,* 234 and 256 ff.

6. See Demandt, *Spätantike,* 261 ff.

7. Demandt, *Spätantike,* 173 ff.

8. Demandt, *Spätantike,* 405 ff., esp. 408 ff., still advocates this view, a common one especially among ancient historians.

9. Cassiodorus, *Variae,* XII 22.

10. Durliat, "Le salaire," 50 f.

11. Demandt, *Spätantike,* 270 f. and 315 ff.

12. Ibid., 269 ff.

13. Jones, *The Later Roman Empire,* 1: 21 ff., 42 ff., 97 ff., 199 ff., 499 ff., and 2: 523 ff., 607 ff., 737 ff., and 795 ff. Compare Durliat, "Le salaire," 21 ff.; and Goffart, "After the Zwettl Conference," 73 ff.; WG 296 f., and id., *Intitulatio* I, 44 ff.; Demandt, "Magister militum," 553 ff., and id., *Spätantike,* 211 ff.; Stroheker, *Adel,* 5 ff.

14. Symmachus, *Epistulae,* I.52.

15. Demandt, *Spätantike,* 275; cf. 251.

16. Demandt, *Spätantike,* 285, 292, 294; Wolfram, "Byzanz," 239.

17. Compare Olympiodorus, *Historiarum,* frag. 44 with Zosimus, Historia, V 29.9.

18. Wolfram, *Splendor,* 111, after Cassiodorus, *Variae,* VIII 2.1 ff.

19. Demandt, *Spätantike,* 350 and 386 f.; compare 286 and 333 ff. (*patrocinium*).

20. Ibid., 405.

21. Durliat, "Le salaire," 51 with note 155.

22. Sidonius Apollinaris, *Epistulae,* IV 17.2.

23. Demandt, *Spätantike,* 291, 358, and 364.

24. Ibid., 329 ff.

25. Ibid., 362.

26. Verlinden, "L'origine de Sclavus," 97 ff., esp. 125, against Demandt, *Spätantike,* 296.

27. Wolfram, "Die Ministerialen und das werdende Land," 8 ff., esp. 11 ff.; id., *Mitteleuropa*, 383 ff.

28. See Chrysos, "Title," 58 f. on Priscus, frag. 8=11.2 (Blockley, *Historians*, 2, 276–278) (the threat of Attila's world supremacy), and Chrysos, "Roman-Persian Legal Relations," 25 ff., esp. 29 and note 3, after Ammianus Marcellinus, *Rerum*, XXV 7.9 ff., and 9.9 ff., as well as Eutropius, *Breviarium*, X 17.1 f.; Procopius, *De bello Persico*, I 19.29 (retreat in Egypt).

29. Dirlmeier et al., *Quellen der Alamannen*, 6, 105 ff.; WG 57 ff.; Zöllner, *Franken*, 16 f.

30. WG 61 f.

31. Ammianus Marcellinus, *Rerum*, XVII 1.11 ff.

32. Ibid., XXX 5.2.

33. WG 64 ff.; esp. after Ammianus Marcellinus, *Rerum*, XXVII 5.7 ff.

34. PLRE 1, 527 f. and 539 (Mallobaudes); Zöllner, *Franken*, 22; Waas, *Germanen*, 108 f.; Dirlmeier et al., *Quellen der Alamannen*, 1, 64 f. and 81 ff., as well as 6, 109 f.; Ammianus Marcellinus, *Rerum*, XVIII 2.15 ff., and XIX 4.2 ff., and XXX 3.1 ff. (Macrianus); Ausonius, "Bissula," 17 ff., after Dirlmeier et al., *Quellen der Alamannen*, 6, 97.

35. PLRE 1, 538 f. (Malarichus and Mallobaudes) and 840 f. (Silvanus), esp. after Ammianus Marcellinus, *Rerum*, XV 5.11 and 16; compare Stroheker, *Germanentum*, 20 f.

36. PLRE 1, 95 ff. (Arbogast), 159 f. (Bauto), 372 f. (Fravitta; compare WG 146 f.), 598 f. (Merobaudes), and 765 f. (Richomeres, Arbogast's uncle); Stroheker, *Germanentum*, 21 ff.

37. Ammianus Marcellinus, *Rerum*, XIV 10.8; Stroheker, *Germanentum*, 42 ff.; PLRE 1.28 f. (Agilo), 372 (Fraomarius), 496 (Latinus), and 810 f. (Scudilo).

38. PLRE 1, 605; WG 131.

39. PLRE 1, 379 f.; WG 148 ff.

40. Ammianus Marcellinus, *Rerum*, XVI 12.25.

41. Ibid., XVI 12.23, 26, and 34.

42. Zöllner, *Franken*, 18, esp. after Ammianus Marcellinus, *Rerum*, XV 13.2.

43. Wolfram, "Gotische Studien II," 303 ff. and 319 with note 121. On the expression *reges Gothorum*, see Ammianus Marcellinus, *Rerum*, XXVI 10.3.

44. Ammianus Marcellinus, *Rerum*, XVI 12.26.

45. WG 95; Wolfram, "Gotische Studien I," 20 ff.

46. See Ammianus Marcellinus, *Rerum*, XVI 12.17 and 34 f.

47. Compare Tacitus, *Germania*, chap. 7 (Much, *Germania*, 157 f.) with Procopius, *De bello Gothico*, II (VI) 14.38; Wenskus, *Stammesbildung*, 68, 314 ff., and 410.

48. WG 24 f.

49. WG 89.

50. WG 89–116; Wolfram, "Gotische Studien II" and "Gotische Studien III."

51. WG 67 f., 75–85, and 112–114.

52. WG 69 ff., 86 ff., and 248 ff.; Maenchen-Helfen, *Huns*, 18 ff. and 414 (Balamber).

53. Ammianus Marcellinus, *Rerum*, XXVIII 5.15.

54. Ibid., XVII 8.3 f.; Zöllner, *Franken*, 18 f.

55. Ammianus Marcellinus, *Rerum*, XXVII 7.8.

56. Symmachus, *Orationes,* II 12 and 14, pp. 325 f.

57. Ammianus Marcellinus, *Rerum,* XXXI 8.9.

58. WG 67–75, 86–89, and esp. 117–131.

59. See most recently Beisel, *Studien,* 28, though his most important source (Ammianus Marcellinus, *Rerum,* XVII 8.3 f.) indicates that it classified the Salians as *dediticii* and not as *foederati.*

60. Zöllner, *Franken,* 34 ff., esp. 41: "Whatever the legal form may have been in which Childeric's cooperation with the Romans may have taken place—there were undoubtedly considerations of *Realpolitik* which led him to adopt the attitude he did." Compare Wolfram, *Intitulatio,* I, 44 with notes 67 f.; Ewig, "Merowinger und das Imperium," 6 ff. On the imperial recognition of 508 see McCormick, *Eternal Victory,* 335 ff., Werner, *Ursprünge,* 328, Zöllner, *Franken,* 66 ff.

61. PLRE 1, 144: Bacurius.

62. PLRE 1, 903: Theodosius 3; CTh VI 14.1 (370 or 373 V 28).

63. Wolfram, "Origo et religio," 20.

64. WG 136 ff.

65. Schwarcz, "Reichsangehörige," 172 f.

66. See Wenskus, *Stammesbildung,* 322 f. and 477.

67. PLRE 1, 539; see also 144: Bacurius.

68. PLRE 1, 928; Stroheker, *Germanentum,* 45 f.

69. PLRE 1, 372.

70. Schmidt, *Ostgermanen,* 266.

71. PLRE 1, 853 ff., and 2, 43 ff.; Schwarcz, "Reichsangehörige," 86 ff. and 171 ff.; WG 136–161.

4. EMPERORSHIP AND KINGSHIP ON ROMAN SOIL

1. Krautschick, "Familie der Könige," 109 ff., esp. 115 ff. (kinship tables); Demandt, *Spätantike,* 504.

2. Demandt, *Spätantike,* 504.

3. Priscus frag. 17 = 20 (Blockley, *Historians*).

4. Claudianus, *De IV consolatu Honorii,* verses 214–224.

5. Wolfram, "Königtum," 19 f.

6. WG 137.

7. Wolfram, "Byzanz," 237 ff., with corrections after WG 222 ff. and 295 ff.

8. Durliat, "Le salaire," 21 ff., with corrections after WG 222 ff. and 295 ff.

9. WG 211 ff. and 290 ff.; Claude, "Comes," 65 ff.

10. Jordanes, *Getica,* 304.

11. WG 239 ff. and 300 ff.; Wenskus, *Stammesbildung,* 346 ff.

5. THE HUNNIC ALTERNATIVE

1. Wenskus, *Stammesbildung,* 652 s.v. "Stammesschwarm."

2. Maenchen-Helfen, *Huns,* 376 ff., esp. 441 (conclusions), argues for a Turkish core group, though this is currently once again highly disputed.

3. Olympiodorus, *Historiarum,* frag. 18 = 19 (Blockley, *Historians*).

4. Jordanes, *Getica,* 226; WG 254 with note 52.

5. Priscus frag. 1=2 (Blockley, *Historians*).

6. Maenchen-Helfen, *Huns,* 126.

7. Priscus frag. 3 = 9.3 (Blockley, *Historians*).

8. Priscus frag. 7 f. = 11.1 and 2 (Blockley, *Historians*).

9. Maenchen-Helfen, *Huns,* 586.

10. Priscus frag. 8 = 11.2–14 (Blockley, *Historians*). The English translation is that of Blockley. Explanations have been inserted in brackets.

11. Priscus frag. 8 = 11.2 (Blockley, *Historians* 2, 276–278); Demandt, "Magister militum," col. 753; PLRE 2, 182 f.

12. WG 176 and 178.; Schmidt, *Ostgermanen,* 471 ff.

13. Unless otherwise indicated, this section relies on Maenchen-Helfen, *Huns,* 59–144, esp. 141 (quote). There can be no doubt that Maenchen-Helfen's *World of the Huns* remained a torso. For example, it lacks a treatment of the history leading up to the battle on the Catalaunian Fields, and section IV, "Society," is surely also incomplete.

14. Priscus frag. 22.3 (Blockley, *Historians*).

15. Jordanes, *Getica,* 255.

16. Jordanes, *Getica,* 254 ff.; the translation is based on that of Maenchen-Helfen, *Huns,* 275.

17. WG 259 ff.

18. WG 264; Maenchen-Helfen, *Huns,* 168; see McCormick, *Eternal Victory,* 60, after *Chronicon Paschale* a. 469 and Marcellinus Comes, *Chronicon,* a. 469.

19. Schröter, "Kopfumformung," 258 ff.

20. Priscus frag. 8 = 11.2 (Blockley, *Historians,* 2, 267), and frag. 8 = 13.3 (Blockley, *Historians*).

21. Priscus frag. 21.1 (Blockley, *Historians*).

22. WG 254 f. and 257 f.

23. Maenchen-Helfen, *Huns,* 270–274.

24. Maenchen-Helfen, *Huns,* 278–280, after Jordanes, *Getica,* 183, and Priscus frag. 12.1 (Blockley, *Historians*).

25. Ammianus Marcellinus, *Rerum,* XVII 12.21.

26. Maenchen-Helfen, *Huns,* 221 f. and 278–280.

27. Jordanes, *Getica,* 183, p. 105 f.; Maenchen-Helfen, *Huns,* 360–364.

28. Maenchen-Helfen, *Huns,* 168.

29. Pohl, "Gepiden," 292 f.

6. THE KINGDOM OF TOULOUSE (418–507)

1. McCormick, *Eternal Victory,* 56 f.

2. WG 161–171.

3. See above 112 ff.

4. Sidonius Apollinaris, *Epistulae,* I 2.

5. Rouche, *L'Aquitaine,* 43.

6. Wolfram, *Intitulatio,* I, 78 with note 10.

7. Wolfram, *Intitulatio,* I, 80 with note 23.

8. Wolfram, *Intitulatio,* I, 54 f. with note 103.

9. McCormick, *Eternal Victory,* esp. 231 ff., and id., "Clovis at Tours," 155 ff.

10. See WG 172–246. On the political-legal position of the Jews in sixth-century Gaul, see Brian Brennan, "The Conversion of the Jews of Clermont in A.D. 576," *The Journal of Theological Studies* NS 36 (Oxford, 1985): 321 ff., esp. 336 f.

7. THE VANDALS (406–534)

1. Piganiol, *L'Émpire chrétien,* 422; see Goffart, "Invasions," 102 note 37.

2. Messmer, "Hispania-Idee," 9–21, esp. 15 and 20 f.; Helbling, *Goten und Wandalen,* 24 f.; Courtois, *Les Vandales,* 58 ff. and 167 ff.

3. Courtois, *Les Vandales,* 168.

4. Ibid., 30 (map).

5. Procopius, *De bello Vandalico,* I (III) 22.3–13.

6. Miltner, "Vandalen," cols. 300 ff.; Courtois, *Les Vandales,* 21 ff.; Schmidt, *Wandalen,* 9 ff.

7. WG 150 ff. and 168 ff.

8. Miltner, "Vandalen," cols. 304 ff.

9. Salvianus of Marseille, *De gubernatione Dei* , chap. 52.

10. WG 170 f.; Miltner, "Vandalen," cols. 300 ff.; Courtois, *Les Vandales,* 51 ff.

11. Miltner, "Vandalen," cols. 309 ff.

12. Claude, "Herrschaftsnachfolge," 334 ff.

13. Jordanes, *Getica,* 168.

14. Procopius, *De bello Gothico,* I (V) 3.24.

15. Ibid., III (VII) 1.4.

16. Salvianus, *De gubernatione Dei,* VII 27 f.

17. Procopius, *De bello Vandalico,* I (III) 3.25; Jordanes, *Getica,* 167 and 169, and id., *Romana,* 330.

18. Durliat, "Le salaire," 40 ff.

19. Claude, "Geiseric."

20. Wolfram, *Intitulatio,* I, 84 with note 43.

21. Prosper, *Chronicon,* 1347; Fichtenau, "Datierungen," 189.

22. Courtois, *Les Vandales,* 105 ff.

23. Ibid., 105 ff.; compare 150 ff., 313 ff., as well as 322 ff.

24. Fichtenau, "Datierungen," 190 f.

25. Mommsen, *Schriften;* Fichtenau, "Datierungen," 189 ff.; compare Procopius, *De bello Vandalico,* I (III) 16.13.

26. McCormick, *Eternal Victory,* 261–267, esp. 261 f. and 263 f. with notes 16–18; Wolfram, *Intitulatio,* I, 81 f.

27. Courtois, *Les Vandals,* 250 ff.; Durliat, "Le salaire," 40 ff.

28. Procopius, *De bello Vandalico,* I (III) 5.21.

29. Wolfram, *Intitulatio,* I: 79 ff.; Claude, "Herrschaftsnachfolge," 349 ff.

30. Mommsen, *Schriften,* 6: 353 f. (*Neues Archiv* 16: 61); Claude, "Geiserich," after Procopius, *De bello Vandalico,* I (III): 16.13; Frank Clover and Evangelos Chrysos have already shown, and will demonstrate in even greater detail, that this assumption about the Vandal kingdom, which has, not least, left seemingly ineradicable traces in the historical atlases, is utterly untenable.

31. Prosper, *Chronicon*, 1348.

32. Jordanes, *Getica*, 169 f. (succession order), and 184 (mutilation of the Visigothic princess).

33. Claude, "Geiserich"; Courtois, *Les Vandales*, 185 ff.; Miltner, "Vandalen," cols. 311 ff.

34. Schwarcz, "Nachrichten," 21.

35. Claude, "Herrschaftsnachfolge," 340 ff.

36. Diesner, "Vandalen," col. 957; Courtois, *Les Vandales*, 262 f., 293 ff., and 395 ff.; Schmidt, *Wandalen*, 108 (reports about Huneric's death).

37. Diesner, "Vandalen," cols. 962 ff.; Courtois, *Les Vandales*, 188 f., 265 f., 334 ff., and 340 ff.

38. Courtois, *Les Vandales*, 99 ff., and 349 ff.; Procopius, *De bello Vandalico*, I (III): 8.24–29.

39. WG 307 f.; Schmidt, *Wandalen*, 118 f. with note 9.

40. Procopius, *De bello Vandalico*, I (III): 9.5; Courtois, *Les Vandales*, 268 with note 2.

41. Procopius, *De bello Vandalico*, I (III): 9.1 ff.; Courtois, *Les Vandales*, 267 ff. and 343.

42. Fichtenau, *Arenga*, 26 ff. and 199 f.

43. Procopius, *De bello Vandalico*, II (IV): 1.6.

44. Procopius, *De bello Vandalico*, I (III): 10.1 ff.; WG 308 with note 347 (weakness of the later Vandal fleet).

45. See Procopius, *De bello Vandalico*, I (III): 11.1, and II (IV): 7.20 f.; compare Claude, *Handel*, 51 note 169 (decline in the importance of the Vandal fleet after Geiseric's death).

46. Procopius, *De bello Gothico*, I (V): 3.17–24, and 4.19.

47. Compare Procopius, *De bello Vandalico*, I (III): 11. 19 f., 20.21–23 with II (IV): 8.1–8.

48. Procopius, *De bello Vandalico*, II (IV): 4.34 ff.

49. Ibid., I (III): 20.21–23.

50. Schmidt, *Wandalen*, 121–141; Procopius, *De bello Vandalico*, I (III): 10.21—II (IV): 7.12.

51. McCormick, *Eternal Victory*, 125.

52. Procopius, *De bello Gothico*, II (VI): 14.8 f.

53. Ibid., 14.13.

54. Ibid., 14.17 ff.

55. Courtois, *Les Vandales*, 336 ff.; compare, for example, Procopius, *De bello Gothico*, II (VI): 10.6 ff.

56. Procopius, *De bello Vandalico*, I (III): 23.1 f., II (IV): 1.8, 4.33 f., 8.25. Compare Schmidt, *Wandalen*, 136 and 144 ff., and Clover, "Symbiosis," 57 ff.

57. Procopius, *De bello Vandalico*, II (IV): 7.20 f.

58. See, for example, Procopius, *De bello Vandalico*, I (III): 25.12f., II (IV): 7.10 ff., esp. 14 f. and 20 f. Compare his *De bello Persico*, II: 19.36. Belisarius is an excellent general because of his good luck as well as his virtue.

59. On the term "teutsch," see Gollwitzer, "Germanismus," 283 f.

60. Schmidt, *Wandalen*, 188.

61. Procopius, *De bello Vandalico*, II (IV): 6.5–9; compare Schmidt, *Wandalen*, 188 f.

62. *De bello Gallico*, VI: 13–18, esp. 21.

63. Compare Procopius, *De bello Vandalico* I (III): 8.16, with II (IV): 6.10–13.

8. ODOVACAR, OR THE ROMAN EMPIRE
THAT DID NOT END

1. Schmidt, *Ostgermanen*, 86 ff.; Much, *Germania*, 528.
2. Castritius, "Sozialgeschichte," 22 ff.
3. Schmidt, *Ostgermanen*, 99.
4. Pohl, "Edika," 446 f.; PLRE 2: 385 f. and 791 ff.
5. See Demandt, *Spätantike*, 496.
6. WG 278 ff.; Wolfram, *Intitulatio*, I: 53 f. and 59 f.; Wolfram, "Königtum," 3 ff.; compare Demandt, *Spätantike*, 175 ff.
7. See especially Demandt, *Spätantike*, 178 ff. and 486 ff.
8. Fichtenau, "Datierungen," 202 ff.
9. Demandt, *Der Fall Roms*, 44–77, especially 62 (which has passages that declare also the end of the res publica, but since they do so under the influence of Christian end-times expectations they do not fully count as political statements).
10. WG 204 with note 259.
11. Suerbaum, *Staatsbegriff*, 261 ff.
12. Procopius, *De bello Gothico*, III (VII): I.4.
13. Lotter, *Severinus von Noricum*, 208 f., has done well assembling the sources and evaluating them for the chronology of events at the Danube. However, I cannot agree with his reflections on the end of the Roman Empire. The interpretation I have offered was developed together with Evangelos Chrysos. See in particular Eugippius, *Vita s. Severini*, chap. 20.1.
14. Demandt, *Spätantike*, 486.
15. Demandt, *Spätantike*, 481 ff.; Wolfram, "Aufnahme," 114 f.; Goffart, "Invasions," 87 ff.; Christ, *Der Untergang des Römischen Reiches*.

9. THEODORIC (451–526) AND
CLOVIS (466/467–511)

1. Von den Steinen, "Chlodwigs Übergang zum Christentum," *MIÖG* Erg. 12 (1933): 417 ff.; id., *Theoderich und Chlodwig. Ein Kapitel deutscher Weltgeschichte* (Tübingen, 1933).
2. Von den Steinen, *Theoderich und Chlodwig*, 420 ff.; Demandt, *Spätantike*, 192 f.
3. See, for example, Staufenberg, "Theoderich und Chlodwig," 420 ff.; Demandt, *Spätantike*, 192 f.
4. Ennodius, *Panegyricus*, chap. 11.
5. WG 330.
6. Demandt, *Spätantike*, 186 ff.
7. WG 267 and 289; Claude, "Königserhebungen," 153 f.
8. Werner, *Les origines*, 286. WG 110 f.

9. See Werner, *Les origines*, 297 and 299; Zöllner, *Franken*, 74 with note 4 and 86 with note 5.

10. Zöllner, *Franken*, 45–48; Werner, *Les origines*, 299 f.

11. Ennodius, *Panegyricus*, 12–14.

12. WG 258–278.

13. Anonymus Valesianus, II 49.

14. Procopius, *De bello Gothico*, I (V) 1.29.

15. Anonymus Valesianus, II 64.

16. Procopius, *De bello Gothico*, I (V) 1.25–39.

17. WG 285 ff. Wolfram, "Königtum," 1 ff.; Procopius, *De bello Gothico*, I (V) 1.26 (Theodoric) and II (VI) 14.38 (Herulian *rhix*).

18. WG 269, 277, and 328 f.

19. Lippold, "Chlodovechus," cols. 153 and 172. Graus, "Lebendige Vergangenheit," esp. 240 ff. Goffart, *Narrators*, 30 f.

20. Jordanes, *Getica*, 315. Courtois, *Les Vandales*, 237.

21. Wolfram, "Fortuna," 4 f.

22. Wolfram, "Überlegungen," 490 ff. Papal claims to Pannonia: JE 2976—Fragmenta registri Iohannis VIII papae n. 21 (873 V).

23. Cassiodorus, *Variae*, XI 1.19; Wolfram, *Splendor*, 108. Id., *Intitulatio*, I, 99 ff. WG 29 ff.

24. Anonymus Valesianus, II 60.

25. Ibid., II 65.

26. Gregory the Great, *Dialogi*, II 1.

27. MGH Auct. ant. 12: 425.

28. WG 325 ff.

29. Gregory of Tours, *Historia Francorum*, II.29. Avitus, *Epistulae*, no. 36.

30. Gregory of Tours, *Historia Francorum*, II.9, and Fredegar, *Chronicon*, III.9.

31. Zöllner, *Franken*, 178 f.

32. Lippold, "Chlodovechus," cols. 153 f.

33. WG 16 f., 166, 197 ff., 210, 232 with note 503.

34. WG 198 f.

35. Gregory of Tours, *Historia Francorum*, II: 31. For an alternative date of Clovis's baptism, see Wood, *Merovingian Kingdoms*, 42 ff.

36. Acts 2.41. WG, 417 note 419.

37. Gregory of Tours, *Historia Francorum*, II: 31 and 41. Zöllner, *Franken*, 57 ff. Lippold, "Chlodovechus," cols. 151 ff.

38. Avitus, *Epistulae ad diversos*, no. 46.

39. WG 19 f. with note 5.

40. Wolfgang Mohr, in *Historische Zeitschrift*, 164 (1941): 563.

41. Lippold, "Chlodovechus," cols. 146 ff.

42. Zöllner, *Franken*, 39 ff. Gregory the Great, *Dialogi*, II: 12.

43. WG 16 f. Demougeot, *La formation*. 2.2: 666 f.

44. Lippold, "Chlodovechus," cols. 146 ff.

45. Gregory of Tours, *Historia Francorum*, II: 29. Tacitus, *Annals*, I: 60; Grönbech, *Kultur und Religion* 2: 43 ff.

46. Gregory of Tours, *Historia Francorum*, III: 18 (murder of her grandsons), and X: 31 (appointment of bishops of Tours).

47. *Concilium Aurelianense,* chap. 10.
48. Zöllner, *Franken,* 183 ff.; WG 192 f.
49. Lippold, "Chlodovechus," col. 164 ff.; Zöllner, *Franken,* 67 ff. and 210.
50. Rouche, *L'histoire* 23 (Paris, 1980): 41 f.
51. WG 279 with note 162, after Jordanes, *Getica,* 292.
52. Wolfram, "Königtum," 3 f.
53. WG 243 f., 267 f., 276 f., 283, 309 f., 327 f., 332 f., and 337 ff.
54. See Werner, *Les origines,* 318; Gregory of Tours, *Historia Francorum,* II: 40–42.
55. Gregory of Tours, *Historia Francorum,* II: 42. Zöllner, *Franken,* 106 f.
56. Gregory of Tours, *Historia Francorum,* II: 27.
57. Ennodius, *Panegyricus,* chap. 92.
58. Ennodius, *Panegyricus,* chaps. 19 f., 32, and 43 f.
59. Snorri Sturlson, *Heimskringla,* preface.
60. Ennodius, *Panegyricus,* chap. 89 f. Karl Hauck in Schramm, *Herrschaftszeichen,* I: 229.
61. Jordanes, *Getica,* 296.
62. Jordanes, *Getica,* 295 ff.; Anonymus Valesianus, II: 63–70. WG 306 f.
63. WG 196 f., 243 ff., 313–322. Lippold, "Chlodovechus," col. 164; Wolfram, *Grenzen und Räume.*
64. See especially McCormick, *Eternal Victory,* 335 f., and "Clovis at Tours," 155 ff. Compare Wolfram, *Intitulatio,* I: 89 (Burgundians) and 108 ff. (Franks). Beisel, "Beziehungen," 88 ff. Ewig, *Merowinger und Imperium,* 10.
65. Suerbaum, *Staatsbegriff,* 261 ff.
66. Procopius, *De bello Gothico,* I (V) 1.31–39.

10. A BATTLE FOR ROME (526/535–552/555)

1. This chapter has been taken from WG 332–336.
2. Demandt, *Spätantike,* 377.
3. Demandt, *Spätantike,* 207.
4. WG 361.
5. Wenskus, *Stammesbildung,* 485 and 494. WG 17 with note 127.

11. BRITAIN TOO WAS NOT CONQUERED

1. Zosimus, *Historia,* VI: 5.2–3.
2. PLRE 2: 504; Constantius, *Vita s. Germani,* chaps. 1 and 18.
3. Claude, *Adel,* 55 ff.
4. *Chronica Gallica* anni CCCCLII, 127; a. 441/442; 660.
5. Jerome, *Epistula,* 133: 9.4.
6. Gildas, *De excidio,* 27. English translation by Michael Winterbottom, *Gildas: The Ruin of Britain and other works.* London, 1978.
7. Gildas, *De excidio,* 23.1–5.
8. WG 299 f.
9. Gildas, *De excidio,* 20. *Chronica Gallica* anni CCCCLII ad annum 441/442; anni DXI ad annum 441/442.

10. Lammers, "Stammesbildung," 286 f.; Wenskus, "Sachsen-Angelsachsen-Thüringer," 528–532 (183–186).

11. Wenskus, "Sachsen-Angelsachsen-Thüringer," 534 (189). Id., *Stammesbildung und Verfassung*, 547–559.

12. Bede, *Historia*, HE I:15.

13. Ibid., V: 9.

14. Jan de Vries, "Ursprungssage," 353 ff.

15. Wolfram, "Origo gentis," 23. On the Vandal-Vandil Alci-Alces see Tacitus, *Germania*, chap. 43.

16. Bede, *Historia*, HE II: 5.

17. Wenskus, "Sachsen-Angelsachsen-Thüringer," 531 (186).

18. Bede, *Historia*, HE I:30.

19. Ibid. II: 5.

20. This chapter is based largely on Chrysos, "Römerherrschaft in Britannien und ihr Ende," 247–276. I'd like to thank Anton Scharer for many suggestions and good advice. See Wood, "End," 1 ff., and "Fall," 251; James Campbell, ed., *The Anglo-Saxons;* Johnson, *Later Roman Britain*. On Bonifatius see Theodor Schieffer, *Winfried-Bonifatius,* and Wallace-Hadrill, *Frankish Church*, 150 ff.

21. *Epistolae Bonifatii,* no. 46; Wenskus, "Sachsen-Angelsachsen-Thüringer," 527 (182).

12. THE BURGUNDIANS

1. Maenchen-Helfen, *Huns,* 82 f., on Socrates VII: 30; and *Chronica Gallica* a. 436, 660.

2. *Chronica Gallica* a. 443, 660.

3. Ennodius, *Vita Epifani,* 166; compare Cesa, *Ennodio,* 195 f.

4. Scheibelreiter, "Vester est populus meus," 206, concerning Avitus, *Epistulae*, 93.

5. Schmidt, *Ostgermanen,* 134 ff.; Beck, "Burgunden," 231 ff.; Anton, "Burgunden," 235 ff.; Durliat, "Le salaire," 49 ff.; Maenchen-Helfen, *Huns,* 82 ff.; Wolfram, *Intitulatio,* I: 87 ff.; Cesa, *Ennodio,* 195 f. (date for the marriage between Sigismund and Ostrogotha); WG 311 ff. The articles in the PLRE that deal with the Burgundian kings fall far below the otherwise excellent standards in this work and are remarkably superficial and uncritical.

6. Anton, "Burgunden," 246.

7. See Jordanes, *Getica,* 259.

8. Schröter, "Kopfumformung," 258 ff., esp. 262 (map of sites).

9. Claude, "Comes," 66; Anton, "Burgunden," 247.

10. Maenchen-Helfen, *Huns,* 82 f.

11. WG 446, note 39.

12. WG 312.

13. Sidonius Apollinaris, *Epistulae,* V: 5.3 f.; Ibid., *Carmina* XII: 1–22.

14. WG 43 f. Compare, for example, Sidonius Apollinaris, *Epistulae,* 5: 1 and 3.

15. Ammianus Marcellinus, *Rerum,* XXVII 5: 11–13.

16. Anton, "Burgunden," 246 ff.; Beck, "Burgunden," 224 ff.; Rosenfeld, "Burgunden," 231 ff.; Schmidt, *Ostgermanen,* 165 ff.

13. THE SPANISH KINGDOM OF THE VISIGOTHS
(507/568–711/725)

1. Ewig, "Teilungen," 125 ff.
2. Claude, *Westgoten,* 55.
3. Zöllner, *Franken,* 84 and 107.
4. Wolfram, *Intitulatio,* I: 78 f.
5. Fredegar, *Chronicon,* IV: 82.
6. WG 295, 309 f., and 336 f.
7. PLRE 2: 680; compare, however, O'Donnell, "Liberius," 67, who considers the Spanish command an invention or misunderstanding of Jordanes. Claude, *Westgoten,* 54 ff., and *Adel,* 47 ff.
8. Schwarcz, "Bemerkungen," 124, shows, however, that there was a limit to Leovigild's willingness to compromise.
9. Compare Iohannes of Biclaro, *Chronica,* a. 585.3, with Gregory the Great, *Dialogi,* III.31.
10. Gregory of Tours, *Historia Francorum,* VI.43.
11. Isidor of Seville, *Historia Gothorum,* 51.; McCormick, *Eternal Victory,* 298–300.
12. WG 220 and 223.
13. Isidor of Seville, *Historia Gothorum,* 51; McCormick, *Eternal Victory,* 298–300.
14. Iohannes of Biclaro, *Chronicon,* a. 590; McCormick, *Eternal Victory,* 303 f.
15. Claude, *Adel,* 77 f.
16. McCormick, *Eternal Victory,* 316 with note 86.
17. Claude, *Westgoten,* 85 f.
18. Wolfram, *Intitulatio,* I: 70 f.
19. McCormick, *Eternal Victory,* 312 with note 69.
20. Fontaine, *Isidore de Seville.* On the anointing see Matthias Becher, "Drogo und die Königserhebung Pippins." FMSt 23 (1989): 131 ff., with numerous references to the literature.
21. Claude, *Adel,* 55 ff., 154 ff.; id., *Westgoten,* 54 ff., 66 ff., 75 ff.; Stroheker, *Germanentum,* 134 ff.
22. Isidor of Seville, *Historia Gothorum,* 62.
23. *Leges Visigothorum,* IX.2.8 f.
24. Claude, *Westgoten,* 95 f.; WG 304.
25. Claude, *Westgoten,* 79; id., "Untersuchungen," 342.
26. Claude, "Untersuchungen," 337 note 23.
27. Wolfram, *Intitulatio,* I: 71 f.
28. Claude, *Westgoten,* 77 and 82 ff.; id., *Adel,* 190 ff.; id., "Untersuchungen," 329 ff.; WG 11. My thanks to Dietrich Claude for a number of very valuable suggestions and corrections in this chapter.

14. THE LONGOBARD EPILOGUE (488–643/652)

1. On this and the following discussion see Wolfram, *Mitteleuropa,* 77 ff.
2. Procopius, *De bello Gothico* III (VII): 33.10 f.
3. Cassiodorus, *Variae* IV: 1.1 f.

4. Paulus Diaconus, *Historia Langobardorum*, I: 21.

5. Procopius, *De bello Gothico*, III (VII): 35.

6. Ibid., IV (VIII): 18.

7. See Paulus Diaconus, *Historia Langobardorum*, II: 6 and 26; Hauptfeld, "Eroberung," 40 ff., esp. 44.

8. Wolfram, *Mitteleuropa*, 69 f. and 77–81.; Pohl, *Awaren*, 52 ff. On the Narses story see the *Origo gentis Langobardorum*, chap. 5, and Paulus Diaconus, *Historia Langobardorum*, II: 5. The story is very common in Latin historiography, a fact that rather tends to argue for its credibility.

9. Paulus Diaconus, *Historia Langobardorum*, II: 6.

10. Jarnut, *Langobarden*, 34.

11. *Historia Langobardorum codices Gothani*, chap. 5.

12. Krahwinkler, *Friaul*, 29, on Paulus Diaconus, *Historia Langobardorum*, II: 8, and *Historia Langobardorum codices Gothani*, chap. 1; compare Deuteronomy 34.1 ff.

13. Paulus Diaconus, *Historia Langobardorum*, II: 6.

14. Wolfram, *Intitulatio*, I: 190 f. WG 290.

15. WG 96 and 101.

16. Krahwinkler, *Friaul*, 31 f.

17. *Origo gentis Langobardorum*, chap. 5.

18. Compare Paulus Diaconus, *Historia Langobardorum*, VII.25.

19. McCormick, *Eternal Victory*, 441 s.v. *occursus*.

20. Paulus Diaconus, *Historia Langobardorum*, IV.6.

21. Hauptfeld, "Eroberung," 87 ff.

22. Demandt, *Spätantike*, 165 f.

23. Wolfram, *Mitteleuropa*, 111; Krahwinkler, *Friaul*, 60 ff.; Hauptfeld, "Eroberung," 47 ff.

24. Paulus Diaconus, *Historia Langobardorum*, II: 26 f., compare 29 (ship links with Ravenna).

25. Wolfram, *Mitteleuropa*, 91; Marius of Avenches, *Chronica*, a. 569; compare Paulus Diaconus, *Historia Langobardorum*, III: 3 f.

26. Hauptfeld, "Eroberung," 64.

27. Paulus Diaconus, *Historia Langobardorum*, II: 28 f.

28. Fröhlich, *Studien*, 70–75.

29. Hauptfeld, "Eroberung," 40 ff., on Paulus Diaconus, *Historia Langobardorum*, II: 6 and III: 6.

30. Durliat, "Le salaire," 48 f., on Paulus Diaconus, *Historia Langobardorum*, II: 32 and III: 16.

31. Hauptfeld, "Eroberung," 41.

32. Fröhlich, *Studien*, I: 82 f.; Schmidt, *Ostgermanen*, 597 f.; Hauptfeld, "Eroberung," 63 ff.

33. Fröhlich, *Studien*, I: 82 f.; Schmidt, *Ostgermanen*, 597 f.; Hauptfeld, "Eroberung," 63 ff.

34. Fröhlich, *Studien*, I: 117, note 1, has all the relevant source passages in addition to Paulus Diaconus quoted here (III: 16).

35. Compare Wolfram, *Intitulatio*, I: 112 with note 26.

36. Wolfram, *Intitulatio*, I: 64 ff. and 90 ff.

37. On Durliat, "Le salaire," 48 f., compare Paulus Diaconus, *Historia Langobardorum*, III: 16; Fröhlich, *Studien*, I: 89–96.
38. Wolfram, *Intitulatio*, II: 14 f.; Elze, "Agilulfkrone," 354 f.
39. Wolfram, *Intitulatio*, I: 185 ff.; Garms-Cornides, "Fürstentitel," 341 ff.
40. Wolfram, *Mitteleuropa*, 322 ff.; Fröhlich, *Studien*, I: 102 ff.
41. Fröhlich, *Studien*, I: 107.
42. Pohl, *Awaren*, 159.
43. Wolfram, *Intitulatio*, II: 14 f.; Elze, "Agilulfkrone," 354 f.
44. Schneider, *Königswahl*, 25 ff.; Fröhlich, *Studien*, I: 89 ff.
45. Fichtenau, *Arenga*, 26 ff., and 199 ff.
46. Dilcher, "Langobardisches Recht," col. 1609.
47. Wolfram, *Intitulatio*, I: 90 ff., and 217 ff.

15. THE TRANSFORMATION
OF THE ROMAN WORLD

1. See chapter 2, note 1.
2. See *The Transformation of the Roman World*, ed. Lynn T. White. UCLA, Center for Medieval and Renaissance Studies. Contributions 3. Berkeley and Los Angeles, 1966.
3. Paulinus of Pella, *Eucharisticos*, v. 303; 303.
4. Pohl, *Awaren*, 2.
5. This section on the Slavs and Avars is based largely on Walter Pohl's book on the Avars. In style and substance, it is the best account of the topic in any language. I am grateful to Walter Pohl for permission to draw on his book.
6. Musset, *Invasions*, II: 83 ff.
7. Pohl, *Awaren*, 94–96.
8. WG 356 f.; Pohl, *Awaren*, 96 f.
9. Procopius, *De bello Gothico*, III (VII): 14.24 ff.
10. Ibid., III (VII): 38.6 and 20 ff.
11. Pohl, *Awaren*, 98 ff.
12. Thus the title of a book by Joachim Hermann (Leipzig, 1971).
13. Pohl, *Awaren*, 117 ff.
14. Wolfram, *Mitteleuropa*, 347–349.
15. Pohl, *Awaren*, 1.
16. Pohl, *Awaren*, 170 f.; Bracher, "Reflexbogen," 137 ff.
17. Priscus frag. 8=11 (Blockley, *Historians*, II: 278).
18. Pohl, *Awaren*, 240 and 249.
19. Pohl, *Awaren*, 248–255.
20. Pohl, *Awaren*, 127.
21. Gregory of Tours, *Historia Francorum* VII: 35. See Demandt, *Spätantike*, 326 ff.
22. Demandt, *Spätantike*, 461 ff.
23. Claude, *Handel*, 52 ff.
24. Eugippius, *Vita Severini*, chap. 28: 2–5.
25. Procopius, *Anecdota*, chaps. 18.8 and 13 f.

26. Claude, *Handel,* 283 ff.; Demandt, *Spätantike,* 376 ff. (Rome), 395 (Constantinople), and 412 f.

27. Ewig, "Résidence," 362 ff.

28. Claude, *Handel,* 309 ff.

29. Malchus frag. 10=14.

30. Wolfram, *Intitulatio,* I: 219 ff. and 225 ff.

31. Werner Goez, *Translatio imperii* (Tübingen, 1958).

32. Wolfram, "Mittelalterliche Politik," 12 ff., esp. 15 with note 75, after Sallust, *Catalinae,* 2.

BIBLIOGRAPHY

SOURCES

Agathias of Myrina. *Historiarum libri V.* Edited by Rudolf Keydell. CFHB 2. Berlin, 1967.

Ammianus Marcellinus. *Rerum gestarum libri XXXI.* Edited by Wolfgang Seyfarth. Vols. 1 and 2. Leipzig, 1978. Edited and translated by J. C. Rolfe, 3 vols., Loeb Classical Library, 1935–1940.

Anagnosticum regis (Acta synhodorum habitarum Romae 14). Edited by Theodor Mommsen. MGH Auctores antiquissimi 12. 1892. Or: *Excerpta Valesiana.* Edited by Jacques Moreau and Velizar Velkov. Leipzig, 1968.

Anonymous Valesianus. *Pars prior* (I). Edited by Theodor Mommsen. MGH Auctores antiquissimi 9: 1–11. 1892.

Augustine. *De civitate Dei libri XXII.* Edited by Bernhard Dombart and Alphons Kalb. CC Ser. Lat. 47 and 48. 5th ed. 1981. Edited and Translated by G. E. McCracken, 7 vols., Loeb Classical Library, 1957–1972.

Avitus of Vienne. *Epistulae.* Edited by Rudolf Peiper. MGH Auctores antiquissimi 6, 2: 29 ff. 1883.

Bede the Venerable. *Historia ecclesiastica gentis Anglorum I-V.* Edited by Charles Plummer. Oxford, 1956. Edited and translated by J. E. King, 2 vols, Loeb Classical Library, 1930.

Beowulf. Edited by Friedrich Klaeber. 3rd ed. Lexington, Mass. 1950.

Blockley, R. C., trans. *The Fragmentary Classicising Historians of the Later Roman Empire: Eunapius, Olympiodorus, Priscus, and Malchus.* Vol. 1: Arca. Classical and Medieval Texts, Papers and Monographs, 6. Liverpool, 1981. Vol. 2: Arca. Classical and Medieval Texts, Papers and Monographs, 10. Liverpool. 1983.

Caesar. *De bello Gallico libri VII.* Edited by Otto Seel, *C. Iulii Caesaris commentarii.* Vol. 1. 1961. Edited and translated by H. J. Edwards, Loeb Classical Library, 1917.

———. *Expositio psalmorum.* Edited by M. Adriaen. CC Ser. Lat. 97 and 98. Turnhout, 1958. Translated by P. G. Walsh. *Cassiodorus: explanation of the Psalms.* 3 vols., New York, 1990–1991.

Cassiodorus. *Variae epistulae.* Edited by Theodor Mommsen. MGH Auctores antiquissimi 12. 1894. Or: Edited by Ake J. Fridh. CC Ser. Lat. 96. 1973. Translated by S. J. B. Barnish. *The Variae of Magnus Aurelius Cassiodorus Senator.* Liverpool: Liverpool University Press, 1992.

Cassius Dio. *Historia Romana.* Edited by U. P. Boisevain. 2d ed. Berlin, 1969. Translated by E. Cary, on the basis of the version of H. B. Foster. 9 vols., Loeb Classical Library, 1961–1969.

Chronica Gallica. Edited by Theodor Mommsen. MGH Auctores antiquissimi 9: 615 ff. 1892.

Chronicon paschale aa. 395–469. See Marcellinus Comes.

Claudius Claudianus. *De IV consolatu Honorii.* Edited by Theodor Birt. MGH Auctores antiquissimi 10: 150 ff. 1892. Edited with translation and commentary by W. Barr. *Claudian's Panegyric on the fourth consulate of Honorius.* Liverpool, 1981.

Codex Theodosianus. Edited by Theodor Mommsen. Reprint of the 2d ed. Berlin, 1954. English translation edited by C. Pharr, *The Theodosian Code.* Princeton, 1952.

Concilium Aurelianense. Edited by C. de Clercq. CC Ser. Lat. 148 A: 4 ff. Turnhout, 1963.

Constantius. *Vita s. Germani episcopi Autissiodorensis.* Edited by Wilhelm Levison. MGH rerum Merovingicarum 7: 247 ff. 1920.

Digestae. Corpus iuris civilis 1. Edited by Theodor Mommsen and Paul Krüger. Berlin, 1902. Translated by C. H. Monro. *The Digest of Justinian.* 2 vols. Cambridge, 1904–1909.

Ennodius. *Panegyricus dictus Theoderico regi.* Edited by Theodor Vogel. MGH Auctores antiquissimi 7: 203 ff. 1885.

————. *Vita Epifani.* Edited by Theodor Vogel. MGH Auctores antiquissimi 7: 84 ff. 1885. Translated by Sister Genevieve Marie Cook. *The Life of Saint Epiphanius by Ennodius.* Washington, D.C., 1942.

Epistolae Bonifatii. Edited by Michael Tangl. MGH Epistolae selectae 1. 1916.

Eugippius. *Vita s. Severini.* Edited by Theodor Mommsen. MGH Scriptores rerum Germanicarum, 1898. Edited by Pius Knoell. CSEL 9, 2. 1886. Edited by Hermann Sauppe. MGH Auctores antiquissimi 1, 2. 1877. *Eugippius: The Life of Saint Severin,* Translated by L. Bieler and L. Krestan. The Fathers of the Church. Vol. 55, Washington, D.C., 1965.

Eutropius. *Breviarium ab urbe condita.* Edited by Hermann Droysen. MGH Auctores antiquissimi 2:8 ff. 1879. Translated by H. W. Bird. *The breviarium ab urbe condita of Eutropius.* Liverpool, 1993.

Excerpta Valesiana. See Anonymus Valesianus.

Fredegar. *Chronicon.* Edited by Bruno Krusch. MGH Scriptores rerum Merovingicarum 2. 1888.

Gildas. *De excidio Britonum.* Edited and translated by Michael Winterbottom. Chichester, 1978.

Gregory the Great. *Dialogi.* Edited by Umberto Moricca. Fonti per la storia d'Italia 57. 1924. Translated by O. J. Zimmerman. *Dialogues.* Washington, D.C., 1977.

Gregory of Tours. *Historia Francorum.* Edited by Bruno Krusch and Wilhelm Levison. MGH Scriptores rerum Merovingicarum 1,1. 2d ed. 1951. Translated by Lewis Thorpe, *The History of the Franks.* London, 1974.

Historia Langobardorum codices Gothani. Edited by Georg Waitz. MGH Scriptores rerum Langobardicarum. 1878.

Iohannes of Biclaro. *Chronica.* Edited by Theodor Mommsen. MGH Auctores antiquissimi 11.2: 211 ff. 1894.

Isidor of Seville. *Etymologiarum sive originum libri XX.* Edited by Wallace Martin Lindsay. 2 vols., Oxford, 1911.

————. *Historia vel Origo Gothorum.* Edited by Theodor Mommsen. MGH Auctores antiquissimi 11: 267 ff. 1894.

Jerome. *Epistula* 133. Edited by Isidor Hilberg. CSEL 56: 241 ff. 1918.

John VIII. *Fragmenta registri.* Edited by Erich Caspar. MGH Epistolae: 273. Reprint, 1978.

Jordanes. *Getica.* Edited by Theodor Mommsen. MGH Auctores antiquissimi 5, 1: 53 ff. 1882. Translated by C. C. Mierow. *The Gothic History of Jordanes.* New York, 1960.

————. *Romana.* Ibid: 1 ff.

Leges Visigothorum. Edited by Karl Zeumer. MGH Leges nationum Germanicarum 1. 1902.

Livy. *Ab urbe condita libri.* Edited by W. Weissenborn and M. Müller. Stuttgart, 1959. Edited and translated by B. O. Foster, vols. 1–5; F. G. Moore, vols. 6–9; Evan T. Sage, vols. 9–11; E. T. Sage and A. C. Schlesinger, vol. 12; A. C. Schlesinger, vol. 13.

Malchus. *Byzantinae historiae librorum VII fragmenta.* In FHG 4: 112 ff. Or: Blockley 2: 401 ff.

Marcellinus Comes. *Chronicon.* Edited by Theodor Mommsen. MGH Auctores antiquissimi 11: 37 ff. 1894.

Marius of Avenches. *Chronica.* Edited by Theodor Mommsen. MGH Auctores antiquissimi 11: 232 ff. 1894. Edited and translated into French by Justin Favrod. Cahiers Lausoannois d'histoire médiévale 4. Lausanne, 1993.

Olympiodorus of Thebes. *Historiarum librorum XXII fragmenta.* In FHG 4: 58 ff. Or: Blockley, 2: 151 ff.

Origo gentis Langobardorum. Edited by Georg Waitz. MGH Scriptores rerum Langobardicarum: 1 ff. 1878.

Orosius. *Historiarum adversum paganos libri VII.* Edited by Karl Zangermeister. 1889. Translated by R. J. Deferrari. *The seven books of history against the pagans.* Fathers of the Church, vol. 50. Washington, D.C., 1964.

Paulinus of Pella. *Eucharisticos.* Edited by Wilhelm Brandes. CSEL 16: 291 ff. 1888.

Paulus Diaconus. *Historia Langobardorum.* Edited by Ludwig Bethmann and Georg Waitz. MGH Scriptores rerum Langobardicarum: 12 ff. 1878. Translated by W. D. Foulke. Edited with introduction by Edward Peters. *History of the Lombards.* Philadelphia, 1974.

Priscus. *Historiae Byzantinae librorum VIII fragmenta.* In FHG 4: 71 ff. Or: Blockley, 2: 221 ff.

Procopius. *Prokop: Werke.* Vols. 1–5. Edited by Otto Veh; *Anecdota.* Vol. 1. 2d ed. 1970; *De bello Gothico* I-IV (V-VIII). Vol. 4, 1971; *De bello Persico* I-II. Vol. 2, 1960; *De bello Vandalico* I-II (III-IV). Vol. 3, 1970. Edited and translated by H. B. Dewing, 7 vols., Loeb Classical Library, 1914–1940.

Prosper Tiro. *Epitoma Chronicon.* Edited by Theodor Mommsen. MGH Auctores antiquissimi 9: 341 ff. 1892.

Sallust. *De Catalinae coniuratione.* Edited by Rudolf Dietsch. Leipzig, 1876. Edited and translated by J. C. Rolfe, Loeb Classical Library, 1921.

Salvianus of Marseille. *De gubernatione Dei.* Edited by Karl Halm. MGH Auctores antiquissimi 1. 1877. Translated by J. F. O'Sullivan. *The writings of Salvian, the presbyter.* Fathers of the Church, vol. 3. Washington, D.C., 1947.

Sidonius Apollinaris. *Carmina.* Edited by Christian Luetjohann. MGH Auctores antiquissimi 8: 173 ff. 1887. Edited and translated by W. B. Anderson, Loeb Classical Library, 1936.

———. *Epistulae.* Ibid.: 1 ff. Edited and translated by W. B. Anderson, 2 vols., Loeb Classical Library, 1936, 1965.

Snorri Sturlson. *Heimskringla.* Translated by Samuel Laing and Peter Foote. 4th ed. London and New York, 1968.

Socrates. *Historia ecclesiastica.* Migne, PG 67: 30 ff. 1859. English translation, *The Ecclesiastical History of Socrates.* London, 1874.

Strabo. *Geographica.* Edited by Wolfgang Aly. Vols. 1–4. Bonn, 1957. Edited and translated by Horace L. Jones, 8 vols., Loeb Classical Library, 1917–1932.

Symmachus. *Epistulae.* Edited by Otto Seeck. MGH Auctores antiquissimi 6,1: 1 ff. 1883.

———. *Orationes.* Ibid.: 318 ff.

Tacitus. *Annalium libri XVI.* Edited by Henry Furneaux. Oxford, 1965. Edited and translated by John Jackson, vol. 5 (Books 13–16), Loeb Classical Library, 1937.

———. *Germania.* Edited by Michael Winterbottom. Oxford, 1975. Edited and translated by M. Hutton, revised by E. H. Warmington, Loeb Classical Library.

Themistius. *Orationes quae supersunt.* Edited by Heinrich Schenkl, Glanville Downey, and Albert Francis Norman. Leipzig, 1965–1974.

XII Panegyrici Latini. Edited by R. A. B. Mynors. Oxford, 1964.

Virgil. *Aeneid.* Edited by Otto Ribbeck. Leipzig, 1903. Edited and translated by H. R. Fairclough, 2 vols., Loeb Classical Library, 1935.

Willibald. *Vita Bonifatii.* Edited by Wilhelm Levison. MGH SS Rerum.

Zosimus. *Historia Nova.* Edited by Ludwig Mendelssohn. 1887. Translated by J. J. Buchanan and H. T. Davis. *Zosimus: Historia Nova—the decline of Rome.* San Antonio: Trinity University Press, 1967.

BOOKS AND ARTICLES

Alföldi, Andreas. *Studien zur Geschichte der Weltkrise des dritten Jahrhunderts nach Christus.* Darmstadt, 1967.

Andronikos, Manolis. *Museum Thessaloniki. Ein neuer Führer durch seine Bestände.* Athens, 1985.

Anton, Hans Hubert. "Burgunden." RGA 4: 235 ff. 2d ed. Berlin and New York, 1981.

Bannert, Herbert. "Der Tod des Kaisers Marcus." In *Marc Aurel.* Wege der Forschung 550: 459 ff. Darmstadt, 1979.

Beck, Heinrich. "Burgunden." RGA 4: 224 ff. 2d ed. Berlin and New York, 1981.

———, ed. *Germanenprobleme aus heutiger Sicht.* RGA suppl. vol. 1. Berlin and New York, 1986.

Beisel, Fritz. *Studien zu den fränkisch-römischen Beziehungen. Von ihren Anfängen bis zum Ausgang des 6. Jahrhunderts.* Geschichtswissenschaftliche Beiträge 105. Idstein, 1987.

Bierbrauer, Volker. "Die Landnahme der Langobarden aus archäologischer Sicht." *Vorträge und Forschungen* 41, 1: 103–172. Sigmaringen, 1993.

Birkhan, Helmut. *Germanen und Kelten bis zum Ausgang der Römerzeit.* Sitzungsberichte der Österreichischen Akademie der Wissenschaften in Wien, Phil.-hist. Kl. 272. 1970.

Bracher, Andreas. "Der Reflexbogen als Beispiel gentiler Bewaffnung." In *Typen der Ethnogenese.* Edited by Herwig Wolfram and Walter Pohl. DsÖAW 201: 137 ff. Vienna, 1990.

Campbell, James, ed. *The Anglo-Saxons.* Oxford, 1982.

Castritius, Helmut. "Von politischer Vielfalt zur Einheit. Zu den Ethnogenesen der Alemannen." In *Typen der Ethnogenese.* Edited by Herwig Wolfram and Walter Pohl. DsÖAW 201: 71 ff. Vienna, 1990.

———. "Zur Sozialgeschichte der Heermeister des Westreiches. Einheitliches Rekrutierungsmuster und Rivalitäten im spätrömischen Militäradel." MIÖG 92: 1 ff. 1984.

Cesa, Maria. *Ennodio. Vita del beatissimo Epifaneo vescovo della chiesa pavese.* Bibliotheca di Athenaeum 6. Como, 1988.

Christ, Karl, ed., *Der Untergang des Römischen Reiches.* Wege der Forschung 269. Darmstadt, 1986.

Chrysos, Evangelos K. "Die Römerherrschaft in Britannien und ihr Ende." *Bonner Jahrbücher* 191: 247–276. 1991.

———. "Some Aspects of Roman-Persian Legal Relations." *Kleronomia* 8. Thessaloniki, 1976.

———. "The Title Basileus in Early Byzantine International Relations." *Dumbarton Oaks Papers* 32: 31 ff. 1978.

Claude, Dietrich. *Adel, Kirche, und Königtum im Westgotenreich.* Sigmaringen, 1971.

———. "Zur Begründung familiärer Beziehungen zwischen dem Kaiser und barbarischen Herrschern." In Evangelos K. Chrysos and Andreas Schwarcz, eds., *Das Reich und die Barbaren:* 25 ff. VIÖG 29. Vienna, 1988.

———. "Comes." RGA 5: 65 ff. 2d ed. Berlin and New York, 1984.

———. "Geiserich." RGA, forthcoming.

———. *Geschichte der Westgoten.* Urban Taschenbücher 128. Stuttgart, 1970.

———. *Der Handel im westlichen Mittelmeer während de Frühmittelalters.* Abhandlungen der Akademie der Wissenschaften in Göttingen, Phil.-hist. Kl. III 144, 1985.

———. "Die ostgotischen Königserhebungen." *Denkschriften der Österreichischen Akademie der Wissenschaften in Wien, Phil.-hist. Kl.* 145: 149 ff. 1980.

———. "Probleme der vandalischen Herrschaftsnachfolge." *Deutsches Archiv* 30: 329 ff. 1974.

———. "Untersuchungen zum Untergang des Westgotenreiches (711 bis 725)." *Historisches Jahrbuch* 108: 329 ff. 1988.

Clover, Frank M. *Felix Carthago: Tradition and Innovation in Late Antiquity.* Madison: University of Wisconsin Press, 1984.

———. "The Symbiosis of Romans and Vandals in Africa." In Evangelos K. Chrysos and Andreas Schwarcz, eds., *Das Reich und die Barbaren:* 57 ff. VIÖG 29. Vienna, 1988.

Clover, Frank M., and R. Stephen Humphreys, eds. *Tradition and Innovation in Late Antiquity.* Madison: University of Wisconsin Press, 1984.

Courtois, Christian. *Les Vandales et l'Afrique.* 2d ed. Paris, 1955.

Demandt, Alexander. *Der Fall Roms. Die Auflösung des römischen Reiches im Urteil der Nachwelt.* Munich, 1984.

————. "Magister militum." RE, suppl. 12: 553–790. 1970.

————. *Die Spätantike. Römische Geschichte von Diocletian bis Justinian, 284–565 n. Chr.* Handbuch der Altertumswissenschaften 3–6. Munich, 1989.

Demougeot, Emilienne. *La formation de l'Europe et les invasions barbares.* Vols. 1–3. Paris, 1969–1979.

Diesner, Hans-Joachim. "Vandalen." RE, supp. 10: 957–992. 1965.

Dilcher, Hans-Joachim. "Langobardisches Recht." HRG 2: cols. 1607 ff. Berlin, 1978.

Dirlmeier, Camilla, et al. *Quellen zur Geschichte der Almannen.* 4 vols. Heidelberg, 1976–1984.

Dobesch, Gerhard. "Zur Ausbreitung des Germanennamens." In *Pro Arte Antiqua. Festschrift für Hedwig Kenner.* Sonderschriften Österreichisches Archäologisches Institut 18.1: 77 ff. Vienna, 1982.

Dove, Alfred. "Studien zur Vorgeschichte des deutschen Volksnamens." *Sitzungsberichte der Heidelberger Akademie der Wissenschaften, Phil.-hist. Kl.,* no. 8, 1916.

Durliat, Jean. "Le salaire de la pax sociale dans les royaumes barbares (Ve-VIe siècles)." *Denkschriften der Österreichischen Akadmie der Wissenschaften in Wien, Phil.-hist. Kl.* 193: 21 ff. 1988.

Elze, Reinhard. "Die Agilulfkrone des Schatzes von Monza." In Helmut Beumann, ed., *Festschrift für Walter Schlesinger:* 248 ff. Mitteldeutsche Forschungen 74. Cologne and Vienna, 1974.

Ewig, Eugen. "Die Civitas Ubiorum, die Francia Rinensis und das Land Ribuarien." *Spätantikes und fränkisches Gallien.* Beihefte der Francia 3,1: 472 ff. Munich and Zurich, 1976.

————. "Die fränkischen Teilungen und Teilreiche (511–613)." *Spätantikes und fränkisches Gallien.* Beihefte der Francia 3,1: 114 ff. Munich and Zurich, 1976.

————. "Die Merowinger und das Imperium." *Rheinisch-Westfälische Akademie der Wissenschaften, Vorträge* G 261: 5 ff. Opladen, 1983.

————. "Résidence et capitale pendant le haut Moyen Age." *Spätantikes und fränkisches Gallien.* Beihefte der Francia 3,1: 362 ff. Munich and Zurich, 1976.

Fichtenau, Heinrich. *Arenga.* MIÖG suppl. vol. 18, 1957.

————. "'Politische' Datierungen des frühen Mittelalters." In his *Beiträge zur Mediävistik. Ausgewählte Aufsätze* 3: 186 ff. 1986.

Fontaine, Jacques. *Isidore de Seville et la culture classique dans l'Espagne wisigothique.* Vols. 1 and 2. Paris, 1959.

Fröhlich, Hermann. *Studien zur langobardischen Thronfolge: Von den Anfängen bis zur Eroberung des italienischen Reiches durch Karl den Großen (774).* Parts 1 and 2. Tübingen, 1980.

Garms-Cornides, Elisabeth. "Die langobardischen Fürstentitel (774 bis 1077)." In Herwig Wolfram, ed., *Intitulatio* II: 341 ff. MIÖG suppl. vol. 24, 1973.

Gärtner, H. "Ammianus Marcellinus." RGA 1: 253 ff. 2d ed. Berlin and New York, 1973.

Geary, Patrick. *Before France and Germany: The Creation and Transformation of the Merovingian World*. New York and Oxford, 1988.

Geuenich, Dieter, and Hagen Keller. "Alamannen, Alamannien, Alamannisch im frühen Mittelalter. Möglichkeiten und Schwierigkeiten des Historikers beim Versuch der Eingrenzung." In Herwig Wolfram and Andreas Schwarcz, eds., *Die Bayern und ihre Nachbarn* I: 135 ff. DsÖAW 179, 1985.

Goez, Werner. *Translatio imperii*. Tübingen, 1958

Goffart, Walter. "After the Zwettl Conference: Comment on the 'Techniques of Accommodation.'" In Herwig Wolfram and Andreas Schwarcz, eds., *Anerkennung und Integration. Zu den wirtschaftlichen Grundlagen der Völkerwanderungszeit. 400–600*: 73 ff. DsÖAW 193. Vienna, 1988.

———. *The Narrators of Barbarian History (a.d. 550 to 800). Jordanes, Gregory of Tours, Bede and Paul the Deacon*. Princeton: Princeton University Press, 1988.

———. "The Theme of 'The Barbarian Invasions' in Late-Antique and Modern Historiography." In Evangelos K. Chrysos and Andreas Schwarcz, eds., *Das Reich und die Barbaren*: 87 ff. VIÖG 29. Vienna, 1988.

Gollwitzer, Heinz. "Zum politischen Germanismus des neunzehnten Jahrhunderts." *Festschrift für Hermann Heimpel*: 282 ff. Veröffentlichungen des Max-Planck-Instituts für Geschichte 36,1. Göttingen, 1971.

Graus, Frantisek. *Lebendige Vergangenheit. Überlieferung im Mittelalter und in den Vorstellungen vom Mittelalter*. Cologne, 1975.

Grönbech, Vilhelm. *Kultur und Religion der Germanen*. Vols. 1 and 2. Reprint of the 10th ed. Darmstadt, 1987.

Hauck, Karl. "Lebensnormen und Kultmythen in germanischen Stammes-und Herrschergenealogien." *Saeculum* 6: 186 ff. 1955.

Hauptfeld, Georg. "Die Gentes im Vorfeld von Ostgoten und Franken im 6. Jahrhundert." In Herwig Wolfram and Andreas Schwarcz, eds., *Die Bayern und ihre Nachbarn* 1: 121 f. DsÖAW 179, 1985.

———. "Zur langobardischen Eroberung Italiens. Das Heer und die Bischöfe." MIÖG 91: 37 ff. 1983.

Helbling, Hanno. *Goten und Wandalen. Wandlung der historischen Realität*. Zurich, 1954.

Herrmann, Bernd, and Rolf Sprandel, eds. *Determinanten der Bevölkerungsentwicklung im Mittelalter*. Weinheim, 1987.

Hoffmann, Dietrich. *Das spätrömische Bewegungsheer und die Notitia dignitatum*. Epigraphische Studien 7, parts 1 and 2. Düsseldorf, 1969–1970.

Höfler, Otto. *Germanisches Sakralkönigtum*. Vol. 1. Tübingen, 1952.

Isaac, Benjamin. "The Meaning of the Terms *Limes* and *Limitanei*." *The Journal of Roman Studies* 78: 125 ff. 1988.

Jänichen, Hans, and Hans Kuhn. "Alemannen." RGA 1: 138 ff. 2d ed. Berlin and New York, 1973.

Jarnut, Jörg. *Geschichte der Langobarden*. Stuttgart: Urban Taschenbuch 339, 1982.

Johnson, Stephen. *Later Roman Britain*. London, 1987.

Jones, A. H. M. *The Later Roman Empire (284–602): A Social, Economic and Administrative Survey*. Vols. 1–3. Oxford, 1964.

———. *The Prosopography of the Later Roman Empire: 260–395*. Vol. 1. Cambridge, 1971.

Keller, Hagen. "Alamannen und Sueben nach den Schriftquellen des 3. bis 7. Jahrhunderts." FMSt 23: 89 ff. 1989.

Köbler, Gerhard. *Gotisches Wörterbuch*. Leiden, 1989.

Krahwinkler, Harald. *Friaul im Frühmittelalter. Geschichte einer Region vom Ende des fünften bis in die Mitte des zehnten Jahrhunderts*. VIÖG 30. Vienna, 1992.

Krautschick, Stefan. "Die Familie der Könige in Spätantike und Frühmittelalter." In Evangelos K. Chrysos and Andreas Schwarcz, eds., *Das Reich und die Barbaren*: 169 ff. VIÖG 29. Vienna, 1988.

Krüger, Bruno, ed. "Asen." RGA 1: 457 f. 2d ed. Berlin and New York, 1973.

————. *Die Germanen. Geschichte und Kultur der germanischen Stämme in Mitteleuropa 2*. Veröffentlichungen des Zentralinstituts für Alte Geschichte und Archäologie der Akademie der Wissenschaften der DDR 4, 2. Berlin, 1983.

Lammers, Walther. "Die Stammesbildung bei den Sachsen." In *Entstehung und Verfassung des Sachsenstammes*: 263 ff. Wege der Forschung 50. Darmstadt, 1967.

Lippold, Adolf. "Chlodovechus." RE, suppl. 13: 139 ff. 1973.

Lotter, Friedrich. *Severinus von Noricum: Legende und historische Wirklichkeit*. Monographien zur Geschichte des Mittelalters 12. Stuttgart, 1976.

Lund, A. A. "Zum Germanenbegriff bei Tacitus." In Heinrich Beck, ed., *Germanenprobleme aus heutiger Sicht*. RGA suppl. vol. 1: 53 ff. Berlin and New York, 1986.

Maenchen-Helfen, Otto. *The World of the Huns*. Berkeley and Los Angeles: University of California Press, 1973.

Martindale, John Robert. *Prosopography of the Later Roman Empire: 395–527*. Vol. 2. Cambridge, 1980.

Matthews, John. *Western Aristocracies and Imperial Court: 364–425*. Oxford, 1975.

McCormick, Michael. "Clovis at Tours: Byzantine Public Ritual and the Origins of Medieval Ruler Symbolism." In Evangelos K. Chrysos and Andreas Schwarcz, eds., *Das Reich und die Barbaren*: 155 ff. VIÖG 29. Vienna, 1988.

————. *Eternal Victory: Triumphal Rulership in Late Antiquity, Byzantium and the Early Medieval West*. Cambridge, 1986.

Messmer, Hans. *Hispania-Idee und Gotenmythos*. Zurich, 1960.

Miltner, Franz. "Vandalen." RE II 15: 298 ff. 1955.

Mommsen, Theodor. "Das römische Militärwesen seit Diocletian." In his *Gesammelte Schriften* 6: 206 ff. Berlin, 1910.

Much, Rudolf. *Die Germania des Tacitus*. 3rd ed. Heidelberg, 1967.

————. "Wandalische Götter." *Mitteilungen der Schlesischen Gesellschaft für Volkskkunde* 27: 20 ff. 1926.

Musset, Lucien. *The Germanic Invasions: The Making of Europe, a.d. 400–600*. Translated by Edward and Columba James. Philadelphia: Pennsylvania State University Press, 1975.

O'Donnell, James J. "Liberius the Patrician." *Traditio* 37: 31 ff. 1981.

Öhlinger, Walter. "'Unser sind der Goten, Vandalen und Franken Triumphe.' Germanenideologien vom 12. Jahrhundert bis heute." Diploma thesis. Vienna, 1988.

Piganiol, André. *L'Émpire chrétien*. Paris, 1947.

Pohl, Walter. *Die Awaren. Ein Steppenvolk in Mitteleuropa. 567 bis 822 n. Chr.* Munich, 1988.

————. "Edika." RGA 6: 446 f. 2d ed. Berlin and New York, 1986.

————. "Die Gepiden und die Gentes an der mittleren Donau nach dem Zerfall des Attilareiches." In Herwig Wolfram and Falko Daim, eds., *Die Völker an der mittleren und unteren Donau im fünften und sechsten Jahrhundert*: 240 ff. DsÖAW 145. Vienna, 1980.

Pretzel, Ulrich, ed. *Das Nibelungenlied*. Stuttgart, 1973.

Reichert, Hermann. "Die Bewertung namenkundlicher Zeugnisse für die Verwendung der gotischen Sprache." In Heinrich Beck, ed., *Germanische Rest-und Trümmersprachen*: 119 ff. RGA suppl. 3. Berlin and New York, 1989.

————. *Nibelungenlied und Nibelungensage*. Böhlau-Studien-Bücher. Quellen-Dokumente-Materialien. Vienna and Cologne, 1985.

Rosenfeld, Hellmuth. "Burgunden." RGA 4: 231 ff. 2d ed. Berlin and New York, 1981.

Rouche, Michel. *L'Aquitaine des Wisigoths aux Arabes, 418–781: Naissance d'une région*. Paris, 1979.

Scheibelreiter, Georg. "Vester est populus meus: Byzantinische Reichsideologie und germanisches Selbstverständnis." In Evangelos K. Chrysos and Andreas Schwarcz, *Das Reich und die Barbaren*: 203 ff. VIÖG 29. Vienna, 1988.

Schieffer, Theodor. *Winfried-Bonifatius und die christliche Grundlegung Europas*. Freiburg, 1954.

Schmidt, Ludwig. *Geschichte der Wandalen*. 2d ed. Munich, 1942.

————. *Die Ostgermanen*. Reprint of the 2d ed. Munich, 1969.

————. *Die Westgermanen*. 2d ed. Vols. 1 and 2. Munich, 1938–1940.

Schneider, Reinhard. *Königswahl und Königserhebung im Frühmittelalter*. Monographien zur Geschichte des Mittelalters 3. Stuttgart, 1972.

Schramm, Percy Ernst, ed. *Herrschaftszeichen und Staatssymbolik*. MGH Schriften 13, 1–3. Stuttgart, 1954.

Schröter, Peter. "Zur beabsichtigten künstlichen Kopfumformung im völkerwanderungszeitlichen Mitteleuropa." In *Die Bajuwaren. Ausstellungskatalog Rosenheim-Mattsee*: 258 ff. Salzburg, 1988.

Schwarcz, Andreas. "Bemerkungen zum historischem Forschungsstand in der Geschichte der Goten vom 4. bis zum 8. Jh. n. Chr." In Jerzy Kmiecinski, ed., *Peregrinatio Gothica*: 105–124. Archeologica Baltica 7. Lódz, 1986.

————. "Nachrichten über den lateinischen Westen bei Prokopios von Kaisareia." Manuscript, Institut für Österreichische Geschichtsforschung. Vienna, 1984.

————. "Reichsangehörige Personen gotischer Herkunft. Prosopographische Studien." Ph.D. dissertation. Vienna, 1984.

See, Klaus von. "Kulturkritik und Germanenforschung zwischen den Weltkriegen." *Historische Zeitschrift* 245: 343 ff. 1987.

————. "Was ist Heldendichtung?" In *Europäische Heldendichtung*: 1 ff. Wege der Forschung 500. Darmstadt, 1978.

Staufenberg, Alexander Schenk von. "Theoderich und Chlodwig." In Siegfried Lauffer, ed., *Macht und Geist. Vorträge und Abhandlungen zur alten Geschichte*: 420 ff. Munich, 1972.

Straub, Johannes. "Christliche Geschichtsapologetik in der Krisis des Römischen Reiches." In his *Regeneratio Imperii: Aufsätze über Roms Kaisertum und Reich im Spiegel der heidnischen und christlichen Publizistik*, Vol. 1: 240 ff. Darmstadt, 1972.

————. "Die Wirkung der Niederlage bei Adrianople auf die Diskussion über das Germanenproblem in der spätrömischen Literatur." Ibid.: 195 ff.

Stroheker, Karl Friedrich. *Germanentum und Spätantike.* Zurich and Stuttgart, 1965.

————. *Der senatorishe Adel im spätantiken Gallien.* 2d ed. Darmstadt, 1970.

Suerbaum, Werner. *Vom antiken zum frühmittelalterlichen Staatsbegriff.* 2d. ed. Münster, 1970.

Uecker, H. "Dahn, Felix." RGA 5: 179 ff. 2d ed. Berlin and New York, 1984.

Verlinden, Charles. "L'origine de Sclavus—esclave." *Archivum Latinitatis Medii Aevii* 17: 97 ff. 1937.

Vries, Jan de. "Die Ursprungssage der Sachsen." In *Entstehung und Verfassung des Sachsenstammes:* 343 ff. Wege der Forschung 50. Darmstadt, 1967.

Waas, Manfred. *Germanen im römischen Dienst im 4. Jahrhundert n. Chr.* Bonn, 1965.

Wagner, Norbert. *Getica.* Berlin, 1967.

Wallace-Hadrill, J. M. *The Frankish Church.* Oxford, 1983.

Weber, G. W. "Jüngere Edda." RGA 6: 394 ff. 2d ed. Berlin and New York, 1986.

Wenskus, Reinhard. *Ausgewählte Aufsätze zum frühen und preußischen Mittelalter. Festgabe zu seinem siebzigsten Geburtstag.* Edited by Hans Patze. Sigmaringen, 1986.

————. "Sachsen-Angelachsen-Thüringer." In *Entstehung und Verfassung des Sachsenstammes:* 483 ff. Wege der Forschung 50. Darmstadt, 1967. Or: *Ausgewählte Aufsätze:* 138 ff.

————. *Stammesbildung und Verfassung. Das Werden der frühmittelalterlichen Gentes.* 2d ed. Cologne, 1977.

Werner, Karl Ferdinand. *Die Ursprünge Frankreichs bis zum Jahre 1000.* Stuttgart, 1989.

White, Lynn T., ed. *The Transformation of the Roman World.* Berkeley and Los Angeles, 1966.

Wolfram, Herwig. "Die Aufnahme germanischer Völker ins Römerreich: Aspekte und Konsequenzen." *Settimane di studio del Centro italiano di studi sull'alto medioevo* 29: 87 ff. Spoleto, 1983.

————. "Byzanz und die Xantha Ethna (400–600)." In Evangelos K. Chrysos and Andreas Schwarcz, eds., *Das Reich und die Barbaren:* 237 ff. VIÖG 29. Vienna, 1988.

————. "Donau." RGA 6: 26 ff. 2d ed. Berlin and New York, 1986.

————. "Einleitung oder Überlegungen zur Origo gentis." In Herwig Wolfram and Walter Pohl, eds., *Typen der Ethnogenese:* 19 ff. DsÖAW 201. Vienna, 1990.

————. "Ethnogenesen im frühmittelalterlichen Donau—und Ostalpenraum (6. bis 10. Jahrhundert)." In Helmut Beumann and Werner Schröder, eds., *Frühmittelalterliche Ethnogenese im Alpenraum:* 97 ff. Sigmaringen, 1985.

————. "Fortuna in mittelalterlichen Stammesgeschichten." MIÖG 72: 1 ff. 1964.

————. *Die Geburt Mitteleuropas.* Vienna, 1987.

————. "Gotische Studien I. Das Richterum Athanarichs." MIÖG 83: 1–32. 1975.

————. "Gotische Studien II. Die terwingische Stammesverfassung und das Bibelgotische (I)." MIÖG 83: 289 ff. 1975.

————. "Gotische Studien III. Die terwingische Stammesverfassung und das Bibelgotische (II)." MIÖG 84: 239 ff. 1976.

————. "Gotisches Königtum und römisches Kaisertum von Theodosius dem Großen bis Justinian I." FMSt 13: 1 ff. 1979.

————. *Grenzen und Räume. Geschichte Österreichs vor seiner Entstehung, 378–907*. Vienna, 1995.

————. *History of the Goths*. Translated by Thomas Dunlap. Berkeley and Los Angeles: University of California Press, 1988.

————. *Intitulatio I. Lateinische Königs—und Fürstentitel bis zum Ende des 8. Jahrhunderts*. MIÖG, supp. vol. 21. 1967.

————, ed. *Intitulatio II. Lateinische Herrcher—und Fürstentitel im neunten und zehnten Jahrhundert*. MIÖG, suppl. vol. 24. 1973.

————. "Die Ministerialen und das werdende Land." *Kuenringer-Katalog*: 8 ff. Vienna, 1981.

————. "Mittelalterliche Politik und adelige Staatssprache." MIÖG 76: 1 ff. 1968.

————. "Origo et religio: Ethnic traditions and literature in early medieval texts." *Early Medieval Europe* 3: 19–38. 1993.

————. *Salzburg, Bayern, Österreich*. Mitteilungen des Instituts für Österreichische Geschichtsforschung, suppl. 3. Vienna, 1995.

————. "The Shaping of the Early Medieval Kingdom." *Viator* 1: 1 ff. 1970.

————. *Splendor Imperii*. MIÖG, suppl. vol. 20.3. Vienna, 1963.

————. "Theogonie, Ethnogenese und ein kompromittierter Großvater im Stammbaum Theoderichs des Großen." In *Festschrift für Helmut Beumann*: 80 ff. Sigmaringen, 1977.

————. "Überlegungen zur politischen Situation der Slawen im heutigen Oberösterreich (8–10. Jahrhundert)." *Schriftenreihe des Oberösterreichischen Musealvereins* 10: 17 ff. 1980.

————. "Zisterziensergründung und Ministerialität am Beispiel Zwettls." *Jahrbuch für Landeskunde von Niederösterreich*, New Series 46–47: 1 f. 1980–1981.

Wood, Ian. "The End of Roman Britain: Continental Evidence and Parallels." In Michael Lapidge and David Dumville, eds., *Gildas: New Approaches*, 1 ff. Studies in Celtic History 5. Woodbridge, 1984.

————. "The Fall of the Western Empire and the End of Roman Britain." *Britannia* 18: 251 ff. 1987.

————. *The Merovingian Kingdoms, 450–751*. London and New York, 1994.

Zeitler, W. M. "Zum Germanenbegriff Caesars: Der Germanenexkurs im sechsten Buch von Caesars Bellum Gallicum." In Heinrich Beck, ed., *Germanenprobleme aus heutiger Sicht*, 41 ff. RGA, suppl. vol. 1. Berlin and New York, 1986.

Zöllner, Erich. *Geschichte der Franken bis zur Mittel des sechsten Jahrhunderts*. Munich, 1970.

INDEX

Note: Page numbers in italics refer to genealogies and chronologies. Alternative spellings of tribal, place, and personal names appear parenthetically.

Maps

Map 1. The territorial development of the Roman Empire up to the end of the second century

I BERA

Porolis-
sum
Napoca
Potaissa
Apulum
D A C I A
Sarmizegetusa
Drobeta
Durostorum
Oescus
Nicopolis
THRACIA
Philippopolis

MOESIA

Olbia
Tyras

REGNUM
BOSPORI

Panticapaeum

Troesmis
Tomi
Tropaeum
Odessus
Mesembria
Apollonia
Byzantium

Chersonesos

MACEDONIA

Troia
Pergamum

Ephesus
Laodicea
Athenae
Miletus

RHODUS

CRETA

BITHYNIA ET PONTUS

Ancyra

G A L A T I A

Sinope

CAPPADOCIA

ARMENIA

ASSYRIA

MESOPOTAMIA

Antiochia
SYRIA
Palmyra

CYPRUS

Tyrus
Damaskus
Bostra

A R A B I A

Petra

CYRENAICA
Cyrene

Alexandria

Memphis

A E G Y P T U S

Thebae

0 100 200 300 400 500 km

Map 2. Europe circa 500 A.D.

BALTHI

ZA

VANDALS

ona

UNS

Arad

rsa
mium
Singi-
dunum
Castra
Martis
Bassianae

Naissus

pidaurum

GOTHS

Sucidava
Oescus
Novae
Nicopolis

GOTHS

Daphne
Transmarisca
Marcianopolis

Serdica

Philippopolis

Lychnidus
(Ochrid)
Stobi
Pella
chium
Bitola
Kyrrhos
Beroia
Methone
Pydna
Dion
Larissa

Europos
Thessaloniki
Cassandrea
Troy

Athens
Corinth
Olympia
Sparta

Ephesus

GOTHS

Adrianople

Constantinople
Heraclea

Nicaea

Olbia

GOTHS

Pityus
Phasis

Trebizond

Neocaesarea

Side

0 100 200 300 400 500 km

Compositor: Prestige Typography
Text: 10/12 Baskerville
Display: Baskerville
Printer and binder: Haddon Craftsmen, Inc.